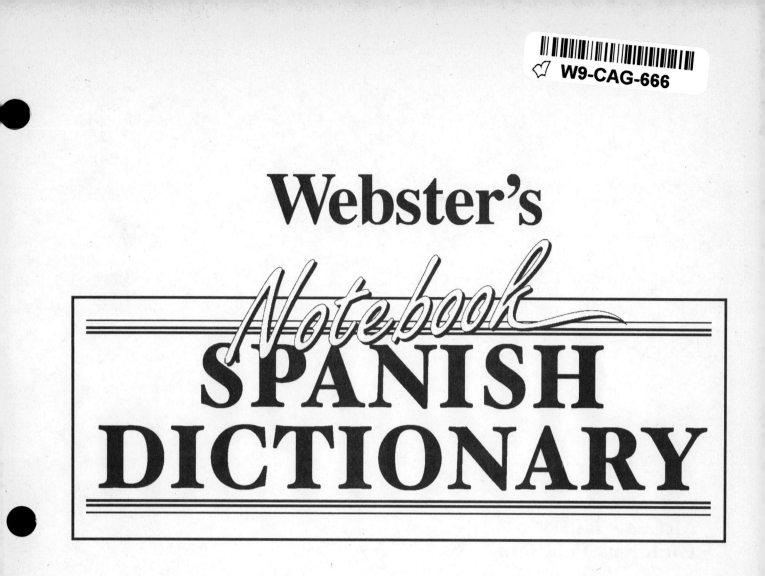

Webster's
Notebook
SPANISH DICTIONARY

McGraw-Hill
Children's Publishing

A Division of The **McGraw·Hill** *Companies*

Copyright © 2003 McGraw-Hill Children's Publishing.

Published by American Education Publishing, an imprint of McGraw-Hill Children's Publishing,
A Division of The McGraw-Hill Companies.

Printed in the United States of America.

Send all inquiries to:
McGraw-Hill Children's Publishing
8787 Orion Place
Columbus, Ohio 43240-4027

ISBN 1-57768-341-2

1 2 3 4 5 6 7 8 9 10 FRY 06 05 04 03 02

ABBREVIATIONS

abbr.—abbreviation

adj.—adjective

adv.—adverb

Amer.—American

coll.—colloquial

conj.—conjunction

contr.—contraction

def. art.—definite article

f.—feminine

indef. art.—indefinite article

infin.—infinitive

interj.—interjection

m.—masculine

n.—noun

obj.—object

pl.—plural

poss.—possessive

prep.—preposition

pron.—pronoun

This is an abridged dictionary, containing a useful selection of words in English and Spanish. It is a portable reference tool for those at all levels of fluency in both languages and is intended as a general guide. To keep this volume's convenient size, we have excluded proper nouns, place names, and historical events, all of which are far more suited to research of greater depth.

Español—Inglés
Spanish—English

A

a *prep.* at; to
a•ba•ce•rí•a *f.* grocery
a•ba•ce•ro *m.* grocer
á•ba•co *m.* abacus
a•bad *m.* abbot
a•ba•de•sa *f.* abbess
a•ba•dí•a *f.* abbey
a•ba•jo *adv.* beneath; down; below; *prep.* down
a•ba•lan•zar *v.* to hurl
a•ban•de•ra•mien•to *m.* registration (nautical)
a•ban•de•rar *v.* to register
a•ban•do•na•do, a *adj.* derelict; careless
a•ban•do•nar *v.* to desert; to forsake; to abandon; to give up
a•ban•do•no *m.* abandonment; neglect
a•ba•ni•car *v.* to fan
a•ba•ni•co *m.* fan
a•ba•ra•jar *v.* to catch
a•ba•ra•tar *v.* to lower; to become cheaper
a•bar•car *v.* to embrace; to comprise; to encompass
a•ba•ti•do, a *adj.* downcast; dejected; despondent; glum
a•ba•ti•mien•to *m.* dejection
a•ba•tir(se) *v.* to knock down; to depress; to discourage
ab•di•car *v.* to abdicate
ab•do•men *m.* abdomen
ab•do•mi•nal *adj.* abdominal
a•be•dul *m.* birch
a•be•ja *f.* bee
a•be•jo•rro *m.* bumblebee

a•be•jón *m.* hornet
a•be•rra•ción *f.* aberration
a•ber•tu•ra *f.* aperture; gap
a•be•to *m.* fir
a•bier•ta•men•te *adv.* outright
a•bier•to, a *adj.* open; clear
a•bi•ga•rra•do, a *adj.* many-colored, variegated; motley
a•bis•mal *adj.* abysmal
a•bis•mo *m.* abyss
ab•ju•rar *v.* to abjure
a•blan•dar(se) *v.* to soften; to mollify
a•bla•ti•vo *m.* ablative
a•blu•ción *f.* ablution
ab•ne•ga•ción *f.* abnegation
ab•ne•gar *v.* to renounce; to abnegate
a•bo•car *v.* to mouth
a•bo•car•dar *v.* to ream
a•bo•chor•na•do, a *adj.* flushed, put to shame
a•bo•fe•tear *v.* to slap
a•bo•ga•cí•a *f.* bar; law; advocacy
a•bo•ga•do *m.* attorney; counsel; lawyer
a•bo•gar *v.* to plead; to advocate
a•bo•len•go *m.* ancestry
a•bo•li•ción *f.* abolition
a•bo•li•cio•nis•ta *m., f.* abolitionist
a•bo•lir *v.* to abolish
a•bo•lla•du•ra *f.* dent
a•bo•llar *v.* to emboss; to dent
a•bo•mi•na•ble *adj.* abominable
a•bo•mi•na•ción *f.* abomination
a•bo•mi•nar *v.* to abominate; to loathe
a•bo•nar *v.* to fertilize; to give credit

a•bo•no *m.* manure; fertilizer; subscription; guarantee
a•bo•ri•gen *adj. m.* aboriginal
a•bo•rre•cer *v.* to hate; to abhor
a•bo•rre•ci•ble *adj.* detestable; abhorrent; loathsome; hateful
a•bo•rre•ci•mien•to *m.* hate; hatred; abhorrence; loathing
a•bor•tar *v.* to abort
a•bor•ti•vo, a *adj.* abortive
a•bor•to *m.* abortion
a•bo•to•nar *v.* to button up
a•bo•za•lar *v.* to muzzle
a•bra *f.* cove
a•bra•sión *adj.* abrasion
a•bra•si•vo *adj.* abrasive
a•bra•za•de•ra *f.* clamp; brace
a•bra•zar(se) *v.* to hug; to cuddle; to embrace
a•bre•car•tas *m.* letter opener
a•bre•var *v.* to soak; to water
a•bre•via•ción *f.* abbreviation
a•bre•viar *v.* to abridge; to abbreviate; to curtail; to condense
a•bri•gar(se) *v.* to shelter; to harbor; to protect
a•bri•go *m.* shelter; coat; overcoat
a•bril *m.* April
a•bri•llan•tar *v.* to polish; to brighten
a•brir(se) *v.* to open up; to spread out; to open
a•bro•char *v.* to button up; to fasten; to buckle
a•bro•ga•ción *f.* abrogation
a•bro•gar *v.* to abrogate; to repeal

a•bru•ma•dor, a *adj.* crushing
a•bru•mar *v.* to overwhelm
a•brup•to, a *adj.* abrupt; steep; blunt
a•bru•ta•do, a *adj.* bestial
abs•ce•so *m.* abscess
ab•so•lu•ción *f.* absolution
ab•so•lu•to, a *adj.* complete; absolute
ab•sol•ven•te *adj.* absolving
ab•sol•ver *v.* to acquit; to clear; to absolve
ab•sor•ben•cia *f.* absorbence
ab•sor•ben•te *m.* absorbent
ab•sor•ber *v.* to soak up; to engross; to absorb
ab•sor•ción *f.* absorption
ab•sor•to, a *adj.* absorbed; intent
abs•ten•ción *f.* abstention
abs•te•ner•se *v.* to abstain; to refrain
abs•ti•nen•cia *f.* abstinence
abs•trac•to, a *adj.* abstract
abs•tra•er *v.* to abstract
abs•tru•so, a *adj.* abstruse
ab•sur•di•dad *f.* absurdity
ab•sur•do, a *adj.* silly; preposterous; absurd
a•bue•la *f.* grandmother
a•bue•lo *m.* grandfather; grandparent
a•bun•da•mien•to *m.* abundance
a•bun•dan•te *adj.* plentiful; abundant; ample
a•bun•dar *v.* to abound
a•bun•do•so *adj.* abundant
a•bu•rri•do *adj.* boring; bored
a•bu•rri•mien•to *m.* boredom
a•bu•rrir *v.* to bore
a•bu•sar *v.* to misuse; to maltreat; to abuse

a•bu•si•vo, a *adj.* abusive

a•bu•so *m.* encroachment; abuse

ab•yec•ción *f.* abjectness

ab•yec•to, a *adj.* abject

a•cá *adj.* here

a•ca•ba•do, a *adj.* end; conclusion

a•ca•bar *v.* to accomplish; to end; to fail

a•ca•de•mia *f.* academy

a•ca•dé•mi•co *adj.* academic

al•ca•li•zar *v.* to alkalize

a•cam•par *v.* to camp

a•ca•ri•ciar *v.* to pet; to pat

a•ca•rrear *v.* to cart

a•ca•rreo *m.* cartage

ac•ce•der *v.* to accede

ac•ce•si•ble *adj.* accessible

ac•ce•so *m.* approach; access

ac•ce•so•rio, a *m.* accessory

ac•ci•den•ta•do, a *adj.* uneven; broken; eventful

ac•ci•den•te *m.* casualty; accident

ac•ción *f.* movement; action

a•ce•bo *m.* holly

a•ce•char *v.* to lurk; to watch for

a•cei•te *m.* oil

a•cei•tu•na *f.* olive

a•ce•le•rar(se) *v.* to speed; to accelerate

a•cen•to *m.* stress; emphasis; accent

a•cen•tuar(se) *v.* to emphasize; to accent; to stress

a•cep•tar *v.* to adopt; to accept; to agree to something

a•cer•car(se) *v.* to bring near; to get close

a•ce•ro *m.* steel

a•cer•ti•jo *m.* riddle

a•cé•ti•co *adj.* acetic

a•ce•to•na *f.* acetone

á•ci•do *m.* acid

á•ci•do bó•ri•co *m.* boric acid

á•ci•do cí•tri•co *m.* citric acid

á•ci•do sul•fú•ri•co *m.* sulfuric acid

a•cla•ma•ción *f.* acclaim

a•cla•ra•ción *f.* clarification

a•cla•rar *v.* to clear; to clarify; to rinse

a•cli•ma•tar *v.* to acclimate

ac•né *m.* acne

a•co•bar•dar(se) *v.* to flinch; to unnerve; to cringe

a•co•gi•da *f.* welcome

a•col•char *v.* to pad

a•có•li•to *m.* altar boy; acolyte

a•co•me•ter *v.* to attempt; to undertake; to cover; to come; attack

a•co•mo•da•di•zo *adj.* easygoing

a•co•mo•da•dor *m.* usher *f.* usherette

a•co•mo•dar *v.* to suit; to accommodate; to put up

a•com•pa•ñan•te *m.* escort, accompanist

a•com•pa•ñar *v.* to escort; to attend; to go with; to accompany

a•con•di•cio•na•dor de ai•re *m.* air conditioner

a•con•se•jar(se) *v.* to advise; to counsel

a•con•te•cer *v.* to chance: to happen

a•con•te•ci•mien•to *m.* occasion; event; occurrence; happening

a•cor•dar(se) *v.* to agree on; to remember; to agree

a•cor•de *m.* chord; in tune; harmony; in accord

a•cor•deón *m.* accordion

a•cor•near *v.* to gore

a•co•rra•lar *v.* to round up; to corral; to intimidate; to pen

a•cor•tar(se) *v.* to clip; to shorten; to lessen; to obstruct

a•co•sar *v.* to harass; to pursue; to beset

a•cos•tar(se) *v.* to lie down; to go to bed

a•cos•tum•brar(se) *v.* to be accustomed to; to be used to; to habituate

a•cre *adj.* acrid; sour

a•cre *m.* acre

a•cre•cen•tar *v.* to advance; to increase

a•cree•dor *m.* creditor

a•cri•mo•nia *f.* acridity

a•cró•ba•ta *m., f.* acrobat

ac•ti•tud *f.* pose; position; attitude

ac•ti•var *v.* to activate

ac•ti•vi•dad *f.* movement; nimbleness; activity

ac•ti•vo, a *adj.* alive; brisk; active; quick

ac•to *m.* event; act; function

ac•tor *m.* actor

ac•triz *f.* actress

ac•tual *adj.* instant; actual

ac•tual•men•te *adv.* at present; now; actually

ac•tuar *v.* to perform; to act; to set in action

a•cua•rio *m.* aquarium

a•cuá•til *adj.* aquatic

a•cu•chi•llar *v.* to slash; to hack; to knife

a•cue•duc•to *m.* aqueduct, waterworks

á•cueo, a *adj.* watery

a•cuer•do *m.* resolution; agreement; accord

a•cu•mu•lar *v.* to amass; to stockpile; to accumulate; to congest

a•cu•ña•ción *f.* coinage

a•cu•ñar *v.* to coin; to mint

a•cu•sar *v.* to impeach; to charge; to indict; to accuse

a•cús•ti•ca *f.* acoustics

a•chi•car *v.* to diminish; to humble; to bail

a•chis•pa•do, a *adj.* tipsy

a•da•gio *m.* proverb; adage

a•da•lid *m.* commander

a•dap•ta•ble *adj.* adaptable; versatile

a•dap•ta•ción *f.* adaptation

a•dap•tar *v.* to fit; to adapt; to adapt oneself to; to adjust

a•de•cua•do, a *adj.* fit; suitable; adequate

a•de•fe•sio *m.* something gaudy; extravagance

a•de•ha•la *f.* tip; bonus

a•de•lan•ta•do, a *adj.* fast; advanced

a•de•lan•tar(se) *v.* to further; to proceed; to overtake

a•de•lan•te *adv.* forwards; forward

a•de•lan•to *m.* progress; advance

a•del•ga•zar(se) *v.* to lose weight; to taper; to make thin; to attenuate; to slim down

a•de•mán *m.* attitude; gesture

a•de•más *adv.* besides; moreover; in addition

a•den•tro *adv.* inside; within

a•dep•to *m.* adept

a•de•re•zar *v.* to adorn; to garnish

a•de•re•zo *m.* finery; adornment; dressing

a•des•trar *v.* adiestrar

a•deu•dar *v.* to debit; to owe

ad•he•ren•cia *f.* bond; adherence

ad•he•ren•te *adj.* adherent; adhesive

ad•he•rir(se) *v.* to cling; to adhere; to stick

ad•he•sión *f.* adherence

ad•he•si•vo, a *adj.* adhesive

a•di•ción *f.* addition

a•di•cio•nal *adj.* more; extra; additional

a•dic•to, a *adj.* addicted

a•dies•trar(se) *v.* to exercise; to train; to practice

a•diós *m.* farewell; goodbye; good day

a•di•po•so, a *m.* fat; adipose

a•di•ta•men•to *m.* attachment; addition

a•di•ti•vo *m.* additive

a•di•vi•nar *v.* to foretell; to guess

ad•je•ti•vo *m.* adjective

ad•ju•di•ca•ción *m.* ward; adjudgement

ad•ju•di•car(se) *v.* to allot; to award

ad•jun•tar *v.* to annex, to attach

ad•mi•nis•tra•ción *f.* administration; management

ad•mi•nis•tra•dor, a *m.* administrator; steward; manager

ad•mi•nis•trar *v.* to manage; to dispense; to administer

ad•mi•nis•tra•ti•vo, a *adj.* administrative

ad•mi•ra•ble *adj.* fine;

excellent; admirable

ad·mi·ra·ción *f.* admiration

ad·mi·rar(se) *v.* to wonder; to admire; to amaze

ad·mi·si·ble *adj.* acceptable; admissible

ad·mi·sión *f.* input; admission

ad·mi·tir *v.* to acknowledge; to permit; to admit

a·do·be *m.* adobe

a·do·les·cen·cia *f.* adolescence

a·dop·tar *v.* to embrace

a·dop·ti·vo, a *adj.* adoptive

a·do·ra·ble *adj.* adorable

a·do·ra·ción *f.* adoration

a·do·rar *v.* to worship; to adore

a·dor·me·cer(se) *v.* to fall asleep; to drowse

a·dor·mi·de·ra *f.* poppy

a·dor·na·mien·to *m.* adornment

a·dor·nar *v.* to adorn, to deck; to decorate; to grace

a·dor·no *m.* adornment; ornament; array

ad·qui·rir *v.* to obtain; to secure; to acquire

a·dre·na·li·na *f.* adrenaline

ads·cri·bir *v.* to assign; to ascribe

a·dua·na *f.* customs

a·dua·ne·ro *m.* customs

a·du·cir *v.* to cite; to adduce

a·du·ja·da *adj.* coiled

a·du·la·ción *f.* flattery; adulation

a·du·la·dor, a *m.* flatterer

a·du·lar *v.* to flatter; to adulate

a·dul·te·ra·ción *f.* adulteration

a·dul·te·ra·dor *m.* adulterator

a·dul·te·rar *v.* to adulterate

a·dul·te·rio *m.* adultery

a·dul·to, a *m.* adult

a·dul·zar *v.* to make sweet

ad·ver·bial *adj.* adverbial

ad·ver·bio *m.* adverb

ad·ver·sa·rio *m.* opponent; adversary

ad·ver·si·dad *f.* adversity

ad·ver·so, a *adj.* averse; unfavorable; adverse

ad·ver·ti·do, a *adj.* skillful; informed; intelligent; capable; sagacious

ad·ver·tir *v.* to notify; to advise; to caution; to take notice of something; to observe

ad·ya·cen·te *adj.* adjacent

ae·ra·ción *f.* aeration

aé·reo, a *adj.* aerial

ae·ro·di·ná·mi·co *adj.* aerodynamic

ae·ro·náu·ti·co, a *adj.* aeronautic

ae·ro·pla·no *m.* airplane

ae·ro·puer·to *m.* airport

a·fa·bi·li·dad *f.* affability

a·fa·ble *adj.* affable; genial; kind

a·fán *m.* anxiety; travail

a·fa·nar *v.* to urge; to toil; to strive

a·fa·no·so, a *adj.* anxious

a·fec·ción *f.* fondness; affection

a·fec·ta·ción *f.* pretense; affectation

a·fec·ta·do, a *adj.* affected

a·fec·tar *v.* to affect

a·fec·to *m.* affection

a·fec·tuo·sa·men·te *adv.* fondly, affectionately

a·fec·tuo·so,a *adj.* affectionate

a·fei·ta·do, a *m.* shave

a·fei·tar *v.* to shave

a·fei·te *m.* shave; cosmetic

a·fe·rrar(se) *v.* to grasp; to furl

a·fian·zar *v.* to bail; to clinch; to guaranty

a·fi·ción *f.* liking; affection; inclination

a·fi·cio·na·do, a *m.* fan; amateur; fancier

a·fi·jo, a *m.* affix

a·fi·lar(se) *v.* to sharpen

a·fi·liar(se) *v.* to join; to affiliate; to adopt

a·fín *adj.* related; contiguous; adjacent

a·fi·na·ción *f.* refining; tuning

a·fi·nar *v.* to refine; to polish; to complete; to tune

a·fi·ni·dad *f.* affinity; relationship

a·fir·mar(se) *v.* to secure; to assert; to contend; to affirm; to make fast

a·fir·ma·ti·vo *adj.* affirmative

a·flic·ción *f.* anxiety; bereavement; affliction

a·fli·gi·do *adj.* stricken

a·fli·gir(se) *v.* to afflict

a·flo·jar(se) *v.* to loosen; to slacken; to weaken

a·flo·rar *v.* to emerge; to sift

a·fluen·cia *f.* affluence; crowd; jam; fluency; abundance

a·fluen·te *adj.* affluent

a·fo·rar *v.* to appraise; to gauge; to measure

a·fo·ris·mo *m.* aphorism; maxim

a·for·tu·na·do, a *adj.* prosperous; lucky; fortunate

a·fren·ta *f.* insult; affront

a·fren·tar(se) *v.* to insult; to affront; to be affronted

a·fro·di·sía·co *adj.* aphrodisiac

a·fue·ra *adv.* outside; outskirts; suburbs

a·ga·char(se) *v.* to crouch; to squat; to bow down

a·ga·lla *f.* gill

a·ga·rrar(se) *v.* to grasp; to seize

a·ga·rre *m.* gripping

a·ga·rro *m.* grip; clutch; grab

a·ga·rro·tar *v.* to compress; to bind tightly

a·ga·sa·ja·dor *adj.* attentive

a·ga·sa·jar *v.* to entertain; to fondle; to welcome

a·gen·cia *f.* bureau; agency

a·gen·ciar *v.* to obtain

a·gen·cio·so *adj.* industrious

a·gen·da *f.* diary; notebook

a·gen·te *m.* officer; agent

á·gil *adj.* nimble; agile; lithe; active; lithesome

a·gi·li·dad *f.* agility

a·gi·ta·ción *f.* flurry; flutter; stir; excitement; agitation

a·gi·tar(se) *v.* to stir up; to churn; to flutter; to shake

a·glo·me·ra·ción *f.*

agglomeration

a·glo·me·ra·do *adj.* agglomerate

a·glo·me·rar *v.* to agglomerate

a·glu·ti·na·ción *f.* agglutination

a·glu·ti·nan·te *m.* cement

a·glu·ti·nar *v.* to agglutinate

a·go·ní·a *f.* pain; agony

a·go·nio·so *adj.* persistent

a·go·rar *v.* to foretell

a·gos·tar *v.* to consume

a·gos·to *m.* August; harvest

a·go·ta·mien·to *m.* exhaustion; depletion

a·go·tar(se) *v.* to drain; to give out; to tire; to exhaust

a·gra·cia·do, a *adj.* graceful

a·gra·ciar *v.* to award; to grace

a·gra·da·ble *adj.* gracious; nice; pleasant; agreeable; delightful

a·gra·dar *v.* to please

a·gra·de·cer *v.* to appreciate; to acknowledge; to thank

a·gra·de·ci·do, a *adj.* thankful; grateful

a·gra·do *m.* liking; taste

a·gra·va·ción *f.* aggravation

a·gra·van·te *adj.* aggravating

a·gra·viar *m.* to harm; to wrong

a·gra·vio *m.* offense; injury; grievance; harm

a·gra·vio·so *adj.* injurious; offensive; insulting

a·gre·dir *v.* to assault

a·gre·sión *f.* aggression

a·gre·si·vo *adj.* aggressive

a·gre·sor, a *m.* aggressor

a·griar *v.* to annoy; to sour

a·gri·cul·tu·ra *f.* farming

a·grie·tar *v.* to split, to crack

a·gri·men·su·ra *f.* surveying

a·grio, a *adj.* acid; sour

a·gro *m.* farming

a·gro·nó·mi·co, a *adj.* agronomical

a·gru·pa·ción *f.* group

a·gru·par(se) *v.* to cluster; to group

a•gua *f.* water
a•gua•ca•te *m.* avocado
a•gua•do, a *adj.* diluted
a•gua•ma•ri•na *f.* aquamarine
a•guan•tar(se) *v.* to support; to endure; to hold
a•guan•te *m.* endurance
a•guar•dar *v.* to await
a•gu•de•za *f.* acuteness; keenness; sharpness; brightness
a•gu•di•zar *v.* to sharpen
a•gu•do, a *adj.* sharp
a•güe•ro *m.* omen
a•gue•rri•do, a *adj.* seasoned
á•gui•la *f.* eagle
a•gu•ja *f.* needle
a•gu•je•ro *m.* hole
a•guo•so, a *adj.* watery
a•gu•zar *v.* to sharpen
a•hí *adv.* there
a•hi•ja•da *f.* goddaughter
a•hi•ja•do *m.* godson
a•hi•jar *v.* to adopt
a•hi•la•do *adj.* faint; soft
a•hi•lar *v.* to faint
a•hi•to, a *adj.* stuffed
a•ho•gar *v.* to oppress; to drown; to choke
a•ho•ra *adv.* now
a•hor•ca•jar(se) *v.* to straddle
a•hor•mar *v.* to fit
a•ho•rrar *v.* to spare, to save
a•ho•rro *m.* savings
a•hue•va•do *adj.* egg-shaped
a•hu•ma•do, a *adj.* smoky; cured; smoked
a•hu•mar *v.* to cure; to smoke
ai•rar *v.* to annoy; to anger
ai•re *m.* aspect; air
ai•re•a•do *adj.* aired out, open
ai•re•ar(se) *v.* to air; to cool
ai•re•o *m.* ventilation
ais•la•do, a *adj.* alone, isolated
ais•lar *v.* to seclude; to isolate
a•ja•do, a *adj.* withered
a•jar *v.* to mar; to spoil
a•je•dre•cis•ta *f., m.* chess player
a•je•drez *m.* chess

a•jen•jo *m.* bitterness
a•je•no, a *adj.* alien; strange; foreign
a•je•tre•o *m.* agitation
a•jo *m.* garlic
a•jus•tar *v.* to settle; to adapt; to adjust; to fix; to tighten
a•jus•te *m.* fitting; accommodation
a•jus•ti•cia•mien•to *m.* execution
a•la *f.* wing
a•la•ban•za *f.* praise
a•la•bar *v.* to commend, to praise
a•la•bas•tro *m.* alabaster
a•la•crán *m.* scorpion
a•la•cri•dad *f.* eagerness
a•la•do, a *adj.* winged
a•lam•bre *m.* wire
á•la•mo *m.* poplar
a•lar•de•o *m.* bragging
a•lar•gar *v.* to stretch; to make longer
a•lar•ma *f.* alarm
a•lar•man•te *adj.* alarming
a•lar•mar *v.* to alarm
al•ba *f.* daybreak
al•ba•ri•co•que *m.* apricot
al•ber•gar *v.* to cherish
al•bi•no, na *adj.* albino
al•bo•ro•ta•do, a *adj.* rowdy; excited
al•bo•ro•tar *v.* to excite; to incite
al•bo•ro•zo *m.* joy
al•ca•cho•fa *f.* artichoke
al•cal•de *m.* mayor
al•ca•li•no, a *adj.* alkaline
al•ca•loi•de *m.* alkaloid
al•can•for *m.* camphor
al•can•zar *v.* to attain; to reach; to pass; to grasp
al•car•cil *m.* artichoke
al•cá•zar *m.* castle
al•ce *m.* moose
al•co•ba *f.* bedroom
al•co•hol *m.* alcohol
al•co•hó•li•co *adj.* alcoholic
a•lea•to•rio *adj.* uncertain
a•le•go•rí•a *f.* allegory
a•le•grar *v.* to make happy; to cheer; to rejoice
a•le•gre *adj.* joyous; gay; glad
a•le•gre•men•te *adv.* gaily

a•le•grí•a *f.* gladness; gaiety
a•le•grón *m.* joy
a•le•ja•mien•to *m.* distance; withdrawal
a•le•la•do *adj.* bewildered
a•len•ta•dor, a *adj.* encouraging
a•len•tar *v.* to encourage
a•ler•gia *f.* allergy
a•lér•gi•co, a *adj.* allergic
a•ler•tar *v.* to alert; to warn
a•le•te•o *m.* flapping
al•fa•bé•ti•co *adj.* alphabetical
al•fa•be•to *m.* alphabet
al•fa•re•rí•a *f.* pottery
al•fi•le•rar *v.* to pin
al•fom•bra *f.* carpet
al•fom•brar *v.* to carpet
al•for•za *f.* pleat
ál•ge•bra *f.* algebra
al•go *pron.* anything; something
al•go•dón *m.* cotton
al•guien *pron.* somebody
al•gún *adj.* some
al•gu•no, a *pron.* anybody
al•ha•ja, a *f.* gem
al•hu•ce•ma *f.* lavender
a•lia•do, a *m.* ally
a•lian•za *f.* alliance
a•li•bi *m.* alibi
a•lie•na•ble *adj.* alienable
a•lie•na•ción *f.* alienation
a•lie•nar *v.* to alienate
a•lien•to *m.* courage
a•li•ge•rar(se) *v.* to relieve
a•li•men•tar *v.* to feed
a•li•men•ti•cio *adj.* nutritious
a•li•men•to *m.* food
a•li•nea•ción *m.* alignment
a•li•ñar *v.* to tidy
a•li•ño *m.* tidiness
a•li•sar *v.* to smooth
a•lis•tar *v.* to alleviate
al•ma *f.* spirit
al•má•ci•ga *f.* nursery
al•me•ja *f.* clam
al•men•dro, a *m.* almond tree
al•mi•dón *m.* starch
al•mi•do•nar *v.* to starch
al•miz•cle *m.* musk
al•mo•ha•da *f.* pillow
al•mor•zar *v.* to lunch
al•muer•zo *m.* lunch

a•lo•ca•do, a *adj.* crazy
a•lo•cu•ción *f.* allocution
a•lo•jar(se) *v.* to house, to stay
al•pi•no *adj.* alpine
al•qui•lar *v.* to hire; rent
al•qui•mia *f.* alchemy
al•qui•mis•ta *m.* alchemist
al•re•de•dor *adv.* around; *prep.* round
al•ta•men•te *adv.* extremely, highly
al•tar *m.* altar
al•te•ra•ción *f.* alteration
al•ter•ca•ción *adj.* altercation
al•ter•na•do *adj.* alternate
al•ter•nar *v.* to rotate; to alternate
al•ter•na•ti•va *f.* alternative
al•ti•me•trí•a *f.* altimetry
al•ti•tud *f.* altitude
al•to, a *adj.* upper; high
al•truís•ta *adj.* altruistic
al•tu•ra *f.* elevation; height
a•lu•ci•nar *v.* to hallucinate
a•lu•ci•na•to•rio *adj.* hallucinatory
a•lu•dir *v.* to allude
a•lum•bra•do *m.* electric lighting
a•lu•mi•nio *m.* aluminum
a•lum•no, a *m.* student; alumnus
a•lu•sión *f.* allusion
al•za•do *adj.* elevated
al•zar *v.* to hoist up; to lift up; to raise
a•llá *adv.* there
a•lla•nar *v.* to overcome; to flatten
a•lle•ga•do, a *adj.* related; close; near
a•llí *adv.* there
a•ma•bi•li•dad *f.* kindness
a•ma•ble *adj.* lovable; amiable; kindly
a•ma•do *adj.* beloved
a•ma•es•trar *v.* to train
a•ma•ne•cer *m.* daybreak
a•man•sar *v.* to soothe; to tame
a•ma•ña•do *adj.* skillful; fixed
a•ma•ño *m.* skill, scheme
a•ma•po•la *f.* poppy
a•mar *v.* to love

a•mar•gar *v.* to make bitter
a•mar•go *m.* bitterness
a•ma•ri•llo *m.* yellow
a•ma•rrar *v.* to fasten; to tie
a•ma•teur *adj.* amateur
a•ma•tis•ta *f.* amethyst
ám•bar *m.* amber
am•bi•ción *f.* ambition
am•bi•cio•so *adj.* ambitious
am•bien•ta•ción *f.* atmosphere
am•bi•güe•dad *f.* ambiguity
am•bi•guo *adj.* uncertain; ambiguous
am•bu•lan•cia *f.* ambulance
am•bu•lan•te *adj.* ambulatory
am•bu•lar *v.* to wander about
a•me•ba *f.* amoeba
a•me•na•za *f.* threat
a•me•na•zar *v.* to menace
a•me•ni•dad *f.* amenity
a•me•ri•ca•no *adj.* American
a•mi•ga *f.* girlfriend
a•mi•gar *v.* to reconcile
a•míg•da•la *f.* tonsil
a•mi•go *m.* boyfriend
a•mi•la•na•do *adj.* intimidated
a•mi•la•nar *v.* to discourage; to intimidate; to scare; to frighten
a•mis•to•so, a *adj.* friendly
a•mo *m.* master; boss
a•mo•lar *v.* to sharpen
a•mol•dar *v.* to adjust; to mold
a•mon•to•nar(se) *v.* to amass; to hoard; to huddle
amor *m.* love
a•mo•ra•li•dad *f.* amorality
a•mo•ro•so, a *adj.* amorous; loving
am•pa•rar *v.* to defend; to protect
am•pliar *v.* to expand; to increase
am•pli•fi•ca•ción *f.* amplification
am•pli•fi•car *v.* to amplify
am•po•lle•ta *f.* hourglass
am•pu•ta•ción *f.* amputation
am•pu•tar *v.* to amputate
a•na•car•do *m.* cashew

a•na•de *m.* duck
a•na•gra•ma *f.* anagram
a•nal•gé•si•co *adj.* analgesic
a•ná•li•sis *m.* analysis
a•na•lis•ta *m.* analyst
a•na•lí•ti•co *adj.* analytical
a•na•li•zar *v.* to analyze
a•na•lo•gí•a *f.* analogy
a•na•ná *m.* pineapple
a•na•quel *m.* shelf
a•na•ran•ja•do, a *adj.* orange
a•nar•quis•ta *m., f.* anarchist
a•na•to•mí•a *f.* anatomy
a•na•tó•mi•co *adj.* anatomic
an•cia•no, a *adj.* aged
an•cla *f.* anchor
an•cho *adj.* broad
an•cho•a *f.* anchovy
an•dar *v.* to go; to ambulate
an•dra•jo•so, a *adj.* ragged
an•droi•de *m.* android
a•néc•do•ta *f.* anecdote
a•nec•do•tis•ta *m.* anecdotist
a•ne•gar *v.* to flood
a•né•mi•co, a *adj.* anemic
a•nes•te•siar *v.* to anesthetize
án•gel *m.* angel
an•gé•li•co, a *adj.* angelical
an•go•ra *adj.* angora
an•gui•la *f.* eel
án•gu•lo *m.* angle
an•gu•lo•so *adj.* angular
an•gu•rria *f.* greed
an•gus•tiar *v.* to anguish
an•he•lar *v.* to long for; to yearn
a•ni•llo *m.* ring
a•ni•ma•ción *f.* animation
a•ni•ma•do, a *adj.* lively; animate
a•ni•mal *m.* animal
a•ni•mar *v.* to become animated; to enliven
a•ni•qui•lar *v.* to destroy; to annihilate
a•ni•ver•sa•rio, a *adj.* anniversary
a•no•che *adv.* last night
a•nó•ni•mo *adj.* anonymous
a•nor•mal *adj.* subnormal; abnormal

a•no•ta•ción *f.* note
a•no•tar *v.* to note
án•sar *m.* goose
an•sia *f.* yearning
an•siar *v.* to long for
an•sie•dad *f.* anxiety
an•te *prep.* before
an•te•bra•zo *m.* forearm
an•te•ce•der *v.* to antecede
an•te•de•cir *v.* to predict
an•te•pa•sa•do *m.* ancestor
an•te•rior *adj.* prior; anterior
an•tes de *adv.* before
an•ti•á•ci•do *adj.* antacid
an•ti•bió•ti•co *m.* antibiotic
an•ti•ci•pa•do *adj.* advanced
an•ti•ci•par *v.* to bring forward; to advance
an•ti•cuer•po *m.* antibody
an•tí•do•to *m.* antidote
an•ti•guo *adj.* ancient; antique
an•tí•lo•pe *m.* antelope
an•ti•na•tu•ral *adj.* unnatural
an•ti•sép•ti•co *m.* antiseptic
an•ti•so•cial *adj.* antisocial
an•ti•tó•xi•co *adj.* antitoxic
an•to•ni•mia *f.* antonymy
an•tro•poi•de *adj.* anthropoid
a•nual *adj.* annual
a•nua•rio *m.* year book
a•nu•lar *v.* to cancel
a•nun•cia•ción *f.* announcement
a•nun•cia•dor *m.* advertiser
a•nun•ciar *v.* to announce
an•zue•lo *m.* fishhook
a•ña•di•do *m.* addition
a•ña•dir *v.* to add
a•ñe•jo, a *adj.* mature
a•ñil *adj., m.* indigo
a•ño *m.* year
a•pa•bu•llar *v.* to squash; to bewilder
a•pa•ci•ble *adj.* gentle
a•pa•ci•guar(se) *v.* to appease
a•pa•dri•nar *v.* to support; to sponsor
a•pa•le•o *m.* thrashing
a•pa•ñar *v.* to mend; to seize; to grasp; to repair
a•pa•ra•to *m.* apparatus
a•pa•ra•to•so *adj.* ostentatious

a•par•car *v.* to park
a•pa•re•cer(se) *v.* to haunt; to come
a•pa•re•jar *v.* to prepare
a•pa•ren•te *adj.* seeming
a•pa•ri•ción *f.* appearance
a•par•ta•do *adj.* isolated
a•par•ta•men•to *m.* apartment
a•par•tar(se) *v.* to divide; to remove; to move away
a•par•te *adv.* aside; apart
a•pa•sio•nar *v.* to excite
a•pa•tí•a *f.* apathy
a•pá•ti•co, a *adj.* apathetic
a•pe•ar *v.* to chock
a•pe•la•ble *adj.* appealable
a•pe•lar *v.* to appeal
a•pe•lli•dar *v.* to name; to be called
a•pe•lli•do *m.* name
a•pe•nar *v.* to pain; to grieve
a•pen•di•ci•tis *m.* appendicitis
a•pe•ro *m.* gear
a•pes•tar *v.* to annoy; to infect
a•pe•ten•cia *f.* appetite
a•pe•ti•to *m.* appetite
a•pe•ti•to•so, a *adj.* delicious
a•pio *m.* celery
a•pla•car *v.* to placate
a•pla•nar *v.* to flatten; to stun
a•plas•tar(se) *v.* to flatten
a•plau•dir *v.* to clap; to applaud
a•plau•so *m.* applause; praise
a•pli•ca•ble *adj.* applicable
a•pli•ca•ción *f.* application
a•pli•car *v.* to apply
a•po•ca•do, a *adj.* timid
a•po•de•rar(se) *v.* to take possession
a•po•do *m.* nickname
a•po•lí•ti•co *adj.* apolitical
a•po•rre•ar(se) *v.* to beat; to fall
a•por•tar *v.* to bring; to contribute
a•po•sen•to *m.* lodging; room
a•po•si•ción *f.* apposition
a•pós•tol *m.* apostle

a·pós·tro·fo *m.* apostrophe
a·po·te·ca·rio *m.* apothecary
a·po·te·o·sis *f.* apotheosis
a·po·yar(se) *v.* to rest on; to support
a·po·yo *m.* support
a·pre·cia·ción *f.* appreciation
a·pre·ciar *v.* to value; to appreciate
a·pre·cio *m.* attention; appraisal
a·pre·hen·der *v.* to seize
a·pre·hen·sión *f.* comprehension; apprehension
a·pren·der *v.* to learn
a·pren·sión *f.* suspicion
a·pre·sar *v.* to seize
a·pre·su·rar *v.* to hurry
a·pre·tar *v.* to crowd; to clutch
a·pro·ba·do, a *adj.* approved
a·pro·bar *v.* to pass
a·pro·pia·do *adj.* appropriate
a·pro·piar(se) *v.* to appropriate
a·pro·vi·sio·nar *v.* to provision
a·pro·xi·mar(se) *v.* to approximate
ap·ti·tud *f.* talent; aptitude
a·pues·ta *f.* wager
a·pun·tar(se) *v.* to aim; to point
a·pun·te *m.* notation; note
a·pu·rar(se) *v.* to worry; to rush
a·que·jar *v.* to distress
a·quel *adj.* that
a·quél *pron.* that one
a·quí *adv.* now; here; then
a·quie·tar *v.* to soothe; to calm down
a·ra *f.* altar
a·ra·ña *f.* spider
ár·bi·trar *v.* to umpire; to arbitrate
ar·bi·tra·rio, a *adj.* arbitrary
ár·bi·tro, a *m.* arbitrator
ár·bol *m.* tree
ar·bo·re·to *m.* arboretum
ar·bus·to *m.* shrub
ar·ca·da *f.* arcade

ar·ca·ís·ta *f.* archaist
ar·cán·gel *m.* archangel
ar·ce *m.* maple tree
ar·co *m.* arch
ar·chi·du·que *m.* archduke
ar·chi·du·que·sa *f.* archduchess
ar·chi·var *v.* to file
ar·chi·vo *m.* archive
ar·der(se) *v.* to burn
ar·dien·te *adj.* ardent; burning
ar·di·lla *f.* squirrel
ar·dor *m.* heat; burning sensation
ar·duo *adj.* arduous
á·rea *f.* area
a·re·no·so *adj.* sandy
a·ren·que *m.* herring
ar·gen·tar *v.* to silver-plate
ar·gen·ta·rio *m.* silversmith
ar·go·lla *f.* ring
ar·güir *v.* to prove; to argue
ar·gu·men·tar *v.* to argue
á·ri·do *adj.* dry
a·ris·co, a *adj.* wild; unfriendly; surly; churlish
a·ris·to·cra·cia *f.* aristocracy
a·ris·tó·cra·ta *m.* aristocrat
a·rit·mé·ti·co *adj.* arithmetic
ar·le·quín *m.* harlequin
ar·ma *f.* weapon
ar·ma·do *adj.* armed
ar·mar *v.* to assemble; to reinforce; to arm; to equip
ar·ma·rio, a *m.* buffet; closet
ar·mi·ño *m.* ermine
ar·mis·ti·cio *m.* armistice
ar·mo·ní·a *f.* accord
ar·mó·ni·co *adj., m.* harmonic
ar·mo·ni·zar *v.* to harmonize
a·ro *m.* hoop; ring
a·ro·ma *m.* fragrance
a·ro·mar *v.* to scent; to perfume
a·ro·má·ti·co *adj.* aromatic
a·ro·ma·ti·zar *v.* to perfume; to scent
a·ro·mo·so *adj.* aromatic
ar·pis·ta *m., f.* harpist
ar·queo·lo·gí·a *f.* archaeology

ar·qui·tec·to *m., f.* architect
ar·qui·tec·tu·ra *f.* architecture
a·rra·ci·ma·do *adj.* bunched
a·rran·car *v.* to seize; to pull up; to obtain; to stem
a·rra·sar *v.* to clear; to level
a·rras·trar(se) *v.* to pull; to crawl; to draw
a·rre·ar *v.* to harness; to herd
a·rre·ba·ta·dor *adj.* exciting
a·rre·ba·to *m.* rage
a·rre·ci·fe *m.* reef
a·rre·gla·do *adj.* neat
a·rre·glar(se) *m.* order; settle
a·rre·glo *m.* understanding; arrangement
a·rre·me·dar *v.* to copy
a·rre·me·ter *v.* to attack
a·rren·dar *v.* to rent
a·rre·o *m.* drove; herd
a·rre·pen·tir·se *v.* to regret
a·rres·ta·do *adj.* arrested
a·rres·to *m.* arrest
a·rri·ba *adv.* above
a·rri·bar *v.* to arrive
a·rri·bis·ta *adj.* social climbing
a·rri·bo *m.* arrival
a·rrien·do *m.* renting
a·rries·ga·do, a *adj.* hazardous; daring
a·rries·gar(se) *v.* to venture; to jeopardize
a·rri·mar *v.* to draw or bring near
a·rri·mo *m.* support
a·rrin·co·na·do *adj.* distant
a·rrin·co·nar *v.* to corner
a·rris·ca·mien·to *m.* boldness; daring
a·rris·car *v.* to fold up; to turn up
a·rrit·mia *f.* lack of rhythm
a·rro·ba·mien·to *m.* rapture; ecstasy
a·rro·bar *v.* to enrapture
a·rro·di·llar(se) *v.* to kneel
a·rro·gan·te *adj.* proud; arrogant
a·rro·jar(se) *v.* to fling; to emit; to throw
a·rro·jo *m.* boldness
a·rro·lla·dor, a *adj.*

overwhelming
a·rro·llar *v.* to carry or sweep away
a·rro·par *v.* to tuck in; to wrap with clothing
a·rro·yo *m.* brook; stream
a·rroz *m.* rice
a·rro·zal *m.* rice paddy or rice field
a·rru·ga *f.* crease; fold; wrinkle line
a·rru·ga·do *adj.* wrinkled
a·rru·gar(se) *v.* to rumple; to wrinkle
a·rrui·nar *v.* to destroy
a·rru·lla·dor *adj.* soothing
a·rru·llar *v.* to lull to sleep; to coo
a·rru·llo *m.* lullaby
a·rru·ma·co *m.* caress
a·rrum·bar *v.* to neglect; to put or cast aside
ar·se·nal *m.* storehouse; shipyard
ar·sé·ni·co *m.* arsenic
ar·te *f.* craft; art
ar·te·fac·to *m.* appliance
ar·te·ria *f.* artery
ar·te·ro *adj.* sly; cunning
ar·te·sa·ní·a *f.* craftsmanship
ar·te·sa·no *m., f.* craftsman or craftswoman
ar·ti·cu·la·ción *f.* joint
ar·ti·cu·lar *v.* to articulate
ar·tis·ta *f., m.* artist
ar·ti·fi·cio *m.* item; article; thing
ar·ti·fi·cial *adj.* artificial
ar·tís·ti·co *adj.* artistic
ar·tri·tis *f.* arthritis
ar·zo·bis·po *m.* archbishop
as *m.* ace
a·sa·do *m.* roasted meat; barbecue
a·sa·dor *m.* grill
a·sa·la·ria·do, a *adj.* salaried worker
a·sa·la·riar *v.* to set a salary for someone
a·sal·ta·dor, a *f., m.* assailant
a·sal·tar *v.* to attack
a·sal·to *m.* attack
a·sam·ble·a *f.* conference; meeting
a·sam·ble·ís·ta *m., f.*

assembly member

as•cen•den•te *adj.* ascending

as•cen•der *v.* to promote; to ascend

as•cen•sión *f.* rise; ascension

as•cen•so *m.* ascent; promotion

as•cen•sor *m.* lift; elevator

as•cen•so•ris•ta *m., f.* one who operates an elevator

as•co *m.* disgust

a•se•ar *v.* to clean; to wash

a•se•char *v.* to trap

a•se•diar *v.* to bother; to pester

a•se•dio *m.* siege

a•se•gu•ra•do *adj.* insured

a•se•gu•rar(se) *v.* to fasten; to assure; to secure

a•se•me•jar(se) *v.* to resemble

a•sen•ta•de•ras *f., pl.* buttocks; behind

a•sen•ta•do *adj.* judicious

a•sen•tar *v.* to record

a•sen•ti•mien•to *m.* consent

a•sen•tir *v.* to agree

a•se•o *m.* tidiness; neatness

a•se•qui•ble *adj.* understandable; accessible

a•ser•ción *f.* affirmation

a•se•rra•de•ro *m.* sawmill

a•se•rrar *v.* to saw

a•se•si•nar *v.* to murder

a•se•si•na•to *m.* murder; assassination

a•se•si•no *adj.* murder, assassin

a•se•sor, a *adj.* advisory; advising

a•se•so•rar *v.* to advise

a•ses•tar *v.* to hit; to punch

a•se•ve•rar *v.* to assert

a•se•ve•ra•ti•vo *adj.* affirmative; assertive

a•se•xua•do *adj.* asexual

as•fal•tar *v.* to spread asphalt

as•fal•to *m.* asphalt

as•fi•xia *f.* suffocation

as•fi•xiar *v.* to asphyxiate

a•sí *adv.* so

a•sien•to *m.* seat

a•sig•nar *v.* to allot; assign

a•sig•nar *v.* to appoint; to assign

a•sig•na•ción *f.* course or subject in school

a•si•lar *v.* to give shelter

a•si•lo *m.* asylum

a•si•mi•lar(se) *v.* to assimilate

a•si•mis•mo *adv.* in a like manner

a•sir(se) *v.* to grip; to hold on to

a•sis•ten•cia *f.* attendance

a•sis•ten•cial *adj.* relief; assisting

a•sis•tir *v.* to accompany; to aid; to attend

as•ma *f.* asthma

as•má•ti•co *adj., m., f.* asthmatic

as•na•da *f.* stupidity

a•so•cia•ción *f.* association

a•so•cia•do *adj.* associated

a•so•ciar(se) *v.* to associate with

a•so•la•dor *adj.* ravaging

a•so•lar *v.* to scorch

a•so•le•a•mien•to *m.* sunstroke

a•so•le•ar *v.* to place in the sun

a•so•mar *v.* to show; to appear

a•som•brar(se) *v.* to amaze; to astonish

as•pi•rar *v.* to breathe; to inhale

as•pi•ri•na *f.* aspirin

as•tro•lo•gí•a *f.* astrology

as•tro•no•mí•a *f.* astronomy

as•tu•ta *adj.* artful; sly; canny; cunning

a•sun•to *m.* issue; concern

a•ta•car *v.* to assault; to charge

a•ta•que *m.* attack

a•tar(se) *v.* to rope; to tie; to brace

a•ten•ción *f.* attention

a•ten•der *v.* to heed; to attend

a•tes•ti•guar *v.* to testify

a•tie•sar(se) *v.* to tighten

at•le•ta *f., m.* athlete

at•lé•ti•co, a *adj.* athletic

a•tó•mi•co *adj.* atomic

á•to•mo *m.* atom

a•trac•ción *f.* attraction

a•trac•ti•vo *adj.* engaging

a•traer *v.* to engage; to lure

a•trás *adv.* aback; back

a•tra•sa•do *adj.* backwards

a•tri•buir *v.* to ascribe

a•tro•ci•dad *f.* atrocity

a•tur•dir(se) *v.* to daze; to bewilder

au•di•ción *f.* audition

au•gus•to *adj.* August

au•men•tar(se) *v.* to augment; to enhance

au•men•to *m.* raise; increase

aún *adv.* still

aun•que *conj.* although

au•sen•te *adj.* missing

au•ten•ti•ci•dad *f.* authenticity

au•to•bús *m.* bus

au•tó•gra•fo *m.* autograph

au•to•mó•vil *m.* car

au•to•ri•za•ción *f.* authorization

a•van•zar(se) *v.* to advance

a•ve *f.* bird

a•ve•ni•da *f.* avenue

a•ven•tu•ra *f.* adventure

a•ver•sión *f.* aversion

a•via•ción *f.* aviation

a•vión *m.* plane; airplane

a•yu•da *f.* aid; help

a•yu•dar *v.* to assist; to help

a•zo•rar *v.* to embarrass

a•zo•rra•do *adj.* foxy

a•zo•ta•do *adj.* whipped

a•zo•tar *v.* to beat upon

a•zo•te *m.* spanking; whip

a•zú•car *m.* sugar

a•zu•ca•ra•do *adj.* sweet

a•zu•fre *m.* sulphur

a•zul *m.* blue

a•zu•la•do *adj.* bluish

a•zu•lar *v.* to color or dye blue

a•zu•le•jo *m.* glazed tile

B

ba•lís•ti•co *adj.* ballistic

ba•lon•ces•to *m.* basketball

ba•lon•ma•no *m.* handball

ba•lon•vo•le•a *m.* volleyball

ba•lo•ta *f.* ballot

bal•sa *f.* balsa

bál•sa•mo *m.* balsam

ba•lle•na *f.* whale

ba•lle•na•to *m.* whale calf

ba•lle•ne•ro, a *adj.* whaling

ba•lles•ta *f.* crossbow

ba•lles•te•ar *v.* to shoot with a crossbow

ba•lles•te•rí•a *f.* archery

bam•ba•le•ar *v.* to sway

bam•bo•le•o *m.* wobble

ba•llet *m.* ballet

bam•bú *m.* bamboo

ba•na•na *f.* banana

ban•ca *f.* banking

ban•ca•rro•ta *f.* bankruptcy

ban•co *m.* bank; band; pew; bench

ban•da•da *f.* flock; group

ban•de•ra *f.* ensign; flag

ban•de•ja *f.* tray

ban•de•ro•la *f.* pennant

ban•di•do *m.* bandit

ban•do•le•ro *m.* bandit

ban•que•ta *f.* stool

ban•que•te *m.* feast

ban•que•tear *v.* to feast

ba•ñar(se) *v.* to bathe

ba•ño *m.* bathtub, bathroom

ba•ra•jar *v.* to shuffle

ba•ra•to *adv.* cheaply; *adj.* inexpensive; cheap

bar•ba *f.* beard

bar•ba•coa *f.* barbecue

bar•ba•do *adj.* bearded

bar•ba•ri•dad *f.* outrage

bár•ba•ra, o *f., m.* savage

bar•bear *v.* to shave

bar•be•ro *m.* barber

bar•bi•lla *f.* chin

bar•bo•tar *v.* to mutter; to mumble

bar•bo•te•o *m.* murmuring

bar•bu•do *adj.* heavily bearded

bar•bu•lla *f.* chatter; jabbering

bar•ca *f.* small boat

bar•ca•za *f.* launch

bar•co *m.* ship; boat

ba•rí•to•no *m.* baritone

bar•niz *m.* glaze; varnish; lacquer

bar•ni•zar *v.* to varnish; to lacquer

ba•ró•me•tro *m.* barometer

ba•rón *m.* baron

ba•ro•ne•sa *f.* baroness

ba•rra *f.* bar

ba•rra•ca *f.* booth

ba•rrer *v.* to sweep

ba·rre·ra *f.* barricade
ba·rri·ga *f.* belly
ba·rril *m.* barrel
ba·rrio *m.* neighborhood
ba·sal·to *m.* basalt
ba·sar *v.* to base
ba·se *f.* foundation
bá·si·co *adj.* basic
ba·sí·li·ca *f.* basilica
bas·quet·bol *m.* basketball
bas·tan·te *adj.* sufficient
bas·tar *v.* to suffice
bas·tar·dear *v.* to debase
bas·to *adj.* rough
bas·tón *m.* baton; stick
ba·su·ra *f.* rubbish
ba·ta *f.* negligee
ba·ta·lla *f.* battle
ba·ta·llar *v.* to battle
ba·ta·llón *m.* battalion
ba·te·rí·a *f.* battery
ba·ti·do *m.* batter
ba·tir(se) *v.* to churn
ba·tu·ta *f.* baton
baúl *m.* trunk
bau·tis·mo *m.* christening
bau·ti·zar *v.* to baptize
ba·ya *f.* berry
ba·yo *adj.* bay
ba·zar *m.* bazaar
ba·zu·ca *f.* bazooka
bea·ti·fi·car *v.* to beatify
bea·tí·fi·co *adj.* beatific
bea·ti·tud *f.* beatitude
be·bé *m.* baby
be·ber *v.* to drink
be·bi·da *f.* beverage
be·ca *f.* scholarship
be·ce·rro *m.* calf
be·far *v.* to taunt
beige *m.* beige
béis·bol *m.* baseball
be·li·co·so, a *adj.* warlike
be·li·ge·ran·te *adj.* belligerent
be·lle·za *f.* beauty
be·llo *adj.* beautiful
be·mol *m.* flat
ben·de·cir *v.* to bless
ben·di·ción *f.* blessing
ben·di·to *adj.* holy
be·ne·fi·ciar(se) *v.* to benefit
be·ne·fi·cio·so *adj.* beneficial
be·né·fi·co *adj.* charitable
be·né·vo·lo *adj.* benevolent

ben·ga·la *f.* flare
be·nig·ni·dad *f.* kindness
be·nig·no *adj.* kind; mild
be·rrin·che *m.* tantrum
be·sar(se) *v.* to smooch; to kiss
be·so *m.* kiss
bes·tia *f.* animal
bes·tial *adj.* bestial
Bi·blia *f.* Bible
bí·bli·co *adj.* Biblical
bi·blio·gra·fí·a *f.* bibliography
bi·blió·gra·fo, a *m.* bibliographer
bi·blio·te·ca *f.* library
bí·ceps *m.* biceps
bi·ci·cle·ta *f.* bicycle
bi·ci·clis·ta *m., f.* bicyclist
bi·cho *m.* bug
bien *m.* good
bien·ve·ni·da *f.* greeting
bi·fur·car·se *v.* to fork
bi·go·te *m.* mustache
bi·la·te·ral *adj.* bilateral
bi·lio·so *adj.* bilious
bi·lis *f.* bile
bi·llar *m.* billiards
bi·lle·te *m.* bill
bi·llón *m.* trillion
bi·na·rio *adj.* binary
bio·gra·fí·a *f.* biography
bio·grá·fi·co *adj.* biographical
bió·gra·fo *m.* biographer
bio·lo·gí·a *f.* biology
bio·ló·gi·co *adj.* biological
bió·lo·go *m.* biologist
biop·sia *f.* biopsy
bi·sa·bue·la, o *f., m.* great-grandmother; great-grandfather
bi·se·car *v.* to bisect
bi·sec·ción *f.* bisection
bi·son·te *m.* bison
biz·quear *v.* to squint
blan·co *adj.* blank; white
blan·dir *v.* to brandish
blan·do *adj.* supple; soft
blan·quear *v.* to whiten
blas·fe·mar *v.* to swear
blas·fe·mia *f.* profanity
blin·da·do *adj.* armored
blo·que *m.* block
blo·quear *v.* to block
blu·sa *f.* blouse
bo·bo *m.* fool; ninny

bo·ca *f.* mouth
bo·ca·di·llo *m.* sandwich
bo·ca·do *m.* bite
bo·da *f.* marriage
bo·de·ga *f.* wine cellar
boi·co·teo *m.* boycott
bo·la *f.* fib; ball
bo·le·tín *m.* bulletin
bo·li·che *m.* bowling
bo·li·ta *f.* pellet
bol·sa *f.* bag; pouch
bol·si·llo *m.* pocket
bol·sis·ta *m.* stockbroker
bol·so *m.* handbag
bo·llo *m.* bump
bom·ba *f.* pump; bomb
bom·bar·de·ro *m.* bomber
bom·bear *v.* to pad; pump
bom·bi·lla *f.* bulb
bom·bón *m.* sweet
bon·dad *f.* kindness
bon·da·do·so, a *adj.* good
bo·ni·to, a *adj.* pretty
bo·que·a·da *f.* gasp
bo·qui·lla *f.* nozzle
bor·de *m.* edge
bor·di·llo *m.* curb
bo·rra·cho *m.* drunkard
bo·rra·dor *m.* eraser
bos·que *m.* woods
bos·que·jar *v.* to outline
bo·ta *f.* wine bag
bo·tá·ni·ca *f.* botany
bo·te *m.* jackpot
bo·te·lla *f.* bottle
bo·ti·ca·rio *m.* druggist
bo·tín *m.* loot
bo·tón *m.* stud, button
bo·to·nes *m.* bellhop
bó·ve·da *f.* vault
bo·vi·no, a *adj.* bovine
bo·xea·dor *m.* boxer
bo·xear *v.* to box
bo·ya *f.* buoy
bo·yan·te *adj.* buoyant
bo·zal *m.* muzzle
bra·man·te *m.* twine
bra·mar *v.* to bellow; to roar
bra·mi·do *m.* bellow
bra·vo, a *adj.* brave
bra·za·do *m.* armful
bra·zo *m.* arm
bre·ve *adj.* short
bre·ve·dad *f.* conciseness
bri·bón *adj.* lazy
bri·llan·te *adj.* bright; shiny
bri·llar *v.* to glow; to beam

bri·llo *m.* glow; shine
brin·car *v.* to jump; to gambol
brí·o *m.* jauntiness
bri·sa *f.* breeze
bro·ca·do *m.* brocade
bro·che *m.* brooch
bro·mear(se) *v.* to joke
bro·mis·ta *f.* joker
bron·ce *m.* bronze
bron·cea·do *m.* suntan; bronze
bron·ce·ar *v.* to tan; to bronze
bron·co *adj.* coarse; rough
bron·quial *adj.* bronchial
bron·quio *m.* bronchial tube
bron·qui·tis *f.* bronchitis
bro·quel *m.* small shield
bro·ta·du·ra *f.* budding; sprouting
bro·tar *v.* to bud
bru·je·rí·a *f.* witchcraft
bru·jo *m.* wizard
brú·ju·la *f.* compass
bru·mo·so *adj.* foggy; misty
bru·ñi·du·ra *f.* polishing; burnishing
bru·ñir *v.* to burnish; to polish
brus·co, a *adj.* sudden
bru·to *m.* beast; brute
bu·bón *m.* swelling or very large tumor
bu·ce·ar *v.* to swim under water
bu·cle *m.* curl; ringlet
bu·dín *m.* pudding
bue·na·ven·tu·ra *f.* good luck; good fortune
bue·no, a *adj.* sound; good
buey *m.* ox
bú·fa·lo *m.* buffalo
bu·fan·da *f.* muffler; scarf
bu·fón *m.* clown; buffoon
bu·ho·ne·ro *m.* hawker; peddler
bui·tre *m.* vulture
bu·jí·a *f.* candle; sparkplug
bul·bo *m.* bulb
bu·le·var *m.* boulevard
bul·to *m.* mass; heft
bu·lla *f.* uproar; brawl; crowd; mob
bu·lli·cio *m.* riot; racket; hubbub
bu·llir *v.* to boil

bu•me•rang *m.* boomerang
bu•ñue•lo *m.* fried dough
bu•que *m.* vessel; ship
bu•qué *m.* bouquet
bur•bu•ja *f.* bubble
bur•de•os *adj.* deep red in color
bur•do *adj.* rough; coarse
bur•gue•sí•a *f.* middle class
bu•ri•lar *v.* to engrave
bur•la *f.* taunt; joke
bur•lar(se) *v.* to gibe; to joke
bur•les•co *adj.* burlesque
bu•ró•cra•ta *f.* bureaucrat
bu•rra *f.* stupid woman
bu•rro *m.* donkey; burro
bur•sá•til *adj.* stock market
bus•ca *f.* search
bus•ca•pié *m.* feeler
bus•car *v.* to look or search for
bus•ca•vi•das *m., f.* busybody
bús•que•da *f.* search
bus•to *m.* bust; chest
bu•ta•ca *f.* armchair
bu•ta•no *m.* butane
bu•ti•le•no *m.* butylene
bu•zo *m.* deep-sea diver
bu•zón *m.* mailbox

C

ca•bal *adj.* fair; precise
cá•ba•la *f.* cabala
ca•bal•gar *v.* to ride on horseback
ca•bal•ga•ta *f.* cavalcade
ca•ba•lle•rí•a *f.* cavalry
ca•ba•lle•ri•za *f.* stable
ca•ba•lle•ro *m.* gentleman
ca•ba•lle•te *m.* easel; sawhorse
ca•ba•lli•to, a *m.* pony, small horse
ca•ba•llo *m.* horse
ca•ba•llón *m.* ridge
ca•ba•ña *f.* cabin
ca•ba•ret *m.* cabaret; night club
ca•be•ci•lla *m.* ringleader
ca•be•lle•ra *f.* head of chair
ca•be•llo *m.* hair
ca•ber *v.* to fit
ca•bes•tri•llo *m.* sling
ca•bes•tro *m.* halter

ca•be•za *f.* skull; head
ca•be•zón, a *adj.* big-headed
ca•be•zo•ta *m., f.* mule
ca•bil•dear *v.* to lobby
ca•bil•do *m.* town council
ca•ble *m.* cable
ca•ble•gra•fiar *v.* to cable
ca•ble•gra•ma *m.* cablegram
ca•ble•vi•sión *f.* cable television
ca•bo *m.* corporal; cape
ca•bra *f.* goat
ca•brí•o *m.* rafter
ca•bri•to *m.* young goat; kid
ca•bro•na•da *f., coll.* dirty trick
ca•ca•hue•te *m.* peanut
ca•cao *m.* cocoa
ca•ca•re•ar *v.* to crow; to cackle
ca•ca•tú•a *f.* cockatoo
ca•ce•ro•la *f.* casserole
ca•ci•que *m.* Indian chief
ca•ci•que•ar *v., coll.* to order people around
ca•co *m.* burglar
cac•to *m.* cactus
ca•cha•lo•te *m.* sperm whale
ca•char *v.* to split; to chip
ca•cha•za *f.* sluggish
ca•che•ar *v.* to frisk; to search
ca•che•te•ar *v., Amer.* to slap; to hit
ca•che•ti•na *f.* fist fight
ca•che•tu•do *adj.* plump or chubby-cheeks
ca•cho•rro *m.* puppy
ca•da *adj.* every; each
ca•dal•so *m.* platform
ca•dá•ver *m.* body; corpse
ca•da•vé•ri•co *adj.* cadaverous
ca•de•na *f.* chain
ca•den•cia *f.* rhythm; cadence
ca•de•ra *f.* hip, hip joint
ca•de•te *m.* cadet
ca•du•co, a *adj.* lapsed; expired
caer(se) *v.* to fall
ca•fé *m.* coffee; cafe
ca•fe•í•na *f.* caffeine
ca•fe•tal *m.* coffee plantation

ca•fe•te•rí•a *f.* cafeteria; cafe
caí•da *f.* downfall; tumble
cai•mán *m.* alligator
ca•ja *f.* cabinet; chest
ca•je•ro *m.* cashier; teller
ca•jis•ta *m., f.* typesetter
cal *f.* lime
ca•la *f.* cove
ca•la•ba•za *f.* pumpkin; gourd; squash
ca•la•bo•zo *m.* jail; underground prison cell
ca•la•dor *m.* driller
ca•la•fa•te•ar *v.* to calk; to caulk
ca•la•mar *m.* squid
ca•lam•bre *m.* cramp
ca•la•mi•dad *f.* calamity; misfortune
ca•la•mi•to•so *adj.* calamitous
ca•la•ña *f.* character; nature
ca•lar(se) *v.* to swoop; to penetrate
cal•ce•te•rí•a *f.* hosiery
cal•ce•tín *m.* sock
cal•ci•fi•ca•ción *f.* calcification
cal•ci•fi•car(se) *v.* to calcify
cal•cio *m.* calcium
cal•co *m.* tracing
cal•co•ma•ní•a *f.* decal
cal•cu•la•dor, a *m., f.* calculator
cal•cu•lar *v.* to estimate; to calculate
cal•cu•lis•ta *m., f.* planner; calculator
cál•cu•lo *m.* calculation
cal•de•ra *f.* boiler
cal•do *m.* soup; broth; stock
ca•le•fac•ción *f.* heating; heat
ca•le•fac•tor *m.* heater
ca•len•da•rio *m.* calendar; schedule
ca•len•ta•dor *adj.* warming; heating
ca•len•tar(se) *v.* to heat or to warm
ca•lien•te *adj.* warm; hot
ca•li•na *f.* haze
ca•lip•so *m.* calypso
cal•ma *f.* calm
cal•man•te *adj.* sedative *m.* tranquilizer
cal•mar(se) *v.* to soothe; to calm; to settle

ca•lo•frí•o *m.* chill; fever
ca•lor *m.* warmth; heat
ca•lo•rí•a *f.* calorie
ca•ló•ri•co *adj.* caloric
ca•lum•nia *f.* slander; calumny
ca•lum•nia•dor, a *adj.* slanderous
ca•lu•ro•so *adj.* warm; hot
cal•va•rio *m.* Calvary
cal•vi•cie *f.* baldness
cal•vo *adj.* bald
cal•za•da *f.* causeway; drive; highway; road
cal•zo•nes *m., pl.* trousers
ca•llar(se) *v.* to keep quiet; to hush
ca•lle *f.* street
ca•lle•jue•la *f.* alley
ca•llo *m.* callus; corn
ca•ma *f.* bed
ca•ma•da *f.* litter; brood
ca•ma•feo *m.* cameo
cá•ma•ra *f.* room; chamber
ca•ma•ra•da *m., f.* comrade
ca•ma•re•ra *f.* waitress
ca•ma•re•ro *m.* waiter
ca•ma•ro•te *m.* cabin
cam•biar(se) *v.* to change; to alter
cam•bia•ví•a *m.* rail switch
cam•bio *m.* shift; change
cam•bis•ta *m., f.* broker; moneychanger
ca•me•le•ar *v. coll.* to deceive
ca•me•lia *f.* camellia
ca•me•llo *m.* camel
ca•me•ro, a *adj.* double bed
ca•mi•lla *f.* stretcher
ca•mi•nar *v.* to walk; to travel
ca•mi•na•ta *f.* hike; walk
ca•mi•no *m.* route; road
ca•mión *m.* truck
ca•mio•ne•ro, a *m., f.* truck driver
ca•mio•ne•ta *f.* van
ca•mi•sa *f.* shirt
ca•mi•se•ta *f.* shirt; undershirt
ca•mi•so•la *f.* camisole
ca•mi•són *m.* nightgown
ca•mo•rra *f., coll.* squabble
ca•mo•rre•ar *v., coll.* to quarrel; to squabble

cam•pa•men•to *m.* camp
cam•pa•na *f.* bell
cam•pa•ña *f.* campaign
cam•pe•si•no, a *adj.* country; peasant
cam•pes•tre *adj.* rural
cam•pis•ta *m., f.* camper
cam•po *m.* country; field
cam•po•san•to *m.* graveyard; cemetery
ca•mu•fla•je *m.* camouflage
ca•mu•flar *v.* to camouflage
ca•nal *m.* canal; channel
ca•na•le•te *m.* paddle
ca•nas•ta *f.* hamper; basket
can•ce•la•ción *f.* cancellation
can•ce•lar *v.* to cancel
can•ci•ller *m.* chancellor
can•ci•lle•rí•a *f.* chancellery
can•ción *f.* song
can•cio•ne•ro *m.* songbook
can•cro *m.* canker
can•da•do *m.* padlock
can•de•la *f.* candle
can•de•le•ro *m.* candlestick
can•di•da•to *m.* candidate
can•di•da•tu•ra *f.* candidacy
cán•di•do *adj.* unsophisticated
ca•ne•la *f.* cinnamon
ca•ne•lón *m.* roof gutter
ca•ne•lo•nes *m., pl.* cannelloni
ca•ne•sú *m.* bodice; yoke
can•gre•jo *m.* crab
can•gu•ro *m.* kangaroo
ca•ní•bal *m.* cannibal
ca•ni•ca *f.* marble
ca•ni•no *adj.* canine
ca•ní•cu•la *f.* midsummer heat; dog days of summer
ca•ni•lla *f.* shinbone
ca•ni•lli•ta *m.* newspaper boy
ca•ni•no, a *adj., m.* canine
can•je *m.* trade; exchange
can•je•a•ble *adj.* exchangeable
can•je•ar *v.* to trade; to exchange
ca•no, a *adj.* gray-haired
ca•noa *f.* canoe; rowboat
ca•ñon *m.* canyon, cannon; barrel
can•sa•do *adj.* weary; tired; rundown

can•san•cio *m.* tiredness
can•sar(se) *v.* to weary; to tire
can•ta•lu•po *m.* cantaloupe
can•tan•te *m., f.* singer
can•tar *v.* to sing; to chant *m.* song
can•ti•dad *f.* quantity; amount
can•tim•plo•ra *f.* canteen
can•to *m.* singing; croak
can•tu•rrear *v.* to croon; to hum
ca•ña *f.* cane; reed
ca•os *m.* chaos
ca•pa *f.* cape; coating; layer
ca•pa•ci•dad *f.* capacity; capability
ca•pa•taz *m.* foreman
ca•paz *adj.* roomy; capable
cap•cio•so *adj.* deceitful
ca•pe•llán *m.* chaplain
ca•pe•ru•za *f.* hood
ca•pi•lar *adj. m.* capillary
ca•pi•la•ri•dad *f.* capillarity
ca•pi•lla *f.* chapel
ca•pi•llo *m.* baby bonnet; cap
ca•pi•ro•ta•zo *m.* flip, as with the finger
ca•pi•tal *m.* capital
ca•pi•ta•lis•mo *m.* capitalism
ca•pi•tán *m.* captain
ca•pi•to•lio *m.* capitol
ca•pí•tu•lo *m.* chapter
ca•pó *m.* bonnet; hood
ca•pón *adj.* castrated
ca•pri•cho *m.* whim; fancy; quick
ca•pri•cho•so *adj.* temperamental; whimsical
cáp•su•la *f.* capsule
cap•tu•ra *f.* capture; catch
ca•pu•cha *f.* hood
ca•pu•llo *m.* cocoon
ca•qui *m.* khaki
ca•ra *f.* face
ca•ra•col *m.* snail
ca•rác•ter *m.* nature; character
ca•rac•te•rís•ti•co, a *adj.* typical
ca•rac•te•ri•za•do, a *adj.* distinguished
ca•rac•te•ri•za•dor, a *adj.* distinguishing
ca•rac•te•ri•zar *v.*

to characterize
ca•ra•cú *m., Amer.* bonemarrow
ca•rám•ba•no *m.* icicle
ca•ra•me•li•zar *v.* to cover with caramel
ca•ra•me•lo *m.* caramel
ca•ra•va•na *f.* caravan
car•bo•hi•dra•to *m.* carbohydrate
car•bón *m.* coal
car•bo•na•to *m.* carbonate
car•bo•no *m.* carbon
car•bun•co *m.* carbuncle
car•bu•ra•dor *m.* carburetor
car•bu•ran•te *m.* fuel
cár•cel *f.* prison; jail
car•de•nal *m.* cardinal
car•dí•a•co *adj.* cardiac
ca•re•cer *v.* to lack
ca•ren•cia *f.* need; lack
ca•rey *m.* sea turtle
car•ga *f.* burden; load
car•ga•de•ro *m.* loading platform
car•ga•men•to *m.* cargo
car•gar(se) *v.* to burden; to load
car•go *m.* charge; burden; load
ca•riar•se *v.* to decay
ca•ri•dad *f.* charity
ca•ri•ño, a *m.* affection; love
ca•ri•ta•ti•vo *adj.* charitable
car•nal *adj.* carnal
car•na•val *m.* carnival
car•ne *f.* pulp; flesh; meat
car•ne•ar *v. Amer.* to slaughter
car•ni•ce•rí•a *f.* slaughter; bloodshed
car•ni•ce•ro *m.* butcher
car•pe•ta *f.* folder
car•pin•te•rí•a *f.* carpentry
car•pin•te•ro *m.* carpenter
ca•rre•ra *f.* career; race
ca•rre•ro *m.* carrier
ca•rre•ta•je *m.* cartage
ca•rre•te *m.* reel; spool; coil; bobbin
ca•rre•te•ra *f.* road; highway
ca•rro•za *f.* coach; chariot
ca•rrua•je *m.* carriage
ca•rru•sel *m.* merry-go-round
car•ta *f.* card; letter
car•ta•pa•cio *m.* notebook

car•tel *m.* poster
car•te•le•ra *f.* billboard
car•te•ra *f.* billfold; wallet
car•te•ro *m.* postman
car•tí•la•go *m.* gristle; cartilage
car•tón *m.* cardboard
car•tu•cho *m.* cartridge
ca•sa *f.* home; house
ca•sa•ca *f.* dress coat
ca•sa•do, a *adj.* married
ca•sar(se) *v.* to wed; to marry
cas•ca•bel *m.* small bell
cas•ca•be•le•ar *v.* to jingle
cas•ca•do, a *adj.* cracked; decrepit
cas•ca•da *f.* cascade
cas•ca•jo *m.* gravel
cás•ca•ra *f.* hull; shell; skin; rind
ca•se•ta *f.* cottage
ca•se•te *m., f.* tape cartridge; cassette
cas•co•te *m.* rubble
ca•si *adj.* almost
ca•si•mir *m.* cashmere
ca•si•no *m.* casino
ca•so *m.* happening; case
cas•pa *f.* dandruff
cas•ta *f.* breed; caste; cast
cas•ta•ñe•te•ar *v.* to chatter
cas•ti•dad *f.* chastity
cas•ti•gar *v.* to punish
cas•ti•llo *m.* castle
cas•tor *m.* beaver
cas•tra•ción *f.* castration
ca•sual *adj.* accidental; coincidental
ca•sua•li•dad *f.* coincidence; chance
ca•ta•le•jo *m.* small telescope; spyglass
ca•ta•lo•gar *v.* to catalog; to catalogue
ca•tar *v.* to taste; to sample
ca•ta•ra•ta *f.* waterfall; cataract
ca•tás•tro•fe *f.* catastrophe
ca•te•dral *f.* cathedral
ca•te•go•rí•a *f.* category
ca•ter•va *f.* gang
ca•té•ter *m.* catheter
ca•tin•ga *f.* body odor
ca•tor•ce *adj.* fourteen
ca•tre *m.* cot made of canvas
cau•ce *m.* channel; riverbed;

ditch
cau•ción *f.* bail; caution
cau•cho *m.* rubber; rubber tree or plant
cau•di•llo *m.* leader
cau•sa *f.* cause
cau•te•la *f.* caution
cau•te•lo•so, a *adj.* cautious
cau•te•ri•zar *v.* to captivate
cau•ti•ve•rio *m.* captivity
cau•ti•vo, a *adj. m., f.* captive
cau•to, a *adj.* cautious
ca•var *v.* to dig
ca•ver•na *f.* cave, cavern
ca•viar *m.* caviar
ca•vi•dad *f.* cavity
ca•vi•la•ción *f.* rumination, pondering
ca•vi•lar *v.* to ruminate; ponder
ca•za *f.* hunt game
ca•za•dor, a *adj.* hunting
ca•zar *v.* to hunt
ca•zo *m.* ladle
ca•zue•la *m.* pan
ce•bar *v.* to fatten
ce•bo•lla *f.* onion
ce•bra *f.* zebra
ce•ce•o *m.* lisp
ce•dro *m.* cedar
cé•du•la *f.* document
cé•fi•ro *m.* zephyr
ce•gar *v.* to blind
ce•gue•ra *f.* blindness
ce•ja *f.* eyebrow
ce•jar *v.* to back up
ce•la•da *f.* ambush
ce•la•dor, a *adj.* vigilant; watchful
ce•lar *v.* to comply with something
cel•da *f.* cell
ce•le•bra•ción *f.* celebration
ce•le•bran•te *adj.* celebrating
ce•le•brar *v.* to celebrate
cé•le•bre *adj.* famous; celebrated
ce•le•bri•dad *f.* celebrity
ce•le•ri•dad *f.* speed
ce•les•te *adj.* sky-blue
ce•les•tial *adj.* heavenly
ce•les•ti•na *f.* madam; procuress
ce•li•ba•to *m.* celibacy

cé•li•be *adj. f.* celibate
ce•lo•fán *m.* cellophane
ce•lo•sí•a *f.* latticework
ce•lo•so, a *adj.* zealous
cé•lu•la *f.* cell
ce•lu•loi•de *m.* celluloid
ce•lu•lo•so *adj.* cellulous
ce•llis•ca *f.* sleet
ce•men•te•rio *m.* cemetery
ce•men•to *m.* cement
ce•na *f.* supper; dinner
ce•na•gal *m.* swamp
ce•nar *v.* to have dinner
cen•ce•rro *m.* cowbell
ce•ni•ce•ro *m.* ashtray
ce•nit *m.* zenith
cen•sor *m.* censor
cen•su•rar *v.* to censor
cen•te•lla *f.* flash
cen•te•lle•an•te *adj.* sparkling
cen•te•na *f.* one hundred
cen•te•nar *m.* one hundred
cen•te•no *m.* rye
cen•té•si•mo *adj.* hundredth
cen•tí•gra•do *adj.* centigrade
cen•tí•me•tro *m.* centimeter
cen•ti•ne•la *m., f.* sentry
cen•to•lla *f.* spider crab
cen•tra•do, a *adj.* centered
cen•tral *adj.* central
cen•tra•li•zar *v.* to centralize
cen•trar *v.* to center
cén•tri•co *adj.* central
cen•tro *m.* core; middle; center
ce•ñir *v.* to encircle; to bind
ce•ño *m.* frown
ce•pa *f.* stump
ce•pi•llo *m.* brush
ce•ra *f.* wax
ce•rá•mi•ca *f.* ceramics
cer•ca *adv.* near; close
cer•ca *f.* fence
cer•ca•ní•a *f.* nearness *pl.* outskirts
cer•ca•no *adj.* near; close
cer•car *v.* to surround; to fence something in
cer•ce•nar *v.* to cut
cer•cio•rar *v.* to assure
cer•co *m.* circle
cer•da *f.* pig; sow
cer•do *m.* pig
cer•do•so *adj.* bristly

ce•real *m.* cereal
ce•re•bral *adj.* cerebral
ce•re•bro *m.* brain
ce•re•mo•nia *f.* ceremony
ce•re•mo•nial *m.* ceremonial
ce•re•za *f.* cherry
ce•ri•lla *f.* match
ce•ro *m.* zero
ce•rra•do *adj.* shut
ce•rra•du•ra *f.* lock
ce•rrar(se) *v.* to close; to seal
ce•rro•jo *m.* bolt
cer•ti•fi•ca•do *m.* certificate
cer•ti•fi•car *v.* to certify
cer•va•to *m.* fawn
cer•ve•za *f.* ale; beer
ce•sar *v.* to cease
ce•sión *f.* grant; cession
cés•ped *m.* grass; sod; lawn
ces•ta *f.* basket
cha•le•co *m.* vest
cha•ma•rra *f.* short jacket
cham•pú *m.* shampoo
chan•ta•je *m.* blackmail
cha•pa *f.* metal plate; sheet
cha•que•ta *f.* jacket
char•la *f.* talk; chat
char•lar *v.* to chat; to talk
char•la•tán *adj.* talkative; gossipy *m.* trickster; charlatan
cha•rol *m.* varnish; *Amer.* tray
cha•ro•la *f. Amer.* tray
chas•qui *m. Amer.* messenger; courier
chas•qui•do *m.* click; snap; crack
cha•val *m.* lad; boy; kid
che•que *m.* cheque; check
chi•ca•no *adj.* Mexican-American
chi•cle *m.* chewing-gum
chi•co *adj.* small; little boy; child
chi•llar *v.* to yell; to scream
chi•me•ne•a *f.* chimney
chis•me *m.* piece of gossip
chis•pa *f.* spark
chis•te *m.* joke, funny story
chis•to•so *adj.* funny; amusing
cho•can•te *adj.* startling; shocking
cho•car *v.* to shock; to startle; to collide

cho•co•la•te *adj.* chocolate
chó•fer *m.* driver; chauffeur
cho•que *m.* impact; crash
chu•bas•co *m.* shower; squall; storm
chus•ma *f.* rabble; mob
chu•tar *v.* to shoot (at goal)
cí•cli•co *adj.* cyclic
ci•clis•ta *m., f.* cyclist
ci•clo *m.* circle
ci•clón *m.* cyclone
ci•cu•ta *f.* hemlock
cie•go *adj.* sightless; blind
cie•lo *m.* heaven; sky
cien *adj.* hundred
cié•na•ga *f.* swamp
cien•cia *f.* science
cien•tí•fi•co *m.* scientist
cien•to *m.* hundred
cie•rre *m.* snap
cier•ta•men•te *adv.* certainly
cier•to, a *adj.* certain; sure
cier•vo *m.* stag, deer
ci•fra *f.* figure; cipher
ci•frar *v.* to cipher
ci•ga•rri•llo *m.* cigarette
ci•lin•dro *m.* cylinder
ci•ma *f.* crest; summit; top
cin•co *adj.* five
cin•cuen•ta *adj.* fifty
ci•ne *m.* movies
cin•ta *f.* tape; ribbon
cin•to *m.* girdle
cin•tu•rón *m.* belt
ci•prés *m.* cypress
cir•co *m.* circus
cir•cu•la•ción *f.* circulation
cir•cu•lar *adj.* circular
cír•cu•lo *m.* circle
cir•cun•ci•dar *v.* to circumcise
cir•cun•ci•sión *f.* circumcision
ci•rio *m.* candle; taper
ci•rro *m.* cirrus
ci•rue•la *f.* plum
ci•ru•gí•a *f.* surgery
ci•ru•ja•no *m.* surgeon
cis•ne *m.* swan
ci•ta *f.* meeting; date; appointment
ci•ta•ción *f.* citation; subpoena
ci•tar(se) *v.* to quote; to summon
ciu•dad *f.* town; city

ciu·da·da·no *m.* citizen
cí·vi·co *adj.* civic
ci·vil *adj.* civilian; civil
ci·vi·li·za·ción *f.* civilization
cla·mor *m.* outcry; noise
cla·mo·ro·so *adj.* clamorous
clan *m.* clan
cla·ra·men·te *adv.* clearly
cla·ri·dad *f.* clarity
cla·ri·fi·car *v.* to clarify
cla·rín *m.* bugle
cla·ri·ne·te *m.* clarinet
cla·ro *adj.* clear; light; lucid
cla·se *f.* grade; class; sort
clá·si·co *adj.* classic; classical
cla·si·fi·ca·ción *f.* classification
cla·si·fi·car(se) *v.* to classify
cla·var(se) *v.* to nail; to thrust; to stick
cla·ve *adj.* key
cla·vel *m.* carnation
cla·vi·ja *f.* peg
cla·vo *m.* spike; nail
cle·men·cia *f.* mercy; clemency
cle·men·te *adj.* clement
cle·ri·cal *adj.* clerical
clé·ri·go *m.* priest; parson
cle·ro *m.* ministry; clergy
clien·te *m., f.* client; customer; patron
cli·ma *m.* climate
clí·max *m.* climax
clí·ni·ca *f.* clinic
clo·quear *v.* to cluck
clo·ro *m.* chlorine
coac·ción *f.* compulsion; constraint
coa·gu·la·ción *f.* coagulation
coa·gu·lar(se) *v.* to coagulate; to clot
coa·li·ción *f.* coalition
co·bal·to *m.* cobalt
co·bar·de *m.* coward
co·bra *f.* cobra
co·bra·dor, a *m.* conductor
co·brar(se) *v.* to cash; to receive
co·bre *m.* copper
co·bro *m.* recovery
co·ca·í·na *f.* cocaine
co·cer *v.* to bake; to cook
co·cien·te *m.* quotient
co·ci·na *f.* kitchen; stove

co·ci·nar *v.* to cook
co·co *m.* coconut
co·co·dri·lo *m.* crocodile
coc·tel *m.* cocktail
co·che *m.* automobile
co·di·cia *f.* greed
co·di·ciar *v.* to covet
co·di·cio·so *adj.* greedy
co·di·fi·car *v.* to codify
có·di·go *m.* code
co·do *m.* elbow
co·e·du·ca·ción *f.* coeducation
coe·tá·neo *m.* contemporary
co·fra·dí·a *f.* gang
co·fre *m.* chest
co·ger *v.* to get; to take
co·gi·da *f.* toss; catch
co·he·char *v.* to bribe
co·he·cho *m.* bribery
co·he·ren·te *adj.* coherent
co·he·te *m.* rocket
coin·ci·den·te *adj.* coincidental
coin·ci·dir *v.* to coincide
coi·to *m.* intercourse
co·jear *v.* to hobble
co·je·ra *f.* limp
co·jín *m.* cushion
co·jo *adj.* lame
col *f.* cabbage
co·la *f.* tail
co·la·bo·ra·ción *f.* collaboration
co·la·bo·rar *v.* to collaborate
co·la·dor *m.* strainer
co·lap·so *m.* collapse
col·cha *f.* quilt; spread
col·chón *m.* mattress
co·lec·ción *f.* collection
co·lec·cio·nar *v.* to collect
co·le·ga *m.* colleague
co·le·gio *m.* academy; college; high school
col·ga·du·ra *f.* drape
co·li·brí *m.* hummingbird
có·li·co *f.* colic
co·li·flor *f.* cauliflower
co·li·na *f.* hill
col·me·na *f.* hive; beehive
col·mi·llo *m.* fang; tusk
col·mo *m.* height; climax
co·lo·ca·ción *f.* location; situation
co·lo·car(se) *v.* to place; to locate; to put
co·lon *m.* colon

co·lo·nia *f.* colony
co·lo·nial *adj.* colonial
co·lo·no *m.* settler
co·lor *m.* color
co·lo·re·te *m.* rouge
co·lum·na *f.* pillar
co·lum·nis·ta *m., f.* columnist
co·lum·piar(se) *v.* to swing
co·lu·sión *f.* collusion
co·ma *f.* comma
co·ma·dre *f.* gossip
co·man·dan·te *f.* commander
co·man·dar *v.* to command
co·ma·to·so *adj.* comatose
com·ba *f.* bend
com·bar(se) *v.* to bend; to sag
com·ba·te *m.* fight
com·ba·tir(se) *v.* to combat
com·bi·na·ción *f.* combination
com·bi·nar(se) *v.* to blend; to combine
com·bus·ti·ble *adj.* combustible
com·pe·ler *v.* to compel
com·pen·sa·ción *f.* compensation
com·pe·ten·cia *f.* competence
com·pe·tir *f.* to compete
com·pi·lar *v.* to compile
com·pin·che *m.* chum
com·pla·cer(se) *v.* to please; to humor
com·ple·men·to *m.* complement
com·ple·tar *v.* to complete
com·ple·to *adj.* full; absolute; thorough; complete
com·pli·ca·ción *f.* complication
com·pli·car(se) *v.* to involve, to complicate
cóm·pli·ce *m.* accessory, accomplice
com·po·ner(se) *v.* to make; to compose
com·por·ta·mien·to *m.* behavior
com·por·tar(se) *v.* to behave
com·po·si·ción *f.* composition
com·prar *v.* to purchase;

to trade
com·pren·sión *f.* comprehension
com·pren·der *v.* to understand
com·pren·si·vo *adj.* comprehensive
com·pre·sión *f.* compression
com·pri·mir *v.* to compress
com·pro·ba·ción *f.* proof
com·pro·bar *v.* to verify
com·pues·to *m.* compound
com·pul·sión *f.* compulsion
com·pu·ta·dor *m.* computer
com·pu·tar *v.* to compute
co·mún *adj.* common
con *prep.* towards; with; by
con·ca·vi·dad *f.* hollow
con·ce·bir *v.* to conceive
con·ce·der *v.* to allow; to accord
con·ce·jo *m.* council
con·cen·tra·ción *f.* concentration
con·cen·trar(se) *v.* to concentrate
con·cep·ción *f.* conception
con·cep·to *m.* concept; notion
con·ce·sión *f.* allowance; concession
con·cien·cia *f.* conscience
con·cier·to *m.* concert
con·cluir(se) *v.* to end; to conclude
con·cor·dar *v.* to tally; to agree
con·cor·dia *f.* concord
con·cre·to *adj.* concrete
con·cu·bi·na *f.* concubine
con·cu·rrir *v.* to meet; to concur
con·cur·san·te *m., f.* participant
con·cur·so *m.* contest
con·da·do *m.* county
con·de *m.* earl; count
con·de·co·rar *v.* to decorate
con·de·na *f.* sentence
con·de·na·ción *f.* condemnation
con·de·sa *f.* countess
con·di·ción *f.* state; condition
con·di·cio·nal *adj.* conditional
con·di·cio·nar *v.*

to condition

con·di·men·to *m.* condiment; seasoning

con·do·len·cia *f.* condolence

con·do·nar *v.* to condone

con·du·cir(se) *v.* to steer; to lead; to conduct; to drive

con·duc·ta *f.* behavior

con·duc·to *m.* duct; conduit

co·nec·tar *v.* to connect

co·ne·ji·to *m.* bunny

co·ne·jo *m.* rabbit

co·ne·xión *f.* connection

con·fec·ción *f.* confection

con·fec·cio·nar *v.* to make up; to concoct

con·fe·de·ra·ción *f.* confederation; confederacy

con·fe·ren·cia *f.* lecture; conference

con·fe·rir *v.* to grant; to bestow

con·fe·sar(se) *v.* to confess; to admit

con·fe·sión *f.* confession; avowal

con·fe·sio·na·rio *m.* confessional

con·fe·sor *m.* confessor

con·fe·ti *m.* confetti

con·fia·ble *adj.* reliable

con·fian·za *f.* dependence; confidence

con·fiar *v.* to trust; to rely; to confide

con·fi·den·cial *adj.* confidential

con·fi·gu·ra·ción *f.* configuration

con·fín *m.* confines; bound

con·fir·ma·ción *f.* corroboration

con·fir·mar *v.* to ratify; to confirm

con·fis·ca·ción *f.* confiscation

con·fis·car *v.* to confiscate

con·fla·gra·ción *f.* conflagration

con·flic·to *m.* clash; conflict

con·for·mar(se) *v.* to adjust; to conform

con·for·me *adj.* similar; agreeable

con·for·mi·dad *f.* conformity

con·for·tar *v.* to comfort

con·fron·ta·ción *f.* confrontation

con·fron·tar *v.* to confront

con·fun·dir(se) *v.* to confound; to perplex; to puzzle; to baffle

con·fu·sión *f.* mess; jumble; confusion

con·fu·tar *v.* to disprove; to confute

con·ge·la·ción *f.* frostbite

con·ge·lar(se) *v.* to freeze; to congeal

con·gé·ni·to *adj.* congenital

con·ges·tión *f.* congestion

con·glo·me·ra·do *m.* conglomerate

con·gre·gar(se) *v.* to flock; to assemble

con·gre·so *m.* convention; congress

con·je·tu·ra *f.* surmise; guess; conjecture

con·je·tu·rar *v.* to conjecture

con·ju·gar(se) *v.* to conjugate

con·jun·ción *f.* conjunction

con·jun·to *m.* whole; ensemble

con·ju·rar *v.* to conjure

con·me·mo·ra·ción *f.* commemoration

con·me·mo·rar *v.* to commemorate

con·me·mo·ra·ti·vo *adj.* memorial

con·mo·ción *f.* stir; commotion

con·mo·ve·dor *adj.* stirring

con·mo·ver·(se) *v.* to shake; to move; to thrill

co·no *m.* cone

cons·truc·ti·vo *adj.* constructive

cons·truir *v.* to build; to construct

con·sue·lo *m.* consolation

con·sul·tar *v.* to consult

con·su·mar *v.* to carry out

con·su·mi·dor *m.* consumer

con·su·mir(se) *v.* to waste away; to consume

con·su·mo *m.* consumption

con·sun·ción *f.* consumption

con·tac·to *m.* contact

con·ta·giar(se) *v.* to catch; to infect

con·ta·gio *m.* contagion

con·ta·gio·so *adj.* catching

con·ta·mi·na·ción *f.* pollution; contamination

con·ta·mi·nar(se) *v.* to contaminate

con·tar(se) *v.* to number; to count; to relate; to tell

con·tem·pla·ción *f.* contemplation

con·tem·plar *v.* to view; to meditate

con·tem·po·rá·neo *adj.* contemporary

con·ten·der *v.* to strive; to content; to contest

con·ten·dien·te *m.* contestant

con·te·ner(se) *v.* to hold; to include; to contain

con·te·ni·do *m.* content

con·ten·to *adj.* happy; contented

con·tes·ta·ción *f.* answer

con·tes·tar *v.* to reply; to answer

con·tien·da *f.* contest; strife; struggle

con·ti·guo *adj.* adjacent

con·ti·nen·tal *adj.* continental

con·ti·nen·te *m.* mainland; continent; container

con·tin·gen·cia *f.* contingency

con·ti·nua·ción *f.* continuation

con·ti·nuar *v.* to continue

con·ti·nuo *adj.* constant; continuous

con·to·near(se) *v.* to strut

con·tor·no *m.* contour; outline

con·tra *prep.* versus; against; *adv.* against

con·tra·ba·jo *m.* bass

con·tra·ban·dis·ta *m., f.* smuggler

con·tra·ban·do *m.* contraband

con·trac·ción *f.* contraction

con·tra·de·cir *v.* to contradict

con·tra·dic·ción *f.* contradiction

con·tra·er(se) *v.* to contract

con·tral·to *m., f.* alto; contralto

con·tra·rie·dad *f.* snag; vexation

con·tra·rio *adj.* adverse; contrary

con·tras·tar *v.* to contrast

con·tras·te *m.* contrast

con·tra·tiem·po *m.* upset; mishap

con·tra·to *m.* contract; agreement

con·tra·ven·ta·na *f.* shutter

con·tri·bu·ción *f.* tax; contribution

con·tri·buir *v.* to contribute

con·trol *m.* control

con·tro·lar *v.* to control

con·tro·ver·sia *f.* controversy

con·tu·sión *f.* bruise; contusion

con·va·le·cen·cia *f.* convalescence

con·va·le·cer *v.* to convalesce

con·va·le·cien·te *m., f.* convalescent

con·ven·cer *v.* to satisfy

con·ven·ción *f.* convention

con·ven·cio·nal *adj.* conventional

con·ve·nien·cia *f.* expediency

con·ve·nien·te *adj.* handy; fitting; convenient

con·ve·nir(se) *v.* to agree; to be fit

con·ven·to *m.* abbey

con·ver·gir *v.* to converge

con·ver·sa·ción *f.* conversation

con·ver·sar *v.* to converse

con·ver·tir(se) *v.* to turn into

con·ve·xo *adj.* convex

con·vic·ción *f.* conviction

con·vi·da·do *m.* guest

con·vi·dar(se) *v.* to invite

con·vi·te *m.* invitation

con·vo·ca·ción *f.* convocation

con·vo·car *v.* to summon

con·voy *m.* convoy

con·vul·sión *f.* convulsion

co·ñac *m.* brandy

co·o·pe·ra·ción *f.* teamwork

co·o·pe·rar *v.* to cooperate
co·or·di·na·ción *f.* coordination
co·or·di·nar *v.* to coordinate
co·pa *f.* goblet
co·pe·te *m.* tuft
co·pia *f.* imitation; copy
co·piar *v.* to copy
co·pio·so *adj.* copious
co·que·ta *f.* coquette
co·que·tear *v.* to flirt
co·ral *adj.* choral
co·ra·zón *m.* heart
co·ra·zo·na·da *f.* hunch
cor·ba·ta· *f.* tie
cor·cel *m.* steed
cor·che·te *m.* clasp
cor·cho *m.* cork
cor·de·ro *m.* lamb
cor·dón *m.* cord
co·reó·gra·fo *m.* choreographer
cor·ne·ta *f.* bugle
cor·ni·sa *f.* cornice
co·ro *m.* chorus
co·ro·la *f.* corolla
co·ro·na *f.* crown
co·ro·nar *v.* to crown
co·ro·na·ria *f.* coronary
cor·pi·ño *m.* bodice
cor·po·ral *adj.* corporal
cor·pó·reo *adj.* bodily
corps *m., pl.* corps
co·rral *m.* corral
co·rrea *f.* strap
co·rrec·ción *f.* propriety
co·rrec·to, a *adj.* right
co·rre·dor *m.* broker
co·rre·gir(se) *v.* to correct
co·rre·rí·a *f.* foray
co·rres·pon·der(se) *v.* to concern
co·rrien·te *adj.* current
co·rroer(se) *v.* to erode
co·rrom·per(se) *v.* to rot
co·rro·sión *f.* corrosion
co·rro·si·vo *adj.* corrosive
co·rrup·ción *f.* corruption
cor·sé *m.* corset
cor·ta·do *adj.* abrupt
cor·ta·du·ra *f.* slit
cor·tan·te *adj.* edged
cor·tar(se) *v.* to chop; to cut; to clip
cor·te *m.* court
cor·tés *adj.* civil; polite
cor·te·sí·a *f.* civility

cor·ti·jo *m.* grange
cor·to *adj.* brief
co·sa *f.* thing, affair
co·se·cha *f.* crop
co·ser *v.* to sew
cos·mé·ti·co *adj.* cosmetic
cos·mos *m.* cosmos
cos·qui·llear *v.* to tickle
cos·ta *f.* coast
cos·tar *v.* to cost
cos·te *m.* price
cos·ti·lla *f.* rib
cos·to·so, a *adj.* expensive
cos·tum·bre *f.* custom
cos·tu·ra *f.* joint
co·ti·dia·no *adj.* daily
co·yo·te *m.* coyote
crá·neo *m.* skull
cra·so *adj.* thick
crá·ter *m.* crater
crea·ción *f.* creation
crea·dor *m.* creator
crear *v.* to make; to create
cre·cer(se) *v.* to increase
cre·cien·te *m.* crescent
cre·ci·mien·to *m.* growth
cré·di·to *m.* credit
cre·do *m.* credo
cré·du·lo *adj.* credulous
cre·en·cia *f.* faith
creer(se) *v.* to think
creí·ble *adj.* plausible
cre·ma *f.* cream
cre·sa *f.* maggot
cres·po *adj.* frizzy
cre·ta *f.* chalk
cria·da *f.* maid
criar(se) *v.* to raise; to nurse
cri·men *m.* felony
crip·ta *f.* crypt
cri·sis *f.* breakdown
cri·sol *m.* crucible
cris·tal *m.* crystal; glass
cris·tia·nis·mo *m.* Christianity
Cris·to *m.* Christ
cri·te·rio *m.* criterion
crí·ti·ca *f.* censure; criticism
cri·ti·car *v.* to criticize
crí·ti·co, a *adj.* critical
cro·má·ti·co *adj.* chromatic
cro·mo *m.* chrome
cró·ni·ca *f.* chronicle
cró·ni·co *adj.* chronic
cro·no·me·trar *v.* to tell time
cro·quet *m.* croquet

cro·que·ta *f.* croquette
cru·ce *m.* intersection
cru·ci·fi·car *v.* to crucify
cru·ci·fi·xión *f.* crucifixion
cru·do *adj.* crude; raw
cruel *adj.* heartless; cruel
cru·ji·do *m.* crack
cru·jir *v.* to crunch
cruz *f.* cross
cru·za·da *f.* crusade
cru·za·do, a *m.* crusader
cru·zar(se) *v.* to cross
cua·dra·do *m.* square
cua·dran·te *m.* quadrant
cua·drar(se) *v.* to tally
cua·dri·lon·go *m.* oblong
cua·dro *m.* square; picture
cua·ja·da *f.* curd
cual *adv.* as; *pron.* which
cua·li·dad *f.* quality
cual·quier *adj.* any; either
cuán *adv.* how
cuan·do *prep.* when; *adv.* when; since
cuan·tí·a *f.* amount
cuan·to *adj.* as much as
cuán·to *adj.* how much
cua·ren·ta *adj.* forty
cua·ren·ta·vo *adj.* fortieth
cua·res·ma *f.* Lent
cuar·te·ar *v.* to cut up; to quarter
cuar·tel *m.* barracks
cuar·to *m.* quarter; fourth
cuar·zo *m.* quartz
cua·si *adv.* almost
cua·te *adj.* twin; alike
cua·tre·re·ar *v.* to rustle or steal
cua·tre·ro *adj.* to steal horses
cua·tro *m.* four
cua·tro·cien·tos *adj.* four hundred
cu·be·ta *f.* bucket
cu·bier·to *f.* casing; cover
cu·bil *m.* den
cu·bi·le·te *m.* tumbler
cu·bo *m.* pail
cu·brir(se) *v.* to conceal; to cover
cu·ca·ra·cha *f.* cockroach
cu·cha·ra *f.* spoon
cu·cha·ra·da *f.* spoonful
cu·che·ta *f.* cabin
cu·chi·che·ar *v.* to whisper
cu·chi·che·o *m.* whispering

cu·cha·ri·lla *f.* teaspoon
cu·chi·lla *m.* knife
cue·llo *m.* collar
cuen·ta *f.* count; bill
cuen·ta·go·tas *m.* eyedropper
cuen·te·ro *adj.* gossipy
cuen·tis·ta *m.* storyteller
cuen·to *m.* tale
cuer·da *f.* cord
cuer·do *adj. m., f.* sensible; sane person
cuer·no *m.* horn
cue·ro *m.* hide
cuer·po *m.* body
cuer·vo *m.* crow
cues·ta *f.* hill; slope
cues·tión *f.* question
cues·tio·na·ble *adj.* debatable; questionable
cues·tio·nar *v.* to debate; to discuss
cues·tio·na·rio *m.* questionnaire
cue·va *f.* cave
cui·da·do *m.* heed, care
cui·da·dor *m., f.* caretaker
cui·da·do·so *adj.* careful
cui·dar(se) *v.* to look after
cui·ta *f.* grief
cu·lan·tro *m.* coriander
cu·le·bra *f.* snake
cu·le·bri·lla *f.* ringworm
cu·li·na·rio, a *adj.* culinary
cul·mi·na·ción *f.* culmination
cul·mi·nan·te *adj.* culminating
cul·mi·nar *v.* to culminate
cul·pa *f.* fault
cul·pa·bi·li·dad *f.* guilt
cul·pa·ble *adj.* guilty
cul·par *v.* to criticize; to accuse
cul·ti·va·ción *f.* cultivation
cul·ti·var *v.* farm; to cultivate
cul·ti·vo *m.* cultivation
cul·to *adj.* cultured
cul·tu·ra *f.* culture
cum·bre *f.* peak; top
cum·plea·ños *m.* birthday
cum·pli·do, a *adj.* perfect; complete
cum·pli·dor *adj.* reliable; trustworthy
cum·pli·men·tar *v.* to compliment

cum·pli·mien·to *m.* fulfillment

cum·plir *v.* to accomplish

cun·dir *v.* to expand; to spread

cu·ña·da *f.* sister-in-law

cu·ña·do *m.* brother-in-law

cu·plé *m.* popular song

cu·po *m.* quota

cu·pón *m.* coupon

cu·ra *f.* cure

cu·ra·ble *adj.* curable

cu·ra·ción *f.* treatment; cure

cu·ran·de·ro, a *m., f.* quack

cu·rar(se) *v.* to heal; to recover

cu·ria *f.* court

cu·rio·se·ar *v.* to pry; to snoop

cu·rio·si·dad *adj.* curiosity

cu·rio·so *adj.* curious

cu·rri·cu·lum vi·tae *m.* resume

cur·sar *v.* to study

cur·si *adj.* vulgar

cur·si·vo *adj.* cursive

cur·so *m.* course

cur·ti·do *m.* tanning as in leather

cur·ti·dor *m.* tanner

cur·tim·bre *m.* tannery

cur·tir(se) *v.* to coarsen

cur·va *f.* bend; curve

cur·va·do, a *adj.* bent; curved

cur·var *v.* to curve

cur·va·tu·ra *f.* curvature

cus·to·dia *f.* keeping

cus·to·diar *v.* to protect; to watch over

cus·to·dio *adj. m.* guardian

cu·tí·cu·la *f.* cuticle

cu·tis *m.* complexion; skin

D

da·ble *adj.* feasible; possible

dac·ti·lo·gra·fí·a *f.* typewriting; typing

dac·ti·ló·gra·fo *m., f.* typist

dá·di·va *f.* gift; present

da·di·vo·si·dad *f.* liberality; generosity

da·di·vo·so, a *adj.* lavish; generous

da·do *m.* die

dal·to·nis·mo *m.* color-blindness

da·ma *f.* lady

da·mi·se·la *f.* damsel

dam·ni·fi·car *v.* to harm; to damage

dam·ni·fi·ca·do, a *adj.* harmed; damaged

dan·za *f.* dance

da·ñar(se) *v.* to hurt; to damage

da·ñi·no, a *adj.* harmful; damaging

da·ño *m.* damage

dar(se) *v.* to give; to allow

dar·do *m.* arrow; dart

dár·se·na *f.* dock; inner harbor; port

da·ta *f.* items; date

da·tar *v.* to date

da·to *m.* fact

de *prep.* of; from; with

de·am·bu·lar *v.* to roam or wander around

de·ba·jo *adj.* underneath; below

de·ba·te *m.* discussion; debate

de·ba·tir *v.* to discuss; to debate

de·be *m.* debit

de·ber *v.* to owe; *m.* obligation or duty

de·bi·da·men·te *adv.* duly; properly

de·bi·do *adj.* fitting; due

dé·bil *adj.* feeble; weak; faint

de·bi·li·dad *f.* weakness

de·bi·li·tar *v.* to weaken

de·but *m.* opening; debut

de·bu·tan·te *f.* debutant; *adj.* beginning

de·ca·den·cia *f.* decline; decadence

de·ca·den·te *adj. m., f.* decadent

de·ca·er *v.* to decay

de·cai·mien·to *m.* feebleness; weakness; dejection

de·ca·no *m.* dean

de·can·ta·ción *f.* pouring off

de·can·tar *v.* to pour off; to decant

de·ca·pi·tar *v.* to behead

de·cen·cia *f.* decency

de·ce·nio *m.* decade

de·cen·te *adj.* decent

de·cep·ción *f.* deception; disappointment

de·cep·cio·nar *v.* to disappoint

de·ce·so *m.* death; decease

de·ci·di·do, a *adj.* resolute; determined

de·ci·dir *v.* to resolve

de·ci·mal *adj.* decimal

de·cir *v.* to state; to say

de·ci·sión *f.* decision; verdict; ruling

de·ci·si·vo *adj.* conclusive; decisive

de·cla·mar *v.* to recite

de·cla·ra·ción *f.* declaration; statement; evidence

de·cla·ra·da·men·te *adv.* openly; manifestly

de·cla·rar(se) *v.* to propose; to declare

de·cli·na·ción *f.* decline

de·cli·nar *v.* to decline; to refuse

de·cli·ve *m.* incline; slope

de·co·lo·ra·ción *f.* discoloration

de·co·lo·ran·te *m.* bleaching agent

de·co·lo·rar *v.* to fade; to discolor

de·co·mi·sar *v.* to seize; to confiscate

de·co·ra·do *m.* scenery or set in a theater

de·co·ra·do, ra *adj.* ornamental; decorative

de·co·rar *v.* to decorate

de·co·ra·ti·vo, a *adj.* ornamental; decorative

de·co·ro *m.* honor; respect

de·co·ro·so, a *adj.* decent; honorable

de·cre·cer *v.* to diminish

de·cre·ci·mien·to *m.* decrease

de·cré·pi·to, a *adj.* aged; decrepit

de·cre·tar *v.* to decree; to order

de·dal *m.* thimble

de·di·car(se) *v.* to devote

de·do *m.* finger

de·du·cir *v.* to conclude; to deduce; to subtract

de·fa·mar *v.* to defame

de·fec·ción *f.* defection

de·fec·to *m.* flaw; defect

de·fec·tuo·so, a *adj.* faulty; defective

de·fen·der *v.* to defend

de·fen·sa *f.* defense

de·fen·sor *m.* supporter

de·fi·cien·cia *f.* lacking; deficient

de·fi·ni·ción *f.* definition; determination

de·fi·nir *v.* to define

de·for·mar(se) *v.* to lose shape

de·frau·da·ción *f.* cheating; fraud

de·frau·dar *v.* to cheat

de·fun·ción *f.* death; demise

de·ge·ne·rar *v.* to decline; to degenerate

de·go·lla·de·ro *m.* windpipe; throat

de·go·llar *v.* to cut the throat

de·gra·dar(se) *v.* to demean

de·gus·ta·ción *f.* sampling; tasting

dei·dad *f.* deity

de·ja·do, a *adj.* negligent; careless

de·jar(se) *v.* to quit; to let

de·jo *m.* abandonment

del *contr. of* de and el

de·lan·te *adv.* ahead; before; in front

de·lan·te·ro *adj.* forward; front

de·la·tar *v.* to inform; to denounce; to expose

de·le·ga·ción *f.* delegation

de·le·gar *v.* to delegate

de·lei·ta·ble *adj.* enjoyable; delightful

de·lei·tar(se) *v.* to delight

del·ga·do *adj.* thin; slim

de·li·be·ra·do, a *adj.* intentional; deliberate

de·li·ca·do, a *adj.* sensitive

de·li·cia *f.* pleasure; delight

de·lin·cuen·te *adj.* delinquent

de·li·ne·ar *v.* to outline; to delineate

de·li·ran·te *adj.* delirious

de·li·rar *v.* to rave; to be delirious

de·man·da *f.* challenge; demand

de·man·dar *v.* to demand; to ask for

de·ma·sí·a *f.* surplus; more than what is needed

de·ma·sia·do *adv.* to much

de·mé·ri·to *m.* demerit

de·mo·cra·cia *f.* democracy

de·mo·le·dor, a *adj.* demolishing

de·mo·ler *v.* to demolish; to destroy

de·mo·li·ción *f.* destruction

de·mo·nio *m.* devil; demon

de·mo·ra *f.* wait; delay

de·mo·rar(se) *v.* to delay

de·mos·trar *v.* to display; to demonstrate

de·mos·tra·ti·vo, a *adj.* demonstrative

de·mu·dar *v.* to change

de·ne·gar *v.* to reject; to refuse

de·no·da·do, a *adj.* bold

de·no·mi·na·ción *f.* denomination

de·no·mi·na·dor, a *adj.* denominative

de·nos·tar *v.* to insult; to abuse

de·no·tar *v.* to denote

den·si·dad *f.* density

den·so *adj.* thick; dense

den·ta·du·ra *f.* denture

den·tal *adj.* dental

den·te·lle·ar *v.* to bite; to nibble

den·te·ra *f.* jealousy; envy

den·tí·fri·co *m.* toothpaste

den·tis·ta *m., f.* dentist

den·tro *adv.* within; inside

de·nue·do *m.* courage; bravery

de·nues·to *m.* insult

de·nun·ciar *v.* to denounce

de·pa·rar *v.* to supply

de·par·ta·men·to *m.* office; department

de·par·tir *v.* to converse; to talk

de·pen·den·cia *f.* dependence; kinship; reliance

de·pen·der *v.* to depend

de·plo·rar *v.* to deplore

de·po·ner *v.* to depose; to put aside

de·por·ta·ción *f.* deportation

de·por·tar *v.* to exile; to deport

de·por·te *m.* sport

de·po·si·tar *v.* to bank

de·pó·si·to *m.* deposit

de·pra·va·ción *f.* corruption

de·pra·va·do, a *adj.* corrupted

de·pra·var *v.* to deprave

de·pre·car *v.* to implore

de·pre·ca·to·rio *adj.* imploring

de·pre·ciar *v.* to depreciate

de·pre·dar *v.* to pillage

de·pre·sión *f.* slump; depression

de·pri·mi·do *adj.* depressed

de·pri·mir *v.* to depress

de·re·cho *adj.* right; upright

de·ri·var(se) *v.* to drift

der·ma·to·lo·gí·a *f.* dermatology

der·ma·tó·lo·go *m., f.* dermatologist

de·rra·mar(se) *v.* to overflow; to spill

de·rri·bar *v.* to overthrow; to knock down

de·rro·char *v.* to waste

de·rro·che *m.* squandering

de·rro·tar(se) *v.* to ruin

des·a·co·plar *v.* to disconnect

des·a·fiar *v.* to defy

des·a·fío *m.* challenge

des·a·gra·dar *v.* to displease

des·a·hu·ciar *v.* to evict

des·ai·re *m.* slight

des·a·len·tar *v.* to dishearten

des·a·ni·mar(se) *v.* to dismay

des·á·ni·mo *m.* depression

des·a·pro·bar *v.* to disapprove

des·a·rre·glar(se) *v.* to derange

des·a·rre·glo *m.* disorder

des·a·rro·llar(se) *v.* to unfold

des·a·rro·llo *m.* development

des·a·so·sie·go *m.* unrest

de·sas·tre *m.* disaster

des·a·tar(se) *v.* to undo

des·a·ten·to *adj.* unthinking

de·sa·ti·no *m.* blunder

des·a·yu·nar(se) *v.* to breakfast

des·a·yu·no *m.* breakfast

des·ca·li·fi·car *v.* to disqualify

des·can·sar *v.* to rest

des·can·so *m.* rest

des·ca·ra·do *adj.* brazen

des·car·gar(se) *v.* to unload

des·cen·den·te *adj.* downward

des·cen·der *v.* to descend

des·ci·frar *v.* to decipher

des·co·lo·rar(se) *v.* to fade

des·com·po·ner(se) *v.* to decompose

des·con·cer·tar(se) *v.* to embarrass

des·con·fiar *v.* to distrust

des·co·no·cer *v.* to disavow

des·con·ten·to *m.* discontent

des·con·ti·nuar *v.* to discontinue

des·cor·tés *adj.* impolite

des·co·ser(se) *v.* to come apart

des·cri·bir *v.* to describe

des·crip·ción *f.* description

des·cu·brir *v.* to find

des·cui·da·do *adj.* remiss

des·cui·dar *v.* to neglect

des·de *prep.* since; from

des·de·ñar *v.* to disdain

des·di·cha *f.* unhappiness

de·sea·ble *adj.* eligible

de·sear *v.* to hope; to wish; to desire

des·e·char *v.* to reject

des·em·bo·car *v.* to land

des·em·bol·sar *v.* to disburse

des·en·cor·var *v.* to unbend

des·en·la·ce *m.* ending

de·seo *m.* craving

de·ser·tar *v.* to defect

de·ser·tor *m.* deserter

des·es·pe·rar *v.* to despair

des·fal·car *v.* to embezzle

des·fi·gu·rar *v.* to blemish; to disfigure

des·fi·le *m.* parade

des·ga·rrar(se) *v.* to tear

des·gas·te *m.* waste

des·gra·cia *f.* misfortune

des·gra·cia·do *m.* unfortunate

des·ha·cer(se) *v.* to unwrap

des·he·lar(se) *v.* to thaw

des·hi·dra·ta·ción *f.* dehydration

des·hon·ra *f.* disgrace

des·hon·rar *v.* to disgrace

des·i·gual *adj.* irregular

des·in·flar *v.* to deflate

des·in·te·rés *m.* disinterest

de·sis·tir *v.* to desist

des·leal *adj.* disloyal

des·li·zar(se) *v.* to glide

des·lum·brar *v.* to blind

des·lus·trar(se) *v.* to dull

des·lus·tre *m.* tarnish

des·ma·yo *m.* swoon

des·mi·ga·jar(se) *v.* to crumble

des·mon·tar(se) *v.* to dismantle

des·na·tar *v.* to skim

des·nu·dar(se) *v.* to undress

des·nu·do, a *adj.* nude; bare

des·nu·tri·ción *f.* malnutrition

des·o·be·de·cer *v.* to disobey

des·o·cu·pa·do *adj.* free

des·o·do·ri·zar *v.* to deodorize

de·so·la·ción *f.* desolation

des·or·den *m.* mess

des·or·ga·ni·zar *v.* to disrupt

des·pa·cio *adv.* slowly

des·pa·char *v.* to speed

des·pe·dir(se) *v.* to dismiss; to see off

des·pei·na·do *adj.* unkempt

des·per·di·ciar *v.* to waste

des·per·tar(se) *v.* to awaken; to wake up

des·pier·to *adj.* awake

des·ple·gar(se) *v.* to unfold

des·po·jar(se) *v.* to strip

des·po·sar(se) *v.* to marry

des·pre·cia·ble *adj.* vile; worthless

des·pre·ciar(se) *v.* to scorn

des·pués *adv.* after; later

des·te·rrar *v.* to banish

des·te·tar(se) *v.* to wean

des·ti·lar *v.* to distill

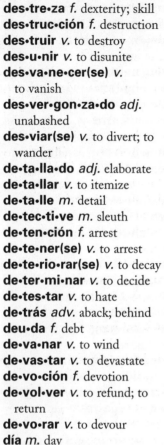

des·tre·za *f.* dexterity; skill
des·truc·ción *f.* destruction
des·truir *v.* to destroy
des·u·nir *v.* to disunite
des·va·ne·cer(se) *v.* to vanish
des·ver·gon·za·do *adj.* unabashed
des·viar(se) *v.* to divert; to wander
de·ta·lla·do *adj.* elaborate
de·ta·llar *v.* to itemize
de·ta·lle *m.* detail
de·tec·ti·ve *m.* sleuth
de·ten·ción *f.* arrest
de·te·ner(se) *v.* to arrest
de·te·rio·rar(se) *v.* to decay
de·ter·mi·nar *v.* to decide
de·tes·tar *v.* to hate
de·trás *adv.* aback; behind
deu·da *f.* debt
de·va·nar *v.* to wind
de·vas·tar *v.* to devastate
de·vo·ción *f.* devotion
de·vol·ver *v.* to refund; to return
de·vo·rar *v.* to devour
dí·a *m.* day
dia·blo *m.* devil
diá·co·no *m.* deacon
dia·frag·ma *m.* diaphragm
diag·nos·ti·car *v.* to diagnose
dia·gra·ma *m.* diagram
dia·lec·to *m.* dialect
dia·man·te *m.* diamond
dia·rio *m.* daily
di·bu·jan·te *m.* cartoonist
di·bu·jar *v.* to sketch
dic·cio·na·rio *m.* dictionary
di·ciem·bre *m.* December
dic·ta·dor *m.* dictator
dic·tar *v.* to dictate
di·cho *m.* remark; saying
die·ci·nue·ve *adj.* nineteen
die·cio·cho *adj.* eighteen
die·ci·séis *adj.* sixteen
die·ci·sie·te *adj.* seventeen
dien·te *m.* tooth
diez *adj.* ten
di·fe·ren·cia *f.* difference
di·fe·ren·te *adj.* different
di·fe·rir *v.* to defer
di·fí·cil *adj.* hard; difficult
di·fun·to *adj.* deceased
di·fu·so *adj.* widespread
di·ge·rir *v.* to digest

di·ges·tión *f.* digestion
dí·gi·to *m.* digit
dig·ni·dad *f.* dignity
di·la·tar(se) *v.* to dilate
di·li·gen·te *adj.* diligent
di·lu·ir *v.* to dilute
di·lu·viar *v.* to pour
di·men·sión *f.* dimension
di·nas·tí·a *f.* dynasty
di·ne·ro *m.* money
dios *m.* god
dio·sa *f.* goddess
di·plo·ma·cia *f.* diplomacy
di·rec·ción *f.* direction
di·rec·ta·men·te *adv.* straight
di·rec·to *adj.* straight
di·ri·gir(se) *v.* to lead; to control
dis·cer·nir *v.* to discern
dis·ci·pli·na *f.* discipline
dis·ci·pli·nar *v.* to discipline
dis·co *m.* record
dis·cre·par *v.* to disagree
dis·cre·to *adj.* discreet
dis·cul·pa *f.* excuse
dis·cul·par *v.* to excuse
dis·cu·sión *f.* discussion
dis·cu·tir *v.* to argue
di·se·mi·nar *v.* to spread
di·se·ñar *v.* to design
dis·fraz *m.* costume
dis·fra·zar *v.* to disguise
dis·gus·tar(se) *v.* to annoy
dis·gus·to *m.* displeasure
dis·lo·ca·ción *f.* dislocation
dis·lo·car(se) *v.* to dislocate
dis·sol·ver(se) *v.* to dissolve
dis·per·sar(se) *v.* to dispel
dis·po·ner(se) *v.* to ready
dis·pues·to *adj.* willing
dis·pu·ta *f.* dispute
dis·pu·tar *v.* to fight; to quarrel
dis·tan·te *adj.* distant
dis·tin·guir *v.* to distinguish
dis·traer(se) *v.* to divert; to distract
dis·tri·buir *v.* to distribute
dis·tur·bio *m.* trouble
di·sua·dir *v.* to deter
di·ván *m.* couch
di·ver·gir *v.* to diverge
di·ver·sión *f.* amusement
di·ver·so *adj.* varied; different
di·vi·dir(se) *v.* to split; to

divide
di·vi·no *adj.* divine
di·vor·ciar(se) *v.* to divorce
do·blar(se) *v.* to fold; to double
do·ce *adj.* twelve
do·ce·na *f.* dozen
dó·cil *adj.* meek
dó·lar *m.* dollar
do·ler(se) *v.* to pain; to hurt
do·lor *m.* ache; pain
do·mes·ti·car(se) *v.* to domesticate
do·min·go *m.* Sunday
do·nan·te *m.* donor
do·nar *v.* to donate
don·de *adv.* where
dor·mir(se) *v.* to sleep
dos *adj.* two
dra·gón *m.* dragon
dra·má·ti·co *adj.* dramatic
dro·ga *f.* drug
du·cha *f.* shower
du·char·se *v.* to shower
du·dar *v.* to hesitate; doubt
due·ño *m.* owner; master
dul·ce *m.* candy
duo·dé·ci·mo *adj.* twelfth
du·pli·car(se) *v.* to duplicate
du·que·sa *f.* duchess
du·ra·de·ro *adj.* durable
du·ran·te *prep.* during
du·ro *adj.* stiff; hard

E

é·ba·no *m.* ebony
e·brie·dad *f.* inebriation
e·brio *m.* drunk
e·cléc·ti·co *adj.* eclectic
e·cle·siás·ti·co *adj.* ecclesiastic
e·clip·sar *v.* to eclipse
e·clip·se *m.* eclipse
e·co *m.* echo
e·co·lo·gí·a *f.* ecology
e·co·no·mí·a *f.* economy
e·co·no·mis·ta *m.* economist
e·co·no·mi·zar *v.* to economize
e·cua·ción *f.* equation
e·cua·dor *m.* equator
e·cuá·ni·me *adj.* impartial
e·cua·to·rial *adj.* equatorial
ec·ze·ma *m.* eczema

e·cha·da *f.* toss
e·char(se) *v.* to throw; to cast away
e·dad *f.* age
e·di·ción *f.* edition
e·dic·to *m.* edict
e·di·fi·car *v.* to edify
e·di·tar *v.* to edict
e·di·tor *m.* editor
e·di·to·rial *m.* editorial
e·du·ca·ción *f.* education
e·du·car *v.* to instruct; to teach; to train; to educate
e·fe·bo *m.* adolescent
e·fec·ti·vi·dad *f.* effectiveness
e·fec·to *m.* result; impact; effect
e·fec·tuar *v.* to make happen, to effect
e·fi·ca·cia *f.* efficacy
e·fi·cien·cia *f.* efficiency
e·fi·cien·te *adj.* efficient
e·fu·sión *f.* effusion
e·fu·si·vo *adj.* effusive
e·go *m.* ego
e·gre·sar *v.* to graduate
e·je·cu·ción *f.* execution
e·je·cu·tar *v.* to execute
e·je·cu·ti·vo *adj.* executive
e·jem·plar *m.* example
e·jem·pli·fi·car *v.* to exemplify
e·jem·plo *m.* example
e·jer·cer *v.* exercise
e·jer·ci·cio *m.* drill; exercise; practice
e·jér·ci·to *m.* army
e·lec·to *adj.* elect
e·lec·to·ra·do *m.* electorate
e·lec·tri·ci·dad *f.* electricity
e·lec·tri·fi·car *v.* to electrify
e·lec·tro·cu·tar *v.* to electrocute
e·lec·trón *m.* electron
e·le·fan·te *m.* elephant
e·le·gan·cia *f.* grace
e·le·gan·te *adj.* elegant
e·le·gi·do *adj.* chosen
e·le·gir *v.* to choose; to elect
e·le·men·tal *adj.* elementary; essential; elemental
e·le·va·ción *f.* elevation
e·le·va·do *adj.* high
e·le·var(se) *v.* to elevate; to lift

e·li·mi·nar *v.* to eliminate
e·lip·se *f.* ellipse
e·líp·ti·co *adj.* elliptical
e·li·xir *m.* elixir
e·lo·cuen·cia *f.* eloquence
e·lo·cuen·te *adj.* eloquent
e·lo·giar *v.* to eulogize
e·lu·ci·dar *v.* to elucidate
e·lu·dir *v.* to elude
e·lla *pron., f.* she
e·llas *pl.pron., f.* them; they
e·llo *pron.* it
e·llos *pl.pron., m.* them; they
e·ma·nar *v.* to emanate
e·man·ci·par *v.* to emancipate
em·ba·ja·da *f.* embassy
em·ba·ja·dor *m.* ambassador
em·bal·sa·mar *v.* to embalm
em·ba·ra·za·da *adj.* pregnant
em·ba·ra·zo, m. embarrassment; pregnancy
em·bar·car(se) *v.* to embark
em·bar·que *m.* shipment
em·bas·tar *v.* to tack; to quilt
em·be·ber *v.* to wet; to absorb
em·be·lle·cer *v.* to embellish
em·bes·tir *v.* to attack
em·blan·que·cer *v.* to bleach
em·ble·ma *m.* emblem
em·bo·lia *f.* embolism
em·bo·rra·char(se) *v.* to get drunk
em·bos·car *v.* to ambush
em·bo·ta·do, a *adj.* dull
em·bo·tar *v.* to dull
em·bo·te·llar *v.* to bottle
em·bra·ve·cer *v.* to infuriate
em·bria·gar(se) *v.* to intoxicate
em·brión *m.* embryo
em·bro·llar *v.* to embroil
e·mer·gen·cia *f.* emergency
e·mi·gra·do *m.* emigrant
e·mi·grar *v.* to emigrate
e·mi·sa·rio *m.* emissary
e·mi·sión *f.* issue
e·mi·tir *v.* to give off; to emit
e·mo·ción *f.* feeling; emotion

e·mo·cio·nar *v.* to affect
e·mo·ti·vo, a *adj.* emotional
em·pal·mar *v.* to splice; to join
em·pa·par(se) *v.* to drench; to wet
em·pa·pe·la·do *m.* lining
em·pa·pe·lar *v.* to line with paper
em·pa·re·da·do *m.* recluse; captive; prisoner
em·pa·tar *v.* to tie
em·pa·te *m.* impediment; draw; connection
em·pe·ci·na·do *adj.* obstinate
em·pe·ci·nar *v.* to be obstinate
em·pe·llar *v.* to push
em·pe·ño *m.* patron; pledge; insistence
em·peo·rar(se) *v.* to become worse
em·pe·ra·dor *m.* emperor
em·pe·ra·triz *f.* empress
em·pe·ro *conj.* however
em·pe·zar *v.* to start; to begin
em·pí·ri·co *adj.* empirical
em·plas·tar *v.* to hamper; to plaster
em·plas·to *m.* plaster
em·ple·a·do *m.* employee
em·ple·a·dor *m.* employer
em·ple·ar(se) *v.* to employ
em·pleo *m.* job; work
em·plu·mar *v.* to feather
em·po·bre·ci·do *adj.* impoverished
em·pren·der *v.* to begin
em·pre·sa *f.* company; business
em·pre·sa·rio *m.* director
em·pu·jar *v.* to thrust; to push
em·pu·je *m.* push
e·mu·la·ción *f.* emulation
e·mul·sión *f.* emulsion
en *prep.* in
e·na·je·na·ble *adj.* alienable
e·na·je·na·ción *f.* alienation
e·na·je·nar *v.* to alienate
e·na·no *m.* dwarf
e·nar·de·cer *v.* to ignite
en·ca·be·za·mien·to *m.* heading; caption

en·ca·be·zar *v.* to enroll; to head
en·ca·jar *v.* to force; to insert
en·ca·je *m.* insertion; lace
en·ca·lle·cer *v.* to develop a callous
en·can·di·lar *v.* to excite; to stir
en·can·ta·do *adj.* happy; delighted
en·can·ta·dor *adj.* charming; enchanting
en·can·ta·mien·to *m.* enchantment
en·can·tar *v.* to charm; to enchant
en·can·to *m.* enchantment
en·ca·po·ta·do *adj.* cloudy
en·ca·po·tar *v.* to become overcast
en·ca·ra·mar *v.* to elevate; to raise; to promote
en·ca·rar *v.* to confront
en·car·gar *v.* to advise; to place in charge; to request
en·car·go *m.* assignment; task; job
en·car·na·ción *f.* incarnation
en·car·nar *v.* to heal; to mix; to embody
en·car·ni·za·do *adj.* bloody
en·ca·rri·llar *v.* to guide
en·ce·fa·li·tis *f.* encephalitis
en·cen·de·dor *m.* lighter
en·cen·der(se) *v.* to ignite
en·ce·rar *v.* to polish
en·ce·rrar(se) *v.* to confine
en·ci·clo·pe·dia *f.* encyclopedia
en·cie·rro *m.* closing; seclusion; enclosure
en·ci·ma *adv.* above
en·ci·ma de *adv.* upon
en·cin·ta *adj.* pregnant
en·co·co·rar *v.* to annoy
en·co·ger *v.* to shrink; to contract; to become smaller
en·co·gi·mien·to *m.* shrinkage; contraction
en·co·lar *v.* to glue
en·co·men·dar(se) *v.* to commend
en·co·miar *v.* to extol
en·co·nar *v.* to irritate; to anger
en·con·trar(se) *v.* to find; to

encounter
en·cor·var *v.* to curve
en·cru·ci·ja·da *f.* intersection
en·cua·der·nar *v.* to bind
en·cua·drar *v.* to frame
en·cu·brir *v.* to hide
en·cuen·tro *m.* meeting; collision; encounter
en·cues·ta *f.* inquiry
en·cum·brar *v.* to honor; to lift; to raise
en·cur·tir *v.* to preserve
en·chi·la·da *f.* enchilada
en·chu·far *v.* to couple; to connect; to merge
en·chu·fe *m.* plug; connection; socket
en·de·ble *adj.* weak
en·dé·mi·co *adj.* endemic
en·de·re·zar *v.* to direct; to straighten
en·dia·bla·do *adj.* diabolical
en·di·bia *f.* endive
en·do·sa·ble *adj.* endorsable
en·do·san·te *m.* endorser
en·do·sar *v.* to endorse
en·do·so *m.* endorsement
en·dul·zar *v.* to sweeten
en·du·re·cer(se) *v.* to toughen
e·ne·mi·go *m.* enemy
e·ne·mis·tad *f.* animosity
e·ner·gí·a *f.* energy
e·nér·gi·co *adj.* energetic
e·ne·ro *m.* January
e·ner·va·ción *f.* enervation
e·ner·var *v.* to weaken
en·fa·dar *v.* to annoy; to anger
én·fa·sis *m.* stress; emphasis
en·fer·mar *v.* to become ill
en·fer·me·dad *f.* sickness
en·fer·me·ra *f.* nurse
en·fer·mo *adj.* ill
en·fer·vo·ri·zar *v.* to encourage; to enliven
en·fi·lar *v.* to string; to point; to direct
en·fo·car(se) *v.* to focus
en·fren·te *adv.* in front of
en·friar(se) *v.* to cool
en·fu·re·cer *v.* to infuriate
en·gan·char *v.* to persuade
en·gan·che *m.* hook
en·ga·ña·di·zo *adj.* credulous

en·ga·ñar(se) *v.* to fool; to deceive

en·ga·ño *m.* mistake; trick; error; fraud

en·ga·ño·so *adj.* tricking; deceitful; deceiving

en·gar·zar *v.* to curl; to mount; to thread

en·gas·te *m.* mounting

en·gen·drar *v.* to breed

en·gen·dro *m.* fetus

en·go·la·do *adj.* arrogant

en·go·lle·ta·do *adj.* proud

en·go·mar *v.* to glue

en·gor·de *m.* fattening

en·go·rro·so *adj.* troublesome

en·gra·nar *v.* to link; to connect

en·gran·de·cer *v.* to praise; to increase; to heighten; to augment; to be promoted; to exaggerate

en·gra·pa·do·ra *f.* stapler

en·gra·sa·do *m.* lubricant

en·gra·se *m.* lubricant

en·gre·í·do *adj.* arrogant

en·gro·sar *v.* to swell; to enlarge

en·ha·ci·nar *v.* to heap

en·he·brar *v.* to connect; to string; to link

en·hi·lar *v.* to arrange; to guide; to thread;

e·nig·má·ti·co *adj.* enigmatic

en·jam·brar *v.* to swarm

en·jam·bre *m.* swarm

en·ju·gar *v.* to settle; to dry

en·jui·ciar *v.* to examine; to indict; to judge

en·jun·dia *f.* fat; grease; vitality

en·la·ce *m.* liaison; link; junction; connection

en·lar·dar *v.* to baste

en·la·zar *v.* to connect; to rope; to lace; to lasso

en·lo·que·cer *v.* to make insane; to drive crazy

en·sor·de·cer *v.* to make deaf

en·su·ciar(se) *v.* to soil

en·sue·ño *m.* daydream

en·ta·bla·do *m.* floor

en·ta·llar *v.* to engrave; to carve; to groove

en·ten·de·dor, a *adj.* sharp; expert

en·ten·der(se) *v.* to understand

en·ten·di·mien·to *m.* understanding

en·te·ra·men·te *adv.* totally; entirely

en·te·rar(se) *v.* to learn

en·te·re·za *f.* fortitude; integrity

en·te·ri·zo *adj.* entire

en·te·ro *adj.* whole; entire

en·ti·dad *f.* concern; entity

en·tie·rro *m.* funeral; burial; grave; internment

en·tin·ta·do *m.* inky

en·tin·tar *v.* to ink

en·to·mo·lo·gí·a *f.* entomology

en·to·nar *v.* to modulate; to intone

en·ton·ces *adv.* then

en·tor·no *m.* environment

en·tor·pe·cer *v.* to deaden; to obstruct; to dull

en·tra·da *f.* entrance

en·tram·par *v.* to ensnare; to trick; to entangle

en·tran·te *adj.* coming; next

en·tra·ña·ble *adj.* beloved; close; dear

en·trar *v.* to go into; to enter

en·tre *prep.* among; between

en·tre·ca·no *adj.* graying

en·tre·cor·tar *v.* to interrupt

en·tre·ga *f.* delivery

en·tre·gar(se) *v.* to deliver

en·tre·na·dor *m.* coach

en·tre·na·mien·to *m.* coaching

en·tre·nar *v.* to train

en·tre·ta·llar *v.* to impede; to carve; to engrave

en·tre·te·ner(se) *v.* to entertain

en·tre·te·ni·do *adj.* entertaining

en·tre·ver *v.* to surmise

en·tre·ve·ro *m.* jumble

en·tre·vis·tar *v.* to interview

en·tu·bar *v.* to put a tube into

en·tuer·to *m.* injustice

en·tur·biar *v.* to cloud

en·tu·sias·mar *v.* to enthuse

en·tu·sias·mo *m.* enthusiasm

e·nu·me·ra·ción *f.* enumeration

e·nu·me·rar *v.* to enumerate

e·nun·cia·ción *f.* enunciation

e·nun·ciar *v.* to enunciate

en·va·sar *v.* to package; to bottle

en·va·se *m.* packaging

en·ver·gar *v.* to fasten

en·via·do *m.* envoy

en·viar *v.* to send

en·vi·dia *f.* envy

en·vi·diar *v.* to envy

en·vi·dio·so *adj.* envious

en·ví·o *m.* dispatch; package

en·vol·tu·ra *m.* wrapper

en·vol·ven·te *adj.* enveloping

en·vol·ver(se) *v.* to wrap up

en·ye·sar *v.* to plaster

en·zi·ma *f.* enzyme

e·ón *m.* aeon

e·pi·cen·tro *m.* epicenter

é·pi·co *f.* epic

e·pi·de·mia *f.* epidemic

e·pi·dé·mi·co *adj.* epidemic

e·pi·dér·mi·co *adj.* epidermic

e·pi·glo·tis *f.* epiglottis

e·pi·lep·sia *f.* epilepsy

e·pí·lo·go *m.* epilogue

e·pi·so·dio *m.* episode

e·pi·te·lio *m.* epithelium

é·po·ca *f.* age; time period

e·po·pe·ya *f.* epic

e·qui·dad *f.* equity

e·qui·lá·te·ro *adj.* equilateral

e·qui·li·bra·do *adj.* well-balanced; reasonable

e·qui·li·brar *v.* to balance

e·qui·li·brio *adj.* equilibrium

e·qui·li·bris·ta *f.* acrobat

e·qui·no *adj.* equine

e·qui·pa·je *m.* baggage

e·qui·par *v.* to equip

e·qui·pa·rar *v.* to compare

e·qui·po *m.* team

e·qui·ta·ti·vo *adj.* fair

e·qui·va·len·te *adj.* equivalent

e·qui·vo·ca·do *adj.* being wrong

e·qui·vo·car(se) *v.* to err

e·quí·vo·co *adj.* equivocal

er·bio *m.* erbium

e·rec·to *adj.* erect

er·guir *v.* to lift up

e·ri·gir *v.* to erect

e·ro·sión *f.* erosion

e·ró·ti·co *adj.* erotic

e·rra·di·car *v.* to uproot; to eradicate

e·rra·do *adj.* mistaken

e·rran·te *adj.* errant

e·rrar(se) *v.* to wander; to miss; to roam; to fail

e·rró·ne·o *adj.* erroneous

e·rror *m.* error

e·ruc·to *m.* burp

e·ru·di·ción *f.* erudition

e·rup·ción *f.* eruption

e·sa *adj.* that

es·bel·to *adj.* slender

es·bo·zo *m.* outline

es·ca·bel *m.* footstool; stool

es·ca·bro·so *adj.* rough; rugged

es·ca·la *f.* range; ladder

es·ca·lar *v.* to climb; to scale

es·ca·le·ra *f.* stairs; staircase

es·cal·far *v.* to poach

es·ca·lo·nar *v.* to stagger

es·ca·par(se) *v.* to escape; to get away

es·car·pa·do, a *adj.* short; abrupt

es·ca·so *adj.* scarce

es·ce·na *f.* scene

es·cla·vi·zar *v.* to enslave

es·cla·vo, a *m.* slave

es·co·ba *f.* broom

es·co·ger *v.* to decide; to choose

es·con·der(se) *v.* to hide

es·cor·pión *m.* scorpion

es·cri·bir *v.* to write

es·cu·char *v.* to listen

es·cue·la *f.* school

es·cul·pir *v.* to carve

es·cul·tu·ra *f.* sculpture

e·se *adj.* that; **e·sos** *pl.* those

e·sen·cial *adj.* essential

es·for·zar(se) *v.* to strive for

es·fuer·zo *m.* exertion; attempt

es·mal·te *m.* enamel

es·me·ral·da *f.* emerald

e·so *pron.* that

e·só·fa·go *m.* esophagus

es·pa·ciar(se) *v.* to spread out

es·pa·cio *m.* space
es·pa·da *f.* sword
es·pa·gue·ti *m.* spaghetti
es·pal·da *f.* back
es·pas·mo *m.* spasm
es·pás·ti·co *adj.* spastic
es·pe·cial *adj.* special
es·pe·cia·li·dad *f.* speciality
es·pe·cia·li·zar(se) *v.*
   to specialize
es·pe·ci·fi·car *v.* to specify
es·pé·ci·men *m.* specimen
es·pec·ta·dor *m.* witness
es·pe·jo *m.* mirror
es·pe·ra *f.* wait
es·pe·rar *v.* to hope; wait
es·piar *v.* to spy
es·pi·na *f.* spine, thorn
es·pi·na·zo *m.* backbone
es·pi·ni·lla *f.* shin
es·pi·ral *adj.* spiral
es·pi·rar *v.* to exhale
es·plén·di·do *adj.* splendid
es·plen·dor *m.* splendor
es·pon·tá·neo *adj.*
   spontaneous
es·po·sa *f.* wife
es·po·so *m.* husband
es·que·le·to *m.* skeleton
es·quí *m.* ski
es·quiar *v.* to ski
es·qui·na *f.* corner
es·ta *adj., f.* this
és·ta *pron, f.* this
es·ta·ble·cer(se) *v.*
   to settle; to establish
es·ta·ción *f.* station; season
es·ta·dio *m.* stadium
es·ta·do *m.* state
es·ta·llar *v.* to explode
es·tam·par *v.* to stamp
es·tam·pi·da *f.* stampede
es·tan·car(se) *v.* to stagnate
es·tan·dar·te *m.* standard
es·tar *v.* to lie; to be
es·ta·tua *f.* statue
es·ta·tu·ra *f.* stature
es·te *adj.* east
és·te *pron.* this; *pl.* these
es·te·ri·li·dad *f.* sterility
es·ti·bar *v.* to stow
es·ti·lo *m.* style
es·ti·mar(se) *v.* to estimate
es·ti·mu·lar *v.* to stimulate
es·ti·rar *v.* to stretch
es·tó·ma·go *m.* stomach
es·tor·bar *v.* to block; to

impede
es·tor·nu·dar *v.* to sneeze
es·tor·nu·do *m.* sneeze
es·tran·gu·lar *v.* to choke
es·tra·te·gia *f.* strategy
es·tra·ti·fi·car(se) *v.*
   to stratify
es·tre·char(se) *v.* to narrow
es·tre·lla *f.* star
es·tre·llar(se) *v.* to smash
   into
es·tre·me·cer(se) *v.*
   to shake
es·tric·to *adj.* strict
es·tro·pa·jo *m.* mop
es·tro·pear(se) *v.* to ruin
es·truc·tu·ra *f.* form
es·truen·do *m.* thunder
es·tu·dian·te *m., f.* student
es·tu·diar *v.* to study
es·tu·dio *m.* studio
es·tu·fa *f.* stove
es·tu·pen·do *adj.*
   stupendous
es·tú·pi·do *adj.* stupid
e·ter·no *adj.* eternal
e·ti·que·ta *f.* label
eu·fo·ria *f.* euphoria
e·va·cua·ción *f.* evacuation
e·va·cuar *v.* to evacuate
e·va·dir *v.* to avoid; to dodge
e·va·lua·ción *f.* evaluation
e·va·po·ra·ción *f.*
   evaporation
e·va·po·rar(se) *v.*
   to evaporate
e·va·sión *f.* evasion
e·vi·den·cia *f.* evidence
e·vi·den·te *adj.* obvious
e·vi·tar *v.* to shun
e·vo·car *v.* to evoke
e·vo·lu·ción *f.* evolution
ex·ac·ta·men·te *adv.*
   exactly
ex·a·ge·ra·ción *f.*
   exaggeration
ex·a·ge·rar *v.* to exaggerate
ex·a·men *m.* test; quiz
ex·a·mi·nar(se) *v.*
   to examine
ex·ca·va·ción *f.* excavation
ex·ce·der(se) *v.* to surpass
ex·ce·len·cia *f.* excellence
ex·ce·len·te *adj.* excellent
ex·cep·to *prep.* unless
ex·ci·tar(se) *v.* to arouse
ex·cla·ma·ción *f.*

exclamation
ex·cla·mar *v.* to exclaim
ex·cluir *v.* to exclude
ex·clu·sión *f.* exclusion
ex·cu·sa *f.* excuse
ex·cu·sar *v.* to excuse
ex·ha·lar *v.* to exhale
ex·i·gir *v.* to require
ex·is·tir *v.* to exist
ex·pan·sión *f.* expansion
ex·pen·der *v.* to expend
ex·pe·rien·cia *f.* experience
ex·pe·ri·men·tar *v.*
   to experiment
ex·per·to *m.* expert
ex·pli·ca·ción *f.* explanation
ex·pli·car(se) *v.* to explain
ex·plo·ra·ción *f.* exploration
ex·plo·rar *v.* to explore
ex·por·ta·ción *f.* export
ex·por·tar *v.* to export
ex·pre·sar(se) *v.* to tell; to
   express
ex·pre·sión *f.* expression
ex·pul·sar *v.* to put out; to
   expel
ex·ten·der(se) *v.* to expand
   out
ex·te·rior *adj.* exterior
ex·tran·je·ro *m.* alien
ex·tra·ño *adj.* odd; strange
ex·tre·mo *adj.* extreme

F

fá·bri·ca *f.* mill
fa·bri·ca·ción *f.* manufacture
fa·bri·car *v.* to manufacture
fá·bu·la *f.* fiction; fable
fa·bu·lo·sa·men·te *adv.*
   fabulously
fa·bu·lo·so *adj.* fabulous
fac·ción *f.* feature; faction
fa·ce·ta *f.* facet
fá·cil *adj.* simple
fa·ci·li·dad *f.* chance; facility
fa·ci·li·tar *v.* to expedite; to
   facilitate
fac·ti·ble *adj.* feasible
fac·tor *m.* factor
fac·to·rí·a *f.* foundry; factory
fac·tu·ra·ción *f.* invoicing
fac·tu·rar *v.* to invoice
fa·cul·tad *f.* power
fa·cul·tar *v.* to empower
fa·cha *f.* appearance

fai·sán *m.* pheasant
fa·ja *f.* sash; band
fa·ja·du·ra *f.* belting
fa·jar *v.* to belt; to wrap
fa·lan·ge *f.* phalanx
fa·laz *adj.* deceptive
fal·da *f.* skirt
fal·dón *m.* tail
fá·li·co *adj.* phallic
fal·se·dad *f.* untruth; lie
fal·si·fi·car *v.*
   to misrepresent
fal·so *adj.* dishonest
fal·ta *f.* fault; shortage; flaw;
   want; lack
fal·tar *v.* to fail; to need
fal·to *adj.* wanting; wretched;
   short
fa·llar *v.* to fail
fa·llo *adj.* judgment; void;
   decision; ruling
fa·ma *f.* fame
fa·mé·li·co *adj.* famished
fa·mi·lia *f.* family
fa·mi·liar *adj.* familiar;
   casual; familial
fa·mo·so *adj.* well-known
fa·na·ti·zar *v.* to fanaticize
fan·fa·rrón *adj.* showy;
   bragging
fan·go *m.* mud
fan·go·si·dad *f.* muddiness
fan·ta·se·ar *v.* to dream
fan·ta·sí·a *f.* fantasy
fan·tás·ti·co *adj.* bizarre;
   fanciful
fa·rán·du·la *f.* business;
   theater
fa·ra·ón *m.* pharaoh
far·do *m.* bale; pack
fa·rin·ge *f.* pharynx
far·ma·céu·ti·co *m.*
   pharmacist
far·ma·cia *f.* pharmacy
fa·ro *m.* beacon; light;
   lighthouse
fa·rol *m.* light; lantern
far·sa *f.* farce
fas·ci·na·ción *f.* fascination
fas·ci·nan·te *adj.*
   fascinating
fas·ci·nar *v.* to intrigue; to
   fascinate
fas·cis·ta *m.* fascist
fas·ti·diar(se) *v.* to annoy; to
   bother
fas·ti·dio *m.* annoyance;

repugnance

fas·ti·dio·so *adj.* annoying; tedious; bothersome

fas·to *m.* splendor

fas·tuo·si·dad *f.* splendor

fa·tal *adj.* fatal

fa·ta·li·dad *f.* fatality

fa·tal·men·te *adv.* fatally; unhappily; wretchedly

fa·ti·ga *f.* fatigue

fa·ti·gar(se) *v.* to fatigue; to tire

fa·ti·go·so *adj.* tiring; fatigued; tired

fa·tuo *m.* fool

fau·na *f.* fauna

fa·vor *m.* favor

fa·vo·ra·ble *adj.* favorable

fa·vo·re·cer *v.* to favor; to help another; to support

fa·vo·ri·to *adj.* favorite

fe *f.* trust; faith

fe·bre·ro *m.* February

fe·bril *adj.* hectic

fé·cu·la *f.* starch

fe·cun·di·dad *f.* fertility

fe·cha *f.* date

fe·char *v.* to date

fe·de·ra·ción *f.* federation

fe·de·ral *adj.* federal

fe·de·ra·lis·ta *adj.* federalist

fe·de·rar *v.* to federate

fe·li·ci·dad *f.* bliss; happiness; felicity

fe·li·ci·ta·ción *f.* congratulation

fe·li·ci·tar *v.* to congratulate

fe·li·no *adj.* feline

fe·liz *adj.* happy

fel·po *m.* rug

fel·po·so *adj.* plush

fel·pu·do *m.* rug

fe·me·ni·no *adj.* feminine

fe·mi·nis·ta *adj.* feminist

fé·mur *m.* femur

fe·ne·cer *v.* to pass away; to settle; to finish

fe·no·bar·bi·tal *m.* phenobarbital

fen·ol *m.* phenol

feo *adj.* ugly

fe·ria *f.* fair; market

fe·ria·do *adj.* holiday

fer·men·ta·ción *f.* fermentation

fer·men·tar *v.* to ferment

fe·ro·ci·dad *f.* ferocity

fe·roz *adj.* fierce

fé·rre·o *adj.* iron

fe·rro·ca·rril *m.* railway

fér·til *adj.* rich

fer·ti·li·zan·te *adj.* fertilizing

fer·ti·li·zar *v.* to fertilize

fér·vi·do *adj.* fervid

fer·vor *m.* fervor

fes·te·jar *v.* to celebrate; to entertain; to court

fes·tín *m.* feast

fes·ti·val *m.* festival

fes·ti·vo, a *adj.* merry; festive; witty

fe·tal *adj.* fetal

fe·ti·che *m.* fetish

fe·ti·dez *f.* fetidness

fe·to *m.* fetus

feu·dal *adj.* feudal

feu·da·lis·mo *adj.* feudalism

fia·ble *adj.* dependable

fia·dor *m.* guarantor

fian·za *f.* guarantor; security; deposit

fiar *v.* to entrust; to guaranty

fias·co *m.* fiasco

fi·bro·so *adj.* stringy; fibrous

fic·ción *f.* fiction

fic·ti·cio *adj.* fictitious

fi·cha *f.* chip; token

fi· de·dig·no *adj.* trustworthy

fi·dei·co·mi·so *m.* trust

fi·de·li·dad *f.* accuracy; fidelity

fie·bre *f.* fever

fiel *adj.* true; loyal; honest; faithful; trustworthy

fiel·tro *m.* felt

fie·re·za *f.* ferocity; deformity; fierceness

fies·ta *f.* feast; party

fi·gu·ra *f.* shape; figure; character

fi·gu·ra·ción *f.* figuration

fi·gu·ra·do *adj.* figurative

fi·gu·rar(se) *v.* to figure

fi·gu·ra·ti·vo *adj.* figurative

fi·ja·dor *adj.* fixative

fi·ja·men·te *adv.* firmly

fi·jar(se) *v.* to determine; to set

fi·jo *adj.* permanent; set; steady; fixed

fi·la *f.* row; file; tier

fi·la·men·to *m.* filament

fi·lán·tro·po *m.* philanthropist

fi·la·te·lis·ta *m.* philatelist

fi·li·gra·na *f.* filigree

fil·mar *v.* to film

fíl·mi·co *adj.* movie; film

fi·lo *m.* edge

fi·lo·lo·gí·a *f.* philology

fi·lo·so·fí·a *f.* philosophy

fi·ló·so·fo *m.* philosopher

fil·tra·ción *f.* filtration

fil·trar(se) *v.* to strain; to filter

fil·tro *m.* filter

fin *m.* finish; end

fi·nal *adj.* ending; last; end; final

fi·na·li·dad *f.* finality

fi·na·lis·ta *m.* finalist

fi·na·li·zar *v.* to conclude

fi·nal·men·te *adv.* finally

fin·ca *f.* land; farm

fi·ne·za *f.* politeness; fineness; affection

fin·gir(se) *v.* to pretend; to sham

fi·ni·to *adj.* finite

fi·no *adj.* acute; fine; elegant; delicate

fir·ma *f.* firm

fir·ma·men·to *m.* firmament

fir·mar *v.* to sign

fir·me *adj.* hard; strong; firm

fis·ca·li·zar *v.* to investigate; to oversee; to snoop

fí·si·co *adj.* physical

fi·sio·lo·gí·a *f.* physiology

fi·sió·lo·go *m.* physiologist

fi·sión *f.* fission

fís·tu·la *f.* fistula

fi·su·ra *f.* fissure

fla·co *adj.* skinny; gaunt

fla·ge·la·do *adj.* whipped

fla·gran·te *adj.* flagrant

fla·me·ar *v.* to flame

flan·co *m.* side

fla·que·ar *v.* to weaken

fla·que·za *f.* weakness; leanness

flau·ta *f.* flute

flau·tín *m.* piccolo

flau·tis·ta *f.* flutist

fle·bi·tis *f.* phlebitis

fle·cha *f.* arrow

fle·ma *f.* phlegm

fle·te *m.* cargo; freight

fle·xi·bi·li·dad *f.* flexibility

fle·xi·ble *adj.* flexible

fle·xor *adj.* flexor

flo·je·dad *f.* laziness; debility

flo·je·ra *f.* carelessness

flo·jo *adj.* limp; weak

flor *f.* blossom; flower; bloom

flo·re·cer *v.* to bloom; to prosper

flo·reo *m.* flourish

flo·ris·ta *m., f.* florist

flo·tar *v.* to float

fluc·tua·ción *f.* fluctuation

fluc·tuar *v.* to fluctuate

flui·do *adj.* fluid

fluir *v.* to flow

fo·co *m.* focus

fo·lí·cu·lo *m.* follicle

fo·lla·je *m.* foliage

fo·lle·to *m.* brochure

fo·men·tar *v.* to encourage

fon·ta·ne·ro *m.* plumber

for·jar *v.* to forge

for·ma *f.* shape; form

for·ma·ción *f.* formation

for·ma·li·dad *f.* formality

for·mar(se) *v.* to make; to shape

for·ta·le·cer(se) *v.* to fortify

for·ta·le·za *f.* fortress

for·tui·to *adj.* casual

for·tu·na *f.* fortune

for·zar *v.* to strain; to force

fó·sil *m.* fossil

fo·to *f.* picture; photograph

fo·to·gra·fí·a *f.* photography

fra·ca·sar *v.* to fail

frac·ción *f.* fraction

frac·tu·ra *f.* break; fracture

frac·tu·rar(se) *v.* to fracture

frá·gil *adj.* frail

fran·ca·men·te *adv.* frankly

fran·cés *adj.* French

fran·co *adj.* open; candid

fran·que·za *f.* frankness

fra·se *f.* sentence

fra·ter·ni·dad *f.* fraternity

frau·de *m.* deception

fre·cuen·cia *f.* frequency

fre·cuen·te *adj.* frequent

fre·gar *v.* to wash; to scrub

freír(se) *v.* to fry

fre·nar *v.* to brake

fren·te *f.* front; forehand

fres·co *adj.* fresh

fric·ción *f.* friction

frí·o *adj.* cold; frigid
fron·tal *adj.* frontal
fron·te·ra *f.* border; limit
frun·cir *v.* to gather
frus·tra·ción *f.* frustration
frus·trar(se) *v.* to frustrate
fue·go *m.* fire
fuen·te *f.* spring; fountain
fue·ra *adv.* outside; off
fuer·te *m.* sturdy; strong
fuer·za *f.* power; force
fu·gar·se *v.* to flee
ful·gu·rar *v.* to gleam
fu·mar *v.* to smoke
fun·da·ción *f.* foundation
fun·dar(se) *v.* to establish
fun·dir(se) *v.* to fuse
fu·ria *f.* fury
fu·rio·so *adj.* furious
fu·tu·ro *m.* future

G

ga·bán *m.* topcoat
ga·bar·di·na *f.* gabardine
ga·bi·ne·te *m.* boudoir
ga·ce·la *f.* gazelle
ga·ce·ta *f.* gazette
ga·chí *f.* girl, bird, chick
ga·cho *adj.* floppy; bent
ga·fas *f.* glasses
ga·ga *adj.* foolish
gai·te·ro *adj.* gaudy
ga·jo *m.* section; bunch
ga·lác·ti·co *adj.* galactic
ga·la·na·men·te *adv.* elegantly
ga·la·ní·a *f.* elegance
ga·lan·te *adj.* gallant
ga·lan·te·o *m.* flirting; courting another
ga·len·te·rí·a *f.* generosity; grace
ga·lar·do·nar *v.* to reward
ga·la·xia *f.* galaxy
ga·le·ón *m.* galleon
ga·le·ra *f.* galley
ga·le·rí·a *f.* gallery
ga·li·ma·tí·as *m.* nonsense
ga·lón *m.* gallon
ga·lo·pan·te *adj.* galloping
ga·lo·par *v.* to gallop
ga·lo·pe *m.* gallop
gal·va·ni·zar *v.* to galvanize
ga·llar·dí·a *f.* gallantry; grace; elegance

ga·llar·do *adj.* graceful; brave
ga·lle·ta *f.* cracker
ga·lli·na *f.* chicken; hen
ga·lli·ne·ro *m.* henhouse; coop
ga·llo *m.* cock; rooster
ga·ma *f.* gamut
gam·ba·do *adj.* bowlegged
gam·be·te·ar *v.* to prance
ga·na *f.* longing; appetite
ga·na·de·ro *m.* cattle raiser, rancher
ga·na·do *m.* livestock
ga·nan·cia *f.* profit
ga·nar *v.* to earn; to win
gan·cho *m.* hook
gan·du·le·rí·a *f.* laziness
gan·glio *m.* ganglion
gan·go·so *adj.* nasal
gan·gre·na *f.* gangrene
ga·no·so *adj.* anxious
gan·so *m.* goose
ga·ra·ba·to *m.* grapple
ga·ra·je *m.* garage
ga·ran·tí·a *f.* warrant; guaranty
ga·ran·tir *v.* to defend; to guarantee
ga·ra·tu·sa *f.* compliment
gar·ban·zo *m.* chickpea
gar·be·ar *v.* to steal; to rob
gar·bi·llo *m.* sieve
gar·bo·so *adj.* graceful; generous
gar·fa *f.* claw
gar·ga·je·ar *v.* to spit
gar·gan·ta *f.* neck
gár·ga·ra *f.* gargling
gar·ga·ri·zar *v.* to gargle
gár·go·la *f.* gargoyle
gar·güe·ro *m.* gullet; windpipe
ga·rra *f.* talon
ga·rra·fal *adj.* enormous
ga·rra·pa·ta *f.* tick
ga·rrai·nar *v.* to grab
ga·rrón *m.* claw
ga·ruar *v.* to drizzle
gas *m.* gas
ga·sa *f.* gauze
ga·si·fi·car *v.* to gasify
ga·so·li·na *f.* gas
gas·ta·do, a *adj.* threadbare; exhausted
gas·tar *v.* to exhaust; to spend; to squander; to wear

gas·tri·tis *f.* gastritis
gas·tro·no·mí·a *f.* gastronomy
gas·tro·nó·mi·co *adj.* gastronomic
ga·te·ar *v.* to climb; to swipe
ga·ti·llo *m.* trigger
ga·to *m.* cat
ga·tu·no *adj.* catlike
gau·cho *adj.* gaucho
ga·ve·ta *f.* drawer
ga·vio·ta *f.* gull
ga·za·pi·na *f.* brawl
gaz·na·te *m.* windpipe; throat
géi·ser *m.* geyser
ge·la·ti·na *f.* gelatin
ge·ma *f.* gem
ge·nea·lo·gí·a *f.* genealogy
ge·ne·ra·ción *f.* generation
ge·ne·ral *m.* general
ge·ne·ra·li·dad *f.* generality
ge·ne·ra·li·za·ción *f.* generalization
ge·ne·ra·li·zar *v.* to generalize
ge·ne·ra·ti·vo *adj.* generative
ge·né·ri·ca·men·te *adv.* generically
ge·né·ri·co *adj.* generic
ge·ne·ro·si·dad *f.* generosity
ge·ne·ro·so, a *adj.* fine; generous
ge·nial *adj.* genial; inspired; pleasant
ge·nio *m.* genius; disposition
ge·no·ci·dio *m.* genocide
ge·no·ti·po *m.* genotype
gen·te *f.* nation; people
gen·til *adj.* genteel; excellent; polite
gen·tí·o *m.* mob
ge·nui·no *adj.* real; true; genuine
geo·fí·si·co *adj.* geophysical
geo·gra·fí·a *f.* geography
ge·ó·gra·fo *m., f.* geographer
geo·lo·gí·a *f.* geology
ge·ó·lo·go *m., f.* geologist
geo·me·trí·a *f.* geometry
ge·ra·nio *m.* geranium
ge·ren·te *m., f.* director
ge·riá·tri·co *adj.* geriatric
ger·ma·nio *m.* germanium

ger·men *m.* germ
ger·mi·na·ción *f.* germination
ger·mi·nar *v.* to germinate
ge·ron·to·lo·gí·a *f.* gerontology
ges·ta·ción *f.* gestation
ges·ti·cu·la·ción *f.* gesture; grimace
ges·ti·cu·lar *v.* to gesture
gey·ser *m.* geyser
gi·bar *v.* to annoy
gi·bón *m.* gibbon
gi·gan·tea *f.* sunflower
gi·gan·te *m.* giant
gi·go·lo *m.* gigolo
gim·na·sia *f.* gymnastics
gim·nas·ta *f., m.* gymnast
gi·mo·te·ar *v.* to whine
gi·ne·co·lo·gí·a *f.* gynecology
gin·gi·vi·tis *f.* gingivitis
gi·rar *v.* to rotate; to spin; to gyrate
gi·ra·to·rio *adj.* rotating
gi·ro *m.* rotation; turn
gi·ros·co·pio *m.* gyroscope
gi·ta·nes·co *adj.* gypsy-like
gla·cia·ción *f.* glaciation
gla·cial *adj.* glacial; icy
gla·ciar *m.* glacier
gla·dia·dor *m.* gladiator
glán·du·la *f.* gland
gla·se·ar *v.* to glaze
glau·co·ma *m.* glaucoma
glo·bal *adj.* global
glo·bo *m.* globe
glo·glo *m.* gurgle
glo·ria *f.* glory
glo·ri·fi·ca·ción *f.* glorification
glo·ri·fi·car(se) *v.* to glorify
glo·rio·so *adj.* glorious
glo·sa *f.* gloss
glo·sar *v.* to gloss
glo·sa·rio *m.* glossary
glo·tis *f.* glottis
glu·co·sa *f.* glucose
glu·ti·no·so *adj.* glutinous
go·ber·na·ción *f.* government
go·ber·na·dor *m.* governor
go·ber·nar *v.* to govern
go·bier·no *m.* government
go·la *f.* throat
golf *m.* golf
gol·fo *m.* gulf

go·lo·si·na *f.* craving; delicacy; longing
gol·pe *m.* blow; hit
gol·pear *v.* to slug; to hit; to beat
gol·pe·te·ar *v.* to pummel; hit; to pound; to beat
go·ma *f.* rubber; gum; rubber band
go·mo·so *adj.* gummy
gón·do·la *f.* gondola
gon·do·le·ro *m.* gondolier
go·no·co·co *m.* gonococcus
gor·do *adj.* fat
gor·go·te·o *m.* gurgle
go·ri·la *m.* gorilla
go·te·o *m.* dripping
go·zar *v.* to enjoy; to rejoice
gra·bar *v.* to engrave
gra·cia *f.* kindness; charm; pardon
gra·cio·so *adj.* funny; charming; amusing
gra·do *m.* step; grade
gra·dual *adj.* gradual
gra·fi·to *m.* graphite
gra·má·ti·co *adj.* grammatical
gra·na·te *adj. m.* garnet
gra·ní·ti·co *adj.* granite
gran·je·ro *m., f.* farmer
gra·pa *f.* staple
gra·ti·fi·car *v.* to gratify
gra·ve *adj.* serious; important; grave
gre·ga·rio *adj.* gregarious
gris *adj.* gray; grey
gri·tar *v.* to yell; to cry
gri·to *m.* yell; scream
gro·se·rí·a *f.* roughness; stupidity; vulgarity
gro·se·ro *adj.* vulgar; coarse
gro·tes·co *adj.* grotesque
gru·nón *adj.* grumble; grunt
gru·po *m.* bunch
guan·te *m.* glove
guan·te·ro *m.* glove maker
gua·pe·tón *adj.* bold; flashy
gua·pe·za *f.* daring
gua·po *adj.* flashy; good-looking
guar·da *f.* custody; guard
guar·dar(se) *v.* to keep; to guard
guar·dia *f.* guard
guar·dián *m., f.* guardian
guar·ne·cer *v.* to supply

gu·ber·na·men·tal *adj.* governmental
gue·rra *f.* war
gue·rre·ar *v.* to fight
guí·a *m., f.* leader; guide
guiar *v.* to steep; to guide
gui·ta·rra *f.* guitar
gu·sa·no *m.* worm
gus·tar *v.* to like
gus·to *m.* zest; taste

H

ha·ber *v.* to have
há·bil *adj.* skillful
ha·bi·li·dad *f.* ability; skill
ha·bi·ta·ción *f.* habitation; lodging
ha·bi·tar *v.* to dwell
ha·bi·tual *adj.* habitual
ha·bi·tuar *v.* to habituate
ha·bla *f.* speech
ha·bla·do *adj.* spoken
ha·bla·du·rí·a *f.* gossip; chatter
ha·blar *v.* to talk; to speak
ha·ce *adv.* ago
ha·cer(se) *v.* to act; to become; to force; to compose
ha·cia *prep.* about; to
ha·cien·da *f.* ranch
ha·ci·na *f.* pile
ha·ci·nar *v.* to pile up
ha·da *f.* fairy
ha·do *m.* fate
ha·la·güe·ño *adj.* promising; attractive; pleasing
ha·lar *v.* to tow
hal·cón *m.* falcon
hal·co·ne·rí·a *f.* falconry
hal·co·ne·ro *m.* falconer
ha·llar(se) *v.* to locate
ham·bre *f.* hunger
ham·brien·to *adj.* hungry; starved
ham·bur·gue·sa *f.* hamburger
ha·ra·po·so *adj.* tattered
ha·rén *m.* harem
har·tar *v.* to annoy; to stuff
has·ta *prep.* until
has·tiar *v.* to annoy; to sicken
he·bra *f.* filament; thread

he·chi·ce·ro *m., f.* charmer; sorceress; sorcerer
he·chi·zo *m.* charm; spell
he·der *v.* to stink; to smell bad
he·dor *m.* stink
he·la·do *m.* ice cream
he·lar *v.* to freeze
he·li·cóp·te·ro *m.* helicopter
he·lio *m.* helium
he·li·puer·to *m.* heliport
hem·bra *f.* female; woman
he·mo·fi·lia *f.* hemophilia
he·mo·glo·bi·na *f.* hemoglobin
he·mo·rra·gia *f.* hemorrhage
hen·der(se) *v.* to crack
he·nil *m.* hayloft
he·no *m.* hay
he·pa·ti·tis *f.* hepatitis
her·ba·rio *adj.* herbal
he·re·di·ta·rio *adj.* hereditary
he·ren·cia *f.* heritage
he·ri·da *f.* wound
he·rir *v.* to hurt; to injure; to wound
her·ma·na *f.* sister
her·man·dad *f.* sisterhood; brotherhood; league
her·ma·no *m.* brother
her·mo·se·ar *v.* to beautify
her·mo·so, a *adj.* beautiful
her·nia *f.* hernia
he·roi·co *adj.* heroic
he·ro·í·na *f.* heroine
her·pes *m.* herpes
he·rre·ro *m.* blacksmith
he·rrum·brar *v.* to rust
he·rrum·bre *m.* rust
her·vor *m.* boiling
he·si·ta·ción *f.* hesitation
he·si·tar *v.* to hesitate
he·xá·go·no *adj.* hexagonal
hi·ber·na·ción *f.* hibernation
hi·ber·nar *v.* to hibernate
hí·bri·do *m.* hybrid
hi·dra·ta·ción *f.* hydration
hi·dra·tar *v.* to hydrate
hi·dro·car·bu·ro *m.* hydrocarbon
hi·dro·fo·bia *f.* hydrophobia
hi·dró·ge·no *m.* hydrogen
hi·dro·te·ra·pia *f.* hydrotherapy

hi·dró·xi·do *m.* hydroxide
hie·dra *f.* ivy
hie·lo *m.* ice
hier·ba *f.* grass
hi·gie·ne *f.* hygiene
hi·gié·ni·co *adj.* hygienic
hi·ja *f.* daughter
hi·jas·tra *f.* stepdaughter
hi·jas·tro *m.* stepson
hi·jo *m.* son
hi·la·dor *m., f.* spinner
hi·lar *v.* to spin
hi·le·ro *m.* current
hi·lo *m.* filament; thread
hi·men *m.* hymen
him·no *m.* hymn
hin·char *v.* to exaggerate; to swell; to blow up
hi·no·jo *m.* knee
hi·pér·bo·la *f.* hyperbola
hi·per·sen·si·ble *adj.* hypersensitive
hi·per·ter·mia *f.* hyperthermia
hip·no·sis *f.* hypnosis
hip·no·tis·mo *m.* hypnotism
hip·no·ti·zar *v.* to hypnotize
hi·po·con·dria *f.* hypochondria
hi·po·cre·sí·a *f.* hypocrisy
hi·pó·cri·ta *f., m.* hypocrite
hi·po·te·ca *f.* mortgage
hi·po·te·car *v.* to mortgage
hi·po·ter·mia *f.* hypothermia
his·te·ria *f.* hysteria
his·to·ria *f.* story; history
ho·ci·car *v.* to smooch; to nuzzle
hoc·key *m.* hockey
ho·gue·ra *f.* bonfire
ho·ja *f.* petal; leaf; sheet
ho·jo·so *adj.* leafy
hol·gan·za *f.* leisure
ho·lo·caus·to *m.* holocaust
hom·bre *m.* man
hom·bre·ra *f.* shoulder pad
hom·bri·llo *m.* yoke
hom·bro *m.* shoulder
ho·mi·ci·da *adj.* homicidal
ho·mi·ci·dio *m.* homicide
ho·mo·ge·nei·zar *v.* to homogenize
ho·mo·ni·mia *f.* homonymy
hon·do *adj.* intense; deep
hon·do·na·da *f.* gorge

ho·nes·ti·dad *f.* honesty
hon·go *m.* mushroom
ho·nor *m.* honor
ho·no·ra·ble *adj.* honorable
hon·ra·dez *f.* honesty
hon·ra·do *adj.* honest
hon·ro·so *adj.* honorable
ho·ra *f.* time; hour
hor·cón *m.* pitchfork
ho·ri·zon·tal *adj.* horizontal
ho·ri·zon·te *m.* horizon
hor·mi·go·ne·ra *f.* cement plant
hor·mo·na *f.* hormone
hor·ne·ar *v.* to bake
hor·ne·ro *m., f.* baker
hor·ni·llo *m.* stove
hor·no *m.* oven
ho·rós·co·po *m.* horoscope
ho·rren·do *adj.* horrendous
ho·rri·ble *adj.* awful; horrible
hó·rri·do *adj.* horrid
ho·rro·ri·zar *v.* to horrify
ho·rror *m.* terror; horror
hor·tí·co·la *adj.* horticultural
hor·ti·cul·tu·ra *f.* horticulture
hos·pi·tal *m.* hospital
hos·pi·ta·li·zar *v.* to hospitalize
hos·te·rí·a *f.* hostel; inn
hos·ti·gar *v.* to harass; to whip
hos·til *adj.* hostile
hos·ti·li·dad *f.* hostility
ho·tel *m.* hotel
hoy *m.* today
ho·ya *f.* hole
hue·co *adj.* deep; hollow
hue·lla *f.* print; footprint
huer·ta *f.* garden
hue·sa *f.* grave
hue·su·do *adj.* bony
hue·vo *m.* egg
huir(se) *v.* to flee; to escape; to avoid; to run from
hu·ma·nar *v.* to humanize
hu·ma·ni·dad *f.* humanity
hu·ma·ni·zar *v.* to humanize
hu·ma·no *m.* human
hu·me·ar *v.* to steam; to smoke
hu·me·dad *f.* humidity
hú·me·do *adj.* humid
hú·me·ro *m.* humerus

hu·mil·dad *f.* humility
hu·mi·lla·ción *f.* humiliation
hu·mi·llan·te *adj.* humiliating
hu·mi·llo *m.* pride
hu·mo *m.* smoke
hu·mo·ris·mo *m.* wit
hu·mo·so *adj.* smoky
hun·dir *v.* to ruin; to sink; to plunge
hu·ra·cán *m.* hurricane
hur·gón *m.* poker
hu·rón *m.* ferret
hur·tar(se) *v.* to steal; to take
hur·to *m.* robbery
hus·me·ar *v.* to pry
hus·me·o *m.* prying

I

i·bis *f.* ibis
i·ce·berg *m.* iceberg
i·co·no·gra·fí·a *f.* iconography
ic·te·ri·cia *f.* jaundice
ic·tió·lo·go *m.* ichthyologist
i·de·a *f.* notion; thought image; idea; picture
i·de·al *m.* ideal
i·dea·lis·ta *adj.* idealist
i·dea·li·zar *v.* to idealize
i·dear *v.* to invent; to plan; to design
i·dén·ti·co *adj.* identical
i·den·ti·dad *f.* identify
i·den·ti·fi·ca·ble *adj.* identifiable
i·den·ti·fi·ca·ción *f.* identification
i·den·ti·fi·car *v.* to identify
i·deo·ló·gi·co *adj.* ideological
i·di·lio *m.* idyll
i·dio·má·ti·co *adj.* idiomatic
i·dio·sin·cra·sia *f.* idiosyncrasy
i·dio·ta *m., f.* idiot; *adj.* idiotic; foolish
i·do·la·trar *v.* to idolize
i·do·la·trí·a *f.* idolatry
í·do·lo *m.* idol
i·gle·sia *f.* church
ig·ni·ción *f.* ignition
ig·no·mi·nio·so *adj.* ignominious
ig·no·ran·cia *f.* ignorance

ig·no·ran·te *adj.* ignorant; unaware; uneducated
ig·no·to *adj.* undiscovered
i·gual *adj.* level; even; alike; like
i·gua·la·mien·to *m.* equalization
i·gua·lar *v.* to make equal; to equate; to smooth
i·gual·dad *f.* equality
i·gual·men·te *adv.* too; equally
i·gua·na *m.* iguana
i·la·ción *f.* cohesiveness
i·le·gal *adj.* unlawful; illegal
i·le·ga·li·dad *f.* illegality
i·le·gi·ble *adj.* illegible
i·le·tra·do *adj.* illiterate
i·ló·gi·co *adj.* illogical
i·lu·mi·na·ción *f.* illumination
i·lu·mi·na·dor *adj.* illuminative
i·lu·mi·nar *v.* to light; illuminate
i·lu·sión *f.* illusion
i·lu·so·rio *adj.* illusory
i·lus·tra·ción *f.* illustration
i·lus·tra·dor *adj.* illustrative
i·lus·trar *v.* to illustrate
i·lus·tre *adj.* illustrious
i·ma·gi·na·ble *adj.* imaginable
i·ma·gi·na·ción *f.* imagination
i·ma·gi·nar(se) *v.* to think up; to conceive
i·ma·gi·na·ti·vo *adj.* imaginative
i·ma·nar *v.* to magnetize
im·be·ci·li·dad *f.* imbecility
i·mi·ta·ble *adj.* imitable
i·mi·ta·ción *f.* imitation
i·mi·tar *v.* to imitate
im·pa·cien·cia *f.* impatience
im·pa·cien·te *adj.* impatient
im·par·cial *adj.* impartial
im·par·tir *v.* to concede
im·pa·si·ble *adj.* impassive
im·pe·ca·ble *adj.* impeccable
im·pe·di·men·to *m.* impediment
im·pe·dir *v.* to deter; to hinder
im·pen·sa·ble *adj.* unimaginable; unthinkable

im·pe·rar *v.* to reign
im·per·do·na·ble *adj.* inexcusable
im·per·fec·ción *f.* imperfection
im·pe·rial *adj.* imperial
im·per·me·a·bi·li·dad *f.* impermeability
im·per·me·a·ble *m.* raincoat
im·per·so·nal *adj.* impersonal
im·pé·ti·go *m.* impetigo
ím·pe·tu *m.* energy; impetus
im·pe·tuo·so *adj.* impetuous; violent
im·pla·ca·ble *adj.* implacable
im·plan·tar *v.* to implant
im·pli·ca·ción *f.* implication; consequence
im·pli·car *v.* to mean; to implicate
im·plo·rar *v.* to invoke
im·po·ner *v.* to charge; to inspire; to inform
im·po·pu·lar *adj.* unpopular
im·por·ta·ción *f.* importation
im·por·tan·cia *f.* authority; importance
im·por·tan·te *adj.* important
im·por·tu·nar *v.* to importune
im·por·tu·no *adj.* inopportune
im·po·si·bi·li·dad *f.* impossibility
im·po·si·ble *adj.* impossible; difficult
im·pos·tor *m.* imposter
im·po·ten·cia *f.* impotence
im·prac·ti·ca·ble *adj.* unfeasible; impracticable
im·pre·ci·so *adj.* imprecise
im·preg·nar *v.* to impregnate
im·pre·sión *f.* impression
im·pre·sio·nan·te *adj.* impressive
im·pre·vis·to *adj.* unexpected; sudden
im·pri·mir *v.* to stamp; to print; to imprint
im·pro·ba·ble *adj.* improbable

im·pro·duc·ti·vo *adj.* unproductive

im·pro·vi·sa·ción *f.* improvisation

im·pu·den·cia *f.* impudence

im·pul·sar *v.* to drive; to impel

im·pul·sión *f.* impulse

im·pul·so *m.* impulse

im·pu·ni·dad *f.* impunity

im·pu·re·za *f.* impurity

im·pu·ro *adj.* impure

in·ac·ción *f.* inaction

in·a·cep·ta·ble *adj.* unacceptable

in·ac·ti·vo *adj.* inactive

in·a·de·cua·do *adj.* inadequate

in·ad·ver·ten·cia *f.* carelessness; inadvertence

in·al·te·ra·ble *adj.* unalterable

i·na·ne *adj.* vain; useless

i·na·ni·dad *f.* inanity

in·a·pli·ca·ble *adj.* inapplicable

in·a·ten·ción *f.* inattention

in·a·ten·to *adj.* inattentive

in·ca·pa·ci·dad *f.* incapacity

in·ca·pa·ci·tar *v.* to incapacitate

in·ca·paz *adj.* unable; incapable

in·cen·dio *m.* incentive

in·ces·to *m.* incest

in·cien·so *m.* incense

in·cier·to *adj.* vague; uncertain; doubtful

in·ci·ne·rar *v.* to incinerate

in·ci·sión *f.* incision

in·ci·tar *v.* to urge; to incite

in·cle·men·te *adj.* inclement

in·cli·na·ción *f.* slant; inclination; slope

in·cli·nar(se) *v.* to slant; to incline; to persuade

in·cluir *v.* to contain; to include

in·clu·sión *f.* inclusion

in·clu·si·vo *adj.* inclusive

in·co·he·ren·te *adj.* incoherent

in·co·mi·ble *adj.* inedible

in·com·pa·ti·ble *adj.* incompatible

in·com·ple·to *adj.* incomplete

in·con·clu·so *adj.* inconclusive

in·cons·tan·te *adj.* fickle

in·cor·po·ral *adj.* incorporeal

in·cor·po·rar *v.* to incorporate

in·co·rrec·to *adj.* incorrect

in·co·rrup·to *adj.* incorrupt

in·cré·du·lo *adj.* incredulous

in·cre·í·ble *adj.* incredible

in·cre·men·tar *v.* to increase

in·cre·men·to *m.* increase

in·cre·par *v.* to reprimand

in·cri·mi·nar *v.* to incriminate

in·crus·tar *v.* to encrust

in·cu·ba·ción *f.* incubation

in·cu·bar *v.* to incubate

in·cul·car *v.* to inculcate

in·cu·ra·ble *adj.* incurable

in·cu·rrir *v.* to incur

in·de·cen·te *adj.* indecent

in·de·ci·sión *f.* indecision

in·de·ci·so *adj.* indecisive

in·de·fen·so *adj.* defenseless

in·de·le·ble *adj.* indelible

in·dem·ne *adj.* unhurt

in·de·pen·di·zar *v.* to liberate

in·de·se·a·ble *adj.* undesirable

in·di·ca·ción *f.* sign; indication; direction

in·di·car *v.* to show; to indicate

in·di·fe·ren·te *adj.* indifferent

in·di·gen·cia *f.* indigence

in·di·gen·te *adj.* indigent

in·di·ges·tión *f.* indigestion

in·dig·nar *v.* to infuriate

in·dig·no *adj.* despicable

ín·di·go *m.* indigo

in·di·rec·to *adj.* hint; indirect

in·dis·cre·ción *f.* indiscretion

in·dis·cu·ti·ble *adj.* indisputable

in·dis·tin·to *adj.* indistinct

in·di·vi·dual *adj.* individual

in·di·vi·duo *m.* individual

in·di·vi·si·ble *adj.* indivisible

in·dó·cil *adj.* indocile

in·do·ci·li·dad *f.* unruliness

in·do·len·cia *f.* indolence

in·do·len·te *adj.* indolent

in·do·ma·ble *adj.* uncontrollable; untamable

in·dó·mi·to *adj.* untamable; indomitable

in·duc·ción *f.* induction

in·du·cir *v.* to induce

in·du·da·ble *adj.* certain

in·dul·gen·te *adj.* indulgent

in·dus·tria *f.* industry

in·dus·trial *adj.* industrial

in·dus·tria·li·zar *v.* to become industrialized

in·dus·trio·so *adj.* industrious

i·ne·fa·ble *adj.* ineffable

in·e·fi·caz *adj.* ineffective

i·nep·ti·tud *f.* ineptitude

i·nep·to *adj.* inept

i·ner·cia *f.* inertia

i·ner·te *adj.* inert

i·nes·pe·ra·do *adj.* unexpected

i·nes·ta·ble *adj.* unstable

i·ne·vi·ta·ble *adj.* inevitable

i·ne·xis·ten·te *adj.* nonexistent; not existing

i·nex·plo·ra·do *adj.* unexplored

in·fa·li·ble *adj.* infallible

in·fa·mar *v.* to slander

in·fa·mia *f.* infamy

in·fan·cia *f.* infancy

in·fan·te *m.* baby; infant

in·fan·til *adj.* childish; baby

in·far·to *m.* infraction

in·fa·tuar *v.* to become conceited

in·fec·ción *f.* infection

in·fec·cio·so *adj.* infectious

in·fec·tar(se) *v.* to infect

in·fe·liz *adj.* wretched

in·fe·ren·cia *f.* inference

in·fe·rior *adj.* under; inferior

in·fe·rio·ri·dad *f.* inferiority

in·fe·rir *v.* to inflict; to infer

in·fes·tar *v.* to infest

in·fiel *adj.* disloyal

in·fier·no *m.* hell

in·fil·trar *v.* to infiltrate

ín·fi·mo *adj.* worst; lowest

in·fi·ni·to *adj. m.* infinite

in·fla·ción *f.* inflation

in·fla·ma·ble *adj.* inflammable

in·fla·mar *v.* to inflame

in·flar *v.* to inflate

in·flex·i·ble *adj.* rigid; unyielding

in·fluen·cia *f.* influence

in·fluen·ciar *v.* to influence

in·flu·jo *m.* influence

in·for·ma·ción *f.* information

in·for·mal *adj.* informal

in·for·mar(se) *v.* to report; to inform; to find out

in·for·me *adj.* formless

in·for·tu·nio *m.* misfortune

in·fra·rro·jo *adj.* infrared

in·fre·cuen·te *adj.* infrequent

in·fruc·tuo·so *adj.* fruitless

in·fun·dir *v.* to infuse

in·fu·sión *f.* infusion

in·ge·nie·rí·a *f.* engineering

in·ge·nie·ro *m.* engineer

in·ge·nio·so *adj.* witty; clever

in·ge·rir *v.* to ingest

in·ges·tión *f.* ingestion

in·glés *m.* English

in·gra·to *adj.* thankless

in·gre·dien·te *m.* ingredient

in·gre·so *m.* entrance

in·ha·bi·li·dad *f.* incompetence

in·ha·lar *v.* to inhale

in·he·ren·te *adj.* inherent

in·hi·bir *v.* to inhibit

in·hu·ma·no *adj.* inhuman

i·ni·cia·ción *f.* initiation

i·ni·cial *adj.* initial

i·ni·ciar *v.* to initiate

i·ni·cio *m.* beginning

i·ni·gua·la·do *adj.* unequaled

i·ni·mi·ta·ble *adj.* inimitable

in·je·rir *v.* to insert

in·jer·to *m.* transplant

in·ju·ria *f.* injury

in·jus·ti·cia *f.* injustice

in·jus·to *adj.* unjust

in·ma·du·ro *adj.* immature

in·me·mo·rial *adj.* immemorial

in·men·so *adj.* immense

in·mer·sión *f.* immersion

in·mi·grar *v.* to immigrate

in·mi·nen·te *adj.* imminent

in·mo·des·to *adj.* immodest

in·mo·lar *v.* to immolate
in·mo·ral *adj.* immoral
in·mor·tal *adj.* immortal
in·mo·vi·ble *adj.* immovable
in·mó·vil *adj.* immobile
in·mun·do *adj.* filthy
in·mu·ni·dad *f.* immunity
in·mu·ni·zar *v.* to immunize
in·mu·ta·ble *adj.* immutable
in·no·ble *adj.* ignoble
in·no·va·ción *f.* innovation
in·no·var *v.* to innovate
i·no·cen·cia *f.* innocence
i·no·cen·te *adj.* innocent
i·no·cu·lar *v.* to inoculate
i·no·cuo *adj.* innocuous
i·no·pe·ra·ble *adj.*
    inoperable
i·nor·gá·ni·co *adj.* inorganic
in·quie·tar *v.* to alarm
in·quie·tud *f.* uneasiness
in·qui·li·no *m., f.* tenant
in·qui·rir *v.* to probe
in·sa·no *adj.* insane
ins·cri·bir(se) *v.* to record;
    to engrave
ins·crip·ción *f.* record;
    inscription
in·sec·to *m.* insect
in·se·gu·ro *adj.* insecure
in·sen·si·ble *adj.* unfeeling;
    unconscious; insensible
in·ser·ción *f.* insertion
in·ser·tar *v.* to insert
in·sig·nia *f.* emblem
in·sin·ce·ro *adj.* insincere
in·sis·ten·te *adj.* insistent
in·sis·tir *v.* to insist
in·so·len·cia *f.* insolence
ins·pec·ción *f.* inspection
ins·pi·rar *v.* to inspire
ins·truc·ción *f.* instruction
ins·truir(se) *v.* to teach; to
    learn; to instruct
in·su·li·na *f.* insulin
in·sul·tar *v.* to insult
in·tac·to *adj.* together; intact
in·te·li·gen·cia *f.* intellect;
    intelligence
in·te·li·gen·te *adj.* smart;
    intelligent
in·ten·si·fi·car *v.*
    to intensify
in·te·re·sar(se) *v.*
    to concern
in·te·rior *m.* inside
in·ter·no *adj.* inside

in·te·rrup·ción *f.*
    interruption
in·ter·ve·nir *v.* to mediate;
    to intervene
ín·ti·mo *adj.* intimate
in·tro·duc·ción *f.*
    introduction
in·va·dir *v.* to invade
in·va·sión *f.* invasion
in·ven·ción *f.* invention
in·ven·tar *v.* to contrive; to
    think up; to invent
in·ves·tir *v.* to invest
in·vier·no *m.* winter
ir(se) *v.* to depart; to leave
i·rre·gu·lar *adj.* irregular
is·la *f.* island
iz·quier·do, a *adj.* left

J

ja·ba·lí *m.* boar
ja·ba·li·na *f.* javelin
ja·bón *m.* soap
ja·bo·na·do *m.* wash
ja·bo·nar *v.* to lather up
ja·bo·ne·ro *m., f.* soapmaker
ja·ca *f.* nag; pony
ja·ca·re·ro *adj.* lively
ja·co *m.* nag
jac·tan·cia *f.* arrogance;
    bragging; boast
jac·tan·cio·so *adj.* arrogant
jac·tar·se *v.* to brag
ja·de *m.* jade
ja·de·ar *v.* to gasp for air
ja·diar *v.* to hope
ja·guar *m.* jaguar
ja·lar *v.* to pull on
ja·le·a *f.* jelly
ja·le·ar *v.* to urge on
ja·leo *m.* racket; uproar
ja·lo·nar *v.* to mark
ja·más *adv.* never; ever;
    never again
jam·ba *f.* jamb
ja·mel·go *m.* nag
ja·món *m.* ham
ja·que *m.* check
ja·que·ar *v.* to check
ja·ra·be *m.* syrup
ja·ra·near *v.* to carouse
jar·ca *f.* acacia
jar·dín *m.* garden
jar·di·ne·ra *f.* gardener
jar·di·ne·ro *m.* gardener

ja·rra *f.* mug; pitcher
ja·rro *m.* jug
ja·rrón *m.* vase
jas·pe *m.* jasper
jau·la *f.* cell; cage
jaz·mín *m.* jasmine
je·fa *f.* master; boss
je·fe *m.* head; boss; master
je·mi·que·ar *v.* to whine
jen·gi·bre *m.* ginger
je·rar·quí·a *f.* hierarchy
je·re·mí·as *m., f.*
    complainer
jer·ga *f.* jargon; slang
je·ri·gon·za *f.* gibberish
je·rin·gar *v.* to pester
je·rin·ga·zo *m.* injection
je·ro·glí·fi·co *m.* hieroglyph
jer·sey *m.* sweater
ji·fia *f.* swordfish
ji·ne·te *m.* equestrian;
    horseman
ji·ne·te·ar *v.* to ride a horse
ji·par *v.* to pant
ji·ra *f.* excursion
ji·ra·fa *f.* giraffe
jo·co·si·dad *f.* joke; wit
jo·co·so *adj.* jocular
jo·cun·di·dad *f.* jocundity
jo·fai·na *f.* washbowl;
    washbasin
jor·na·da *f.* trip
jor·nal *m.* wage
jo·ro·ba *f.* hump
jo·ro·bar *v.* to annoy; to
    bother
jo·rrar *v.* to haul
jo·ven *m.* youth
jo·vial *adj.* jovial
jo·ya *f.* gem; jewel
jo·ye·ra *f.* box for jewelry
jo·ye·rí·a *f.* jewelry store
jo·ye·ro *m.* jeweler
ju·bi·la·do *m., f.* retired one
ju·bi·lar(se) *v.* to retire
ju·bi·leo *m.* jubilee
jú·bi·lo *m.* joy
ju·bi·lo·so *adj.* joyful
ju·dí·a *f.* bean
jue·go *m.* play; game
jue·ves *m.* Thursday
juez *m.* judge
ju·gar *v.* to game; to play
ju·gue·te·ar *v.* to play
ju·gue·tón *adj.* playful
jui·cio *m.* verdict; judgment
ju·lio *m.* July

jun·co *m.* junk
ju·nio *j* June
jun·ta *f.* union
jun·ta·men·te *adv.* together
jun·tar(se) *v.* to connect; to
    join
jun·to *adv.* together
ju·ra·do *m.* jury
ju·rar *v.* to vow; to swear; to
    curse
ju·ris·ta *f.* jurist
jus·ta·men·te *adv.* fairly
jus·ti·cia *f.* justice
jus·ti·fi·car *v.* to warrant
jus·to *adj.* fair
ju·ve·nil *adj.* youthful,
    juvenile
ju·ven·tud *f.* youth
juz·gar *v.* to try; to judge

K

ki·lo *m.* kilo
ki·lo·ci·clo *m.* kilocycle
ki·lo·gra·mo *m.* kilogram
ki·lo·mé·tri·co *adj.*
    kilometric
ki·ló·me·tro *m.* kilometer
ki·lo·va·tio *m.* kilowatt
kirsch *m.* cherry brandy
kum·mel *m.* cumin brandy

L

la *def. art.* the
la·be·rin·to *m.* labyrinth
la·bia *f.* eloquence
la·bio *m.* lip
la·bor *f.* work
la·bo·ra·ble *adj.* working
la·bo·ral *adj.* labor
la·bo·rar *v.* to work
la·bo·ra·to·rio *m.*
    laboratory
la·bo·re·ar *v.* to work
la·bo·rio·so *adj.* arduous
la·bra·do, a *adj.* plowed;
    cultivated; wrought
la·bra·dor, a *adj.* farming
    m. farmer; peasant
la·bran·za *f.* farmland; farm
la·brar *v.* to carve; to work;
    to plow; to cultivate; to tool
la·ca *f.* shellac; lacquer; hair

spray

la·ca·yo *m.* valet; attendant

la·ce·ra·ción *f.* laceration

la·ce·rar *v.* to injure; to lacerate

la·ce·ria *f.* want; toil

la·cio *adj.* limp; straight

la·có·ni·co, a *adj.* laconic

la·cra *f.* scar

la·cre *m.* a sealing wax

la·cri·mó·ge·no, a *adj.* tear producing

la·cri·mo·so, a *adj.* tearful; sad; sorrowful

lac·ta·ción *f.* nursing

lac·tan·cia *f.* lactation

lac·tar *v.* to suckle

lác·ti·co, a *adj.* lactic

lac·to·sa *f.* lactose

la·de·ar *v.* to tilt

la·de·o *m.* inclination

la·de·ra *f.* slope

la·di·no, a *adj.* astute

la·do *m.* side; **de** next to; beside; alongside

la·drar *v.* to snarl at something; to growl

la·dri·llo *m.* brick

la·drón *m.* robber

la·dro·ne·rí·a *f.* theft

la·gar·ti·ja *f.* a small lizard

la·gar·to *m.* lizard

la·go *m.* lake

lá·gri·ma *f.* tear

la·gri·me·ar *v.* to tear; to weep; to cry

la·gri·mo·so, a *adj.* tearful; watery

la·gu·na *f.* lagoon

lai·cal *adj.* laical

la·ja *adj. f.* laical

la·ja *f.* slab of stone

la·me·du·ra *f.* licking

la·men·ta·ble *adj.* lamentable

la·men·ta·ción *f.* lamentation

la·men·tar *v.* to be sorry for; to regret something

la·men·to *m.* lament

la·men·to·so, a *adj.* mournful

la·mer *v.* to lap up

la·me·ta·da *f.* lick

la·mi·do, a *adj.* polished

la·mi·na·ción *f.* lamination

la·mi·nar *v.* to laminate

lám·pa·ra *f.* lamp

lam·pa·ri·lla *f.* little or small lamp

lam·pa·rón *m.* stain

lam·pi·ño, a *adj.* hairless

la·na *f.* wool

la·na·do, a *adj.* fleecy

lan·ce *m.* argument; move; occurrence

lan·ce·ar *v.* to lance

lan·ce·ta *f.* lancet

lan·cha *f.* boat

lan·che·ro *m.* boatman

lan·chón *m.* barge

la·ne·ro, a *adj.* woolen

lan·gui·de·cer *v.* to languish

lan·gui·dez *f.* feebleness; lethargy

lán·gui·do, a *adj.* languid

lan·guor *m.* languor

la·no·li·na *f.* lanolin

la·no·so, a *adj.* woolly

lan·za *f.* spear

lan·za·da *f.* wound due to a lance

lan·za·mien·to *m.* throwing

lan·zar *v.* to hurt; to fire; to release; to vomit; to throw; to shoot

lá·pi·da *f.* tombstone

la·pi·da·rio, a *adj.* concise; lapidary

lá·piz *m.* pencil

lap·so, a *m.* interval; lapse

la·que·ar *v.* to varnish

lar·do *m.* fat; land

lar·gar *v.* to let go; to dismiss; to release; to hurt; to throw

lar·go *adj.* lengthy; long; abundant

lar·gor *m.* length

lar·gue·za *f.* length

lar·gui·ru·cho, a *adj.* lanky

la·rin·ge *f.* larynx

la·rin·gi·tis *f.* laryngitis

lar·va *f.* larva

lar·val *adj.* larval

las *pron.* them; *art.* the

la·ser *m.* laser

la·si·tud *f.* lassitude

la·so *adj.* weak; limp

lás·ti·ma *f.* compassion; shame; pity

las·ti·ma·du·ra *f.* wound

las·ti·mar *v.* to hurt; to offend; to injure

las·ti·me·ro, a *adj.* pitiful

la·ta *f.* can; tin; pest

la·te·ar *v.* to bend

la·ten·te *adj.* latent

la·te·ral *adj.* lateral

la·ti·do *m.* beating; throbbing; beat

la·tien·te *adj.* throbbing

la·ti·gue·ar *v.* to whip; to crack the whip

la·tir *v.* to throb

la·ti·tud *f.* breadth; extent; width; scope

la·ti·tu·di·nal *adj.* latitudinal

la·to, a *adj.* wide

la·tón *m.* brass

la·to·ne·ro *m.* brassworker

la·to·so, a *adj.* bothersome

la·tro·ci·nio *m.* theft

lau·da·ble *adj.* laudable

lau·de *f.* tombstone

lau·do *m.* verdict

lau·rel *m.* bay; laurel

láu·re·o *adj.* laurel

la·va *f.* lava

la·va·ble *adj.* washable

la·va·da *f.* washing

la·va·de·ro *m.* laundry

la·va·do *m.* wash

la·va·dor *m.* washer

la·van·da *f.* lavender

la·van·de·ra *f.* laundry woman

la·van·de·ro *m.* laundryman

la·va·pla·tos *m.* dishwasher

la·var *v.* to wash; to clean

la·va·ti·va *f.* enema

la·xar *v.* to slacken

la·xa·ti·vo *adj.* laxative

la·zar *v.* to rope

la·za·ri·no, a *adj.* leprous

la·zo *m.* lasso; knot; trap; snare

le *pron.* him

le·al *adj.* faithful

le·al·tad *f.* loyalty

lec·ción *f.* lesson

lec·tor, a *adj.* reading

lec·tu·ra *f.* reading

le·cha·da *f.* grout; whitewash

le·char *v.* to milk

le·che *f.* milk

le·che·rí·o, a *adj.* dairy; milky

le·cho *m.* layer; bed

le·cho·so *adj.* milky

le·chu·ga *f.* lettuce

le·er *v.* to read

le·ga·ción *f.* legation

le·ga·do *m.* legacy

le·ga·jo *m.* file

le·gal *adj.* legal

le·ga·li·dad *f.* legality

le·ga·lis·ta *f.* legalist

le·ga·li·za·ción *f.* legalization

le·ga·li·zar *v.* to legalize

le·gar *v.* to delegate; to bequeath

le·gi·ble *adj.* legible

le·gión *f.* legion

le·gis·la·ción *f.* legislation

le·gis·la·dor *m.* legislator

le·gis·la·tu·ra *f.* legislative

le·jos *adv.* far away

len·gua *f.* language

le·ón *m.* lion

le·o·na *f.* lioness

le·o·par·do *m.* leopard

les *pron.* for them; for you

le·tal *adj.* lethal

le·tra *f.* letter

le·van·tar *v.* to lift up; to erect

ley *f.* rule; law

li·be·ra·ción *f.* liberation

li·be·ral *adj.* liberal

li·ber·tad *f.* freedom

li·bre *adj.* single; open; free

li·bro *m.* book

li·gar *v.* to commit; to bind

li·mi·ta·ción *f.* limitation

li·mi·ta·do *adj.* limited

li·mi·tar *v.* to restrict; to limit

li·món *m.* lemon

lim·piar *v.* to clear; to clean

lim·pie·za *f.* neatness; cleaning

lim·pio *adj.* pure; clean

lí·nea *f.* outline; line; boundary

lis·ta *f.* list

lis·to *adj.* ready

li·tro *m.* liter

li·via·no, a *adj.* faithless; light

li·vi·dez *f.* lividness

lí·vi·do *adj.* livid

lo *def. art.* the

lo·a *f.* praise

lo·a·ble *adj.* praiseworthy

lo·ar *v.* to praise

lo·ba *f.* the female wolf
lo·bo *m.* the male wolf
ló·bre·go *adj.* somber; dark
ló·bu·lo *m.* lobe
lo·ca·ción *f.* leasing
lo·cal *adj.* local
lo·ca·li·dad *f.* locality
lo·ca·li·zar *v.* to find; to locate
lo·ción *f.* lotion
lo·co *adj.* crazy; extraordinary
lo·grar *v.* to take; to obtain
lo·ro *m.* parrot
los *pron.* them; *art.* the
lú·ci·do *adj.* shining
lu·cir *v.* to illuminate; to light
lue·go *adv.* later; then
lu·na *f.* moon
lu·nar *adj.* lunar
lus·trar *v.* to shine
luz *f.* day; light

M

ma·ca·bro *adj.* macabre
ma·ca·dam *m.* macadam
ma·ca·rrón *m.* macaroon
ma·ce·ra·ción *f.* maceration
ma·ce·rar *v.* to macerate
ma·ce·ta *f.* flowerpot or holder
ma·ci·len·to, a *adj.* lean; thin; emaciated
ma·ci·zo, a *adj.* solid
ma·cro·bió·ti·co *f.* macrobiotics
má·cu·la *f.* spot
ma·cha·ca *f.* pounder
ma·cha·ca·dor, a *adj.* pounding
ma·cha·car *v.* to beat; to pound; to bother
ma·cha·cón, a *adj.* tiresome *m., f.* pest
ma·cha·da *f.* stupidity
ma·cha·do *m.* hatchet
ma·che·te *m.* machete
ma·che·te·ar *v.* to injure or cut with a machete
ma·cho *adj.* manly; male; tough; virile
ma·chu·ca·du·ra *f.* beating; bruising
ma·chu·car *v.* to beat
ma·de·ra *f.* timber; wood;

lumber
ma·de·ra·da *f.* raft
ma·de·re·rí·a *f.* lumberyard
ma·de·re·ro, a *adj.* timber
ma·de·ro *m.* log
ma·dras·tra *f.* stepmother
ma·dre *f.* mom; mother
ma·dre·sel·va *f.* honeysuckle
ma·dri·gue·ra *f.* hole; burrow; lair
ma·dri·na *f.* bridesmaid; godmother; patroness
ma·dru·ga·dor, a *m., f.* early riser
ma·dru·gar *v.* to anticipate; to get up early
ma·du·ra·ción *f.* ripening
ma·du·ra·dor, a *adj.* ripening
ma·du·rar *v.* to mature; to ripen; to maturate
ma·du·rez *f.* maturity; ripeness
ma·es·tre *m.* master
ma·es·tro, a *adj.* expert; teacher; master
ma·gan·ce·rí·a *f.* trickery
ma·gia *f.* magic
má·gi·co, a *adj.* magic
ma·gis·tra·do *m.* magistrate
ma·gis·tral *adj.* imposing; masterful; magisterial
mag·na·te *m.* magnate
mag·ne·sia *f.* magnesia
mag·ne·sio *m.* magnesium
mag·né·ti·co, a *adj.* magnetic
mag·ne·tis·mo *m.* magnetism
mag·ne·to·fó·ni·co, a *adj.* magnetic
mag·ni·fi·ca·dor, a *adj.* magnifying
mag·ni·fi·car *v.* to exalt; to magnify; to glorify
mag·ni·fi·cen·cia *f.* magnificence
mag·ni·fi·cen·te *adj.* magnificent
mag·ní·fi·co, a *adj.* excellent; magnificent
mag·ni·tud *f.* size; importance; magnitude
mag·no·lia *f.* magnolia
ma·go, a *adj.* magic
ma·gu·llar *v.* to batter

ma·íz *m.* corn
ma·ja·de·ro, a *adj.* foolish
ma·ja·du·ra *f.* pounding
ma·jar *v.* to pound; to bother; to mash
ma·jes·tad *f.* grandeur; majesty
ma·jo, a *adj.* pretty, nice
mal *adv.* wrongly; badly
ma·la·bar *v.* to juggle
ma·la·ba·ris·ta *m.* juggler
mal·a·cos·tum·bra·do, a *adj.* ill-mannered; having poor or bad habits; spoiled
ma·lan·drín, a *adj.* evil
ma·la·ria *f.* malaria
ma·la·ven·tu·ra *f.* misfortune
ma·la·ven·tu·ran·za *f.* fortune
mal·ba·ra·tar *v.* to squander
mal·co·mer *v.* to eat badly or poorly
mal·co·mi·do *adj.* underfed
mal·con·ten·to, a *adj.* unhappy; rebellious
mal·cria·do, a *adj.* ill-bred
mal·criar *v.* to spoil
mal·dad *f.* evil
mal·de·cir *v.* to slander; to curse
mal·di·cien·te *adj.* defaming; slandering *m., f.* curser; slanderer
mal·di·ción *f.* curse
mal·di·to, a *adj.* wicked; bad
ma·le·a·bi·li·dad *f.* malleability
ma·le·a·ble *adj.* malleable
ma·le·an·te *adj.* corrupting; wicked
ma·le·ar *v.* to ruin; to corrupt; to pervert
ma·le·di·cen·cia *f.* slander
ma·le·fi·cen·cia *f.* evil
ma·le·fi·cen·te *adj.* maleficent
ma·les·tar *m.* uneasiness; malaise
ma·le·ta *f.* suitcase; baggage; luggage
ma·le·vo·len·cia *f.* malevolence
mal·for·ma·ción *f.* malformation
mal·gas·tar *v.* to waste

mal·ha·da·do, a *adj.* unfortunate
mal·he·rir *v.* to injure
mal·hu·mo·ra·do, a *adj.* bad-tempered
mal·hu·mo·rar *v.* to irritate; to bother; to annoy
ma·li·cia *f.* cunning; wickedness; slyness
ma·li·cio·so, a *adj.* malicious; cunning
ma·lig·ni·dad *f.* malignancy
ma·lig·no, a *adj.* malignant
mal·mi·ra·do, a *adj.* disfavored
ma·lo *adj.* harmful; nasty; bad
ma·lo·grar *v.* to fail; to loose; to waste
ma·lo·gro *m.* failure
mal·pa·rar *v.* to harm; to damage
mal·quis·tar *v.* to estrange
mal·quis·to, a *adj.* unpopular
mal·so·nan·te *adj.* harsh
mal·tra·ta·mien·to *m.* mistreatment
mal·tra·tar *v.* to mistreat
mal·va·do, a *adj.* wicked
mal·ver·sa·dor, a *m., f.* embezzler
mal·ver·sar *v.* to embezzle
ma·má *f.* mommy
ma·mar *v.* to nurse; to suck
ma·ma·rio, a *adj.* mammary
ma·me·lón *m.* nipple
ma·na·da *f.* herd; bunch
ma·na·de·ro, a *m., f.* spring
ma·nan·to *adj.* running
ma·nar *v.* to flow
man·car *v.* to disable
man·ci·lla *f.* blemish
man·ci·llar *v.* to blemish
man·ci·par *v.* to enslave
man·co *adj.* one-armed; disabled
man·co·mu·nar *v.* to join together; to combine
man·co·mu·ni·dad *f.* union; association
man·cha *f.* blot; stain
man·char *v.* to stain; to spot; to soil
man·da *f.* bequest
man·da·do *m.* errand; task; order

man·da·mien·to *m.* command; order

man·dar *v.* to leave; to order

man·da·ri·na *f.* mandarin orange

man·da·to *m.* trust; command; order

man·dí·bu·la *f.* mandible

man·do *m.* leadership; power

man·do·li·na *f.* mandolin

man·dria *adj.* timid; worthless; useless

man·dril *m.* mandrel

ma·ne·ar *v.* to hobble around

ma·ne·ja·ble *adj.* manageable

ma·ne·jar *v.* to handle; to manage

ma·ne·jo *m.* operation; handling; management

ma·ne·ra *f.* style; way; manner; type

man·ga *f.* strainer; hose

man·ga·ne·so *m.* manganese

man·gar *v.* to swipe; to mooch

man·gos·ta *f.* mongoose

man·gue·ar *v.* to startle

man·gue·ra *f.* garden hose

man·gui·ta *f.* cover

ma·ní *m.* peanut

ma·ní·a *f.* habit; craze

ma·ní·a·co, a *adj.* maniac

ma·ni·fes·ta·ción *f.* manifestation

ma·ni·fes·tar *v.* to reveal; to manifest

ma·ni·fies·to, a *adj.* manifest

ma·ni·lla *f.* bracelet

ma·ni·pu·la·ción *f.* manipulation

ma·ni·pu·la·dor, a *m.* manipulator

ma·ni·pu·lar *v.* to manipulate; to manage

ma·ni·quí *m.* mannequin

ma·no *f.* hand

ma·no·jo *m.* handful; bunch

ma·no·se·ar *v.* to touch

man·so, a *adj.* mild; tame

man·ta *f.* shawl; blanket

man·te·ca *f.* fat; lard

man·tel *m.* tablecloth

man·te·nen·cia *f.* support; maintenance

man·te·ner *v.* to support; to keep; to feed; to maintain

man·te·ni·mien·to *m.* support; sustenance

man·te·que·rí·a *f.* dairy

man·te·que·ro *m.* dairyman

man·te·qui·lla *f.* butter

man·to *m.* mantle; robe; cloak; cover

ma·nual *adj.* manual

ma·nu·fac·tu·rar *v.* to manufacture

ma·nu·ten·ción *f.* maintenance

man·za·na *f.* apple

man·za·nar *m.* apple orchard

man·za·no *m.* apple tree

ma·ña *f.* dexterity; skill

ma·ña·na *f.* morning

ma·ne·jar *v.* to manage

ma·ñe·ro *adj.* shrewd

ma·pa *f.* map

ma·pa·che *m.* raccoon

ma·que·ar *v.* to varnish

má·qui·na *f.* machine

ma·qui·na·ción *f.* machination

ma·qui·na·dor *m., f.* schemer

ma·qui·nar *v.* to scheme

ma·qui·nis·ta *m.* machinist

mar *m.* sea; tide

ma·ra·tón *m.* marathon

ma·ra·vi·lla *f.* marvel; astonishment; wonder

ma·ra·vi·llar *v.* to astonish; to be amazed

ma·ra·vi·llo·so, a *adj.* marvelous

mar·ca *f.* brand; mark; stamp; trademark

mar·ca·do *adj.* notable

mar·ca·dor, a *adj.* marking

mar·car *v.* to stamp; to mark; to note

mar·cial *adj.* military; martial

mar·cha *f.* march; velocity; speed; progress

mar·char *v.* to run; to walk

mar·chi·tar *v.* to weaken; to wilt; to languish

mar·chi·to, a *adj.* wilted

ma·re·ar *v.* to sail; to bother

ma·re·ja·da *f.* turbulence

ma·re·o *m.* nausea

mar·ga·ri·na *f.* margarine

mar·ga·ri·ta *f.* daisy

mar·gen *m.* fringe; margin

mar·gi·nal *adj.* marginal

mar·gi·nar *v.* to marginate

ma·ri·dar *v.* to wed

ma·ri·do *m.* spouse

ma·ri·nar *v.* to marinate

ma·ri·ne·rí·a *f.* sailoring

ma·ri·ne·ro, a *adj.* marine; seaworthy

ma·ri·no *adj.* marine

ma·ri·po·sa *f.* butterfly

ma·ri·qui·ta *f.* ladybug

ma·ris·cal *m.* marshal

ma·ris·co *m.* shellfish; seafood

ma·ri·tal *adj.* marital

ma·rí·ti·mo, a *adj.* maritime

mar·qués *m.* marquis

ma·rra·no *adj.* filthy

ma·rrar *v.* to fail; to miss something

ma·rrón *adj.* brown

ma·rru·lle·ro, a *m., f.* conniver

mar·so·pa *f.* porpoise

mar·su·pial *adj.* marsupial

mar·tes *m.* Tuesday

mar·ti·llar *v.* to hammer

mar·ti·llo *m.* hammer

már·tir *m.* martyr

mar·ti·rio *m.* martyrdom

mar·zo *m.* March

más *adv.* rather; more

ma·sa·crar *v.* to massacre

ma·sa·cre *m.* massacre

ma·sa·je *m.* massage

ma·sa·jis·ta *m.* masseur

mas·car *v.* to chew

más·ca·ra *f.* mask

mas·ca·ra·da *f.* masquerade

mas·co·ta *f.* mascot

mas·cu·li·ni·dad *f.* masculinity

mas·cu·li·no *adj.* manly; male

ma·si·vo, a *adj.* massive

mas·ti·car *v.* to masticate; to ruminate

más·til *m.* mast

mas·toi·des *adj.* mastoid

ma·ta *f.* shrub

ma·ta·dor, a *m., f.* killer

ma·ta·fue·go *m.* fire extinguisher

ma·tan·za *f.* massacre; killing; slaughtering

ma·tar *v.* to extinguish; to kill; to slaughter

ma·ta·ri·fe *m.* slaughterer

ma·ta·se·llar *v.* to cancel

ma·te·má·ti·co, a *adj.* mathematical

ma·te·ria *f.* matter

ma·te·rial *adj.* material

ma·te·ria·li·dad *f.* materiality

ma·te·ria·lis·ta *adj.* materialistic

ma·ter·nal *adj.* maternal

ma·ter·ni·dad *f.* maternity

ma·ter·no *adj.* motherly

ma·ti·nal *adj.* morning

ma·tiz *m.* tint

ma·ti·zar *v.* to tint

ma·tre·ro, a *adj.* shrewd

ma·triar·ca·do *m.* matriarchy

ma·triar·cal *adj.* matriarchal

ma·tri·ci·dio *m.* matricide

ma·trí·cu·la *f.* list

ma·tri·cu·la·ción *f.* registration

ma·tri·cu·lar *v.* to matriculate

ma·tri·mo·nial *adj.* matrimonial

ma·tri·mo·nio *m.* matrimony

ma·triz *f.* uterus

ma·tro·na *f.* matron

ma·tro·nal *adj.* matronly

má·xi·ma·men·te *adv.* chiefly

má·xi·me *adv.* principally

má·xi·mo *adj.* maximum

ma·yo *m.* May

ma·yo·ne·sa *f.* mayonnaise

ma·yor *adj.* greatest; larger; older

ma·yo·rí·a *f.* majority

ma·yo·ri·dad *f.* majority

ma·yús·cu·lo, a *adj.* important; capital

maz·mo·rra *f.* dungeon

ma·zo *m.* bunch

me *pron.* me

me·cá·ni·co, a *adj.* mechanical

me·ca·ni·zar *v.* to mechanize

me·ce·do·ra *f.* rocking chair
me·cer *v.* to sway; to rock
me·cha *f.* match; wick
me·che·ra *f.* shoplifter
me·chón *m.* tuft
me·da·lla *f.* medal
me·da·llón *m.* medallion
me·dia *f.* stocking
me·dia·dor, a *m., f.* mediator
me·dia·ne·ro, a *adj.* mediating
me·dia·no·che *f.* midnight
me·diar *v.* to intercede
me·di·ca·ción *f.* medication
me·di·car *v.* to medicate
me·di·ci·na *f.* medicine
me·di·ci·nal *adj.* medicinal
me·di·ci·nar *v.* to cure; to treat with medicine
mé·di·co, a *m., f.* doctor
me·di·da *f.* measurement
me·die·val *adj.* medieval
me·dio *adj.* middle; half
me·dio·cre *adj.* mediocre
me·dio·cri·dad *f.* mediocrity
me·dio·día *m.* noon
me·dir *v.* to weigh; to measure
me·di·ta·ción *f.* mediation
me·di·tar *v.* to meditate
me·di·ta·ti·vo, a *adj.* meditative
mé·dium *m.* medium
me·drar *v.* to thrive; to prosper
me·dro·so, a *adj.* timorous
mé·du·la *f.* medulla
me·du·sa *f.* jellyfish
me·gá·fo·no *m.* megaphone
me·ga·tón *m.* megaton
me·ji·lla *f.* cheek
me·jor *adj.* superior; better
me·jo·ra *f.* betterment
me·jo·rar *v.* to make better
me·jo·rí·a *f.* improvement
me·lan·co·lí·a *f.* melancholy
me·la·za *f.* molasses
me·lin·dre·rí·a *f.* affectation
me·lo·co·tón *m.* peach
me·lo·co·to·ne·ro *m.* peach tree
me·lo·dí·a *f.* tune
me·ló·di·co *adj.* tuneful
me·lo·dio·so, a *adj.* melodious
me·lo·dra·ma *m.* melodrama
me·lo·dra·má·ti·co, a *adj.* melodramatic
me·lón *m.* melon
me·lo·te *m.* molasses
me·llar *v.* to nick; to chip
mem·bra·na *f.* membrane
me·mo·ra·ble *adj.* memorable
me·mo·rar *v.* to recall
me·mo·ria *f.* remembrance; memory
me·mo·rial *m.* memorial
me·mo·ri·za·ción *f.* memorization
me·mo·ri·zar *v.* to memorize
men·ción *f.* mention
men·cio·nar *v.* to mention
me·ne·ar *v.* to sway
men·gua *f.* poverty
men·gua·do *adj.* decreased; timid
men·guar *v.* to wane; to diminish
me·nin·gi·tis *f.* meningitis
me·no·pau·sia *f.* menopause
me·nor *adj.* lesser; least; less; younger
me·nos *adv.* least; less
me·nos·ca·bar *v.* to impair
me·nos·ca·bo *m.* damage; diminishing
me·nos·pre·cia·ble *adj.* despicable
me·nos·pre·cio *m.* underestimation; contempt
men·sa·je *m.* message
men·sa·je·ro, a *adj.* messenger
men·sual *adj.* monthly
men·su·ra *f.* measurement
men·su·ra·ble *adj.* measurable
men·su·rar *v.* to measure
men·ta *f.* mint
men·ta·do, a *adj.* renowned
men·tal *adj.* mental
men·ta·li·dad *f.* mentality
men·tar *v.* to mention
men·te *f.* intellect; mind
men·tir *v.* to lie
men·ti·ra *f.* falsehood
men·ti·ro·so, a *adj.* lying
men·tor *m.* mentor
me·nu·do *adj.* little; insignificant
mer·ca·de·o *m.* marketing
mer·ca·do *adj.* merchant
mer·can·til *adj.* mercantile
mer·car *v.* to buy
mer·ced *f.* gift
mer·ce·na·rio, a *adj.* mercenary
mer·cu·rial *adj.* mercurial
mer·cu·rio *m.* mercury
me·re·ci·mien·to *m.* worth
me·ri·dia·no, a *adj.* meridian
me·rien·da *f.* snack
mé·ri·to *m.* value; worth
me·ri·to·rio, a *adj.* meritorious
mer·mar *v.* to diminish
me·ro, a *adj.* pure
me·ro·de·ar *v.* to plunder
mes *m.* month
me·sa *f.* table
me·són *m.* tavern
me·so·ne·ro, a *m., f.* innkeeper
me·su·ra *f.* moderation
me·su·ra·do, a *adj.* moderate
me·ta·bó·li·co, a *adj.* metabolic
me·ta·bo·lis·mo *m.* metabolism
me·tá·fo·ra *f.* metaphor
me·ta·fó·ri·co, a *adj.* metaphoric
me·tal *m.* metal
me·tá·li·co *adj.* metallic
me·ta·li·zar *v.* to metallize
me·ta·mór·fi·co, a *adj.* metamorphic
me·ta·no *m.* methane
me·te·ó·ri·co, a *adj.* meteoric
me·teo·ri·to *m.* meteorite
me·teo·ro *m.* meteor
me·teo·ro·lo·gí·a *f.* meteorology
me·teo·ro·lo·gis·ta *m., f.* meteorologist
me·ter *v.* to insert into; to cause
me·ti·cu·lo·so, a *adj.* meticulous
me·ti·lo *m.* methyl
me·tó·di·co, a *adj.* methodical
mé·to·do *m.* method
me·to·do·lo·gí·a *f.* methodology
mé·tri·co *adj.* metric
me·tro·po·li·ta·no, a *adj.* metropolitan
mez·cla·dor *adj.* blending
mez·clar *v.* to mingle; to blend
mez·quin·dad *f.* miserliness
mez·qui·no, a *adj.* petty; wretched; miserly
mez·qui·ta *f.* mosque
mí *pron.* me
mi·cro·bio *m.* microbe
mi·cro·bio·lo·gí·a *f.* microbiology
mi·cro·fil·me *m.* microfilm
mi·cró·fo·no *m.* microphone
mi·cros·có·pi·co, a *adj.* microscopic
mi·cros·co·pio *m.* microscope
mie·do *m.* dread
mie·do·so, a *adj.* cowardly
miel *f.* honey
miel·ga *f.* alfalfa
miem·bro *m.* member
mien·tras *adj.* meanwhile; *conj.* while
miér·co·les *m.* Wednesday
mies *f.* grain
mi·ga *f.* substance; scrap
mi·gra·ción *f.* migration
mi·gra·ña *f.* migraine
mil *adj.* thousand
mi·la·gro *m.* miracle
mi·la·gro·so *adj.* miraculous
mi·li·cia *f.* militia
mi·li·cia·no, a *adj.* military
mi·li·gra·mo *m.* milligram
mi·lí·me·tro *m.* millimeter
mi·li·tar *m.* soldier
mi·lla *f.* mile
mi·llón *m.* million
mi·mar *v.* to fondle; to pamper
mí·mi·co, a *adj.* mimic
mi·mo·so *adj.* spoiled
mi·na *f.* mine
mi·na·dor *adj.* mining
mi·nar *v.* to mine
mi·ne·ral *adj.* mineral
mi·ne·ra·lo·gis·ta *m., f.* mineralogist
mi·ni·fal·da *f.* miniskirt
mi·ni·mi·zar *v.* to minimize

mí·ni·mo, a *adj.* least; minimal; minute

mi·nis·te·rial *adj.* ministerial

mi·nis·te·rio *m.* ministry

mi·nis·tro *m.* minister

mi·no·rar *v.* to reduce

mi·no·rí·a *f.* minority

mi·no·ri·ta·rio *adj.* minority

mi·nu·cio·so, a *adj.* minute

mi·nús·cu·lo, a *adj.* tiny; small

mi·nu·ta *f.* record; note

mi·nu·to *m.* minute

mí·o, a *adj.* mine

mio·pí·a *f.* myopia

mi·ra *f.* sight; intention

mi·ra·do, a *adj.* regarded; cautious

mi·rar *v.* to watch; to look at; to observe

mi·ra·sol *m.* sunflower

mi·rí·a·da *f.* myriad

mir·lo *m.* blackbird

mis·ce·lá·neo, a *adj.* miscellaneous

mi·se·ra·ble *adj.* miserable; poor

mi·se·ria *f.* suffering; miserliness; misery

mi·sil *m.* missile

mi·sión *f.* mission

mi·sio·nal *adj.* missionary

mis·mo *adj.* likewise; same thing

mis·te·rio *m.* mystery

mis·te·rio·so *adj.* mysterious

mís·ti·co, a *adj.* mystic

mis·ti·fi·car *v.* to mystify

mis·tu·ra *f.* mixture

mi·tad *f.* half

mi·ti·ga·ción *f.* mitigation

mi·ti·gar *v.* to mitigate

mi·to *m.* myth

mi·tón *m.* mitten; mitt

mi·tra *f.* miter

mix·to, a *adj.* mixed

mix·tu·rar *v.* to mix up

mo·bi·lia·rio, a *adj.* movable

mo·bla·je *m.* furnishing

mo·ce·dad *f.* youth

mo·ción *f.* motion

mo·cho, a *adj.* hornless

mo·da *f.* fashion

mo·de·lo *m.* model

mo·de·ra·ción *f.* moderation

mo·de·ra·do *adj.* moderate

mo·de·rar *v.* to regulate; to restrain

mo·der·ni·za·ción *f.* modernization

mo·der·ni·zar *v.* to modernize

mo·der·no *adj.* modern

mo·des·tia *f.* modesty

mó·di·co, a *adj.* moderate

mo·di·fi·ca·ción *f.* modification

mo·di·fi·ca·dor *adj.* modifying

mo·di·fi·car *v.* to modify

mo·dis·te·rí·a *f.* shop for dresses

mo·do *m.* way

mo·do·so, a *adj.* well-mannered

mo·du·la·ción *f.* modulation

mo·du·la·dor, a *m., f.* modulator

mo·far *v.* to drench; to dip; to wet

mol·de *m.* pattern; mold

mol·de·ar *v.* to shape

mo·le·cu·lar *adj.* molecular

mo·ler *v.* to grind

mo·les·tar *v.* to annoy; to disrupt

mo·les·tia *f.* annoyance; trouble

mo·les·to *adj.* bothered; annoying

mo·men·to *m.* moment

mo·na *f.* a female monkey

mo·nas·te·rio *m.* monastery

mo·ni·tor *m.* monitor

mo·no *m.* male monkey

mo·no·gra·ma *m.* monogram

mons·truo *m.* monster

mons·truo·so *adj.* monstrous

mon·ta·ña *f.* mountain

mon·tar *v.* to mount

mo·nu·men·to *m.* monument

mo·ral *f.* morale

mo·ra·li·dad *f.* morality

mo·ra·li·zar *v.* to moralize

mo·rar *v.* to dwell; to live

mór·bi·do *adj.* morbid

mor·fi·na *f.* morphine

mo·rir *v.* to kill

mor·tal *adj.* fatal; mortal

mor·tuo·rio *m.* mortuary

mos·ca *f.* fly

mos·qui·to *m.* mosquito

mos·ta·za *f.* mustard

mos·trar *v.* to exhibit; to appear; to show

mo·tor *m.* engine

mo·ver *v.* to move

mo·vi·mien·to *m.* movement

mu·cha·cha *f.* girl

mu·cha·cho *m.* boy

mu·cho *adj.* many; a lot

muer·te *f.* death

muer·to *adj.* dead

mu·jer *f.* female; woman

múl·ti·ple *adj.* multiple

mul·ti·pli·car *v.* to multiply

mun·do *m.* world

mu·ni·ci·pal *adj.* municipal

mu·ñe·ca *f.* wrist; doll

mús·cu·lo *m.* muscle

mú·si·ca *f.* music

mu·si·cal *adj.* musical

mus·lo *m.* thigh

muy *adv.* much; greatly

N

na·bo *m.* turnip; mast

na·ca·ri·no *adj.* nacreous; pearly

na·cer *v.* to be born; to be conceived

na·ci·do, a *adj.* born

na·cien·te *adj.* recent; growing; initial; nascent

na·ci·mien·to *m.* hatching; origin; birth; spring

na·ción *f.* nation

na·cio·nal *adj.* domestic; national

na·cio·na·li·dad *f.* nationality

na·cio·na·lis·ta *m., f.* nationalist

na·cio·na·li·za·ción *f.* nationalization

na·da *pron.* no; not anything; none; nothing

na·da·dor *m., f.* swimmer

na·dar *v.* to swim

na·die *pron.* no one; nobody

nai·pe *m.* playing card

nal·ga *f.* behind; buttocks

ña·me *m.* yam

ña·pa *f.* tip; bonus

ña·que *m.* junk

na·ran·ja *f.* orange

na·ran·jal *m.* orange grove

na·ran·je·ro *adj.* orange

na·ran·jo *m.* orange tree

nar·có·ti·co, o *adj.* narcotic

nar·co·ti·zar *v.* to narcotize

na·riz *f.* nostril; nose

na·rra·ción *f.* narration; narrative

na·rra·dor, a *adj.* narrating

na·rrar *v.* to narrate

na·rra·ti·vo, a *adj.* narrative

na·ta·ción *f.* swimming

na·tal *adj.* natal

na·ta·li·dad *f.* natality

na·ti·vi·dad *f.* Christmas

na·ti·vo *adj.* native

na·to, a *adj.* born

na·tu·ra *f.* nature

na·tu·ral *adj.* native; innate; natural

na·tu·ra·le·za *f.* nature

na·tu·ra·li·dad *f.* naturalness

na·tu·ra·li·za·ción *f.* naturalization

nau·fra·gar *v.* to shipwreck

náu·sea *f.* nausea

nau·se·ar *v.* to feel nauseous

náu·ti·co, a *adj.* nautical

na·val *adj.* naval

na·ve·ga·ble *adj.* navigable

na·ve·ga·ción *f.* navigation

na·ve·gar *v.* to sail

na·vi·dad *f.* Christmas

na·ví·o *m.* vessel; boat

ne·bli·na *f.* fog

ne·bli·no·so, a *adj.* foggy

ne·bu·lo·si·dad *f.* haziness

ne·ce·dad *f.* nonsense

ne·ce·sa·rio *adj.* necessary

ne·ce·si·dad *f.* need; poverty; necessity

ne·ce·si·tar *v.* to want; to require; to need

ne·cio, a *adj.* foolish; stubborn

ne·cro·lo·gí·a *f.* necrology

nec·tar *m.* nectar

nec·ta·ri·na *f.* nectarine

ne·fri·tis *f.* nephritis

ne·ga·ble *adj.* refutable

ne·ga·ción *f.* denial; refusal; negation

ne·gar *v.* to refuse; to deny;

to forbid
ne·ga·ti·vi·dad *f.* negativity
ne·gli·gen·cia *f.* disregard; negligence
ne·go·cia·ble *adj.* negotiable
ne·go·cia·ción negotiation; transaction
ne·go·ciar *v.* to deal; to negotiate
ne·go·cio *m.* job; work; business; transaction
ne·gro, a *adj.* black
ne·gru·ra *f.* darkness
ne·gruz·co, a *adj.* dark
ne·ne, a *m., f.* neophyte
ne·ón *m.* neon
ne·o·na·to *m.* neonate
ner·vio *m.* nerve
ner·vio·si·dad *f.* nervousness
ne·to, a *adj.* simple; pure
neu·má·ti·co, a *adj.* pneumatic
neu·ro·ci·ru·gí·a *f.* neurosurgery
neu·ró·lo·go *m.* neurologist
neu·ró·ti·co, a *adj.* neurotic
neu·to·nio *m.* newton
neu·tral *adj.* neutral
neu·tra·li·dad *f.* neutrality
neu·tra·li·zar *v.* to neutralize
neu·tro, a *adj.* neutral
neu·trón *m.* neutron
ne·va·do, a *adj.* snow-covered
ne·var *v.* to snow
ne·ve·ra *f.* refrigerator
ne·xo *m.* link
ni *conj.* neither; nor
ni·co·ti·na *f.* nicotine
ni·cho *m.* vault; recess
ni·dal *m.* nest
ni·do *m.* nest; liar; den
nie·bla *f.* mist
nie·ta *f.* granddaughter
nie·to *m.* grandson
nie·ve *f.* snow
ni·hi·lis·ta *adj.* nihilistic
ni·lón *m.* nylon
nim·bo *m.* halo
ni·mio, a *adj.* insignificant
nin·fa *f.* nymph
nin·fo *m.* dandy
nin·fo·ma·ní·a *f.* nymphomania

nin·gu·no, a *adj.* no; none
ni·ñe·rí·a *f.* childish
ni·ñez *f.* infancy; childhood
ni·ño, a *m., f.* child
ní·quel *m.* nickel
ni·que·lar *v.* to nickel
ní·ti·do, a *adj.* clear
ni·tra·to *m.* nitrite
ni·tri·to *m.* nitrite
ni·tró·ge·no *m.* nitrogen
ni·tro·gli·ce·ri·na *f.* nitroglycerin
ni·vel *m.* height; standard
ni·ve·lar *v.* to make level
no *adv.* no
no·ble *adj.* honorable; noble
no·ble·za *f.* nobleness; nobility
no·ción *f.* notion
no·ci·vi·dad *f.* harmfulness
noc·tur·nal *adj.* nocturnal
noc·tur·no, a *adj.* sad; nocturnal
no·che *f.* night
nó·du·lo *m.* nodule
no·gal *m.* walnut
nó·ma·da *adj.* nomadic
nom·bra·mien·to *m.* nomination; naming
nom·brar *v.* to name; to nominate
no·men·cla·tu·ra *f.* nomenclature
nó·mi·na *f.* roll
no·mi·na·ción *f.* nomination
no·mi·nal *adj.* nominal
no·mi·nar *v.* to nominate
non *adj.* uneven
no·na·da *f.* trifle
ño·ñe·rí·a *f.* timidity
ño·ñez *f.* bashfulness
ño·ño, a *m., f. adj.* timid; bashful
no·no, a *adj.* ninth
nor·ma *f.* rule
nor·mal *adj.* normal
nor·ma·li·dad *f.* normality
nor·ma·li·za·ción *f.* normalization
nor·ma·li·zar *v.* to normalize
no·ro·es·te *m.* northwest
nor·te *m.* north
nos *pron.* us
no·ta·ble *adj.* outstanding; notable
no·tar *v.* to observe; to note

no·ti·fi·car *v.* to notify
no·ve·no *adj.* ninth
no·ven·ta *adj.* ninety
no·via *f.* girlfriend
no·vio *m.* boyfriend
nu·bo·si·dad *f.* cloudiness
nu·ca *f.* nape
nu·do *m.* knot
nues·tro *adj.* our
nue·ve *adj.* nine
nue·vo *adj.* new
nú·me·ro *m.* number
nun·ca *adv.* not ever
nu·trir *v.* to feed

O

o *conj.* or
o·a·sis *m.* oasis
ob·ce·ca·mien·to *adv.* blindly
ob·ce·car *v.* to blind
o·be·de·cer *v.* to obey
o·be·dien·cia *f.* obedience
o·be·dien·te *adj.* obedient
o·ber·tu·ra *f.* overture
o·be·si·dad *f.* obesity
ó·bi·ce *m.* obstacle
o·bis·po *m.* bishop
ob·je·ción *f.* objection
ob·je·ta·ble *adj.* objectionable
ob·je·tar *v.* to object
ob·je·ti·var *v.* to objectify
ob·je·ti·vi·dad *f.* objectivity
ob·je·to *m.* theme; object
o·bli·cuo, a *adj.* oblique
o·bli·ga·ción *f.* responsibility; obligation
o·bli·gar *v.* to force; to oblige; to favor
o·bli·ga·to·rio, a *adj.* obligatory
o·blon·go, a *adj.* oblong
o·bo·e *m.* oboe
o·bra *v.* to act; to work
o·bre·ro, a *adj.* working
obs·ce·ni·dad *f.* obscenity
obs·ce·no, a *adj.* obscene
ob·se·quio *m.* present; kindness; gift
ob·se·quio·so, a *adj.* obsequious; attentive
ob·ser·va·ción *f.* observation
ob·ser·var *v.* to watch; to

observe
ob·se·sión *f.* obsession
ob·se·sio·nan·te *adj.* obsessive
ob·se·sio·nar *v.* to obsess about something
obs·ti·na·ción *f.* obstinacy
obs·ti·na·do, a *adj.* obstinate
obs·truc·ción *f.* obstruction
obs·truir *v.* to obstruct
ob·ten·ción *f.* obtaining
ob·te·ner *v.* to get; to have; to obtain
ob·tu·so, a *adj.* obtuse
ob·viar *v.* to prevent
ob·vio, a *adj.* obvious
o·ca·sión *f.* cause; occasion; circumstance
o·ca·sio·nar *v.* to cause; to provoke; to occasion
oc·ci·den·tal *adj.* occidental
oc·ci·pi·tal *adj.* occipital
o·cé·a·no *m.* ocean
o·ce·a·no·gra·fí·a *f.* oceanography
o·ce·a·no·grá·fi·co, a *adj.* oceanographic
o·cio *m.* leisure; idleness
oc·ta·vo *adj.* eighth
oc·te·to *m.* octet
oc·to·gé·si·mo *adj.* eightieth
oc·tó·go·no, a *adj.* octagonal
oc·tu·bre *m.* October
o·cul·tar *v.* to conceal; to silence; to hide
o·cul·tis·mo *m.* occultism
o·cul·to, a *adj.* concealed; occult
o·cu·pa·ción *f.* trade; occupation; job
o·cu·pa·do *adj.* occupied
o·cu·pan·te *adj.* occupying
o·cu·par *v.* to fill; to occupy; to employ; to pay attention to something
o·cu·rren·cia *f.* occurrence
o·cu·rrir *v.* to happen; to take place
o·chen·ta *adj.* eighty
o·chen·ta·vo, a *adj.* eightieth
o·cho *adj.* eight
o·cho·cien·tos *adj.* eight hundred

o·da *f.* ode

o·da·lis·ca *f.* odalisque

o·diar *v.* to loathe

o·dio *m.* loathing

o·dio·so, a *adj.* odious

o·di·se·a *f.* odyssey

o·don·tó·lo·go, a *m., f.* odontologist

o·es·te *m.* west

o·fen·der *v.* to hurt; to offend

o·fen·sa *f.* offense

o·fen·si·vo, a *adj.* offensive

o·fen·sor *adj.* offending

o·fer·tar *v.* to tender

o·fi·cial *m.* officer

o·fi·cia·li·dad *f.* officers

o·fi·cian·te *m.* officiant

o·fi·ci·na *f.* office

o·fi·ci·nis·ta *m., f.* office clerk

o·fi·cio *m.* work; office

o·fi·cio·so *adj.* obliging; diligent

o·fre·ci·mien·to *m.* offering

o·fren·da *f.* gift

o·fren·dar *v.* to give an offering for

of·tal·mo·lo·gí·a *f.* ophthalmology

of·tal·mó·lo·go *m.* ophthalmologist

o·fus·ca·ción *f.* confusion; dazzling

o·fus·car *v.* to bewilder; to blind

o·í·do *m.* ear

o·ír *v.* to listen; to hear; to attend

o·jal *m.* buttonhole

o·je·a·da *f.* glimpse

o·je·ri·za *f.* grudge

o·jo *m.* eye

o·jo·ta *f.* sandal

o·le·a·da *f.* wave

o·le·a·je *m.* waves

o·ler *v.* to smell

ol·fa·to *m.* instinct

ol·fa·to·rio, a *adj.* olfactory

o·li·va *f.* olive

o·li·var *f.* olive grove

o·li·vo *m.* olive tree

ol·mo *m.* elm tree

o·lor *m.* smell

o·lo·ro·so, a *adj.* fragrant

ol·vi·da, ·da *adj.* forgetful; ungrateful

ol·vi·dar *v.* to omit; to forget; to leave out

ol·vi·do *m.* forgetfulness

o·lla *f.* kettle

om·bli·go *m.* navel

o·mi·sión *f.* omission

o·mi·tir *v.* to omit

óm·ni·bus *m.* omnibus

om·ni·po·ten·cia *f.* omnipotence

om·ni·po·ten·te *adj.* omnipotent

o·na·nis·mo *m.* onanism

on·ce *adj.* eleven

on·ce·no *adj.* eleventh

on·co·lon·gí·a *f.* oncology

on·dear *v.* to flutter; to ripple

on·du·la·ción *f.* undulation

on·du·lar *v.* to undulate

o·ne·ro·so, a *adj.* onerous

ó·nix *f.* onyx

o·no·ma·to·pe·ya *f.* onomatopoeia

on·za *f.* ounce

on·za·vo *adj.* eleventh

o·pa *adj.* foolish

o·pa·ci·dad *f.* opacity

o·pa·co, a *adj.* opaque

ó·pa·lo *m.* opal

op·ción *f.* option

op·cio·nal *adj.* optional

ó·pe·ra *f.* opera

o·pe·ra·ción *f.* operation

o·pe·ran·te *adj.* operating

o·pe·rar *v.* to operate

o·pe·ra·ti·vo, a *adj.* operative

o·pi·nión *f.* opinion

o·pio *m.* opium

o·po·ner *v.* to oppose

o·por·tu·na·men·te *adv.* opportunely

o·por·tu·ni·dad *f.* chance

o·por·tu·nis·ta *adj.* opportunist

o·por·tu·no, a *adj.* opportune; fitting

o·po·si·ción *f.* opposition

o·po·si·tor, a *m., f.* opponent

o·pre·sión *f.* oppression

o·pre·si·vo, a *adj.* oppressive

o·pre·so, a *adj.* oppressed

o·pri·mi·do, a *adj.* oppressed

o·pri·mir *v.* to press; to oppress

o·pro·bio *m.* disgrace

o·pro·bio·so, a *adj.* disgraceful

op·tar *v.* to select

óp·ti·co, a *adj.* optical

op·ti·mis·ta *adj.* optimistic

óp·ti·mo, a *adj.* optimal

op·tó·me·tra *m., f.* optometrist

op·to·me·trí·a *f.* optometry

o·pues·to *adj.* contrary; opposite

o·pu·len·cia *f.* opulence

o·ra *conj.* now

o·ra·ción *f.* oration; speech; sentence

o·rá·cu·lo *m.* oracle

o·ral *adj.* oral

o·ran·gu·tán *m.* orangutan

o·rar *v.* to speak; to pray

o·ra·to ·rio, a *adj.* oratorical

or·be *m.* orb

or·den *m.* order

or·de·na·ción *f.* ordination; ordering

or·de·na·da *f.* ordinate

or·de·nar *v.* to command; to put into order

or·de·ñar *v.* to milk

or·di·nal *adj.* ordinal

or·di·na·riez *f.* ordinary; uncouth; coarse

o·re·ar *v.* to ventilate

or·fa·na·to *m.* orphanage

or·fe·li·na·to *m.* orphanage

or·gá·ni·co *adj.* organic

or·ga·nis·mo *m.* organism

or·ga·nis·ta *m., f.* organist

or·ga·ni·za·dor, a *m., f.* organizer

or·ga·ni·zar *v.* to organize

ór·ga·no *m.* organ

or·gu·llo *m.* conceit

o·rien·ta·ción *f.* orientation

o·rien·tal *adj.* oriental

o·rien·tar *v.* to orient

o·ri·fi·cio *m.* opening

o·ri·gen *m.* source

o·ri·gi·nal *adj.* authentic; original; new

o·ri·gi·na·li·dad *f.* originality

o·ri·gi·nar *v.* to originate

o·ri·gi·na·ria·men·te *adv.* originally

o·ri·lla *f.* edge

o·ri·llar *v.* to edge

o·rín *m.* rust

o·ri·nal *m.* urinal

o·ri·nar *v.* to urinate

or·lar *v.* to edge

or·na·men·tal *adj.* ornamental

or·na·men·tar *v.* to ornament; to decorate

or·na·men·to *m.* ornament

or·nar *v.* to embellish

or·ni·tó·lo·go *m., f.* ornithologist

o·ro *m.* gold

or·ques·ta *f.* orchestra

or·ques·ta·ción *f.* orchestration

or·ques·tal *adj.* orchestral

or·ques·tar *v.* to orchestrate

or·quí·de·a *f.* orchid

or·ti·ga *f.* nettle

or·to·do·xo, a *adj.* orthodox

or·to·gra·fí·a *f.* orthographic

or·to·pe·dis·ta *m., f.* orthopedist

o·ru·ga *f.* caterpillar

o·ru·jo *m.* residue

os *pron.* you

o·sa·dí·a *f.* audacity

o·sa·do, a *adj.* daring

o·sa·men·ta *f.* bones

o·sar *v.* to dare

os·ci·la·ción *f.* wavering; swinging

os·ci·lar *v.* to oscillate; to swing

ós·cu·lo *m.* kiss

os·cu·re·cer *v.* to dim; to obscure; to shade

os·cu·re·ci·mien·to *m.* darkening

os·cu·ri·dad *f.* haziness; obscurity

os·cu·ro, a *adj.* unclear; dark, obscure

o·si·fi·car·se *v.* to ossify

ós·mo·sis *f.* osmosis

o·so *m.* bear

os·ten·si·ble *adj.* ostensible

os·ten·ta·ción *f.* ostentation

os·ten·tar *v.* to flaunt; to show

os·te·ó·lo·go, a *m., f.*

os·tra *f.* oyster

os·tra·cis·mo *m.* ostracism

o·te·ar *v.* to survey

o·to·ñal *adj.* autumnal

o·to·ño *m.* autumn
o·tor·gar *v.* to give; to grant
o·tro *adj.* other
o·va·ción *f.* ovation
o·va·cio·nar *v.* to give an ovation
o·val *adj.* oval
ó·va·lo *m.* oval
o·va·rio *m.* ovary
o·ve·ja *f.* the female sheep
o·ver·tu·ra *f.* overture
o·vi·llo *m.* snarl; ball
o·vi·no *m.* ovine
o·vu·la·ción *f.* ovulation
o·vu·lar *adj.* ovular
o·xi·da·ción *f.* oxidation
o·xi·dar *v.* to oxidize
ó·xi·do *m.* oxide
o·xi·ge·na·do, a *adj.* oxygenated
o·xi·ge·nar *v.* to give oxygen; to oxygenate
o·xí·ge·no *m.* oxygen
o·yen·te *adj.* listening *m., f.* listener
o·zo·no *m.* ozone

P

pa·be·llón *m.* banner; pavilion
pa·bi·lo *m.* candle wick
pá·bu·lo *m.* pabulum; support
pa·cer *v.* to graze
pa·cien·cia *f.* patience
pa·cien·te *adj.* patient
pa·ci·fi·ca·ción *f.* pacification
pa·ci·fi·ca·dor, a *m., f.* pacifier
pa·ci·fi·car *v.* to pacify
pa·cí·fi·co *adj.* pacific
pa·ci·fis·ta *adj.* pacifist
pa·cho·rra *f.* sluggishness
pa·de·cer *v.* to bear; to suffer; to endure
pa·dras·tro *m.* stepfather
pa·dre *m.* dad; father
pa·dri·llo *m.* stallion
pa·dri·no *m.* godfather
pa·ga *f.* payment
pa·ga·de·ro, a *adj.* payable
pa·ga·no, a *adj.* pagan
pa·gar *v.* to repay; to pay
pá·gi·na *f.* page

pa·gi·nar *v.* to paginate
pa·go *adj.* paid
país *m.* land
pai·sa·je *m.* landscape
pa·ja *f.* straw
pa·jar *m.* barn
pa·ja·re·ra *f.* cage for birds
pa·ja·re·rí·a *f.* bird store
pá·ja·ro *m.* bird
pa·la *f.* blade; spade; shovelful
pa·la·bra *f.* word
pa·la·bre·o *m.* chatter
pa·la·cie·go, a *adj.* magnificent
pa·la·cio *m.* palace
pa·la·da *f.* shovelful
pa·la·de·ar *v.* to relish
pa·la·dio *m.* palladium
pa·la·fre·ne·ro *m.* groom
pa·lan·ca *f.* shaft; lever
pa·lan·ga·na *f.* washbasin
pa·le·ar *v.* to shovel
pa·le·on·to·lo·gí·a *f.* paleontology
pa·le·ta *f.* trowel; palette
pa·lia·ti·vo, a *adj.* palliative
pa·li·dez *f.* pallor
pá·li·do, a *adj.* pallid
pa·li·to *m.* small stick
pa·li·za *f.* thrashing
pal·ma *f.* palm
pal·ma·do, a *adj.* palm-shaped
pal·mar *m.* palm grove
pal·me·a·do, a *adj.* palm-shaped
pal·me·ar *v.* to applaud
pal·me·ra *f.* palm tree
pal·mo *m.* palm
pal·mo·te·ar *v.* to applaud
pa·lo *m.* pole; handle
pa·lo·ma *f.* pigeon
pa·lo·mi·ta *f.* popcorn
pa·lo·te *m.* drumstick
pal·pa·ble *adj.* palpable
pal·par *v.* to feel
pal·pi·ta·ción *f.* palpitation
pal·pi·tan·te *adj.* palpitating
pal·pi·tar *v.* to palpitate; to beat
pal·ta *f.* avocado
pa·lu·dis·mo *m.* malaria
pa·lur·do, a *m., f.* boor
pam·pa *f.* pampa
pan *m.* bread
pa·na *f.* corduroy

pa·na·de·rí·a *f.* bakery
pa·na·de·ro, a *m., f.* baker
pa·nal *m.* honeycomb
pán·cre·as *m.* pancreas
pan·cre·á·ti·co, a *adj.* pancreatic
pan·cho, a *adj.* unruffled
pan·da *f.* panda
pan·de·mo·nio *m.* pandemonium
pan·de·ro *m.* tambourine
pan·di·lla *f.* gang
pan·fle·to *m.* pamphlet
pa·no·ra·ma *f.* panorama
pa·no·rá·mi·co, a *adj.* panoramic
pan·ta·lo·nes *m.* slacks; pants
pan·ta·lla *f.* movie screen; lamp shade
pan·ta·no *m.* difficulty
pan·te·ón *m.* pantheon
pan·te·ra *f.* panther
pan·to·mi·ma *f.* pantomime
pan·to·rri·lla *f.* calf
pa·ño *m.* cloth
pa·ño·le·ta *f.* scarf
pa·ño·lón *m.* shawl
pa·ñue·lo *m.* handkerchief
pa·pá *f.* potato
pa·pa·ga·yo *m.* parrot
pa·pal *adj.* papal
pa·par *v.* to gape
pa·pa·ya *f.* papaya
pa·pel *m.* paper
pa·pe·le·ro, a *adj.* paper
pa·pe·le·ta *f.* card
pa·pe·ra *f.* goiter
pa·pi·la *f.* papilla
pa·pi·ro *m.* papyrus
pa·que·te *m.* packet; pack; package
pa·que·te·rí·a *f.* elegance
pa·qui·der·mo *m.* pachyderm
par *adj.* paired; equal
pa·ra *prep.* for; to; towards
pa·rá·bo·la *f.* parable
pa·ra·bri·sas *m.* windshield
pa·ra·di·sí·a·co, a *adj.* heavenly
pa·ra·do, a *adj.* stopped; stationary; idle
pa·ra·do·ja *f.* paradox
pa·ra·dó·ji·co, a *adj.* paradoxical
pa·ra·fi·na *f.* paraffin

pa·ra·guas *m.* umbrella
pa·ra·í·so *m.* paradise
pa·ra·je *m.* area
pa·ra·le·lo *m.* parallel
pa·ra·le·lo·gra·mo *m.* parallelogram
pa·rá·li·sis *f.* paralysis
pa·ra·lí·ti·co, a *adj.* paralytic
pa·ra·li·za·ción *f.* paralyzation
pa·ra·li·zar *v.* to paralyze
pa·ra·mé·di·co, a *adj.* paramedical
pa·rá·me·tro *m.* parameter
pa·ra·no·ia *f.* paranoia
pa·ra·noi·co, a *adj.* paranoid
pa·ra·plé·ji·co, a *adj.* paraplegic
pa·rar *v.* to halt; to check; to stop
pa·ra·sí·ti·co, a *adj.* parasitic
pa·rá·si·to, a *adj.* parasitic
pa·ra·sol *m.* parasol
par·ce·la *f.* parcel
par·cial *adj.* partial
par·cia·li·dad *f.* partiality
par·do *adj.* brown
pa·re·ar *v.* to pair
pa·re·cer *m.* view; appearance
pa·re·ci·do *adj.* similar
pa·red *f.* wall
pa·re·jo, a *adj.* equal; smooth; alike
pa·ren·te·la *f.* relatives
pa·ren·tes·co *m.* kinship
pa·rén·te·sis *m.* parenthesis
pa·ri·dad *f.* parity
pa·ri·ta·rio, a *adj.* joint
par·la·men·ta·rio *adj.* parliamentary
par·la·men·to *m.* parliament
par·lar *v.* to chatter
par·lo·te·o *m.* chatter
pa·ro *m.* unemployment
pa·ro·dia *f.* parody
pa·ro·dis·ta *m., f.* parodist
pa·ro·xis·mo *m.* paroxysm
par·pa·de·ar *v.* to twinkle
pár·pa·do *m.* eyelid
par·que *m.* park
par·que·o *m.* parking
par·que·dad *f.* moderation

pa·rra *f.* grapevine
pá·rra·fo *m.* paragraph
pa·rri·ci·dio *m.* parricide
pa·rro·quial *adj.* parochial
par·si·mo·nio·so, a *adj.* parsimonious
par·te *f.* share; part
par·te·ra *f.* midwife
par·ti·ción *f.* partition
par·ti·ci·pa·ción *f.* participation
par·ti·ci·par *adj.* to inform
par·tí·ci·pe *adj.* participating
par·tí·cu·la *f.* particle
par·ti·cu·lar *adj.* particular
par·ti·cu·la·ri·dad *f.* peculiarity
par·ti·cu·lar·men·te *adv.* particularly
par·ti·dis·ta *adj.* party
par·ti·da *adj.* group; leaving; departure
par·ti·do *m.* party
par·tir *v.* to depart; to leave
par·ti·ti·vo, a *adj.* partitive
par·ti·tu·ra *f.* score
pa·sa·di·zo *m.* passage
pa·sa·do *m.* past
pa·sa·dor *adj.* passing
pa·sa·je *m.* passage
pa·sa·por·te *m.* passport
pa·sar *v.* to elapse; to occur; to happen
pa·sa·tiem·po *m.* pastime
pa·se *m.* pass
pa·se·o *m.* stroll; outing
pa·sión *f.* passion
pa·so *m.* footstep; pace
pas·ta *f.* paste
pas·tel *m.* cake
pas·teu·ri·zar *v.* to pasteurize
pas·teu·ri·za·ción *f.* pasteurization
pas·to *m.* pasture; grass
pa·ta *f.* foot; leg; paw; female duck
pa·ta·da *f.* kick
pa·ta·ta *f.* potato
pa·te·ar *v.* to kick
pa·ten·tar *v.* to register
pa·ten·te *adj.* patent; evident; obvious
pa·ter·nal *adj.* paternal
pa·ter·ni·dad *f.* paternity
pa·ti·llas *f.* sideburns

pa·tín *m.* skate
pa·ti·nar *v.* to skate
pa·tio *m.* patio
pa·to *m.* duck
pa·tó·lo·go, a *m., f.* pathologist
pa·triar·ca *m.* patriarch
pa·trio·ta *m., f.* patriot
pa·trió·ti·co, a *adj.* patriotic
pa·tro·ci·nar *v.* to patronize
pa·trón *m.* host
pa·tro·nal *adj.* management
pa·tro·na·to *m.* patronage
pa·tru·llar *v.* to patrol
pau·la·ti·no, a *adj.* gradual
pau·sa *f.* interruption
pau·ta *f.* rule
pa·va·da *f.* foolishness
pa·vi·men·ta·ción *f.* paving
pa·vi·men·to *m.* pavement
pa·vo *m.* turkey
pa·vor *m.* terror
pa·ya·so *m.* clown
paz *f.* peace
paz·gua·to, a *adj.* foolish
pe·car *v.* to sin
pe·ce·ra *f.* aquarium
pec·ti·na *f.* pectin
pec·to·ral *adj.* pectoral
pe·cu·liar *adj.* peculiar
pe·cu·lia·ri·dad *f.* peculiarity
pe·cu·lio *m.* savings
pe·cu·nia *f.* money
pe·char *v.* to pay
pe·cho *m.* breast; chest
pe·dal *m.* pedal
pe·da·le·o *m.* pedaling
pe·dan·te·rí·a *f.* pedantry
pe·da·zo *m.* bit; piece
pe·der·nal *m.* flint
pe·des·tal *m.* pedestal
pe·des·tre *adj.* pedestrian
pe·dia·trí·a *f.* pediatrics
pe·di·gre·e *m.* pedigree
pe·dir *v.* to order; to beg; to charge
pe·dre·go·so, a *adj.* rocky
pe·dris·ca *f.* hail
pe·ga·di·zo, a *adj.* catching
pe·ga·jo·so, a *adj.* catching; adhesive
pe·gar *v.* to glue; to attach; to cleave
pei·na·do *m.* hairdresser
pei·ne *m.* comb
pe·la·do, a *adj.* bare; bald

pe·la·du·ra *f.* peeling
pe·la·gra *f.* pellagra
pe·lar *v.* to peel; to cut
pe·le·a·dor *adj.* fighting
pe·lí·ca·no *m.* pelican
pe·lí·cu·la *f.* film; movie
pe·li·gro *m.* danger
pe·li·gro·so *adj.* dangerous
pe·lo *m.* fur; hair
pe·lo·ta *f.* ball
pel·tre *m.* pewter
pe·lu·ca *f.* wig
pe·lu·do, a *adj.* shaggy
pel·vis *f.* pelvis
pe·lliz·car *v.* to nibble
pe·llón *m.* sheepskin
pe·na *f.* anxiety; penalty; distress
pe·na·cho *m.* crest
pe·na·do, a *adj.* grieved
pe·na·li·zar *v.* to penalize
pe·nar *v.* to punish
pen·den·ciar *v.* to quarrel; to argue
pen·der *v.* to hover
pen·dien·te *adj.* hanging
pe·ne·tra·ble *adj.* penetrable
pe·ne·tra·ción *f.* penetration
pe·ne·tran·te *adj.* piercing; penetrating
pe·ne·trar *v.* to pierce; to penetrate
pe·ni·ci·li·na *f.* penicillin
pe·nín·su·la *f.* peninsula
pe·ni·que *m.* penny
pe·ni·ten·cia *f.* penitence
pe·ni·ten·te *adj.* penitent
pe·no·so *adj.* grievous; wearing
pen·sa·mien·to *m.* thought
pen·san·te *adj.* thinking
pen·sar *v.* to think about
pen·sa·ti·vo *adj.* thoughtful; pensive
pen·sio·nar *v.* to pension
pe·ña *f.* circle
pe·ñas·co·so, a *adj.* rocky
pe·or *adj.* worse
pe·pi·no *m.* cucumber
pép·ti·co, a *adj.* peptic
pe·que·ño *adj.* tiny; small
pe·ra *f.* pear
pe·ral *m.* pear tree
per·cep·ción *f.* perception
per·cep·ti·vo, a *adj.* perceptive

per·ci·bir *v.* to sense; to perceive
per·cu·dir *v.* to dull
per·cu·sión *f.* percussion
per·cu·tir *v.* to percuss
per·cha *f.* hanger; prop
per·der *v.* to waste; to lose
pér·di·da *f.* waste
per·di·do *adj.* missing
per·diz *f.* partridge
per·dón *m.* pardon
per·do·nar *v.* to remit; to excuse; to pardon
per·du·rar *v.* to last
pe·re·cer *v.* to perish
pe·re·gri·na·ción *f.* pilgrimage
pe·re·jil *m.* parsley
pe·ren·ne *adj.* perennial
pe·re·za *f.* laziness
pe·re·zo·so, a *adj.* lazy
per·fec·ción *f.* perfection
per·fec·cio·nar *v.* to make something perfect
per·fec·cio·nis·ta *adj.* perfectionist
per·fec·to *adj.* perfect
pér·fi·do, a *adj.* unfaithful
per·fi·lar *v.* to profile
per·fo·ra·ción *f.* perforation
per·fi·lar *v.* to profile
per·fo·ra·ción *f.* perforation
per·fo·ra·dor *adj.* perforating
per·fo·rar *v.* to perforating
per·fo·rar *v.* to perforate
per·fu·mar *v.* to perfume
per·fu·me *m.* perfume
per·fu·me·rí·a *f.* perfumery
pe·ri·car·dio *m.* pericardium
pe·ri·cia *f.* skill
pe·ri·co *m.* parakeet
pe·rí·me·tro *m.* perimeter
pe·rió·di·ca·men·te *adv.* periodically
pe·rió·di·co *m.* periodical
pe·rio·dis·mo *m.* journalism
pe·rio·dis·ta *m., f.* journalist
pe·rí·o·do *m.* period
pe·ri·qui·to *m.* parakeet
pe·ris·co·pio *m.* periscope
pe·rís·to·le *f.* peristalsis
pe·ri·to·ne·o *m.* peritoneum
per·ju·di·car *v.* to harm
per·ju·di·cial *adj.* harmful
per·ju·rio *m.* perjury

per·la *f.* pearl
per·ma·ne·cer *v.* to remain
per·ma·nen·te *adj.*
  permanent
per·mi·si·ble *adj.*
  permissible
per·mi·si·vo *adj.* permissive
per·mi·so *m.* consent
per·mi·tir *v.* to allow; to
  give; to permit
per·mu·tar *v.* to exchange
per·ni·cio·so, a *adj.*
  pernicious
per·no *m.* pin
pe·ro *conj.* but
pe·ro·né *m.* fibula
pe·ró·xi·do *m.* peroxide
per·pe·tra·ción *f.*
  perpetration
per·ple·ji·dad *f.* perplexity
per·ple·jo, a *adj.* perplexed
pe·rro *m.* dog
per·se·cu·ción *f.*
  persecution
per·se·guir *v.* to follow; to
  hound; to pursue
per·se·ve·ran·cia *f.*
  perseverance
per·se·ve·ran·te *adj.*
  persevering
per·sia·na *f.* blind
per·sig·nar *v.* to cross
per·sis·ten·cia *f.* persistence
per·sis·tir *v.* to cross
per·sis·ten·cia *f.* persistence
per·sis·tir *v.* to persist
per·so·na *f.* person
per·so·na·li·dad *f.*
  personality
per·so·na·li·zar *v.*
  to personalize
per·so·ni·fi·ca·ción *f.*
  personification
pers·pec·ti·va *f.* perspective
per·sua·dir *v.* to persuade
per·sua·sión *f.* persuasion
per·sua·si·vo, a *adj.*
  persuasive
per·te·ne·cer *v.* to belong
per·te·ne·cien·te *adj.*
  pertaining
per·ti·nen·cia *f.* relevancy;
  relevance
per·ti·nen·te *adj.* relevant
per·tre·char *v.* to equip
per·tur·ba·ción *f.*
  disturbance

per·tur·bar *v.* to upset
per·ver·si·dad *f.* perversity
per·ver·sión *f.* perversion
per·ver·ti·do, a *adj.*
  perverted
pe·sa·di·lla *f.* nightmare
pe·sa·do *adj.* dull; heavy;
  boring
pe·sar *v.* to grieve
pes·ca *f.* fishing
pes·ca·de·rí·a *f.* fish market
pes·ca·di·lla *f.* whiting
pes·ca·do *m.* fish
pes·ca·dor *m.* fisherman
pes·car *v.* to fish
pe·se·bre *f.* manger
pe·si·mis·ta *adj.* pessimistic
pe·so *m.* weight
pes·que·ro, a *adj.* fishing
pes·ta·ña *f.* eyelash
pes·ta·ñe·ar *v.* to wink
pes·ta·ñe·o *m.* winking
pes·te *f.* plague
pé·ta·lo *m.* petal
pe·ti·ción *f.* petition
pé·tre·o, a *adj.* rocky
pe·tri·fi·car *v.* to petrify
pe·tró·le·o *m.* petroleum
pe·tu·lan·cia *f.* arrogance
pe·tu·lan·te *adj.* arrogant
pe·tu·nia *f.* petunia
pez *m.* fish
pia·nis·ta *m., f.* pianist
pia·no *m.* piano
piar *v.* to chirp
pi·can·te *adj.* spicy
pi·car *v.* to sting; to chip; to
  bite
pi·ca·res·co, a *adj.*
  mischievous
pí·ca·ro, a *adj.* wicked; sly
pi·ca·zón *f.* itching
pi·co *m.* spout; beak
pi·cor *m.* itching
pi·co·te·ar *v.* to pick; to peck
pic·tó·ri·co, a *adj.* pictorial
pie *m.* foot
pie·dra *f.* stone
piel *f.* fur; skin
pie·za *f.* piece
pi·fiar *v.* to miscue
pig·men·tar *v.* to pigment
pig·me·o *adj.* pygmy
pi·ja·ma *m.* pajamas
pi·lar *m.* pillar
pi·le·ta *f.* sink
pi·lo·tar *v.* to pilot

pi·lo·to *m.* pilot
pi·llar *v.* to plunder
pi·llue·lo, a *adj.* mischievous
pi·men·tón *m.* paprika
pi·mien·ta *f.* pepper
pim·pan·te *adj.* spruce;
  graceful
pi·ná·cu·lo *m.* pinnacle
pi·nar *m.* pine grove
pin·cel *m.* brush
pin·cha·du·ra *f.* puncture
pin·char *v.* to puncture
pin·gui·no *m.* penguin
pi·no *m.* pine
pin·tar *v.* to paint
pin·to, a *adj.* speckled
pin·tor, a *m., f.* painter
pin·to·res·co, a *adj.*
  picturesque
pin·tu·ra *f.* painting
pi·ña *f.* pine cone
pio·jo *m.* louse
pio·la *f.* cord
pi·pa *f.* barrel
pi·pe·ta *f.* pipette
pi·que·ta *f.* pick
pi·que·te *m.* picket
pi·ra·mi·dal *adj.* pyramidal
pi·rá·mi·de *f.* pyramid
pi·ra·ta *m.* pirate
pi·ri·ta *f.* pyrites
pi·rue·ta *f.* pirouette
pi·sa·da *f.* footprint
pi·sar *v.* to walk upon
pis·ci·na *f.* swimming pool
pi·so *m.* story; flat
pi·són *m.* tamper
pi·so·te·ar *v.* to trample
pis·ta *f.* runway; trial
pis·ta·cho *m.* pistachio
pis·to·la *f.* pistol
pis·tón *m.* piston
pi·ti·do *m.* whistle
pi·ti·llo *m.* cigarette
pi·to *m.* whistle
pi·tón *m.* python
pi·to·ni·sa *f.* fortune-teller
pi·tui·ta·rio, a *adj.* pituitary
pi·vo·te *m.* pivot
pla·ca *f.* plaque
pla·ce·bo *m.* placebo
pla·cen·te·ro, a *adj.*
  pleasant; agreeable
pla·cer *m.* gratification;
  pleasure
plá·ci·do *adj.* placid
pla·gar *v.* to plague

plan *m.* scheme; plan
plan·cha *f.* sheet
plan·cha·do, a *adj.* ironing
plan·char *v.* to iron
pla·ne·ar *v.* to plan
pla·ne·ta *f.* planet
pla·ne·ta·rio, a *adj.*
  planetary
pla·ni·cie *f.* plain
pla·ni·fi·ca·ción *f.* planning
pla·ni·fi·car *v.* to plan
pla·no *adj.* plane
plan·ear *v.* to start; to
  expound; to plan
pla·ña·do *m.* lament
plan·tar *v.* to plant
plas·ma *f.* plasma
plas·mar *v.* to mold
plás·ti·co, a *adj.* plastic
plas·ti·fi·car *v.* to shellac
pla·ta *f.* silver
pla·ta·for·ma *f.* platform
plá·ta·no *m.* banana
pla·te·ar *v.* to silver-plate
pla·te·ro *m.* silversmith
pla·ti·car *v.* to talk
pla·ti·no *m.* platinum
pla·to *m.* dish; plate
pla·tó·ni·co, a *adj.* platonic
plau·si·ble *adj.* plausible
pla·ya *f.* beach
ple·ga·ble *adj.* collapsible
ple·ga·do *m.* folding
ple·gar *v.* to fold; to bend; to
  pleat
pleu·re·sí·a *f.* pleurisy
pli·sa·do *m.* pleat
plo·me·ro *m.* plumber
plo·mo, a *adj.* lead
plu·ma *f.* pen; feather
plu·ral *adj.* plural
plu·ra·li·dad *f.* plurality
plu·ra·li·zar *v.* to pluralize
plu·to·nio *m.* plutonium
po·bla·ción *f.* population;
  town
po·bla·do *m.* village
po·blar *v.* to populate
po·bre *adj.* poor
po·bre·za *f.* poverty
po·ción *f.* potion
po·co *adv.* little
po·dar *v.* to prune
po·der *v.* to be able; can
po·de·rí·o *m.* power
po·dia·tra *m.* podiatrist
poe·ma *m.* poem

po•e•sí•a *f.* poetry
po•e•ta *m.* poet
poé•ti•co *adj.* poetical
po•e•ti•sa *f.* poetess
pó•ker *m.* poker
po•lar *m.* polar
po•la•ri•za•ción *f.* polarization
po•la•ri•zar *v.* to polarize
po•len *m.* pollen
po•li•cí•a *f.* constable; police
po•li•cial *adj.* police
po•li•fo•ní•a *f.* polyphony
po•lí•go•no *m.* polygon
po•li•lla *f.* moth
po•li•ni•za•ción *f.* pollination
po•li•no•mio *m.* polynomial
pó•li•po *m* polyp
po•lí•ti•ca *f.* policy
po•lí•ti•co *adj.* political
po•li•ti•zar *v.* to politicize
po•lo *m.* pole
pol•trón, a *adj.* lazy
po•lu•ción *f.* pollution
pol•vo *m.* powder
po•llo *m.* chicken
po•ma•da *f.* pomade
pom•pa *f.* pomp
pom•po•si•dad *f.* pomposity
pom•po•so, a *adj.* pompous
pon•che *m.* punch
pon•cho *m.* poncho
pon•de•ra•ble *adj.* ponderable
pon•de•rar *v.* to consider
po•ner *v.* to place; to don
pon•ti•fi•car *v.* to pontificate
pon•zo•ño•so, a *adj.* poisonous
po•pu•la•cho *m.* masses
po•pu•lar *adj.* popular
po•pu•la•ri•dad *f.* popularity
po•pu•la•ri•zar *v.* to popularize
po•pu•rrí *m.* potpourri
po•quer *m.* poker
por *prep.* from; via; for
por•cen•ta•je *m.* percentage
por•cen•tual *adj.* percentage
por•ción *f.* part; portion
por•che *m.* porch
por•fia•do, a *adj.* stubborn
po•ro•si•dad *f.* porosity
po•ro•so, a *adj.* porous
por•que *conj.* because
por•qué *m.* why

por•tal *m.* porch
por•tá•til *adj.* portable
por•ten•to•so, a *adj.* marvelous
por•ve•nir *m.* future
po•sar *v.* to rest; to lodge
pos•da•ta *f.* postscripts
po•se•er *v.* to have
po•se•í•do, a *adj.* possessed
po•se•si•vo, a *adj.* possessive
po•se•so, a *adj.* possessed
pos•fe•cha *f.* postdate
po•si•bi•li•tar *v.* to make something possible
po•si•ble *adj.* possible
po•si•ción *f.* place; status
pos•po•ner *v.* to postpone
pos•ta *f.* slice
pos•tal *adj.* postal
pos•te *m.* post
pos•te•ga•ción *f.* postponement
pos•te•gar *v.* to postpone
pos•te•rior *adj.* posterior
pos•te•rio•ri•dad *f.* posteriority
pos•ti•zo, a *adj.* artificial
post•o•pe•ra•to•rio, a *adj.* postoperative
pos•tor *m.* bidder
pos•trar *v.* to debilitate; to humiliate
pos•tre *m.* dessert
pos•tre•ro, a *adj.* final
pos•tu•ra *f.* posture
po•ta•ble *adj.* potable
po•ta•sio *m.* potassium
po•te *m.* pot
po•ten•cia *f.* potency
po•ten•cial *adj.* potential
po•ten•ta•do *m.* potentate
po•ten•te *adj.* potent; powerful
po•tre•ar *v.* to frolic
po•tre•ro *m.* pasture
po•tri•llo *m.* colt
po•tro *m.* colt
prác•ti•ca *f.* custom; practice
prac•ti•car *v.* to practice
prác•ti•co *adj.* practical
pra•de•ra *f.* meadow
pre•ám•bu•lo *m.* preamble
pre•ca•rio, a *adj.* precarious
pre•cau•ción *f.* precaution
pre•ca•vi•do, a *adj.* cautious
pre•ce•den•te *adj.* preceding

pre•ce•der *v.* to forgo
pre•cep•to *m.* precept
pre•cep•tor, a *m., f.* tutor
pre•cin•ta•do, a *adj.* sealed
pre•cin•tar *v.* to stamp
pre•cio *m.* fare; cost; price
pre•cio•si•dad *f.* beauty
pre•cio•so *adj.* precious
pre•ci•pi•ta•ción *f.* precipitation
pre•ci•pi•tar *v.* to hasten
pre•ci•sa•men•te *adj.* precisely
pre•ci•sar *v.* to set; to explain
pre•ci•sión *f.* precision
pre•co•ci•dad *f.* precocity
pre•cog•ni•ción *f.* precognition
pre•con•ce•bir *v.* to preconceive
pre•co•ni•zar *v.* to recommend something
pre•coz *adj.* precocious
pre•de•ce•sor, a *m., f.* predecessor
pre•de•cir *v.* to foretell
pre•des•ti•na•ción *f.* predestination
pre•de•ter•mi•nar *v.* to predetermine
pré•di•ca *f.* sermon
pre•di•ca•do *m.* predicate
pre•di•car *v.* to preach
pre•dic•ción *f.* prediction
pre•di•lec•to, a *adj.* favorite
pre•dio *m.* property
pre•dis•po•ner *v.* to predispose
pre•dis•po•si•ción *f.* predisposition
pre•do•mi•nan•te *adj.* predominant
pre•do•mi•nar *v.* to prevail
pre•do•mi•nio *m.* predominate
pre•fa•bri•ca•do, a *adj.* prefabricated
pre•fa•bri•car *v.* to prefabricate
pre•fa•cio *m.* preface
pre•fec•tu•ra *f.* prefecture
pre•fe•ren•te *adj.* preferable
pre•fe•ren•te•men•te *adv.* preferably
pre•fe•ri•do *adj.* preferred
pre•fe•rir *v.* to prefer

pre•go•nar *v.* to divulge; to proclaim
pre•gun•ta *f.* question
pre•gun•tar *v.* to ask; to question
pre•his•to•ria *f.* prehistory
pre•his•tó•ri•co, a *adj.* pre historic
pre•juz•gar *v.* to prejudge
pre•lu•dio *m.* prelude
pre•ma•tu•ro, a *adj.* premature
pre•me•di•ta•ción *f.* premeditation
pre•me•di•ta•da•men•te *adv.* deliberately
pre•me•di•tar *v.* to premeditate
pre•miar *v.* to reward
pre•mio *m.* prize
pre•mi•sa *f.* premise
pre•mo•ni•ción *f.* premonition
pre•mu•ra *f.* urgency
pre•na•tal *adj.* prenatal
pren•da *f.* token; guaranty
pren•der *v.* to catch
pren•sa *f.* press
pren•sar *v.* to press
pre•nup•cial *adj.* prenuptial
pre•ñez *f.* pregnancy
pre•o•cu•pa•ción *f.* concern
pre•o•cu•par *v.* to mind; to occupy
pre•pa•rar *v.* to ready; to fix
pre•pon•de•ran•te *adj.* preponderant
pre•po•si•ción *f.* preposition
pre•po•ten•cia *f.* power; dominance
pre•po•ten•te *adj.* powerful; dominant
pre•pu•cio *m.* prepuce
pre•sa *f.* victim; capture
pres•cin•den•cia *f.* omission
pres•cin•di•ble *adj.* nonessential
pres•cin•dir *v.* to ignore
pres•cri•bir *v.* to prescribe
pre•sen•cia *f.* presence
pre•sen•ciar *v.* to witness
pre•sen•ta•ción *f.* presentation
pre•sen•tar *v.* to introduce; to feature
pre•sen•te *adj.* current
pre•ser•va•ción *f.* preserve

pre·ser·va·ti·vo, a *adj.*
preservative
pre·si·den·cia *f.* presidency
pre·si·den·cial *adj.*
presidential
pre·si·den·ta *f.* president
pre·si·den·te *m.* president
pre·si·dia·rio *m.* convict
pre·si·dio *m.* prison
pre·si·dir *v.* to preside
pre·sión *f.* pressure
pres·ta·ción *f.* services
pres·ta·dor, a *adj.* lending
pres·ta·men·te *adj.* quickly
prés·ta·mo *m.* loan
pres·tar *v.* to loan
pres·te·za *f.* promptness
pres·ti·gio *m.* prestige
pres·ti·gio·so, a *adj.*
prestigious
pres·to, a *adj.* prompt
pre·su·mi·ble *adj.*
presumable
pre·su·mir *v.* to presume
pre·sun·ción *f.* presumption
pre·sun·tuo·so, a *adj.*
presumptuous
pre·su·po·ner *v.*
to presuppose
pre·su·po·si·ción *f.*
presupposition
pre·su·pues·ta·rio, a *adj.*
budgetary
pre·su·ri·zar *v.* to pressurize
pre·ten·cio·so, a *adj.*
pretentious
pre·ten·der *v.* to attempt; to
pretend
pre·ten·dien·te *adj.*
pretending to
pre·ten·sión *f.* desire
pre·ten·sio·so, a *adj.*
pretentious
pre·va·le·cer *v.* to prevail
pre·ven·ción *f.* prevention
pre·ve·nir *v.* to prepare; to
prevent
pre·ven·ti·vo, a *adj.*
preventive
prez *m.* glory
pri·ma, o *f., m.* cousin
pri·ma·rio, a *adj.* primary
pri·ma·te *m* . primate
pri·ma·ve·ra *f.* spring
pri·mo *adj.* prime; first
pri·mi·ti·vo *adj.* primitive
pri·mo·ro·so *adj.* delicate;

exquisite
prin·ce·sa *f.* princess
prin·ci·pa·do *m.* principality
prin·ci·pal *adj.* leading;
master; principal
prin·ci·pal·men·te *adv.*
principally
prín·ci·pe *m.* prince
prin·ci·pes·co, a *adj.*
princely
prin·ci·piar *v.* to begin
prin·ci·pio *m.* beginning
prin·go·so, a *adj.* greasy
prio·ri·dad *f.* priority
pri·sa *f.* haste
pri·sión *f.* prison
pri·sio·ne·ro, a *m., f.*
prisoner
pris·ma *m.* prism
prís·ti·no, a *adj.* pristine
pri·va·do *adj.* private
pri·va·ti·zar *v.* to privatize
pri·vi·le·gio *m.* privilege
pro·ba·bi·li·dad *f.*
probability
pro·ba·ble *adj.* probable
pro·bar *v.* to prove; to try
pro·bi·dad *f.* probity
pro·ble·ma *m.* problem
pro·ble·má·ti·co, a *adj.*
problematic
pro·bo, a *adj.* upright
pro·ce·di·mien·to *m.*
procedure
pro·ce·sar *v.* to prosecute
pro·ce·sión *m.* action
pro·cla·ma·ción *f.*
proclamation
pro·cla·mar *v.* to announce;
to proclaim
pro·cre·a·ción *f.* procreation
pro·cre·ar *v.* to produce; to
procreate
pro·di·gar *v.* to waste
pró·di·go *adj.* lavish;
spendthrift
pro·di·gio·so, a *adj.*
marvelous
pro·duc·ción *f.* turnout;
production
pro·du·cir *v.* to yield; to
produce
pro·duc·ti·vi·dad *f.*
productivity
pro·duc·ti·vo, a *adj.*
productive
pro·duc·to, a *m.* product

pro·fa·nar *v.* to disgrace
pro·fe·sar *v.* to teach; to
practice
pro·fe·sión *f.* vocation; job;
profession
pro·fe·sio·nal *adj.*
professional
pro·fe·sor, a *m., f.*
professor; teacher
pro·fi·la·xis *f.* prophylaxis
pro·fun·di·dad *f.* profundity
pro·fun·do, a *adj.* profound;
deep
pro·fu·sión *f.* profusion
pro·fu·so, a *adj.* profuse
pro·gra·ma *m.* program
pro·gra·ma·ción *f.*
programming
pro·gra·mar *v.* to program
pro·gre·sar *v.* to progress
pro·gre·sión *f.* progress
pro·gre·sis·ta *adj.*
progressive
pro·gre·so *m.* progress
pro·hi·bi·ción *f.* prohibition
pro·hi·bi·do, a *adj.*
forbidden
pro·hi·bir *v.* to prohibit
something
pro·hi·bi·ti·vo, a *adj.*
prohibitive
pro·li·fe·ra·ción *f.*
proliferation
pro·li·fe·rar *v.* to proliferate
pro·lí·fi·co, a *adj.* prolific
pró·lo·go *m.* prologue
pro·lon·ga·do, a *adj.*
prolonged
pro·lon·gar *v.* to lengthen
pro·me·dio *m.* average
pro·me·sa *f.* vow; promise
pro·me·te·dor, a *adj.*
promising
pro·me·ter *v.* to promise
pro·mi·nen·te *adj.*
prominent
pro·mi·so·rio, a *adj.*
promising
pro·mo·ción *f.* promotion
pro·mo·cio·nar *v.*
to promote
pro·mo·ve·dor, a *adj.*
promoting
pro·mo·ver *v.* to promote
pro·no, ·na *adj.* prone
pro·no·mi·nal *adj.*
pronominal

pro·nos·ti·car *v.* to predict
pron·ti·tud *f.* promptness
pron·to *adj.* prompt
pro·nun·cia·ción *f.*
pronunciation
pro·nun·ciar *v.*
to pronounce
pro·pa·ga·ción *f.*
propagation
pro·pa·lar *v.* to divulge
pro·pen·so, a *adj.* prone
pro·pie·dad *f.* estate
pro·pi·na *f.* gratuity
pro·pio *adj.* proper
pro·po·ne·dor, a *adj.*
proposing
pro·po·ner *v.* to intend
pro·por·ción *f.* proportion
pro·por·cio·nal *adj.*
proportional
pro·po·si·ción *f.* motion;
proposition
pro·pó·si·to *m.* purpose;
intention
pro·pues·ta *f.* proposal
pro·pug·nar *v.* to push
pro·pul·sión *f.* propulsion
pro·rra·te·ar *v.* to extend
pro·sa *f.* prose
pro·sai·co, a *adj.* prosaic
pros·cri·bir *v.* to proscribe
pros·crip·ción *f.*
proscription
pros·pec·to *m.* prospectus
pros·pe·rar *v.* to thrive; to
prosper
pros·pe·ri·dad *f.* prosperity
prós·pe·ro, a *adj.*
prosperous
prós·ta·ta *f.* prostate
pros·ti·tu·ción *f.*
prostitution
pro·tec·ción *f.* protection
pro·tec·tor, a *adj.*
supporting; protective
pro·te·ger *v.* to defend; to
protect
pro·te·í·na *f.* protein
pro·tes·ta *f.* protest
pro·tes·tar *v.* to protest
pro·tes·to *m.* protest
pro·tón *m.* proton
pro·to·ti·po *m.* prototype
pro·ve·cho *m.* profit; benefit
pro·ve·cho·so *adj.*
profitable
pro·veer *v.* to cater; to fill; to

provide
pro·vi·den·cial *adj.* providential
pro·vi·sión *f.* provision
pro·vo·ca·ción *f.* provocation
pro·vo·car *v.* to antagonize
próx·i·mo *adj.* near
pru·den·cia *f.* prudence
psi·co·lo·gí·a *f.* psychology
pu·bli·ca·ción *f.* publication
pu·bli·car *v.* to publish
pú·bli·co *m.* public
pue·blo *m.* nation; town
puer·ta *f.* entrance
pues *conj.* then; for
pul·gar *m.* thumb
pu·lir *v.* to shine; to polish
pul·món *m.* lung
pun·ta *m.* dot; point
pu·ro *adj.* pure
púr·pu·ra *f.* purple

Q

quan·tum *m.* quantum
que *pron.* that; whom
qué *adj.* what; which
que·bra·da *f.* gap; ravine
que·bra·di·zo, a *adj.* fragile
que·bra·do *adj.* rough; broken; bankrupt
que·bra·du·ra *f.* rupture; fracture; crack
que·bra·jar *v.* to crack
que·bran·ta·dor, a *adj.* crushing; breaking
que·bran·to *m.* sorrow; loss
que·brar *v.* to break
que·da·men·te *adv.* calmly
que·dar *v.* to stay; to be; to remain
que·jar·se *v.* to complain; to whine
que·ji·do *m.* groan
que·jo·so *adj.* complaining
que·ma *f.* burning
que·ma·de·ro *m.* incinerator
que·ma·do, a *adj.* burnt; burned out
que·ma·zón *f.* burning
que·re·lla *f.* lament; quarrel
que·re·llan·te *adj.* complaining
que·rer *v.* to desire; to want;

to love
que·ri·do, a *adj.* beloved
que·so *m.* cheese
quie·bra *f.* crack
quien *pron.* who
quie·to, a *adj.* quiet
quí·mi·ca *f.* chemistry
quí·mi·co *adj.* chemical
quin·ce *adj.* fifteen
quin·to *adj.* fifth
qui·tar *v.* to remove; to take away

R

rá·ba·no *m.* radish
ra·bí *m.* rabbi
ra·bia *f.* rabies
ra·biar *v.* to have rabies; to rage
ra·bi·no *m.* rabbi
ra·bio·so *adj.* furious
ra·bo *m.* stern; tail
ra·cial *adj.* racial
ra·ci·mo *m.* bunch; cluster
ra·ción *f.* allowance; ration
ra·cio·nal *adj.* rational
ra·cio·na·li·dad *f.* rationality
ra·cio·na·lis·mo *m.* rationalism
ra·cio·na·lis·ta *adj.* rationalist
ra·cio·na·li·zar *v.* to rationalize about
ra·cio·nar *v.* to ration
ra·cha *f.* gust
ra·da *f.* bay
ra·dar *m.* radar
ra·dia·ción *f.* radiation
ra·diac·ti·vi·dad *f.* radioactivity
ra·diac·ti·vo, a *adj.* radioactive
ra·dia·dor *m.* radiator
ra·dial *adj.* radial
ra·dian·te *adj.* radiant
ra·diar *v.* to radiate
ra·di·cal *adj.* radical
ra·dio *m.* radio; radius
ra·dio·di·fun·dir *v.* to broadcast
ra·dio·gra·fí·a *f.* radiography; x-ray
ra·dio·gra·ma *f.* radiogram
ra·dio·lo·gí·a *f.* radiology
ra·dió·lo·go, ·ga *m., f.*

radiologist
ra·dios·co·pia *f.* radioscopy
ra·er *v.* to scrape
ra·í·do, a *adj.* worn
ra·ja *f.* split; crack
ra·ja·du·ra *f.* crack
ra·jar *v.* to sliver; to crack
ra·lo, a *adj.* thin
ra·llar *v.* to grate
ra·ma *f.* branch
ra·ma·da *f.* grove
ra·mal *m.* flight; strand
ram·bla *f.* boulevard
ra·mi·fi·ca·ción *f.* ramification
ra·mi·fi·car·se *v.* to branch
ra·mi·lle·te *m.* cluster
ra·mo *m.* bouquet
ra·mo·ne·ar *v.* to graze
ram·pa *f.* ramp
ra·na *f.* frog
ran·ci·dez *f.* rancidity
ra·par *v.* to crop; to shave
rá·pi·da·men·te *adv.* rapidly
rá·pí·do *adj.* fast; express; rapid
rap·so·dia *f.* rhapsody
rap·to *m.* rapture
ra·que·ta *f.* racket
ra·qui·tis·mo *m.* rickets
ra·ra·men·te *adv.* rarely
ra·re·za *f.* rarity
ra·ro *adj.* rare; bizarre; odd
ra·sar *v.* to brush
ras·ca·cie·los *m.* skyscraper
ras·ca·du·ra *f.* scratch
ras·car *v.* to scrape
ras·ca·zón *f.* itch
ras·ga·du·ra *f.* tear
ras·gar *v.* to tear
ras·gu·ñar *v.* to scratch
ras·gu·ño *m.* scratch
ra·so, a *adj.* level; flat
ras·pa·dor *m.* scraper
ras·pa·du·ra *f.* rasping
ras·pan·te *adj.* abrasive
ras·par *v.* to erase; to scrape
ras·tra *f.* trail
ras·tre·ar *v.* to trail
ras·tri·llo *m.* rake
ra·su·ra *f.* shaving
ra·su·rar *v.* to shave
ra·ta *f.* rat
ra·te·ro, a *m., f.* thief
ra·ti·fi·ca·to·rio, a *adj.* ratifying

ra·to *m.* while
ra·tón *m.* mouse
ra·ya *f.* stripe; line
ra·yar *v.* to rule; to streak
ra·yo *m.* beam; ray
ra·yón *m.* rayon
ra·za *f.* race
ra·zón *f.* cause
ra·zo·na·ble *adj.* rational; reasonable
ra·zo·na·do, a *adj.* reasoned
ra·zo·nar *v.* to reason
re·ac·ción *f.* reaction
re·ac·cio·nar *v.* to react
re·ac·ti·va·ción *f.* reactivation
re·ac·ti·var *v.* to reactivate
re·a·dap·ta·ción *f.* readaptation
re·a·dap·tar *v.* to readapt
re·a·fir·mar *v.* to reaffirm
re·a·jus·tar *v.* to readjust
real *adj.* true; real; royal
re·a·le·za *f.* royalty
rea·li·dad *f.* reality
rea·lis·ta *adj.* realistic
re·a·li·za·dor, a *adj.* fulfilling
rea·li·zar *v.* to accomplish; to realize
re·al·zar *v.* to enhance
re·a·ni·mar *v.* to reanimate
re·a·nu·da·ción *f.* resumption
re·a·nu·dar *v.* to resume
re·a·pa·re·cer *v.* to reappear
rea·ta *f.* rope
re·a·vi·var *v.* to revive
re·ba·ja *f.* reduction
re·ba·jar *v.* to reduce
re·ba·na·da *f.* slice
re·ba·nar *v.* to slice
re·ba·ño *m.* flock
re·be·lar·se *v.* to rebel; to revolt
re·bel·de *adj.* rebel
re·be·lión *f.* revolt
re·bor·de *m.* border
re·bo·tar *v.* to bounce
re·buz·no *m.* braying
re·ca·bar *v.* to request
re·ca·do *m.* message
re·ca·er *v.* to relapse
re·cal·car *v.* to squeeze
re·ca·len·ta·mien·to *m.* reheating
re·ca·len·tar *v.* to reheat

re·ca·pa·ci·tar v. to reconsider

re·ca·pi·tu·la·ción m. recapitulation

re·ca·pi·tu·lar v. to recapitulate

re·car·gar v. to overload; to reload

re·cau·dar v. to collect

re·cau·do m. collection

re·ce·lar v. to suspect

re·ce·lo m. jealousy; mistrust; suspicion

re·ce·lo·so, a adj. suspicious

re·cep·ción f. reception

re·cep·cio·nis·ta m., f. receptionist

re·cep·ti·vo adj. receptive

re·ce·tar v. to prescribe

re·ci·bi·dor, a adj. receiving

re·ci·bi·mien·to m. reception

re·ci·bir v. to accept; to receive

re·ci·bo m. receipt

re·ci·clar v. to recycle

re·cien·te adj. recent

re·cien·te·men·te adv. recently

re·cio, a adj. severe; strong

re·ci·pro·car v. to reciprocate

re·ci·pro·ci·dad f. reciprocity

re·ci·ta·ción f. complaint

re·cla·ma·dor adj. claiming

re·cla·mar v. to reclaim

re·cli·nar v. to rest on

re·cluir v. to imprison

re·clu·sión f. imprisonment

re·clu·so m. recluse

re·clu·ta f. recruitment

re·clu·ta·mien·to m. recruitment

re·clu·tar v. to recruit

re·co·brar v. to regain; to recover

re·co·bro m. recovery

re·co·do m. bend

re·co·ge·dor, a adj. collecting

re·co·ger v. to collect; to gather; to shorten

re·co·gi·mien·to m. retirement

re·co·lec·ción f. collection

re·co·lec·tar v. to gather

re·co·men·da·ble adj. advisable

re·co·men·da·ción f. recommendation

re·co·men·dar v. to recommend

re·com·pen·sa f. reward

re·com·pen·sar v. to compensate

re·con·ci·lia·ble adj. reconcilable

re·con·ci·lia·ción f. reconciliation

re·con·ci·liar v. to reconcile

re·con·for·tar v. to comfort

re·co·no·ci·do, a adj. gratitude; recognition

re·con·quis·tar v. to recover

re·con·si·de·rar v. to reconsider

re·cons·truc·ción f. reconstruction

re·cons·ti·tuir v. to reconstruct

re·con·tar v. to recount

re·co·pi·la·ción f. compilation

re·co·pi·la·dor m. compiler

re·co·pi·lar v. to compile

re·cor·da·ción f. memory

re·cor·dar v. to remember

re·co·rrer v. to travel

re·cor·tar v. to reduce

re·cre·a·ción f. recreation

re·cre·ar v. to re-create

re·crea·ti·vo adj. recreational

re·creo m. recreation

re·cri·mi·na·ción f. recrimination

re·cru·de·ci·mien·to m. worsening

rec·tal adj. rectal

rec·ta·men·te adv. justly

rec·tan·gu·lar adj. rectangle

rec·tán·gu·lo adj. rectangular

rec·ti·fi·ca·ción f. rectification

rec·ti·fi·car v. to rectify

rec·ti·tud f. honesty

rec·to adj. right; upright

re·cu·brir v. to cover

re·cuen·to m. recount

re·cuer·do m. memory; remembrance

re·cu·la·da f. backing up

re·cu·pe·ra·ble adj. recoverable

re·cu·pe·ra·ción f. recovery

re·cu·pe·rar v. to recover

re·cu·rren·te adj. recurrent

re·cu·rrir v. to return

re·cur·so m. remedy; resource

re·cu·sa·ción f. rejection

re·cu·sar v. to refuse

re·cha·za·mien·to m. rejection

re·cha·zar v. to reject; rebuff

re·cha·zo m. rejection

re·chi·fla f. hissing

re·chi·flar v. to hiss

re·dac·ción f. writing

re·dac·tar v. to edit

re·da·da f. roundup

re·de·ci·lla f. mesh

re·den·ción f. redemption

re·dil m. fold

re·di·mir v. to redeem

ré·di·to m. rent

re·di·tuar v. to yield

re·do·blar v. to fold

re·don·dez f. roundness

re·don·do, a adj. round

re·duc·ción f. reduction

re·du·ci·do adj. reduced

re·du·cir v. to shorten; to reduce

re·duc·tor, a adj. reducing

re·dun·dan·cia f. redundancy

re·dun·dan·te adj. redundant

re·dun·dar v. to overflow

re·e·le·gir v. to re-elect

re·em·bol·sa·ble adj. reimbursable

re·em·bol·so m. reimbursement

re·em·pla·zar v. to replace

re·em·pla·zo m. substitution

re·en·car·na·ción f. reincarnation

re·es·truc·tu·ra·ción restructuring

re·es·truc·tu·rar v. to restructure

re·fec·to·rio m. refectory

re·fe·ren·cia f. reference

re·fe·ren·te adj. referring

re·fe·rir v. to refer; to tell

re·fi·na·do, a adj. refined

re·fi·na·mien·to m. refinement

re·fi·nar v. to refine

re·fi·ne·rí·a f. refinery

re·fle·jar v. to speculate; to reflect

re·fle·xión f. reflection

re·fle·xi·vo, a adj. reflective

re·for·ma f. reform

re·for·ma·ción f. reformation

re·for·ma·to·rio, a adj. reformatory

re·for·mis·ta adj. reformist

re·for·za·do, a adj. reinforced

re·for·zar v. to reinforce

re·frac·ción f. refraction

re·frac·tar v. to refract

re·fre·nar v. to restrain

re·fres·can·te adj. refreshing

re·fres·car v. to refresh

re·fres·co m. refreshment

re·fri·ge·ra·ción f. refrigeration

re·fri·ge·ra·dor m. refrigerator

re·fri·ge·rar v. to refrigerate

re·fri·to, a adj. refried

re·fuer·zo m. reinforcement

re·fu·gia·do, a adj. refugee

re·fu·gio m. shelter; refuge

re·ful·gen·te adj. refulgent

re·fun·fu·ñar v. to grumble

re·fun·fu·ño m. grumble

re·fu·ta·ción f. rebuttal

re·fu·tar v. to rebut

re·ga·la·do, a adj. easy; dainty

re·ga·lar v. to give away

re·ga·liz m. licorice

re·ga·lo m. present

re·ga·ñar v. to argue

re·gar v. to bathe; to water

re·ga·zo m. lap

re·ge·ne·ra·ción f. regeneration

re·ge·ne·ra·dor, a m., f. regenerator

re·ge·ne·rar v. to regenerate

re·gen·tar v. to direct

ré·gi·men m. regimen

re·gi·men·tar v. to regiment

re·gio, a adj. regal

re·gión f. area; region

re·gio·nal adj. regional

re·gio·na·lis·mo *m.* regionalism

re·gir *v.* to govern

re·gis·tra·dor, a *m., f.* register; *adj.* registering

re·gis·trar *v.* to record; to register

re·gla *f.* rule

re·gla·men·ta·ción *f.* regulation

re·gla·men·tar *v.* to regulate

re·glar *v.* to regulate

re·go·ci·jo *m.* joy

re·go·de·o *m.* pleasure

re·gre·sar *v.* to return

re·gre·sión *f.* regression

re·gre·si·vo *adj.* regressive

re·gre·so *m.* return

re·gue·ro *m.* trail; stream

re·gu·la·ción *f.* regulation

re·gu·la·dor *m.* regulator

re·gu·lar *adj.* regular

re·gu·la·ri·zar *v.* to regularize

re·gu·lar·men·te *adv.* regularly

re·gur·gi·ta·ción *f.* regurgitation

re·gur·gi·tar *v.* to regurgitate

re·ha·bi·li·ta·ción *f.* rehabilitation

re·ha·bi·li·tar *v.* to rehabilitate

re·ha·cer *v.* to remake

re·ho·gar *v.* to brown

re·huir *v.* to avoid

re·hu·sar *v.* to refuse

re·im·pri·mir *v.* to reprint

rei·na *f.* queen

rei·na·do *m.* reign

rei·nan·te *adj.* ruling

rei·nar *v.* to reign

re·in·ci·den·te *adj.* relapsing

re·in·ci·dir *v.* to relapse

re·in·cor·po·ra·ción *f.* reincorporation

re·in·gre·sar *v.* to re-enter

rei·no *m.* kingdom

re·ins·ta·la·ción *f.* reinstallation

re·ins·ta·lar *v.* to reinstall

re·in·te·gra·ción *f.* reintegration

re·in·te·grar *v.* to reintegrate

re·in·te·gro *m.* reintegration

re·ír(se) *v.* to laugh

rei·te·ra·ción *f.* reiteration

rei·te·rar *v.* to reiterate

rei·te·ra·ti·vo, a *adj.* reiterative

rei·vin·di·car *v.* to recover

re·jun·tar *v.* to gather

re·ju·ve·ne·cer *v.* to rejuvenate

re·la·ción *f.* account; relation

re·la·cio·na·do, a *adj.* related

re·la·ja·ción *f.* relaxation

re·la·ja·do, a *adj.* relaxed

re·la·jar *v.* to relax

re·la·mer *v.* to lick

re·lám·pa·go *m.* lightning

re·lám·pa·gue·o *m.* lightning

re·lap·so, ·sa *adj.* relapsed

re·la·tar *v.* to narrate

re·la·ti·vi·dad *f.* relativity

re·la·ti·vo, a *adj.* relative

re·la·to *m.* story; narration

re·le·gar *v.* to relegate

re·le·var *v.* to relieve; to praise

re·li·ca·rio *m.* reliquary

re·lie·ve *m.* relief

re·li·gión *f.* religion

re·li·gio·si·dad *f.* religiosity

re·li·gio·so *adj.* religious

re·loj *m.* watch; clock

re·lo·je·rí·a *f.* clockmaking

re·lo·je·ro, a *m., f.* watchmaker

re·lu·cir *v.* to shine

re·lum·bran·te *adj.* dazzling

re·lum·brar *v.* to dazzle

re·lle·nar *v.* to refill

re·ma·llar *v.* to mend

re·mar *v.* to row

re·ma·tar *v.* to use up

re·ma·te *m.* conclusion

re·me·dar *v.* to mimic

re·me·dia·ble *adj.* remediable

re·me·diar *v.* to cure; to remedy

re·mem·bran·za *f.* remembrance

re·me·mo·ra·ción *f.* remembrance

re·me·mo·rar *v.* to remember something

re·men·dar *v.* to mend; to repair

re·men·dón, a *m., f.* cobbler; mender

re·mi·sión *f.* remission

re·mi·so, a *adj.* remiss

re·mi·ten·te *adj.* remitting

re·mi·tir *v.* to forgive; to remit; to diminish

re·mo·la·cha *f.* beet

re·mol·car *v.* to tow

re·mo·lo·ne·ar *v.* to loaf

re·mol·que *m.* tow truck

re·mon·tar *v.* to remount; to surmount

re·mor·di·mien·to *m.* remorse

re·mo·to *adj.* faraway

re·mo·ver *v.* to remove; to move; to dismiss

re·mo·zar *v.* to rejuvenate

re·mu·ne·ra·ción *f.* remuneration

re·mu·ne·ra·ti·vo, a *adj.* remunerative

re·na·ci·mien·to *m.* revival

re·nal *adj.* renal

ren·ci·lla *f.* quarrel

ren·cor *m.* spite; bitterness; rancor

ren·co·ro·so *adj.* bitter; resentful

ren·di·do *adj.* submissiveness; yield

ren·dir *v.* to yield; to surrender; to defeat

ren·gue·ar *v.* to limp

re·no *m.* reindeer

re·nom·bra·do, a *adj.* renowned

re·nom·bre *m.* renown

re·no·va·ción *f.* renovation

re·no·va·do *adj.* renewed

re·no·var *v.* to renovate; to reform

ren·ta *f.* interest; rent; income

ren·ta·ble *adj.* profitable

ren·tar *v.* to rent

re·nuen·cia *f.* reluctance

re·nuen·te *adj.* reluctant

re·nun·cia *f.* renunciation

re·nun·cia·ción *f.* renunciation

re·nun·ciar *v.* to reject; to surrender; to waive; to renounce

re·ñi·dor, a *adj.* quarrelsome

re·ñir *v.* to fight; to quarrel with another

re·or·ga·ni·za·ción *f.* reorganization

re·or·ga·ni·zar *v.* to reorganize

re·pa·ra·ción *f.* repair

re·pa·ra·dor, a *m., f.* repairer

re·pa·rar *v.* to mend; to repair

re·pa·ro *m.* protection; objection

re·par·ti·ción *f.* sharing

re·par·ti·dor, a *m., f.* distributor

re·par·tir *v.* to share; to divide

re·par·to *m.* delivery

re·pa·sar *v.* to review; to revise

re·pa·so *m.* review

re·pa·tria·ción *f.* repatriation

re·pa·triar *v.* to repatriate

re·pe·len·te *adj.* repellent

re·pe·ler *v.* to repel

re·pen·te *m.* start

re·pen·ti·no, a *adj.* repercussion

re·per·cu·sión *f.* repercussion

re·per·cu·tir *v.* to reverberate

re·per·cu·to·rio *m.* repertoire

re·pe·ti·ción *f.* repetition

re·pe·tir *v.* to repeat

re·pe·ti·ti·vo, a *adj.* repetitive

re·pi·que·te·ar *v.* to beat; to ring

re·pi·sa *f.* shelf

re·plan·tar *v.* to replant

re·plan·te·ar *v.* to restate

re·ple·to, a *adj.* full

ré·pli·ca *f.* answer

re·pli·car *v.* to reply; to respond

re·po·bla·ción *f.* repopulation

re·po·blar *v.* to repopulate

re·po·llo *m.* cabbage

re·po·ner *v.* to replace; to revive

re·por·te·ro, a *adj.* reporting

re·po·sa·do *adj.* quiet
re·po·sar *v.* to lie
re·po·si·ción *f.* reposition
re·po·so *m.* repose
re·pren·der *v.* to reprimand
re·pren·sión *f.* reprimand
re·pre·sa·lia *f.* reprisal
re·pre·sen·tan·te *adj.* representing
re·pre·sen·tar *v.* to represent; to appear to be
re·pre·sen·ta·ti·vo, a *adj.* representative
re·pre·sión *f.* repression
re·pre·si·vo, a *adj.* repressive
re·pri·men·da *f.* reprimand
re·pri·mir *v.* to repress
re·pro·char *v.* to reproach
re·pro·che *m.* rebuke; reproach
re·pro·duc·ción *f.* reproduction
re·pro·du·cir *v.* to reproduce
rep·tar *v.* to crawl
rep·til *v.* reptile
re·pú·bli·ca *f.* republic
re·pu·bli·ca·no, a *adj.* republican
re·pu·dia·ción *f.* repudiation
re·pu·diar *v.* to repudiate
re·pug·nan·te *adj.* repugnant
re·pul·gar *v.* to hem
re·pul·sar *v.* to reject
re·pul·sión *f.* repulsion
re·pul·si·vo, a *adj.* repulsive
re·pun·tar *v.* to turn
re·pun·te *adj.* turning
re·que·brar *v.* to break something again
re·que·ri·mien·to *m.* requirement
re·que·rir *v.* to want; to require
ré·quiem *m.* requiem
re·qui·sar *v.* to requisition
re·qui·si·ción *f.* requisition
re·qui·si·to *m.* requirement
re·sa·la·do, a *adj.* charming
re·sar·cir *v.* to indemnify
res·ba·lar *v.* to glide
res·ca·tar *v.* to rescue; to recover
res·ca·te *m.* rescue
res·cin·dir *v.* to rescind
res·ci·sión *f.* rescission

re·sen·ti·do, a *adj.* resentful
re·sen·ti·mien·to *m.* resentment
re·sen·tir·se *v.* to feel hurt
re·se·ña *f.* account; inspection
re·se·ñar *v.* to review; to inspect
re·ser·va *f.* reserve
re·ser·va·ción *f.* reservation
re·ser·va·do, a *adj.* reserved; confidential
re·ser·var *v.* to reserve
res·fria·do *m.* cold
res·friar *v.* to cool
res·guar·do *m.* guard; protection
re·si·den·cia *f.* residence
re·si·den·cial *adj.* residential
re·si·den·te *m., f.* resident
re·si·dir *v.* to live; to reside
re·si·duo *m.* residue
re·sig·na·ción *f.* resignation
re·sis·ten·cia *f.* endurance; resistance
re·sis·ten·te *adj.* resolute
re·sol·ver *v.* to settle; to solve; to resolve
re·so·nan·cia *f.* resonance
re·so·nan·te *adj.* resounding
re·so·nar *v.* to resound
re·so·pli·do *m.* puffing
res·pal·dar *v.* to back something or someone
res·pal·do *m.* back
res·pec·ti·vo *adj.* respective
res·pec·to *m.* respect
res·pe·ta·ble *adj.* respectable
res·pe·tar *v.* to respect
res·pe·to *m.* respect
res·pe·tuo·so, a *adj.* respectful
res·pi·ra·ción *f.* respiration
res·pi·ra·dor *m.* respirator
res·pi·rar *v.* to breath
res·pi·ro *m.* respite
res·plan·dor *m.* glow; brightness
res·pon·der *v.* to reply; to respond
res·pon·sa·ble *adj.* responsible
res·pues·ta *f.* answer; response
res·que·brar *v.* to crack

res·que·mor *m.* remorse
res·ta·ble·cer *v.* to reestablish
res·ta·ble·ci·mien·to *m.* reestablishment
res·ta·llar *v.* to crack
res·tau·ran·te *m.* restaurant
res·tau·rar *v.* to restore
res·ti·tu·ción *f.* restitution
res·to *m.* remainder
res·tric·ción *f.* restriction
res·tric·ti·vo, a *adj.* restrictive
res·trin·gir *v.* to restrict
re·su·ci·tar *v.* to resuscitate
re·sul·ta *f.* result
re·sul·ta·do *m.* issue; result
re·sul·tar *v.* to result
re·su·mir *v.* to summarize
re·sur·gir *v.* to reappear
re·su·rrec·ción *f.* resurrection
re·tar·dar *v.* to delay
re·ten·ción *f.* retention
re·te·ner *v.* to keep; to retain
re·ti·na *f.* retina
re·ti·ni·tis *f.* retinitis
re·ti·ra·da *f.* retreat
re·ti·ra·do, a *adj.* retired
re·ti·rar *v.* to retire; to withdraw; to retract
re·ti·ro *m.* retreat; withdrawal
re·to *m.* challenge
re·to·ñar *v.* to sprout
re·tor·cer *v.* to twist
re·tor·ci·do, a *adj.* twisted
re·tor·ci·mien·to *m.* twisting
re·tó·ri·co, a *adj.* rhetorical
re·tor·nar *v.* to return
re·to·zar *v.* to frolic
re·to·zo *m.* frolic
re·to·zón, a *adj.* frolicsome
re·trac·ción *f.* retraction
re·trac·tar *v.* to recant; to retract
re·trác·til *adj.* retractable
re·tra·er *v.* to dissuade
re·tra·í·do, a *adj.* withdrawn
re·trai·mien·to *m.* seclusion
re·trans·mi·tir *v.* to retransmit
re·tra·sar *v.* to delay
re·tra·to *m.* portrait
re·tre·ta *f.* retreat

re·tri·bu·ción *f.* retribution
re·tri·bu·ir *v.* to reward
re·tro·ac·ti·vo, a *adj.* retroactive
re·tró·gra·do, a *adj.* retrograde
re·tros·pec·ción *f.* retrospection
re·tum·bar *v.* to resound
reu·má·ti·co *adj.* rheumatic
reu·ma·tis·mo *m.* rheumatism
reu·nión *f.* meeting; reunion
reu·nir *v.* to gather; to mass; to meet
re·va·li·da·ción *f.* revalidation
re·va·li·dar *v.* to revalidate
re·va·lo·ri·zar *v.* to revalue
re·van·cha *f.* revenge
re·ve·la·ción *f.* revelation
re·ve·la·dor, a *adj.* revealing
re·ve·lar *v.* to betray; to reveal
re·ven·der *v.* to resell
re·ven·tar *v.* to blow; to burst
re·ven·tón *m.* burst
re·ver *v.* to review
re·ver·be·rar *v.* to reverberate
re·ve·ren·cia *f.* reverence
re·ve·ren·ciar *v.* to revere
re·ve·ren·do, a *adj.* reverend
re·ve·ren·te *adj.* respectful
re·ver·so *m.* reverse
re·ver·tir *v.* to revert
re·ves·tir *v.* to cover
re·vi·sar *v.* to review
re·vi·sión *f.* revision
re·vi·si·ta *f.* revision
re·vi·sor, a *m., f.* inspector
re·vis·ta *f.* magazine
re·vis·te·ro, a *m., f.* reviewer
re·vi·ta·li·zar *v.* to revitalize
re·vi·vi·fi·car *v.* to revive
re·vi·vir *v.* to revive
re·vo·ca·ción *f.* revocation
re·vo·car *v.* to repeal; to revoke
re·vol·cón *m.* fall
re·vo·lo·te·ar *v.* to flutter
re·vo·lu·ción *f.* revolution
re·vo·lu·cio·nar *v.* to revolutionize

re·vo·lu·cio·na·rio *adj.* revolutionary

re·vol·ver *v.* to revolve; to mix; to shake

re·vól·ver *m.* revolver; gun; pistol

re·vo·que *m.* plaster

re·vue·lo *m.* commotion

rey *m.* king

re·zar *v.* to pray; to say something

re·zon·gar *v.* to grumble

ri·be·ra *f.* shore

ri·be·te·a·do *adj.* trimmed

ri·be·te·ar *v.* to hem

ri·ca·men·te *adv.* richly

ri·co *adj.* wealthy; rich

ri·dí·cu·la·men·te *adv.* ridiculously

ri·di·cu·li·zar *v.* to ridicule

ri·dí·cu·lo *adj.* ridiculous

riel *m.* rail

rien·da *f.* rein

ries·go *m.* danger; risk

ri·fa *f.* raffle

ri·far *v.* to raffle off

ri·fle *m.* rifle

rí·gi·do *adj.* stiff; rigid

ri·gor *m.* rigor

ri·gu·ro·so *adj.* severe; rigorous

ri·ma *f.* rhyme

ri·mar *v.* to rhyme

rim·bom·ban·te *adj.* echoing

rin·cón *m.* corner

ri·no·ce·ron·te *m.* rhinoceros

ri·ña *f.* quarrel

ri·ñón *m.* kidney

río *m.* river

ri·que·za *f.* riches

ri·sa *f.* laughter

ri·si·ble *adj.* laughable

ris·tra *f.* string

ri·sue·ño, a *adj.* smiling

rít·mi·co *adj.* rhythmical

ri·to *m.* ceremony

ri·tual *m.* ritual

ri·val *m.* rival

ri·va·li·dad *f.* rivalry

ri·va·li·zar *v.* to rival

ri·zar *v.* to curl up

ro·bar *v.* to steal

ro·ble *m.* oak

ro·bo *m.* robbery

ro·bus·te·cer *v.* to make strong; to strengthen

ro·bus·to *adj.* hardy; strong

ro·ciar *v.* to sprinkle

ro·cín *m.* donkey

ro·cí·o *m.* sprinkle

ro·dar *v.* to tumble; to roll

ro·de·ar *v.* to circle; to ring

ro·de·o *m.* to go around

ro·de·te *m.* bun

ro·di·lla *f.* knee

ro·e·dor, a *adj.* gnawing

ro·er *v.* to gnaw

ro·gar *v.* to request; to pray

ro·jo *adj.* red

ro·llo *m.* roll

ro·ma·no, a *adj.* Roman

ro·mán·ti·co *adj.* romantic

rom·bo *m.* rhombus

ro·me·ro *m.* rosemary

rom·per *v.* to smash; to break

ron *m.* rum

ron·car *v.* to snore

ron·co, a *adj.* hoarse

ron·que·dad *f.* hoarseness

ro·ño·so, a *adj.* filthy

ro·pa *f.* clothing

ro·pe·ro *m.* closet

ro·sa *f.* rose

ro·sa·do, a *adj.* pink

ro·sal *m.* rosebush

ro·sa·le·da *f.* rose garden

ros·bif *m.* roast beef

ros·ca *f.* coil; ring

ros·tro *m.* face

ro·ta·ción *f.* rotation

ro·ta·to·rio, a *adj.* rotating

ro·ton·da *f.* rotunda

ro·tor *m.* rotor

ro·tu·la·do *m.* label

ro·tu·lar *v.* to label

ro·tu·la·dor, a *adj.* labeling

ro·za·mien·to *m.* rubbing

ro·zar *v.* to scrape; to skim

ru·bé·o·la *f.* rubella

ru·bí *m.* ruby

ru·bi·cun·do, a *adj.* ruddy

ru·bio *adj.* blonde

ru·bor *m.* blush

ru·bo·ri·zar·se *v.* to blush

ru·da *f.* rue

ru·de·za *f.* rudeness

ru·di·men·tal *adj.* rudimentary

ru·di·men·ta·rio, a *adj.* rudimentary

ru·di·men·to *m.* rudiment

ru·do, a *adj.* rude

rue·da *f.* wheel

rue·do *m.* hem; edge

rue·go *m.* request

ru·gi·do *m.* roar

ru·gien·te *adj.* roaring

ru·go·so, a *adj.* winkled

rui·do *m.* sound; rattle; noise

rui·do·so, a *adj.* noisy

ruin *adj.* poor; despicable

rui·na *f.* ruin

rui·nar *v.* to ruin

rum·bo *m.* direction

ru·mor *m.* rumor

rup·tu·ra *f.* rupture

ru·ral *adj.* rural

ru·ti·lar *v.* to shine

ru·ti·na *f.* route

S

sá·ba·do *m.* Saturday

sá·ba·na *f.* sheet for a bed

sa·ber *v.* to inform; to know

sa·bi·do, a *adj.* known

sa·bi·du·rí·a *f.* knowledge

sa·bio, a *adj.* learned

sa·ble *m.* saber

sa·bor *m.* flavor; taste

sa·bo·re·ar *v.* to taste

sa·bo·ta·je *m.* sabotage

sa·bo·te·a·dor, a *adj.* sabotaging

sa·bo·te·ar *v.* to sabotage

sa·bro·so *adj.* delightful

sa·ca·cor·chos *m.* corkscrew

sa·ca·pun·tas *m.* pencil sharpener

sa·car *v.* to pull out; to get out

sa·ca·ri·na *f.* saccharin

sa·cer·do·cio *m.* priesthood

sa·cer·do·te *m.* priest

sa·cer·do·ti·sa *f.* priestess

sa·co *m.* bag

sa·cra·men·to *m.* sacrament

sa·cri·fi·car *v.* to sacrifice

sa·cri·fi·cio *m.* sacrifice

sa·cri·le·gio *m.* sacrilege

sa·cro *adj.* sacred

sa·cu·di·da *f.* tremor; shake

sa·cu·dir *v.* to beat; to tug

sá·di·co, a *adj.* sadistic

sa·ga *f.* saga

sa·ga·ci·dad *f.* sagacity

sa·gaz *adj.* sagacious

sa·gra·do, a *adj.* sacred

sal *f.* salt

sa·la *f.* living room of a house

sa·la·do, a *adj.* salted; salty

sa·la·man·dra *f.* salamander

sa·laz *f.* salacious

sal·chi·chón *m.* sausage

sal·dar *v.* to pay off something

sal·do *m.* payment

sa·le·ro *m.* saltshaker

sa·li·da *f.* exit; solution

sa·lien·te *adj.* salient; projecting

sa·li·no, a *adj.* saline

sa·lir *v.* to get out; to leave

sa·li·va *f.* saliva

sa·li·val *adj.* salivary

sa·li·var *v.* to salivate

sal·mo *m.* psalm

sal·món *m.* salmon

sa·lo·bre *adj.* briny

sal·pi·car *v.* to splash

sal·pi·men·tar *v.* to season

sal·sa *f.* sauce

sal·ta·dor *m.* jumper

sal·ta·mon·tes *m.* grasshopper

sal·tar *v.* to jump; to leap; to bounce

sal·te·ar *v.* to skip

sal·to *m.* jump

sa·lu·bre *adj.* healthful

sa·lud *f.* health

sa·lu·da·ble *adj.* healthy

sa·lu·dar *v.* to salute

sa·lu·ta·ción *f.* greeting

sal·va·ción *f.* salvation

sal·va·guar·dar *v.* to safeguard

sal·va·guar·dia *f.* safeguard

sal·va·ja·da *f.* savagery

sal·va·je *adj.* untamed; wild; uncivilized

sal·var *v.* to avoid; to save; to cover

sal·via *f.* sage

sal·vo *adj.* safe

sa·na·men·te *adv.* sincerely

sa·nar *v.* to heal

san·ción *f.* sanction

san·cio·nar *v.* to sanction

san·da·lia *f.* sandal

sán·da·lo *m.* sandalwood

san·dez *f.* nonsense

san·dí·a *f.* watermelon

sa·ne·a·mien·to *m.* sanitation

sa·ne·ar *v.* to right

san·grar *v.* to bleed

san·gre *f.* blood

san·grí·a *f.* sangria

san·grien·to *adj.* bloody

san·gui·jue·la *f.* leech

san·gui·na·rio, a *adj.* cruel

sa·ni·dad *f.* healthiness

sa·ni·ta·rio, a *adj.* sanitary

sa·no *adj.* unharmed; wholesome

san·ti·dad *f.* sanctify

san·ti·fi·car *v.* to sanctify

san·to *adj.* blessed

san·tua·rio *m.* sanctuary

sa·pien·cia *f.* wisdom

sa·pien·te *adj.* wise

sa·po *m.* toad

sa·que·ar *v.* to plunder

sa·que·o *m.* plundering

sa·ram·pión *m.* measles

sar·cas·mo *m.* sarcasm

sar·cás·ti·co *adj.* sarcastic

sar·di·na *f.* sardine

sar·dó·ni·co, a *adj.* sardonic

sar·gen·to *m.* sergeant

sar·no·so, a *adj.* scabby

sa·rro *m.* crust

sar·ta *f.* string

sa·sa·frás *m.* sassafras

sa·té·li·te *m.* satellite

sa·tén *m.* satin

sa·ti·na·do, a *adj.* satiny

sá·ti·ra *f.* satire

sa·tí·ri·co, a *adj.* satirical

sa·ti·ri·zar *v.* to satirize

sá·ti·ro *m.* satyr

sa·tis·fac·ción *f.* satisfaction

sa·tis·fa·cer *v.* to satisfy

sa·tis·fac·to·rio, a *adj.* satisfactory

sa·tu·ra·ción *f.* saturation

sa·tu·ra·do, a *adj.* saturated

sa·tu·rar *v.* to saturate

sa·xo·fón *m.* saxophone

sa·yo *m.* tunic

sa·zón *f.* season

sa·zo·na·do *adj.* flavorful

sa·zo·nar *v.* to season

se *pron.* herself; oneself; yourself; himself

se·bá·ce·o, a *adj.* sebaceous

se·bo *m.* fat

se·bo·rre·a *f.* seborrhea

se·ca·do *m.* drying

se·ca·do·ra *f.* clothes dryer

se·can·te *adj.* drying

se·car *v.* to dry

sec·ción *f.* section

sec·cio·nar *v.* to section

se·ce·sión *f.* secession

se·ce·sio·nis·ta *adj.* secessionist

se·co *adj.* dried

se·cre·sión *f.* secretion

se·cre·ta·men·te *adv.* secretly

se·cre·ta·ria *f.* secretary

se·cre·te·ar *v.* to whisper

se·cre·te·o *m.* whispering

se·cre·to *m.* secret

sec·ta·rio, a *adj.* sectarian

sec·tor *m.* sector

sec·to·rial *adj.* sectorial

se·cue·la *f.* consequence

se·cuen·cia *f.* sequence

se·cues·trar *v.* to kidnap

se·cues·tro *m.* kidnapping

se·cu·lar *adj.* secular

se·cu·la·ri·zar *v.* to secularize

se·cun·dar *v.* to second

se·cun·da·rio, a *adj.* secondary

sed *f.* thirst

se·da *f.* silk

se·dan·te *n.* sedative

se·dar *v.* to soothe

se·dar *v.* to sedate

se·da·ti·vo *adj.* sedative

se·den·ta·rio, a *adj.* sedentary

se·di·ción *f.* sedition

se·dien·to, a *adj.* thirsty

se·di·men·to *m.* sediment

se·do·so *adj.* silky

se·duc·ción *f.* seduction

se·du·cir *v.* to seduce

se·duc·ti·vo, a *adj.* seductive

se·ga·dor, a *adj.* seductive

se·gar *v.* to mow; to harvest

se·glar *adj.* secular

seg·men·ta·ción *f.* segmentation

seg·men·to *m.* segment

se·gre·ga·ción *f.* segregation

se·gre·ga·cio·nis·ta *adj.* segregationist

se·gre·gar *v.* to segregate

se·gui·da·men·te *adv.* continuously

se·gui·do *adj.* consecutive

se·gui·dor, a *m., f.* follower

se·guir *v.* to chase; to follow; to watch

se·gún *prep.* according to

se·gun·do *adj.* second

se·gur *m.* sickle

se·gu·ra·men·te *adv.* probably

se·gu·ri·dad *f.* safety

se·gu·ro *adj.* sure; certain

seis *adj.* six

seis·cien·tos, as *adj.* six hundred

se·lec·ción *f.* selection

se·lec·cio·nar *v.* to select

se·lec·ti·vo, a *adj.* selective

se·lec·to, a *adj.* select

sel·va *f.* forest; jungle

se·llar *v.* to stamp

se·llo *m.* stamp

se·ma·na *f.* week

se·ma·nal *adj.* weekly

se·ma·nal·men·te *adv.* weekly

se·ma·na·rio, a *adj.* weekly

se·mán·ti·co, a *adj.* semantic

sem·bra·dor, a *adj.* sowing

sem·brar *v.* to sow

se·me·jan·te *adj.* similar

se·me·jan·za *f.* similarity

se·men·tar *v.* to seed

se·mes·tral *adj.* semiannual

se·mes·tre *m.* semester

se·mi·au·to·má·ti·co, a *adj.* semiautomatic

se·mi·cír·cu·lo *m.* semicircle

se·mi·fi·na·lis·ta *adj.* semifinalist

se·mi·lla *f.* seed

se·mi·lle·ro *m.* nursery for plants

se·mi·nal *adj.* seminal

se·mi·na·rio *m.* seminary

se·mi·na·ris·ta *m.* seminarian

sé·mo·la *f.* semolina

sem·pi·ter·no, a *adj.* everlasting

se·na·do *m.* senate

se·na·dor *m.* senator

sen·ci·lla·men·te *adv.* simply

sen·ci·llez *f.* simplicity

sen·ci·llo, a *adj.* simple; easy

sen·da *f.* path; trail

se·nil *adj.* senile

se·no *m.* cavity; hollow

sen·sa·ción *f.* sensation

sen·sa·cio·nal *adj.* sensational

sen·sa·to *adj.* sensible

sen·si·bi·li·dad *f.* sensibility; sensitiveness

sen·si·bi·li·zar *v.* to sensitize

sen·si·ble *adj.* sentimental; sensitive

sen·so·rio, a *adj.* sensorial

sen·sual *adj.* sensual

sen·sua·li·dad *f.* sensuality

sen·ta·do, a *adj.* settled; seated

sen·tar *v.* to sit

sen·ten·cia *f.* sentence

sen·ten·ciar *v.* to sentence

sen·ten·cio·so, a *adj.* sententious

sen·ti·do, a *adj.* heartfelt

sen·ti·men·tal *adj.* sentimental

sen·ti·mien·to *m.* sentiment

sen·tir *v.* to feel; to sense; to experience

se·ña *f.* signal; sign

se·ñal *f.* sign

se·ña·lar *v.* to point; to determine

se·ña·li·zar *v.* to put up signs

se·ñe·ro *adj.* solitary

se·ñor *adj.* Mr.; Mister

se·ño·rí·o *m.* domain; solemnity

se·ño·ri·ta *f.* lady; girl

se·ño·ri·to *m.* boy; young man

se·ñue·lo *m.* trap; bait

se·pa·ra·ción *f.* separation

se·pa·ra·da·men·te *adv.* separately

se·pa·ra·do *adj.* separated

se·pa·rar *v.* to divide

se·pa·ra·tis·ta *adj.* separatist

se·pe·lio *m.* burial

sép·ti·co, a *adj.* septic

sep·tiem·bre *m.* September

sép·ti·mo *adj.* seventh

sep·tua·ge·na·rio, a *adj.*

septuagenarian
sep·tua·gé·si·mo *adj.*
seventieth
se·pul·tar *v.* to bury
se·pul·to, a *adj.* buried
se·pul·tu·ra *f.* burial
se·que·dad *f.* dryness
se·quí·a *f.* drought
ser *v.* to be; to come from
se·ra·fín *m.* angel
se·re·nar *v.* to calm
se·re·na·ta *f.* serenade
se·re·ni·dad *f.* serenity
se·ria·men·te *adv.* seriously
se·rie *f.* series
se·rie·dad *f.* seriousness
se·rio *adj.* serious
ser·món *m.* sermon
ser·mo·ne·ar *v.* to lecture
ser·pien·te *f.* snake
se·rra·do, a *adj.* sawed
se·rra·ní·a *f.* mountains
se·rrar *v.* to saw
se·rre·rí·a *f.* sawmill
se·rru·cho *m.* saw
ser·vi·cio *m.* help; service
ser·vi·dor, a *m., f.* servant
ser·vil *adj.* servile
ser·vi·lle·ta *f.* napkin
ser·vir *v.* to serve
sé·sa·mo *m.* sesame
se·sen·ta *adj.* sixty
se·sen·ta·vo, a *adj.* sixtieth
ses·go *m.* slant
se·sión *f.* session
se·so *m.* brain
se·su·do, a *adj.* wise
se·te·cien·tos, as *adj.*
seven hundred
se·ten·ta *adj.* seventy
se·ten·ta·vo, a *adj.*
seventieth
se·tiem·bre *m.* September
seu·dó·ni·mo, a *m.*
pseudonym
se·ve·ra·men·te *adv.*
relentlessly; severely
se·ve·ro, a *adj.* unyielding;
severe
se·xa·gé·si·mo, a *adj.*
sixtieth
sex·te·to *m.* sextet
sex·to *adj.* sixth
se·xual *adj.* sexual
se·xua·li·dad *f.* sexuality
si *conj.* if; *adv.* yes
si·bi·lan·te *adj.* sibilant

si·co·mo·ro *m.* sycamore
sie·ga *f.* harvesting
siem·bra *f.* sowing
siem·pre *adv.* forever;
always
sien *f.* temple
sie·rra *f.* saw
sier·vo *m.* servant; serf
sies·ta *f.* nap in the
afternoon
sie·te *adj.* seven
sí·fi·lis *f.* syphilis
si·fi·lí·ti·co, a *adj.* syphilitic
si·gi·lo *m.* secrecy
si·gla *f.* acronym
si·glo *m.* century
sig·ni·fi·ca·ción *f.*
significance
sig·ni·fi·ca·do, a *adj.*
significant
sig·ni·fi·can·te *adj.*
significant
sig·ni·fi·car *v.* to signify; to
indicate
sig·ni·fi·ca·ti·vo, a *adj.*
significant
sig·no *m.* sign
si·guien·te *adj.* next
sí·la·ba *f.* syllable
si·la·be·ar *v.* to syllable
si·la·be·o *m.* syllabication
sil·ba·to *m.* whistle
sil·bi·do *m.* whistle
si·len·cia·dor *m.* silencer
si·len·ciar *v.* to silence
si·len·cio *m.* silence
si·len·cio·so *adj.* silent
si·li·co·na *f.* silicone
si·lo *m.* silo
si·lo·gís·ti·co, a *adj.*
stylogistic
si·lue·ta *f.* outline
sil·ves·tre *adj.* wild
sil·vi·cul·tor *m.* forester
si·lla *f.* chair
si·llín *m* seat; saddle
si·llón *m.* armchair
sim·bio·sis *f.* symbiosis
sim·bió·ti·co, a *adj.*
symbiotic
sim·bo·li·zar *v.* to symbolize
sím·bo·lo *m.* symbol
si·me·trí·a *f.* symmetry
si·mé·tri·co, a *adj.*
symmetric
si·mien·te *f.* seed
sí·mil *adj.* similar

si·mi·li·tud *f.* similarity
sim·pa·tí·a *f.* congeniality;
affection
sim·pá·ti·co, a *adj.* pleasant
sim·pa·ti·zan·te *adj.*
sympathizing
sim·ple *adj.* simple
sim·ple·za *f.* simplicity
sim·pli·ci·dad *f.* simplicity
sim·pli·fi·ca·ción *f.*
simplification
sim·pli·fi·car *v.* to simplify
sim·po·sio *m.* symposium
si·mu·la·ción *f.* pretense
si·mu·la·dor, a *m., f.*
simulator
si·mul·tá·ne·o, a *adj.*
simultaneous
sin *prep.* without
si·na·go·ga *f.* synagogue
sin·ce·ri·dad *f.* sincerity
sin·ce·ro, a *adj.* sincere
sín·co·pa *f.* syncope
sin·co·pa·do, a *adj.*
syncopated
sín·co·pe *m.* syncope
sin·cro·ní·a *f.* synchrony
sin·cro·ni·za·ción *f.*
synchronization
sin·cro·ni·zar *v.*
to synchronize
sin·di·ca·li·za·ción *f.*
unionization
sin·di·ca·li·zar *v.*
to unionize
sín·dro·me *m.* syndrome
si·ner·gia *f.* synergy
sin·fo·ní·a *f.* symphony
sin·fó·ni·co, a *adj.*
symphonic
sin·gu·lar *adj.* single
sin·gu·la·ri·zar *v.*
to distinguish
sin·nú·me·ro *m.* countless
si·no *conj.* but; fate
si·nó·ni·mia *f.* synonymy
si·nó·ni·mo, a *adj.*
synonymous
si·nóp·sis *f.* synopsis
si·nóp·ti·co, a *adj.* synoptic
sin·ta·xis *m.* syntax
sín·te·sis *f.* synthesis
sin·té·ti·co, a *adj.* synthetic
sin·te·ti·za·dor *m.*
synthesizer
sin·te·ti·zar *v.* to synthesize
sín·to·ma *m.* symptom

sin·to·má·ti·co, a *adj.*
symptomatic
sin·to·ni·zar *v.* to tune
si·nuo·si·dad *f.* sinuosity
si·nuo·so, a *adj.* sinuous
si·quia·tra *m., f.* psychiatrist
si·quia·trí·a *f.* psychiatry
sí·qui·co *adj.* psychic
si·quie·ra *adv.* at least
sir·vien·ta *f.* maid
sir·vien·te *m.* servant
sís·mi·co, a *adj.* seismic
sis·mo *m.* earthquake
sis·mó·gra·fo *m.*
seismograph
sis·te·ma *m.* system
sis·te·ma·ti·za·ción *f.*
systematization
sis·te·ma·ti·zar *v.*
to systematize
sís·to·le *f.* systole
si·tio *m.* place
si·to *m.* site
si·tua·ción *f.* situation
si·tuar *v.* to place
so·ba·co *m.* armpit
so·bar *v.* to thrash; to knead
so·be·o *m.* strap
so·be·ra·no, a *adj.*
sovereign
so·ber·bio, a *adj.* superb
so·bor·nar *v.*
to bribe another
so·bor·no *m.* bribery
so·bra *f.* excess
so·bra·do, a *adj.* plenty
so·bran·te *adj.* surplus
so·brar *v.* to surpass
so·bre *prep.* over; on; above
so·bre·a·bun·dan·cia *f.*
superabundance
so·bre·car·ga *f.* overload
so·bre·car·gar *v.*
to overload
so·bre·ce·jo *m.* frown
so·bre·co·ger *v.* to scare
so·bre·en·ten·di·do, a *adj.*
understood
so·bre·ex·ci·tar *v.* to
overexcite
so·bre·lle·nar *v.* to overfill
so·bre·lle·var *v.* to bear
so·bre·na·tu·ral *adj.*
supernatural
so·bre·nom·bre *m.*
nickname
so·bren·ten·der *v.*
to understand

so·bre·pa·sar v. to surpass
so·bre·pe·so m. overload
so·bre·pre·cio m. surcharge
so·bre·sa·lien·te adj. outstanding
so·bre·sa·lir v. to project
so·bre·sal·tar v. to startle
so·bre·sal·to m. fright
so·bres·cri·to m. address
so·bres·ti·mar v. to overestimate
so·bre·to·do m. coat; overcoat
so·bre·vi·vien·te adj. surviving
so·bre·vi·vir v. to survive
so·bri·na f. niece
so·bri·no m. nephew
so·ca·rrón, a m., f. one who is sarcastic
so·ca·rro·ne·rí·a f. sarcasm
so·ca·var v. to excavate
so·cia·bi·li·dad f. friendliness
so·cia·ble adj. sociable
so·cie·dad f. society
so·cio, a m., f. member
so·cio·e·co·nó·mi·co, a adj. socioeconomic
so·cio·lo·gí·a f. sociology
so·cio·ló·gi·co, a adj. sociological
so·ció·lo·go, a m., f. sociologist
so·co·rrer v. to aid
so·co·rro m. aid
so·dio m. sodium
so·fá f. sofa
so·fis·ma m. sophism
so·fis·ta adj. sophistic
so·fis·ti·ca·ción f. sophistication
so·fis·ti·ca·do, a adj. sophistication
so·fo·ca·ción f. suffocation
so·fo·ca·dor, a adj. suffocating
so·fo·car v. to suffocate; to suppress
so·ga f. rope
so·ja f. soybean
so·juz·gar v. to subjugate
sol m. sun
so·la·men·te adv. only
so·la·no m. the east wind
so·lar adj. solar
so·la·rium m. solarium

so·laz m. relaxation
sol·da·do m. soldier
sol·da·dor m. welder
sol·da·du·ra f. welding
sol·dar v. to join; to weld
so·le·a·do adj. sunny
so·le·cis·mo m. solecism
so·le·dad f. loneliness
so·lem·ne adj. solemn
so·lem·ni·dad f. solemnity
so·le·van·tar v. to lift
so·li·ci·ta·ción f. request
so·li·ci·tan·te m., f. petitioner
so·li·ci·tar v. to ask for; to request
so·lí·ci·to, a adj. solicitous
so·li·ci·tud f. request; solicitude
so·li·da·ri·dad f. solidarity
so·li·dez f. solidity
so·li·di·fi·ca·ción f. solidification
so·li·di·fi·car v. to solidify
só·li·do adj. solid
so·li·lo·quio m. soliloquy
so·lis·ta f. soloist
so·li·vian·tar v. to irritate
so·li·viar v. to lift something
so·lo adj. alone
sol·sti·cio m. solstice
sol·tar v. to let go; to loosen
sol·te·ro adj. single
sol·tu·ra f. confidence; looseness
so·lu·ble adj. soluble
so·lu·ción f. solution
so·lu·cio·nar v. to solve
sol·ven·cia f. solvency
sol·ven·tar v. to resolve
sol·ven·te adj. solvent
so·má·ti·co, a adj. somatic
so·ma·ti·za·ción f. somatization
som·bra f. shade
som·brar v. to shade
som·bre·ro m. hat
som·brí·o, a adj. sullen
so·me·ter v. to subordinate
so·me·ti·mien·to m. submission
som·no·len·cia f. somnolence
so·na·do, a adj. crazy
so·nar v. to sound
son·da f. sounding
son·de·ar v. to sound

son·de·o m. survey
so·ne·to m. sonnet
so·ni·do m. sound
so·no·ri·dad f. sonority
so·no·ro, a adj. sonority
so·no·ro, a adj. sound
son·re·ír v. to smile
son·rien·te adj. smiling
son·ri·sa f. smile
son·ro·jo m. blush
son·ro·sar v. to turn pink
son·sa·car v. to wheedle
so·ña·do, a adj. dream
so·ña·dor, a m., f. dreamer
so·ñar v. to dream
so·ño·len·cia f. somnolence
so·ño·lien·to, a adj. sleepy
so·pa f. soup
so·pa·pe·ar v. to slap
so·pa·po m. slap
so·pe·sar v. to weigh
so·pla·dor, a adj. blowing
so·plar v. to blow
so·por m. sleepiness
so·por·ta·ble adj. bearable
so·por·tar v. to support
so·por·te m. support
so·pra·no m. soprano
sor·ber v. to absorb
sor·be·te m. sherbet
sor·bo m. sip
sor·de·ra f. deafness
sor·di·dez f. squalor
sór·di·do, a adj. squalid
sor·do, a adj. deaf
sor·na f. sarcasm
sor·pren·den·te adj. surprising
sor·pren·der v. to surprise
sor·pre·si·vo, a adj. unexpected
sor·ti·ja f. ring
so·se·ga·do, a adj. peaceful
so·se·gar v. to calm down
so·sie·go m. quiet
sos·la·yo, a adj. slanted
so·so, a adj. dull
sos·pe·cha f. suspicion
sos·pe·cho·so, a adj. suspicious
sos·tén m. support; sustenance
sos·te·ne·dor m. supporter
sos·te·ner v. to uphold; to support
sos·te·ni·do, a adj. sustained

sos·te·ni·mien·to m. sustenance; support
so·ta·na f. soutane
só·ta·no m. basement
Sr. abbr. **Señor**, m. Mr.
Sra. abbr. **Señora**, f. Mrs.
su, sus adj. her; his; its; your
sua·ve adj. sweet, soft
sua·vi·dad f. smoothness; sweetness
sua·vi·za·dor, a adj. softening
sua·vi·zar v. to smooth; to soften
su·bal·ter·no, a adj. subordinate
su·ba·rren·dar v. to sublet
su·ba·rrien·do m. sublease
su·bas·ta f. auction
su·bas·tar v. to auction
sub·co·mi·sión f. subcommittee
sub·cons·cien·te adj. subconscious
sub·cu·tá·ne·o, a adj. subcutaneous
sub·di·vi·sión f. subdivision
su·bes·ti·mar v. to underestimate
su·be y ba·ja m. seesaw
su·bi·do, a adj. deep
su·bir v. to raise; to go up; to come
sú·bi·ta·men·te adv. suddenly
sú·bi·to adj. hasty
sub·je·ti·vi·dad f. subjectivity
sub·je·ti·vo, a adj. subjective
su·ble·var v. to rebel
su·bli·ma·ción f. sublimation
su·bli·mar v. to sublimate
sub·ma·ri·no adj. submarine
su·bor·di·na·ción f. subordination
su·bor·di·na·do, a adj. subordinate
su·bor·di·nar v. to subordinate
sub·sa·nar v. to correct
subs·cri·bir v. to subscribe to; to sign
subs·crip·ción f. subscription

subs·crip·tor, a *m., f.* subscriber
sub·se·cuen·te *adj.* subsequent
sub·si·diar *v.* to subsidize
sub·si·dio *m.* subsidy
sub·sis·ten·cia *f.* subsistence
sub·sis·tir *v.* to subsist
subs·tan·cia *f.* substance
subs·tan·cial *adj.* substantial
subs·tan·ciar *v.* to substantiate
subs·tan·cio·so, a *adj.* substantial
subs·ti·tu·ción *f.* substitution
subs·ti·tuir *v.* to substitute
subs·ti·tu·ti·vo, a *adj.* substitute
subs·trac·ción *f.* subtraction
subs·tra·er *v.* to subtract; to deduce
sub·sue·lo *m.* basement
sub·te·rrá·ne·o, a *adj.* underground
sub·tí·tu·lo *m.* subtitle
su·bur·ba·no, a *adj.* suburban
sub·ven·ción *f.* subsidy
sub·ven·cio·nar *v.* to subsidize
sub·yu·gar *v.* to subjugate
suc·ción *f.* suction
su·ce·dá·ne·o, a *adj.* substitute
su·ce·der *v.* to succeed
su·ce·sión *f.* succession
su·ce·si·va·men·te *adv.* successively
su·ce·si·vo, a *adj.* consecutive
su·ce·so *m.* event
su·ce·sor, a *adj.* succeeding
su·cie·dad *f.* filthiness
su·cio, a *f.* dirty
su·cu·len·to, a *adj.* succulent
su·cum·bir *v.* to succumb
sud *m.* south
su·dar *v.* to sweat
su·des·te *m.* southeast
su·do·es·te *m.* southwest
su·dor *m.* sweat
su·do·rí·fe·ro, a *adj.* sudoriferous; secreting sweat

su·do·ro·so, a *adj.* sweaty
sue·gra *f.* mother-in-law
sue·gro *m.* father-in-law
sue·lo *m.* floor; soil; ground
suel·to, a *adj.* nimble; loose
sue·ño *m.* dream; sleep
sue·ro *m.* serum
suer·te *f.* luck
su·fi·cien·te *adj.* sufficient
su·fi·jo *m.* suffix
su·fra·gio *m.* suffrage
su·fra·gis·ta *f., m.* suffragist
su·fri·do, a *adj.* patient
su·frir *v.* to suffer; to endure something
su·ge·ren·cia *f.* suggestion
su·ge·rir *v.* to suggest
su·ges·tión *f.* suggestion
su·ges·ti·vo, a *adj.* suggestive
sui·ci·da *adj.* suicidal
sui·ci·dio *m.* suicide
su·je·ción *f.* subjection
su·je·tar *v.* to subject; to fasten
su·je·to, a *adj.* subject
sul·fu·ro *m.* sulphide
su·ma·men·te *adv.* extremely
su·mar *v.* to add up
su·ma·ria·men·te *adv.* summarily
su·ma·rio, a *adj.* brief
su·mer·gir *v.* to submerge
su·mi·de·ro *m.* drain
su·mi·nis·trar *v.* to supply
su·mi·nis·tro *m.* supply
su·mir *v.* to submerge
su·mi·sión *f.* submission
su·mi·so, a *adj.* submissive
sun·tuo·si·dad *f.* sumptuousness
sun·tuo·so, a *adj.* sumptuous
su·pe·di·tar *v.* to subordinate
su·per·a·bun·dar *v.* to superabound
su·pe·rar *v.* to surpass; to beat
su·per·es·truc·tu·ra *f.* superstructure
su·per·fi·cial *adj.* superficial
su·per·fi·cie *f.* surface
su·per·fi·no, a *adj.* very fine
su·per·fluo, a *adj.* superfluous

su·pe·rin·ten·den·te *m., f.* superintendent
su·pe·rior *adj.* superior; better
su·pe·rio·ri·dad *f.* superiority
su·per·mer·ca·do *m.* supermarket
su·per·po·bla·ción *f.* overpopulation
su·per·só·ni·co, a *adj.* supersonic
su·pers·ti·ción *f.* superstition
su·pers·ti·cio·so, a *adj.* superstitious
su·per·vi·sar *v.* to supervise
su·per·vi·sión *f.* supervision
su·per·vi·ven·cia *f.* survival
su·pi·no, a *adj.* supine
su·plan·tar *v.* to supplant
su·ple·men·tal *adj.* supplemental
su·plen·te *adj.* substitute
su·pli·car *v.* to implore
su·po·ner *v.* to imagine; to suppose
su·po·si·ción *f.* supposition
su·po·si·to·rio *m.* suppository
su·pre·mo, a *adj.* supreme
su·pri·mir *v.* to eliminate
su·pues·to, a *adj.* supposed; assumed
su·pu·rar *v.* to suppurate
sur *m.* south
sur·car *v.* to plow
sur·gir *v.* to arise
su·rre·a·lis·ta *adj.* surrealistic
sur·ti·dor, a *m.* supplier
sur·tir *v.* to supply something
sus·cep·ti·bi·li·dad *f.* susceptibility
sus·cep·ti·ble *adj.* susceptible
sus·pen·der *v.* to interrupt
sus·pen·sión *f.* suspension
sus·pen·si·vo, a *adj.* suspensive
sus·pen·so·rio, a *adj.* suspensory
sus·pi·ca·cia *f.* distrust
sus·pi·caz *adj.* being distrustful
sus·pi·rar *v.* to sigh
sus·pi·ro *m.* sigh

sus·ten·ta·mien·to *m.* sustenance
sus·ten·tar *v.* to uphold; to sustain
sus·to *m.* scare
su·su·rran·te *adj.* rustling
su·su·rrar *v.* to murmur; to whisper
su·su·rro *m.* whisper
su·til *adj.* subtle
su·ti·le·za *f.* subtlety
su·tu·ra *f.* suture
su·tu·rar *v.* to suture a wound
su·yo, a *adj.* their; her; his; your

T

ta·ba *f.* bone of the ankle
ta·ba·cal *m.* field for tobacco
ta·ba·ca·le·ro, a *m., f.* tobacco dealer
ta·ba·co *m.* tobacco
tá·ba·no *m.* gadfly
ta·ba·que·rí·a *f.* tobacco shop
ta·ber·na *f.* tavern
ta·ber·ná·cu·lo *m.* tabernacle
ta·ber·ne·ro, a *m., f.* bartender
ta·bi·que *m.* partition
ta·bla *f.* table
ta·ble·a·do, a *m.* pleats
ta·ble·ro *m.* board
ta·ble·ta *f.* tablet
ta·bu·la·dor *m., f.* tabulator
ta·bu·re·te *m.* stool
ta·co *m.* pad; wedge
ta·cón *m.* heel
tác·ti·co, a *adj.* tactical
tác·til *adj.* tactile
tac·to *m.* touch; tact
ta·cha *f.* flaw
ta·char *v.* to cross something out
ta·cho *m.* can
ta·chue·la *f.* tack
ta·fe·tán *m.* taffeta
ta·hur *m.* cardsharp
tai·ma·do, a *adj.* crafty
ta·ja·da *f.* profit
ta·jan·te *adj.* sharp

ta·jar *v.* to slice
ta·jo *m.* cut
tal *adj.* such
ta·la *f.* ruin
ta·la·dor, a *adj.* cutting
ta·la·drar *v.* to drill
ta·la·dro *m.* drill
ta·lar *v.* to cut something down
tal·co *m.* talc
ta·le·ga *f.* wealth
ta·len·to *m.* talent
ta·len·to·so, a *adj.* talented
ta·lis·mán *m.* talisman
ta·lón *m.* talon; heel
ta·lo·na·rio *m.* checkbook
ta·lla *f.* size; height
ta·lla·do, a *adj.* engraved; carved
ta·lla·dor *m.* engraver
ta·llar *v.* to carve
ta·lle *m.* figure; shape
ta·ller *m.* shop
ta·llo *m.* stern
ta·ma·ño, a *adj.* very big
ta·ma·ño *m.* size
tam·ba·le·an·te *adj.* staggering
tam·ba·le·ar *v.* to stagger
tam·bién *adv.* too; also
tam·bor *m.* drum
tam·bo·ra *f.* drum
tam·bo·ri·le·ar *v.* to beat
tam·bo·ri·le·o *m.* beating
ta·miz *m.* sieve
ta·mi·zar *v.* to filter
tam·po·co *adv.* nor; neither
tan *adv.* as; so
tan·da *f.* shift; turn
tan·gen·te *adj.* tangent
tan·gi·ble *adj.* tangible
tan·go *m.* tango
tan·gue·ar *v.* to tango
tan·que *m.* tanker
tan·te·ar *v.* to consider; to test
tan·to, a *adj.* so many
ta·ñer *v.* to play
ta·pa *f.* cover; lid
ta·pa·do *m.* coat
ta·par *v.* to block something
ta·pe·te *m.* carpet
ta·piar *v.* to wall something in
ta·pi·ce·ro, a *m., f.* upholsterer
ta·pio·ca *f.* tapioca

ta·piz *m.* tapestry
ta·pi·zar *v.* to upholster; to hang tapestries
ta·pón *m.* cork
ta·qui·gra·fí·a *f.* stenography
ta·qui·gra·fiar *v.* to write using shorthand
ta·quí·gra·fo, a *m., f.* stenographer
ta·ra *f.* defect
ta·rán·tu·la *f.* tarantula
ta·ras·car *v.* to bite
tar·dan·za *f.* delay
tar·dar *v.* to delay
tar·de *f.* afternoon
tar·dí·o, a *adj.* late
ta·re·a *f.* homework
ta·ri·fa *f.* tariff
ta·ri·far *v.* to give or apply a tariff to something
tar·je·ta *f.* card
ta·rro *m.* jar
tar·ta *f.* pie
tar·ta·mu·de·o *m.* stammering
tar·tán *m.* tartan
tár·ta·ro, a *adj.* tartar
ta·sa *f.* rate
ta·sa·ción *f.* appraisal
ta·sa·dor, a *adj.* appraising
ta·sa·je·ar *v.* to jerk something
ta·sa·jo *m.* jerky
tas·ca *f.* joint
ta·ta·ra·bue·la *f.* great-great-grandmother
ta·ta·ra·bue·lo *m.* great-great-grandfather
ta·ta·ra·nie·ta *f.* great-great-granddaughter
ta·ta·ra·nie·to *m.* great-great-grandson
ta·tua·je *m.* tattoo
ta·tuar *v.* to tattoo
tau·ro·ma·quia *f.* bullfighting
ta·xi *m.* taxi
ta·xi·der·mia *f.* taxidermy
ta·xis·ta *m., f.* one who drives a taxi
ta·xo·no·mí·a *f.* taxonomy
ta·za *f.* bowl; cup
te *pron.* you
te·a *f.* torch
te·a·tral *adj.* theatrical
te·a·tra·li·dad *f.*

theatricality
te·a·tro *m.* theater
te·cla *f.* key
te·cla·do *m.* keyboard
téc·ni·co, a *adj.* technical
tec·no·cra·cia *f.* technocracy
tec·no·lo·gí·a *f.* technology
tec·no·ló·gi·co, a *adj.* technological
te·char *v.* to roof a building
te·cho *m.* ceiling; roof
te·dio *m.* tedium
te·dio·so, a *adj.* tedious
te·ja *f.* tile
te·jar *v.* to tile
te·jer *v.* to knit
te·ji·do *m.* weave
te·jón *m.* badger
te·la *f.* fabric; film
te·la·ra·ña *f.* spider's web
te·le·co·mu·ni·ca·ción *f.* telecommunication
te·le·di·fun·dir *v.* to telecast
te·le·di·fu·sión *f.* to telecast
te·le·fo·na·zo *m.* telephone call
te·le·fo·ne·ar *v.* to phone someone
te·le·fó·ni·ca·men·te *adv.* by a phone
te·le·fo·nis·ta *m., f.* telephone operator
te·lé·fo·no *m.* telephone
te·le·fo·to *m.* telephoto
te·le·gra·fí·a *f.* telegraphy
te·le·gra·fiar *v.* to telegraph
te·le·grá·fi·co, a *adj.* telegraphic
te·le·gra·fis·ta *m., f.* telegrapher
te·lé·gra·fo *m.* telegraph
te·le·gra·ma *f.* telegram
te·le·man·do *m.* remote control
te·le·me·trí·a *f.* telemetry
te·le·pa·tí·a *f.* telepathy
te·le·pá·ti·co, a *adj.* telepathic
te·les·có·pi·co, a *adj.* telescopic
te·les·co·pio *m.* telescope
te·le·ti·po *m.* teletype
te·le·vi·sar *v.* to televise
te·le·vi·sión *f.* television
te·le·vi·sor *m.* television
te·lón *m.* curtain
te·lu·rio *m.* tellurium

te·ma *f.* subject; obsession
te·má·ti·co, a *adj.* thematic
tem·blar *v.* to tremble
tem·ble·que·ar *v.* to tremble
tem·blor *m.* earthquake; tremor
te·mer *v.* to be afraid of
te·me·ro·so, a *adj.* frightening
te·mor *m.* fear
tem·pe·ra·men·tal *adj.* temperamental
tem·pe·ra·men·to *m.* weather
tem·pe·ran·cia *f.* temperance
tem·pe·rar *v.* to calm
tem·pe·ra·tu·ra *f.* temperature
tem·pes·tad *f.* storm
tem·pes·tuo·so, a *adj.* stormy
tem·pla·do, a *adj.* mild
tem·plan·za *f.* moderation
tem·plar *v.* to temper; to tune; to appease
tem·ple *m.* mood; temper
tem·plo *m.* temple
tem·po·ra·da *f.* season
tem·po·ral *adj.* temporal
tem·po·rá·ne·o, a *adj.* temporary
tem·pra·ne·ro, a *adj.* early
tem·pra·no, a *adj.* early
te·na·ci·dad *f.* tenacity
te·naz *f.* tenacious
ten·den·cia *f.* tendency
ten·der *v.* to stretch something out
ten·di·do, a *adj.* spread out
ten·dón *m.* tendon
te·ne·bro·so, a *adj.* obscure; dark
te·ne·dor *m.* one who owns
te·nen·cia *f.* possession
te·ner *v.* to contain; to have; to keep
te·nia *f.* tapeworm
te·nien·te *m.* lieutenant
te·nis *m.* tennis
te·nis·ta *m., f.* one who plays tennis
ten·sar *v.* to stretch
ten·sión *f.* tension
ten·so, a *adj.* tense
ten·ta·ción *f.* temptation

ten·tá·cu·lo *m.* tentacle
ten·ta·dor, a *adj.* tempting
ten·ta·ti·vo, a *adj.* tentative
te·ñir *v.* to make dark
te·o·cra·cia *f.* theocracy
te·ó·lo·go, a *m., f.* theologian
te·o·re·ma *m.* theorem
te·o·rí·a *f.* theory
te·ó·ri·co *adj.* theoretical
te·o·ri·zar *v.* to theorize
te·ó·so·fo, a *m., f.* theosophist
te·qui·la *f.* tequila
te·ra·peu·ta *m., f.* therapist
te·ra·péu·ti·co, a *adj.* therapeutic
te·ra·pia *f.* therapy
ter·ce·ro, a *adj.* third
ter·cio, a *adj.* third
ter·cio·pe·lo *m.* velvet
ter·co, a *adj.* stubborn
ter·gi·ver·sar *v.* to distort
ter·mal *adj.* thermal
ter·mi·na·ción *f.* ending; termination
ter·mi·nal *adj.* terminal
ter·mi·nar *v.* to complete; to end something
tér·mi·no *m.* ending
ter·mi·no·lo·gí·a terminology
ter·mi·ta *m.* termite
ter·mo·di·ná·mi·ca *f.* thermodynamics
ter·mo·e·léc·tri·co, a *adj.* thermoelectric
ter·mó·me·tro *m.* thermometer
ter·mos·ta·to *m.* thermostat
ter·no *m.* a set of three things
ter·nu·ra *f.* tenderness
te·rra·plén *m.* embankment
te·rrá·que·o, a *adj.* terrestrial
te·rra·za *f.* terrace
te·rre·mo·to *m.* earthquake
te·rre·nal *adj.* earthly
te·rre·no *adj.* earthly
te·rres·tre *adj.* terrestrial
te·rri·ble *adj.* terrible
te·rri·to·rial *adj.* territorial
te·rri·to·rio *m.* territory
te·rror *m.* terror
te·rro·rí·fi·co, a *adj.* terrifying

te·rro·ris·ta *m., f.* terrorist
ter·so, a *adj.* smooth
te·sis *f.* thesis
te·són *m.* tenacity
te·so·ne·ro, a *adj.* tenacious
te·so·re·rí·a *f.* treasury
te·so·re·ro, a *m., f.* treasurer
te·so·ro *m.* treasure
tes·tí·cu·lo *m.* testicle
tes·ti·fi·car *v.* to testify
tes·ti·mo·nio *m.* testimony
te·ta *f.* udder
té·ta·no *m.* tetanus
te·ti·lla *f.* teat
tex·til *adj.* textile
tex·to *m.* textbook
tex·tu·ra *f.* texture
tez *f.* complexion
ti *pron.* yourself
tí·a *f.* aunt
tia·ra *f.* tiara
ti·bia *f.* tibia
ti·bu·rón *m.* shark
tiem·po *m.* weather; time
tien·da *f.* store; shop
tien·to *m.* caution; touch
tier·no, a *adj.* tender
tie·rra *f.* land; country
tie·so, a *adj.* arrogant
ties·to *m.* flowerpot
ti·foi·de·o, adj. typhoid
ti·fón *m.* typhoon
ti·fus *m.* typhus
ti·gre *m.* tiger
ti·gre·sa *f.* tigress
ti·je·re·te·ar *v.* to snip
ti·je·re·te·o *m.* snipping
ti·ma·dor, a *m., f.* cheat
ti·mar *v.* to cheat
tim·bra·do, a *adj.* stamped
tim·brar *v.* to stamp
tim·bre *m.* ring
ti·mi·dez *f.* timidity
tí·mi·do, a *adj.* timid
ti·mo *m.* thymus
ti·mo·ra·to, a *adj.* shy
tin·gla·do *m.* platform
ti·no *m.* good judgment
tin·ta *f.* dye
tin·te *m.* dye
tin·te·ro *m.* inkwell
tin·ti·nar *v.* to clink something
tin·tu·ra *f.* tincture
ti·ña *f.* ringworm
tí·o *m.* uncle

tí·pi·co, a *adj.* typical
ti·pi·fi·car *v.* to typify
ti·po *m.* type; kind
ti·po·gra·fí·a *f.* typography
ti·ra·da *f.* distance
ti·ra·ní·a *f.* tyranny
ti·ra·ni·zar *v.* to tyrannize
ti·ra·no, a *adj.* tyrannical
ti·ran·te *adj.* tight
ti·ran·tez *f.* tightness
ti·rar *v.* to throw
ti·ri·tar *v.* to shiver
ti·ro *m.* shot; throw
ti·ro·te·o *m.* shooting
ti·sis *f.* tuberculosis
tí·te·re *m.* puppet
ti·ti·lar *v.* to quiver
ti·ti·le·o *m.* quivering
ti·ti·ri·tar *v.* to tremble
ti·tu·be·o *m.* staggering
ti·tu·la·do, a *adj.* titled
tí·tu·lo *m.* title
ti·za *f.* chalk
tiz·nar *v.* to smudge
to·a·lla *f.* towel
to·bi·llo *m.* ankle
to·bo·gán *m.* sled
to·ca·dor *m.* dressing room
to·car *v.* to ring; to handle; to touch
to·da·ví·a *adv.* still
to·do, a *adj.* all; every
to·le·ran·cia *f.* tolerance
to·le·ran·te *adj.* tolerant
to·le·rar *v.* to tolerate
to·lon·drón, a *m., f.* scatterbrain
to·ma *f.* intake; taking
to·ma·dor, a *adj.* drinking
to·mar *v.* to have; to take
to·ma·te *m.* tomato
to·na·da *f.* tune
to·na·li·dad *f.* tonality
to·nel *m.* barrel
to·ne·la·da *f.* ton
to·ne·la·je *m.* tonnage
to·ni·fi·car *v.* to tone
to·ni·na *f.* tuna
to·no *m.* tone
ton·te·rí·a *f.* foolishness
ton·to *m.* fool
tó·pi·co *m.* topic
to·po *m.* mole
to·po·gra·fí·a *f.* topography
to·pó·gra·fo *m.* topographer
to·que *m.* beat; touch
to·que·te·ar *v.* to handle

to·que·te·o *m.* handling
to·rá·ci·co, a *adj.* thoracic
tor·ce·du·ra *f.* twist
tor·cer *v.* to sprain; to bend
to·re·a·dor *m.* bullfighter
to·re·ar *v.* to bullfight
to·re·o *m.* bullfighting
tor·men·to *m.* torment
tor·men·to·so, a *adj.* stormy
tor·na·do *m.* tornado
tor·na·sol *m.* sunflower
tor·na·so·la·do, a *adj.* iridescent
tor·ne·ar *v.* to turn on the lathe
tor·ne·o *m.* tournament
tor·ni·llo *m.* screw
tor·ni·que·te *m.* tourniquet
to·ro *m.* bull
to·ron·ja *f.* grapefruit
tor·pe·de·ar *v.* to torpedo
tor·pe·za *f.* stupidity
tor·por *m.* torpor
to·rrar *v.* to roast
to·rre *f.* castle
to·rren·cial *adj.* torrential
to·rren·te *m.* torrent
tó·rri·do, a *adj.* torrid
tor·sión *f.* torsion
tor·so *m.* torso
tor·ta *f.* cake
tór·to·la *f.* turtledove
tor·tu·ga *f.* turtle
tor·tuo·so, a *adj.* tortuous
tor·tu·ra *f.* torture
tor·tu·rar *v.* to torture
tos *f.* coughing
to·ser *v.* to cough
tos·que·dad *f.* coarseness
tos·ta·do, a *adj.* roasted
tos·ta·dor, a *m., f.* toaster
tos·tar *v.* to roast; to toast
to·tal *adj.* total
to·ta·li·dad *f.* totality
to·ta·li·ta·rio, a *adj.* totalitarian
to·ta·li·zar *v.* to total
to·xe·mia *f.* toxemia
to·xi·ci·dad *f.* toxicity
tó·xi·co, a *adj.* poison
to·xi·có·lo·go, a *m., f.* toxicologist
to·xi·na *f.* toxin
to·zu·do, a *adj.* stubborn
tra·ba *f.* obstacle; bolt
tra·ba·ja·dor *m.* worker

tra·ba·jar *v.* to work
tra·ba·jo *m.* job; work
tra·ba·jo·so, a *adj.* demanding
tra·bar *v.* to fasten; to bolt
tra·bu·car *v.* to mix up
trac·ción *f.* traction
trac·tor *m.* tractor
tra·di·ción *f.* tradition
tra·di·cio·nal *f.* traditional
tra·duc·ción *f.* translation
tra·du·cir *v.* to express
tra·duc·tor, a *m.* translator
tra·fi·car *v.* to deal
trá·fi·co *m.* traffic
tra·ga·luz *m.* skylight
tra·gar *v.* to devour; to swallow
tra·ge·dia *f.* tragedy
trá·gi·co, a *adj.* tragic
tra·gi·co·me·dia *f.* tragicomedy
tra·go *m.* gulp
trai·ción *f.* treason
trai·cio·nar *v.* to betray another
tra·je *m.* dress
tra·je·a·do, a *adj.* dressed
tra·je·ar *v.* to dress
tra·ji·nar *v.* to carry
tra·ma *f.* plot
tra·ma·dor, a *m.,f.* weaver
tra·mar *v.* to scheme
tra·mi·ta·ción *f.* transaction
tra·mi·tar *v.* to negotiate
tra·mo *m.* flight
tram·pa *f.* trap
tram·pe·ar *v.* to cheat
tram·po·lín *m.* trampoline
tram·po·so, a *adj.* tranquilizing
tran·qui·lo, a *adj.* tranquil
tran·sac·ción *f.* transaction
tran·sat·lán·ti·co, a *adj.* transatlantic
trans·cen·den·cia *f.* transcendence
trans·cen·der *v.* to transcend
trans·con·ti·nen·tal *adj.* transcontinental
trans·fe·ren·cia *f.* transfer
trans·fe·rir *v.* to transfer
trans·fi·gu·ra·ción *f.* transfiguration
trans·for·ma·ción *f.* transformation

trans·for·ma·dor, a *adj.* transforming
trans·for·mar *v.* to convert; to transform
trans·fun·dir *v.* to transfuse
trans·fu·sión *f.* transfusion
trans·gre·dir *v.* to transgress
trans·gre·sión *f.* transgression
tran·si·ción *f.* transition
tran·sis·tor *m.* transistor
tran·si·tar *v.* to travel
tran·si·ti·vo, a *adj.* transitive
trán·si·to *m.* traffic
tran·si·to·rio, a *adj.* temporary
trans·la·ción *f.* translation
trans·lú·ci·do, a *adj.* translucent
trans·mi·gra·ción *f.* transmigration
trans·mi·grar *v.* to transmigrate
trans·mi·tir *v.* to transmit
trans·mu·tar *v.* to transmute
trans·pa·ren·te *adj.* transparent
trans·pi·ra·ción *f.* perspiration
trans·pi·rar *v.* to perspire
trans·plan·tar *v.* to transplant
trans·po·ner *v.* to transplant; to move
trans·por·ta·ción *f.* transportation
trans·por·tar *v.* to transport
trans·po·si·ción *f.* transposition
trans·ver·so, a *adj.* transverse
tran·ví·a *m.* streetcar
tra·pe·cio *m.* trapezoid
tra·pe·zoi·de *m.* trapezoid
trá·que·a *f.* trachea
tras *prep.* behind; after
tras·at·lán·ti·co, a *adj.* transatlantic
tras·cen·den·te *adj.* transcendent
tras·cen·der *v.* to extend
tra·se·gar *v.* to decant
tras·fon·do *m.* background
tra·sie·go *m.* decanting
tras·la·ción *f.* translation
tras·la·dar *v.* to transcribe; to move

tras·la·do *m.* transfer
tras·no·cha·do, a *adj.* trite
tras·pa·pe·lar *v.* to misplace something
tras·pa·pe·la·do, a *adj.* misplaced
tras·pa·sar *v.* to break
tras·pa·so *m.* transfer
trans·plan·tar *v.* to transplant
tras·qui·lar *v.* to shear
tras·to·car *v.* to twist
tras·tor·nar *v.* to disrupt
tras·tro·car *v.* to twist
tra·sun·tar *v.* to summarize
tra·ta·mien·to *m.* treatment; process
tra·tar *v.* to process; to handle
tra·to *m.* treatment
trau·ma *m.* trauma
trau·má·ti·co, a *adj.* traumatic
trau·ma·ti·zar *v.* to traumatize
tra·ve·sí·a *f.* crosswind; crossroad
tra·ve·su·ra *f.* mischief
tra·vie·so, a *adj.* mischievous
tra·yec·to *m.* way
tra·yec·to·ria *f.* trajectory
tra·za *f.* plan
tra·zar *v.* to outline something
tra·zo *m.* line
tré·bol *m.* clover
tre·ce *adj.* thirteen
tre·cho *m.* in parts; stretch
tre·gua *f.* rest
trein·ta *adj.* thirty
trein·ta·vo *f.* thirtieth
trein·te·na *f.* thirty
tre·men·do, a *adj.* terrible; horrible
tre·men·ti·na *f.* turpentine
tre·mo·lar *v.* to wave
tre·mo·li·na *f.* rustling
tre·mor *m.* tremor
tren *m.* train
tren·ci·lla *f.* braid
tren·za *f.* braid
tre·pi·dar *v.* to vibrate
tres *adj.* three
tres·cien·tos *adj.* three hundred

tre·za·vo, a *adj.* thirteenth
trí·a·da *f.* triad
trian·gu·lar *adj.* triangular
trián·gu·lo *m.* triangular
tri·bal *adj.* tribal
tri·bu *f.* tribe
tri·bu·la·ción *f.* tribulation
tri·bu·no *m.* tribune
tri·bu·ta·rio, a *adj.* tributary
tri·bu·to *m.* tribute
tri·cen·te·na·rio *m.* tricentennial
tri·ci·clo *m.* tricycle
tri·co·lor *adj.* tricolor
tri·cús·pi·de *adj.* tricuspid
tri·gal *m.* field of wheat
tri·gé·si·mo, a *adj.* thirtieth
tri·go *m.* wheat
tri·go·no·me·trí·a *f.* trigonometry
tri·lin·güe *adj.* trilingual
tri·lo·gí·a *f.* trilogy
tri·lla·dor, a *adj.* threshing
tri·lli·zo *m.* triplet
tri·mes·tral *adj.* quarterly
trin·cha·dor, a *adj.* carving
trin·char *v.* to carve
tri·no·mio *m.* trinomial
trí·o *m.* trio
tri·ple *adj.* triple
tri·pli·ca·ción *f.* triplication
tri·pli·ca·do *m.* triplicate
tri·pli·car *v.* to triplicate
tri·plo, a *adj.* triple
trí·po·de *m., f.* tripod
tri·qui·no·sis *f.* trichinosis
tris·ca *f.* crack
tris·car *v.* to stamp
tris·te *adj.* miserable; sad
tris·te·za *f.* sorrow
tri·tu·rar *v.* to chew; to triturate
triun·fa·dor, a *adj.* triumphant
triun·fan·te *adj.* triumphant
triun·fo *m.* triumph
tri·vial *adj.* trivial
tri·via·li·dad *f.* triviality
tri·za *f.* piece
tro·car *v.* to barter
tro·fe·o *m.* trophy
tro·glo·di·ta *adj.* barbarous
tro·le *m.* trolley
trom·bón *m.* trombone
trom·bo·sis *f.* thrombosis
trom·pa *f.* horn
trom·pe·ar *v.* to punch

trom·pe·ta *f.* trumpet
trom·pe·tis·ta *m., f.* trumpeter
trom·pi·car *v.* to trip
trom·po *m.* top
tro·na·da *f.* thunderstorm
tro·na·dor, a *adj.* thundering
tro·nan·te *adj.* thundering
tro·nar *v.* to thunder
tron·co *m.* trunk
tron·cha *f.* slice
tro·pel *m.* confusion
tro·pe·lí·a *f.* violence
tro·pe·zar *v.* to trip
tro·pi·cal *adj.* tropical
tró·pi·co *m.* tropic
tro·pie·zo *m.* stumble
tro·po *m.* trope
tro·que·lar *v.* to mint
tro·ta·da *f.* trot
tro·ta·dor, a *adj.* trotting
tro·va *f.* ballad
tro·zo *m.* chunk; part; piece
tru·co *m.* trick
true·no *m.* thunder
tru·far *v.* to lie
tú *pron.* you
tu·ba *f.* tuba
tu·ber·cu·li·na *f.* tuberculin
tu·ber·cu·lo·sis *f.* tuberculosis
tu·be·ro·so, a *adj.* tuberous
tu·bo *m.* tube
tu·bu·la·do, a *adj.* tubular
tu·bu·lar *adj.* tubular
tu·cán *m.* toucan
tues·te *m.* toasting
tu·fo *m.* fume
tu·li·pán *m.* tulip
tu·llir *v.* to cripple
tum·ba *f.* tomb
tum·bar *v.* to knock out
tum·bo *m.* jolt
tu·mor *m.* tumor
tú·mu·lo *m.* tomb
tu·mul·to *m.* tumult
tu·mul·tuo·so, a *adj.* tumultuous
tu·nan·ta *adj.* cunning
tun·da *f.* beating
tun·de·ar *v.* to beat
tun·di·dor, a *m., f.* one who shears
tun·di·du·ra *f.* shearing
tun·dir *v.* to shear
tun·dra *f.* tundra

tú·nel *m.* tunnel
tungs·te·no *m.* tungsten
tú·ni·ca *f.* tunic
tu·pé *m.* toupee
tu·pi·do, a *adj.* dense; thick
tu·pir *v.* to weave close together
tur·ba *f.* mob
tur·ba·ción *f.* confusion
tur·ba·dor, a *adj.* disturbing
tur·ban·te *m.* turban
tur·bar *v.* to embarrass; to upset another
tur·bie·dad *f.* opaqueness
tur·bi·na *f.* turbine
tur·bio, a *adj.* turbulent; muddy
tur·bión *m.* shower
tur·bu·len·cia *f.* turbulence
tur·bu·len·to, a *adj.* turbulent
tu·ris·ta *f.* tourist
tu·rís·ti·co, a *adj.* tourist
tur·nar *v.* taking turns at something
tur·no *m.* turn
tur·que·sa *f.* turquoise
tu·ru·la·to, a *adj.* being stunned
tu·sa *f.* cornhusk
tu·sar *v.* to trim
tu·te·ar *v.* to address another as "tu"
tu·tor, a *m., f.* guardian
tu·yo, a *adj.* yours

U

u·bé·rri·mo, a *adj.* luxuriant
u·bi·ca·ción *f.* placing
u·bi·car *v.* to locate
u·bre *f.* udder
u·fa·nar·se *v.* to boast about something
u·fa·no, a *adj.* please
úl·ti·mo, a *adj.* final; last
ul·tra *adv.* besides
ul·tra·de·re·cha *f.* the far right
ul·tra·jan·te *adj.* outrageous
ul·tra·jar *v.* to insult
ul·tra·je *m.* insult
ul·tra·ma·ri·no, a *adj.* overseas
ul·tra·mo·der·no, a *adj.* ultramodern

ul·tra·só·ni·co, a *adj.* ultrasonic
ul·tra·so·ni·do *m.* ultrasound
ul·tra·vio·le·ta *adj.* ultraviolet
um·bi·li·cal *adj.* umbilical
um·bral *m.* threshold
um·brí·o, a *adj.* shady
um·bro·so, a *adj.* shady
un *indef. art.* an; a
u·na *indef. art.* an; a
u·ná·ni·me *adj.* unanimous
u·na·ni·mi·dad *f.* unanimity
un·cir *v.* to yoke
un·dé·ci·mo, a *adj.* eleventh
un·du·lar *v.* to undulate
un·güen·to *m.* ointment
u·ni·ce·lu·lar *adj.* unicellular
u·ni·ci·dad *f.* uniqueness
ú·ni·co, a *adj.* single; sole
u·ni·cor·nio *m.* unicorn
u·ni·dad *f.* unity; each
u·ni·do, a *adj.* united
u·ni·fi·ca·ción *f.* unification
u·ni·fi·car *v.* to unify
u·ni·for·mar *v.* to make something uniform
u·ni·for·me *adj.* even; uniform
u·ni·for·mi·dad *f.* uniformity
u·ni·la·te·ral *adj.* unilateral
u·nión *f.* joint; unity
u·nir(se) *v.* to unite together
u·ni·se·xo *adj.* unisex
u·ní·so·no, a *adj.* to be in unison with
u·ni·ta·rio, a *adj.* unified
u·ni·ver·sal *adj.* worldwide; universal
u·ni·ver·sa·li·dad *f.* universality
u·ni·ver·sa·li·zar *v.* to universalize
u·ni·ver·si·dad *f.* university
u·ni·ver·si·ta·rio, a *adj.* university
u·ni·ver·so *m.* universe
u·no, a *adj.* one
un·tar *v.* to spread; to grease
un·to *m.* grease
un·tuo·si·dad *f.* greasiness
un·tuo·so, a *adj.* greasy
un·tu·ra *f.* greasing

u·ña *f.* toenail; fingernail
u·ra·nio *m.* uranium
ur·ba·ni·dad *f.* urbanity
ur·bate·o·rí·a *f.* theory
ur·ba·ni·za·ción *f.* urbanization
ur·ba·ni·zar *v.* to develop
ur·ba·no, a *adj.* urban
u·rea *f.* urea
u·re·tra *f.* urethra
ur·gen·cia *f.* urgency
ur·gen·te *adj.* urgent
u·ri·na·rio, a *adj.* urinary
u·san·za *f.* custom
u·sar *v.* to use
u·so *m.* use
us·ted *pron.* you
u·sual *adj.* usual
u·su·ra *f.* usury
u·sur·par *v.* to usurp
u·ten·si·lio *f.* utensil
ú·til *adj.* useful

V

va·ca *f.* cow
va·ca·ción *f.* vacation
va·can·te *adj.* vacant
va·cia·de·ro *m.* dump
va·cia·do *m.* cast
va·ciar *v.* to void; to empty; to drain
va·ci·la·ción *f.* vacillation; hesitation
va·ci·lan·te *adj.* hesitating
va·ci·lar *v.* to falter; to vacillate
va·cío, a *adj.* devoid; empty; void; hollow
va·cui·dad *f.* vacuity
va·cu·na·ción *f.* vaccination
va·cu·nar *v.* to vaccinate
va·cu·no, a *adj.* bovine
va·cuo, a *adj.* vacuous
va·de·ar *v.* to overcome
va·ga·bun·do, a *adj.* vagabond
va·ga·men·te *adv.* vaguely
va·gan·cia *f.* vagrancy
va·gar *v.* to roam; to stray; to wander
va·gi·do *m.* cry
va·go, a *adj.* hazy; wandering; vague
va·gón *m.* van
va·gue·ar *v.* to wander

va·gue·dad *f.* vagueness
va·ho *m.* vapor; steam
vai·ni·lla *f.* vanilla
vai·vén *m.* fluctuation
va·le *m.* voucher
va·le·de·ro, a *adj.* valid
va·len·cia *f.* valence
va·len·tí·a *f.* courage; valor; bravery
va·len·tón, a *adj.* boastful
va·len·to·na *f.* boast
va·ler *v.* to be of value; to have authority over; to be of worth
va·le·ro·so, a *adj.* valorous; courageous
va·lí·a *f.* worth
va·li·da·ción *f.* validation
va·li·dar *v.* to validate
va·li·dez *f.* validity
vá·li·do, a *adj.* good
va·lien·te *adj.* brave; valiant
va·li·ja *f.* suitcase
va·lio·so, a *adj.* valuable
va·lor *m.* valor; worth; importance
va·lo·ra·ción *f.* appraisal
va·lo·ri·zar *v.* to appraise something
vals *m.* waltz
va·luar *v.* to value something
vál·vu·la *f.* valve
va·llar *v.* to put a fence around; to fence in
va·lle *m.* valley
vam·pi·ro *m.* vampire
va·na·glo·ria *f.* pride
va·na·glo·rio·so, a *adj.* boastful
va·na·men·te *adv.* foolishly; vainly
van·da·lis·mo *m.* vandalism
va·ni·dad *f.* vanity
va·ni·do·so, a *adj.* one who is vain
va·no, a *adj.* vain
va·por *m.* steam
va·po·ri·za·dor *m.* vaporizer
va·po·ri·zar *v.* to vaporize
va·po·ro·so, a *adj.* steamy; vaporous
va·que·ta *f.* hide of a cow
va·ra *f.* rod; stalk
va·rar *v.* to beach
va·re·a·dor, a *m., f.* cowhand

va·re·ar *v.* to cudgel
va·ria·ble *adj.* variable
va·ria·ción *f.* change; variation
va·ria·do, a *adj.* varied
va·rien·te *adj.* varying
va·riar *v.* to change
va·rie·dad *f.* variety
va·ri·lla *f.* rod
va·rio, a *adj.* varied
va·rón *m.* man
va·ro·nil *adj.* virile
va·sa·llo, a *adj.* subordinate
vas·cu·lar *adj.* vascular
va·sec·to·mí·a *f.* vasectomy
va·si·ja *f.* container
va·so *m.* vessel; glass
vas·to, a *adj.* vast
va·ti·ci·nar *v.* to predict
va·ti·ci·nio *m.* prediction
va·tio *m.* watt
ve·ci·nal *adj.* local
ve·ci·na·men·te *adv.* next
ve·cin·dad *f.* vicinity
ve·ci·no, a *adj.* near; next
vec·tor *m.* vector
ve·da *f.* prohibition
ve·da·do, a *adj.* prohibited
ve·dar *v.* to suspend; to prohibit
ve·ge·ta·ción *f.* vegetation
ve·ge·tal *adj.* vegetable
ve·ge·tar *v.* to vegetate
ve·ge·ta·ria·no, a *adj.* vegetarian
ve·ge·ta·ti·vo, a *adj.* vegetative
ve·he·men·cia *f.* vehemence
ve·he·men·te *adj.* vehement
ve·hí·cu·lo *m.* vehicle
vein·te *adj.* twenty
ve·ja·ción vexation
ve·ja·men *m.* vexation
ve·jar *v.* to persecute; to vex
ve·jez *f.* old age
ve·ji·ga *f.* bladder
ve·la *f.* sail
ve·la·da *f.* evening
ve·la·do, a *adj.* veiled
ve·lar *v.* to guard
ve·lei·do·so, a *adj.* fickle
ve·lo *m.* veil
ve·lo·ci·dad *f.* velocity
ve·loz *adj.* swift
ve·llo *m.* fuzz
ve·llón *m.* sheepskin

ve·llu·do, a *adj.* hairy
ve·na *f.* vein
ve·na·blo *m.* javelin
ven·ce·dor, a *m., f.* conqueror
ven·cer *v.* to conquer; to beat another
ven·ci·do, a *adj.* conquered; defeated
ven·ci·mien·to *m.* defeat; collapse
ven·da·je *m.* bandage
ven·dar *v.* to bandage
ven·de·dor, a *m., f.* seller
ven·der *v.* to sell
ven·di·mia·dor, a *m., f.* one who picks grapes
ve·ne·no *m.* poison
ve·ne·no·si·dad *f.* poisonousness
ve·ne·no·so, a *adj.* poisonous
ve·ne·ra·ble *adj.* venerable
ve·ne·ra·ción *f.* veneration
ve·ne·rar *v.* to venerate
ven·gan·za *f.* revenge; vengeance
ven·gar *v.* to avenge
ve·nia *f.* forgiveness
ve·nial *adj.* venial
ve·ni·da *f.* return
ve·ni·de·ro, a *adj.* upcoming
ve·nir *v.* to come
ven·ta *f.* sale
ven·ta·ja *f.* benefit
ven·ta·jo·so, a *adj.* advantageous
ven·ta·na *f.* window
ven·ti·la·ción *f.* ventilation
ven·ti·la·dor *m.* fan
ven·ti·lar *v.* to air
ven·tis·ca *f.* blizzard
ven·tis·que·ro *m.* blizzard
ven·to·si·dad *f.* gas
ven·to·so, a *adj.* windy
ven·tri·cu·lar *adj.* ventricular
ven·trí·cu·lo *m.* ventricle
ven·trí·lo·cuo, a *m., f.* ventriloquist
ven·tu·ra *f.* happiness
ven·tu·ro·so, a *adj.* fortunate
ver *v.* to sight; to see
ve·ra *f.* edge
ve·ra·ci·dad *f.* veracity

ve·ra·ne·o *m.* vacationing
ve·ra·no *m.* summer
ve·ras *f.* earnestness
ve·raz *adj.* truthful
ver·bal *adj.* verbal
ver·bal·men·te *adv.* verbally
ver·bo *m.* verb
ver·bo·rre·a *f.* verbosity
ver·bo·si·dad *f.* verbosity
ver·bo·so, a *adj.* verbose
ver·dad *f.* truth
ver·da·de·ro, a *adj.* truthful
ver·de *adj.* green
ver·dor *m.* verdancy
ver·do·so, a *adj.* greenish
ver·du·ra *f.* greenery
ve·re·dic·to *m.* verdict
ver·gel *m.* orchard
ver·gon·zo·so, a *adj.* shameful
ver·güen·za *f.* shyness
ve·rí·di·co, a *adj.* true
ve·ri·fi·ca·ción *f.* verification
ve·ri·fi·ca·dor, a *m., f.* checker
ver·mi·ci·da *adj.* vermicidal
ver·nal *adj.* vernal
ve·ro·si·mi·li·tud *f.* probability
ver·sa·do, a *adj.* versed
ver·sá·til *adj.* versatile
ver·sa·ti·li·dad versatility
ver·sí·cu·lo *m.* versicle
ver·si·fi·car *v.* to versify
ver·sión *f.* version
ver·so *m.* version
ver·so *m.* verse
vér·te·bra *f.* vertebra
ver·te·bra·do, a *adj.* vertebrate
ver·te·bral *adj.* vertebral
ver·ter *v.* to shed
ver·ti·cal *adj.* vertical
ver·ti·ca·li·dad *f.* verticality
ver·tien·te *f.* spring
vér·ti·go *m.* vertigo
ve·sí·cu·la *f.* vesicle
ve·si·cu·lar *adj.* vesicular
ves·ti·do *m.* clothing; dress
ves·ti·du·ra *f.* garment
ves·ti·gio *m.* vestige
ves·ti·men·ta *f.* clothes
ves·tir *v.* to attire; to wear; to dress
ve·tar *v.* to veto

ve·te·ar *v.* to streak
ve·te·ra·no, a *m., f. adj.* veteran
ve·te·ri·na·rio, a *m., f.* veterinarian
vez *f.* time
vía *f.* means; way
via·ble *adj.* viable
via·jar *v.* to journey; to travel
via·je *m.* journey; trip
vial *adj.* traffic
vian·da *f.* food
ví·bo·ra *f.* viper
vi·bra·ción *f.* vibration
vi·brar *v.* to shake; to vibrate
vi·ce·pre·si·den·cia *f.* vice presidency
vi·ce·pre·si·den·te *m.* vice president
vi·ciar *v.* to corrupt; to falsify; to pollute
vi·cio *m.* vice
vi·cio·so, a *adj.* depraved
vi·ci·si·tud *f.* vicissitude
víc·ti·ma *f.* victim
vic·to·ria *f.* victory
vic·to·rio·so, a *adj.* victorious
vid *f.* grapevine
vi·da *f.* life
vi·de·o *m.* video
vi·de·o·ca·se·te *m.* videocassette
vi·de·o·cin·ta *f.* videotape
vi·dria·do, a *adj.* glazed
vi·drie·ro, a *m., f.* glazier
vi·drio *m.* glass
vi·drio·so, a *adj.* glassy
vie·jo, a *adj.* aged; old
vien·to *m.* wind
vier·nes *m.* Friday
vi·gen·cia *f.* force
vi·gi·lan·cia *f.* vigilance
vi·gi·lan·te *adj.* heedful; vigilant
vi·gi·lar *v.* to guard
vi·gi·lia *f.* vigil
vi·gor *m.* strength; vigor
vi·go·ro·so, a *adj.* forceful; vigorous
vi·hue·la *f.* guitar
vi·le·za *f.* vileness
vi·lla *f.* village
vi·lla·no, a *adj.* peasant
vi·na·gre *m.* vinegar
vi·na·gre·ta *f.* vinaigrette
vin·cu·lar *v.* to link

vin·di·ca·ción *f.* vindication
vin·di·car *v.* to vindicate
vi·ni·lo *m.* vinyl
vi·no *m.* wine
vi·ñe·do *m.* vineyard
vio·la *f.* viola
vio·lá·ce·o, a *adj.* violet
vio·la·ción *f.* violation
vio·lar *v.* to violate
vio·len·cia *f.* violence; rape
vio·len·tar *v.* to force; to distort; to break into
vio·len·to, a *adj.* violent
vio·le·ta *f., adj.* violet
vio·lín *f.* violin
vio·li·nis·ta *m., f.* violinist
vio·lón *m.* double bass player; double bass
vi·pe·ri·no *adj.* venomous
vi·ra·je *m.* turning point; veering turn
vi·rar *v.* to turn; to tone; to swerve
vir·gen *adj. f.* virgin
vi·ril *adj.* virile
vir·tual *adj.* virtual
vi·ru·len·to, a *adj.* virulent
vi·rus *m.* virus
vi·ru·ta *f.* shavings
vi·sar *v.* to sight; to endorse
vis·co·si·dad *f.* viscosity
vi·se·ra *f.* visor
vi·si·llo *m.* window curtain
vi·sión *f.* vision
vi·si·tar *v.* to visit
vis·ta *f.* sight; view
vis·to·so, a *adj.* colorful
vi·sual *adj.* visual
vi·tal *adj.* vital
vi·ta·mi·na *f.* vitamin
vi·to·re·ar *v.* to cheer
vi·tral *m.* stained-glassed window
viu·da *f.* widow
viu·do *m.* widower
vi·vaz *adj.* lively
vi·ven·cia *f.* experience
ví·ve·res *m., pl.* provisions
ví·ve·ro *m.* fish hatchery; nursery
vi·ve·za *f.* liveliness; sharpness; quickness
ví·vi·do, a *adj.* vivid
vi·vien·da *f.* dwelling; housing
vi·vien·te *adj.* living
vi·vi·fi·ca·dor, a *adj.*

vivifying
vi·vir *v.* to reside; to live
vi·vo, a *adj.* vivid; lively
vo·ca·blo *m.* term
vo·ca·bu·la·rio *m.* vocabulary
vo·ca·ción *f.* job; occupation; vocation
vo·cal *adj.* vocal
vo·ca·li·za·ción *f.* vocalization
vo·ce·ar *v.* to shout
vo·ce·o *m.* shouting
vo·ce·ro, a *m., f.* spokesman; spokeswoman
vo·la·da *f.* short flight
vo·lan·do *adv.* in a flash
vo·lan·te *adj.* flying; *m.* steering wheel
vo·lar *v.* to fly; to blow up; to disappear
vo·la·tín *m.* acrobatic stunt
vo·la·ti·ne·ro, a *m., f.* tightrope walker
vol·cán *m.* volcano
vo·le·ar *v.* to scatter
vo·li·ción *f.* volition
vol·ta·je *m.* voltage
vol·tear *v.* to upset; to turn over
vol·te·re·ta *f.* somersault
vol·tí·me·tro *m.* voltmeter
vol·tio *m.* volt
vo·lu·men *m.* volume
vo·lun·tad *f.* will; wish; intention
vo·lun·ta·rio, a *adj.* voluntary
vo·lun·ta·rio·so, a *adj.* willing; willful
vo·lup·tuo·si·dad *f.* voluptuousness
vol·ver *v.* to turn; to return; to recur; to restore
vo·mi·tar *v.* to spew; to vomit; to spill
vo·mi·ti·vo, a *adj., m.* vomitive
vo·ra·ci·dad *f.* voracity
vo·rá·gi·ne *f.* whirlpool
vo·ra·gi·no·so, a *adj.* turbulent
vo·raz *adj.* voracious
vór·ti·ce *m.* center of cyclone; vortex
vos *pron. m., f.* you
vo·se·ar *v.* to address

vo·se·o *m.* used in addressing someone
vo·so·tras *pron. f.* you
vo·so·tros *pron. m.* you
vo·ta·ción *f.* voting; vote
vo·tan·te *m., f.* voter
vo·tar *v.* to vote
vo·ti·vo *adj.* votive
voz *f.* voice
vo·za·rrón *m.* booming voice
vuel·co *m.* turn; overturning
vue·lo *m.* flight
vuel·to, a *m., f.* revolution
vues·tra *adj.* your
vul·ca·ni·zar *v.* to vulcanize
vul·gar *adj.* vulgar; common
vul·ga·ri·dad. *f.* vulgarity
vul·ga·ris·mo *m.* vulgarism
vul·ga·ri·zar *v.* to popularize; to vulgarize
vul·go *m.* masses
vul·ne·ra·bi·li·dad *f.* vulnerability
vul·ne·rar *v.* to violate; to wound
vul·va *f.* vulva

W

wat *m.* watt
wel·ter *m.* welterweight
whis·ky *m.* whiskey

X

xe·no·fo·bia *f.* xenophobia
xi·ló·fo·no *m.* xylophone
xi·lo·gra·fí·a *m.* xylography

Y

ya·ca·ré *m.* alligator
ya·cer *v.* to lie; to be
ya·guar *m.* jaguar
yám·bi·co *adj.* iambic
yan·qui *adj. m., f.* Yankee
yar·da *f.* yard
ya·te *m.* yacht
ye·gua *f.* mare
ye·gua·da *f.* herd of horses
yel·mo *m.* helmet

ye·ma *f.* yolk
yen *m.* yen
yer·ba *f.* grass
yer·bal *m., f.* field of mate
yer·mar *v.* to strip
yer·mo, a *adj.* barren
yer·no *m.* son-in-law
ye·rra *f.* cattle branding
ye·rro *m.* fault; sin
yer·to *adj.* frozen stiff
ye·se·ro *adj.* plaster
ye·so *m.* gypsum
yo *pron.* I; me
yo·da·do, a *adj.* iodized
yo·do *m.* iodine
yo·du·ro *m.* iodide
yo·ga *m.* yoga
yo·g(h)i *m.* yogi
yo·gur(t) *m.* yogurt
yo·yo *m.* yo-yo
yu·ca *f.* yucca
yu·cal *m.* yucca field
yu·do *m.* judo
yu·ga·da *f.* day's plowing;
  yoke
yu·gu·lar *adj. f.* jugular
yun·que *m.* anvil
yun·ta *f.* yoke
yu·te *m.* jute
yux·ta·po·ner *v.*
  to juxtapose
yux·ta·po·si·ción *f.*
  juxtaposition
yu·yal *m.* weed patch
yu·yo *m.* weed
yu·yu·ba *f.* jujube

Z

za·far(se) *v.* to loosen
za·gal *m.* boy; lad
za·ga·la *f.* lass
za·ma·rro *m.* sheepskin
zam·bu·lli·da *f.* dive
zam·bu·llir *v.* to plunge into
za·na·ho·ria *f.* carrot
zan·ja *f.* trench; ditch
za·pa·te·rí·a *f.* shoestore
za·pa·te·ro *m.* shoemaker
za·pa·ti·lla *f.* slipper
za·pa·to *m.* shoe
zar *m.* czar
za·ri·na *f.* czarina
zar·za·mo·ra *f.* blackberry
zo·co *adj.* left-handed
zo·dí·a·co *m.* zodiac

zo·na *f.* zone
zoo·lo·gí·a *f.* zoology
zoo·ló·gi·co *adj.* zoological
zoó·lo·go *m.* zoologist
zo·rra *f.* fox
zo·rro *m.* fox
zo·zo·brar *v.* to overturn
zum·bar *v.* to whiz; to buzz
zu·mo *m.* juice
zu·mo·so *adj.* juicy
zur·cir *v.* to stitch

English—Spanish
Inglés—Español

A

a *indef. art.* una; un
a·back *adv.* atrás
a·ba·cus *n.* ábaco
a·ban·don *v.* abandonar
a·base *v.* humillar; rebajar
a·bate *v.* disminuir; reducir
ab·bey *n.* monasterio
ab·bre·vi·a·tion *n.* abreviación
ab·di·cate *v.* abdicar
ab·do·men *n.* abdomen
ab·duct *v.* secuestrar
ab·er·ra·tion *n.* aberración
a·bet *v.* instigar; ayudar
ab·hor *v.* aborrecer
a·bide *v.* cumplir; soportar
a·bil·i·ty *n.* habilidad
ab·ject *adj.* abyecto
ab·jure *v.* abjurar
a·ble *adj.* capaz; competente
ab·ne·gate *v.* renunciar; negar
ab·nor·mal *adj.* anormal
a·board *adv., prep.* a bordo
a·bode *n.* domicilio
a·bol·ish *v.* abolir
a·bom·i·nate *v.* abominar
ab·o·rig·i·nes *n.* aborígenes
a·bor·tion *n.* aborto
a·bound *v.* abundar
a·bout *prep.* sobre; alrededor de
a·bove *prep.* sobre; encima de
a·bra·sion *n.* abrasión
a·breast *adv.* de frente; al lado
a·bridge *v.* abreviar; resumir
a·broad *adv.* fuera de casa; en el extranjero
ab·ro·gate *v.* abrogar

ab·rupt *adj.* brusco
ab·scess *n.* absceso
ab·scond *v.* fugarse
ab·sent *adj.* ausente
ab·so·lute *adj.* completo; absoluto
ab·solve *v.* absolver
ab·sorb *v.* absorber
ab·stain *v.* abstenerse
ab·ste·mi·ous *adj.* abstemio
ab·stract *v.* abstraer
ab·surd *adj.* absurdo
a·bun·dant *adj.* abundante
a·buse *v.* insultar; maltratar
a·but *v.* limitar; bordear
a·byss *n.* abismo
ac·a·dem·ic *adj.* academico
a·cad·e·my *n.* academia
ac·cede *v.* acceder; consentir; subir
ac·cel·er·ate *v.* acelerar
ac·cent *n.* acento
ac·cept *v.* recibir
ac·cess *n.* acceso
ac·ces·si·ble *adj.* accesible
ac·ces·so·ry *n., pl.* accesorio; cómplice
ac·ci·dent *n.* accidente
ac·claim *v.* aclamar
ac·cli·mate *v.* aclimatar
ac·co·lade *n.* acolada
ac·com·mo·date *v.* acomodar
ac·cord *n.* acuerdo
ac·cor·di·on *n.* acordeón
ac·count *v.* explicar
ac·count·a·ble *adj.* responsable
ac·cum·u·late *v.* acumular
ac·cu·ra·cy *n.* exactitud
ac·cu·rate *adj.* exacto; fiel
ac·cuse *v.* acusar; culpar
ac·cus·tom *v.* acostumbrar
a·ce·tic *adj.* acético
ace·tone *n.* acetona
ache *n.* dolor
a·chieve *v.* acabar

acid *adj.* ácido
ac·knowl·edge *v.* reconocer; confesar; agradecer
ac·me *n.* cima
ac·ne *n.* acné
ac·o·lyte *n.* acólito
a·corn *n.* bellota
a·cous·tics *n.* acústica
ac·quaint *v.* enterar
ac·quaint·ance *n.* conocido
ac·qui·esce *v.* consentir
ac·quire *v.* adquirir
ac·quit *v.* absolver
a·cre *n.* acre
ac·rid *adj.* acre
ac·ri·mo·ny *n.* acrimonia
ac·ro·bat *n.* acróbata
a·cross *prep.* a través de
act *v.* fingir; hacer
ac·tion *n.* acción
ac·ti·vate *v.* activar
ac·tive *adj.* activo
ac·tor *n.* actor
ac·tress *n.* actriz
ac·tu·al *adj.* actual; real
a·cu·i·ty *n.* agudeza
a·cu·men *n.* agudeza
a·cute *adj.* agudo; fino
ad·age *n.* adagio
ad·a·mant *adj.* firme
a·dapt *v.* adaptar
add *v.* sumar; añadir
ad·di·tion *n.* adición
ad·dress *v.* dirigir (se a)
a·dept *n., adj.* experto
ad·e·quate *adj.* adecuado; suficiente
ad·here *v.* adherirse; pegarse; cumplir
ad·he·sive *adj., n.* adhesivo
ad·ja·cent *adj.* adyacente
ad·jec·tive *n.* adjetivo
ad·join *v.* juntar; estar contiguo
ad·journ *v.* suspender
ad·judge *v.* juzgar; sentenciar
ad·just *v.* ajustar; adaptar

ad·ju·tant *n.* ayudante
ad·lib *v.* improvisar
ad·min·is·ter *v.* administrar
ad·min·is·tra·tion *n.* administración
ad·mire *v.* admirar
ad·mis·si·ble *adj.* admisible
ad·mis·sion *n.* entrada; confesión
ad·mit *v.* confesar; admitir
ad·mon·ish *v.* amonestar
a·do·be *n.* adobe
ad·o·les·cence *n.* adolescencia
a·dopt *v.* adoptar; aceptar
a·dore *v.* adorar
a·dorn *v.* adornar
a·dren·a·line *n.* adrenalina
a·droit *adj.* hábil; diestro
ad·u·la·tion *n.* adulación
a·dult *adj.* mayor
a·dul·ter·y *n.* adulterio
ad·vance *v.* avanzar
ad·van·tage *n.* ventaja
ad·ven·ture *n.* aventura
ad·ven·ture·some *adj.* aventurado
ad·verb *n.* adverbio
ad·ver·sar·y *n.* adversario
ad·verse *adj.* adverso; contrario
ad·ver·si·ty *n.* adversidad
ad·ver·tise *v.* publicar
ad·vice *n.* consejo
ad·vise *v.* avisar
ad·vo·cate *v.* abogar
adz, adze *n.* azuela
ae·gis *n.* patrocinio
aer·ate *v.* airear
aer·i·al *adj.* aéreo
aer·o·naut·ics *n., pl.* aeronáutica
aes·thete *n.* esteta
aes·thet·ic *adj.* estético
a·far *adv.* lejos
af·fa·ble *adj.* afable; cortés
af·fair *n.* asunto

af·fect *v.* afectar
af·fec·ta·tion *n.* afectación
af·fec·tion *n.* afección
af·fec·tion·ate *adj.* cariñoso
af·fi·ance *v.* desposarse
af·fi·da·vit *n.* declaración;
  jurada
af·fil·i·ate *v.* afiliar
af·fin·i·ty *n.* afinidad
af·firm *v.* afirmar
af·firm·a·tive *n.* aserción
af·fix *v.* añadir; fijar
af·flic·tion *n.* aflicción
af·flu·ence *n.* afluencia
af·flu·ent *adj.* rico; opulento
af·ford *v.* tener medios para;
  dar
af·front *v.* afrentar
a·fire *adj., adv.* ardiendo
a·flame *adj., adv.* en llamas
a·float *adj., adv.* a flote
a·foul *adj., adv.* enredado
a·fraid *adj.* atemorizado
a·fresh *adv.* de nuevo; otra
  vez
aft *adj., adv.* en (a) popa
af·ter *prep.* detrás de
af·ter·birth *n.* secundinas
af·ter·noon *n.* tarde
af·ter·ward *adv.* después
a·gain *adv.* otra vez
a·gainst *prep.* contra
a·gape *adj., adv.*
  boquiabierto
age *n.* edad
a·ged *adj.* viejo
a·gen·cy *n.* agencia; acción;
  medio
a·gen·da *n., pl.* orden del
  dia
a·gent *n.* agente;
  representante
ag·glom·er·ate *v.* aglomerar
ag·gran·dize *v.* engrandecer
ag·gra·vate *v.* agravar
ag·gre·gate *v.* agregar;
  juntar
ag·gres·sion *n.* agresión
ag·gres·sive *adj.* agresivo
a·ghast *adj.* horrorizado
ag·ile *adj.* ágil
a·gil·i·ty *n.* agilidad
ag·i·tate *v.* agitar; inquietar
a·glow *adj.* ardiente
ag·nos·tic *n.* agnóstico
a·go *adj.* pasado
ag·o·ny *n.* agonía; angustia

a·grar·i·an *adj.* agrario
a·gree *v.* acordar
a·gree·a·ble *adj.* agradable;
  conforme
a·gree·ment *n.* acuerdo
ag·ri·cul·ture *n.* agricultura
a·gron·o·my *n.* agronomía
a·ground *adv.* encallado
a·head *adv.* al frente
aid *n.* ayuda
ail·ment *n.* enfermedad;
  dolencia
aim *v.* aspirar
air *n.* aire
air con·di·tion·er *n.*
  acondicionador de aire
air·plane *n.* avión
air·port *n.* aeropuerto
air·raid *n.* ataque aéreo
air·y *adj.* ligero; alegre
aisle *n.* nave lateral; pasillo
a·jar *adj., adv.* entreabierto
a·kin *adj.* semejante; consan
  guíneo
al·a·bas·ter *n.* alabastro
a·lac·ri·ty *n.* alacridad
a·larm *n.* alarma
a·larm·ist *n.* alarmista
al·ba·tross *n.* albatros
al·be·it *conj.* aunque
al·bi·no *n.* albino
al·bum *n.* álbum
al·bu·men *n.* albumen
al·bu·min *n.* albúmina
al·che·my *n.* alquimia
al·co·hol *n.* alcohol
ale *n.* cerveza
a·lee *adv.* a sotavento
a·lert *adj.* alerte
al·fal·fa *n.* alfalfa
al·ga *n.* alga
al·ge·bra *n.* álgebra
a·li·as *n.* alias
al·i·bi *n.* coartada; excusa
a·lien *n.* extranjero
a·light *v.* bajar; posarse
a·lign *v.* alinera; aliar
a·like *adj.* semejante
al·i·ment *n.* alimento
al·i·men·ta·ry *adj.*
  alimenticio
al·i·mo·ny *n.* alimentos
a·live *adj.* activo
all *adj.* todo
al·lay *v.* aliviar; aquietar
al·le·ga·tion *n.* alegación
al·lege *v.* alegar; declarar

al·leged *adj.* supuesto;
  alegado
al·le·giance *n.* lealtad
al·le·go·ry *n.* alegoría
al·ler·gy *n.* alergia
al·le·vi·ate *v.* calmar
al·le·vi·a·tion *n.*
  aligeramiento
al·ley *n.* callejuela
al·li·ance *n.* alianza
al·li·ga·tor *n.* caimán
al·lo·cate *v.* asignar
al·lo·ca·tion *n.* reparto; cupo
al·lot *v.* asignar; distribuir;
  adjudicar
al·low *v.* dar; permitir
al·low·ance *n.* ración;
  permiso
al·loy *n.* aleación
al·lude *v.* aludir
al·lure *v.* tentar
al·lu·sion *n.* alusión
al·lu·vi·um *n.* derrubio
al·ly *n.* aliado; confederado
al·ma·nac *n.* almanaque
al·might·y *adj.* omnipotente;
  todopoderoso
al·mond *n.* almendra;
  almendro
al·most *adv.* casi
alms *n.* limosna
a·loft *adv.* en alto
a·lone *adj.* solo
a·long *adv., conj., prep.*
  a lo largo
a·loof *adv.* lejos reservado
a·loud *adv.* en voz alta; alto
al·pha·bet *n.* alfabeto
al·read·y *adv.* ya
al·so *adv.* también; además
al·tar *n.* altar
al·ter *v.* cambiar; alterar;
  modificar
al·ter·a·tion *n.* alteración
al·ter e·go *n.* álter ego
al·ter·nate *v.* alternar
al·ter·na·tive *n.* alternativa
al·though *conj.* aunque
al·tim·e·ter *n.* altímetro
al·ti·tude *n.* altura; altitud
al·to *n.* alto; contralto
al·to·geth·er *adv.* en total
a·lu·mi·num *n.* aluminio
a·lum·na *n.* graduada
a·lum·nus *n.* graduado
al·ways *adv.* siempre
a.m. *abbr. adj.*

  antemeridiano
a·mal·gam *n.* amalgama
a·mal·gam·ate *v.*
  amalgamar
a·mass *v.* acumular;
  amontonar
am·a·teur *n.* aficionada
am·a·to·ry *adj.* amatorio
a·maze *v.* asombrar
a·maze·ment *n.* sorpresa
am·a·zon *n.* amazona
am·bas·sa·dor *n.*
  embajador
am·ber *n.* ámbar
am·bi·dex·trous *adj.*
  ambidextro
am·bi·gu·i·ty *n.*
  ambigüedad; doble sentido
am·big·u·ous *adj.* ambiguo
am·bi·tion *n.* ambición
am·bi·tious *adj.* ambicioso
am·biv·a·lence *n.*
  ambivalencia
am·ble *v.* amblar; andar
  lentamente
am·bu·late *v.* andar;
  ambular
am·bu·la·to·ry *adj.*
  ambulante
am·bus·cade *n.* emboscada
am·bush *n.* emboscada
a·me·ba *n.* amiba
a·mel·io·rate *v.* mejorar;
  mejoramiento
a·men *int.* amén
a·me·na·ble *adj.* dócil
a·mend *v.* enmendar;
  corregir
a·mends *n., pl.*
  compensación
a·men·i·ty *n.* amenidad
A·mer·i·can *adj.* americano
am·e·thyst *n.* amatista
a·mi·a·ble *adj.* amable
am·i·ca·ble *adj.* amistoso
a·mid *prep.* en medio de;
  entre
a·mid·ships *adv.* en medio
  del navío
a·miss *adv., adj.*
  impropiamente
am·mo·nia *n.* amoníaco
am·ne·sia *n.* amnesia
am·nes·ty *n.* amnistía
a·moe·ba *n.* amiba
a·mong *prep.* en medio de
a·mor·al *adj.* amoral

am·o·rous *adj.* amoroso
a·mor·phous *adj.* amorfo
am·or·tize *v.* amortizar
a·mount *n.* cantidad; suma
am·pere *n.* amperio
am·phib·i·an *adj., n.* anfibio
am·phib·i·ous *adj.* anfibio
am·phi·the·a·ter *n.* anfiteatro
am·ple *adj.* abundante
am·pli·fy *v.* amplificar
am·pli·tude *n.* amplitud; abundancia
am·pu·tate *v.* amputar
am·pu·ta·tion *n.* amputación
a·muck *adv.* furiosamente
am·u·let *n.* amuleto
a·muse·ment *n.* pasatiempo
an *indef. art.* una; un; uno
a·nach·ro·nism *n.* anacronismo
an·a·con·da *n.* anaconda
a·nae·mi·a *n.* anemia
an·a·gram *n.* anagrama
a·nal *adj.* anal
an·al·ge·sic *adj.* analgésico
a·nal·o·gize *v.* analogizar
a·nal·o·gy *n.* analogía
a·nal·y·sis *n.* análisis
an·a·lyst *n.* analizador
an·a·lyze *v.* analizar
an·ar·chism *n.* anarquismo
an·ar·chist *n.* anarquista
an·ar·chy *n.* anarquía
a·nat·o·my *n.* anatomía
an·ces·tor *n.* antepasado
an·ces·try *n.* linaje; abolengo
an·chor *n.* ancla; áncora
an·cho·vy *n.* anchoa
an·cient *ajd.* antiguo
and *conj.* y
an·ec·dote *n.* anécdota
a·ne·mi·a *n.* anemia
an·e·mom·e·ter *n.* anemómetro
an·es·the·sia *n.* anestesia
an·es·the·tic, *adj.* anestésico
a·new *adv.* de nuevo; otra vez
an·gel *n.* ángel
an·gel·ic *adj.* angélico
an·ger *n.* ira; cólera
an·gle *n.* ángulo

an·gle·worm *n.* lombriz
An·glo·Saxon *v., adj.* anglosajón
an·gor·a *n.* angora
an·gry *adj.* enfadado
an·guish *n.* angustia; ansiedad
an·gu·lar *adj.* angular; anguloso
an·hy·drous *adj.* anhidro
an·i·mad·ver·sion *n.* animadversión
an·i·mad·vert *v.* censurar
an·i·mal *n.* animal
an·i·mal·ize *v.* animalizar
an·i·mate *v.* dar vida
an·i·ma·tion *n.* animación
an·i·mos·i·ty *n.* animosidad
an·ise *n.* anís
an·kle *n.* tobillo
an·nals *n., pl.* anales
an·neal *v.* templar
an·nex *v.* anexar; adjuntar
an·nex·a·tion *n.* anexión
an·ni·hi·late *v.* aniquilar
an·ni·hi·la·tion *n.* aniquilación
an·ni·ver·sa·ry *n.* aniversario
an·no·tate *v.* anotar
an·nounce *v.* proclamar
an·nounce·ment *n.* anuncio
an·noy *v.* molestar
an·noy·ance *n.* fastidio
an·nu·al *adj.* anual
an·nu·i·ty *n.* renta vitalicia
an·nul *v.* anular
an·nul·ment *n.* anulación
an·nun·ci·ate *v.* anunciar
an·nun·ci·a·tion *n.* anunciación
an·ode *n.* ánodo
a·noint *v.* untar; ungir
a·nom·a·lous *adj.* anómalo
a·nom·a·ly *n.* anomalía
a·non·y·mous *adj.* anónimo
an·oth·er *adj., pron.* otro
an·swer *v.* contestar; responder
ant *n.* hormiga
ant·ac·id *n.* antiácido
an·tag·o·nist *n.* antagonista
an·tag·o·nize *v.* contender
ant·arc·tic *adj.* antártico
ant·eat·er *n.* oso hormiguero
an·te·cede *v.* anteceder
an·te·date *v.* antedatar;

preceder
an·te·di·lu·ve·an *adj.* antediluviano
an·te·lope *n.* antílope
an·ten·na *n.* antena
an·te·ri·or *adj.* anterior
an·te·room *n.* antecámara
an·them *n.* antífona;
an·ther *n.* antera
an·thol·o·gy *n.* antología
an·thra·cite *n.* antracita
an·thrax *n.* ántrax
an·thro·poid *adj.* antropoide
an·thro·pol·o·gist *n.* antropólogo
an·thro·pol·o·gy *n.* antropología
an·ti *prefix* anti; contra
an·ti·bi·ot·ic *n.* antibiótico
an·ti·bod·y *n.* anticuerpo
an·tic *n.* travesura; cabriola
an·tic·i·pate *v.* anticipar; esperar
an·tic·i·pa·tion *n.* anticipación; expectativa
an·ti·cli·max *n.* anticlímax
an·ti·dote *n.* antídoto
an·tip·a·thy *n.* antipatía
an·tip·odes *n.* antípoda
an·ti·quate *v.* anticuar
an·ti·quat·ed *adj.* viejo; anticuado
an·tique *adj.* antiguo
an·tiq·ui·ty *n.* antigüedad
an·ti·sem·i·tism *n.* antisemitismo
an·ti·sep·tic *adj., n.* antiséptico
an·ti·so·cial *adj.* antisocial
an·tith·e·sis *n.* antítesis
an·ti·tox·in *n.* antitoxina
ant·ler *n.* cuerno; asta
an·to·nym *n.* antónimo
a·nus *n.* ano
an·vil *n.* yunque
anx·i·e·ty *n.* inquietud; ansia
anx·ious *adj.* impaciente
an·y *adj., pro.* alguno; algún
an·y·bod·y *pron.* alguien
an·y·how *adv.* de cualquier modo; de todas formas
an·y·one *pron.* alguien; alguno
an·y·thing *pron.* algo
an·y·way *adv.* de cualquier

modo; de todas fromas
an·y·where *adv.* en todas partes; dondequiera
a·or·ta *n.* aorta
a·part·ment *n.* apartamento
ap·a·thet·ic *adj.* indiferente
ap·a·thy *n.* apatía
ape *n.* mono
ap·er·ture *n.* abertura
a·pex *n.* ápice
aph·o·rism *n.* aforismo
aph·ro·dis·i·ac *n.* afrodisíaco
a·pi·a·rist *n.* colmenero
a·pi·ar·y *n.* colmenar
a·piece *adv.* cada uno; por persona
a·plomb *n.* aplomo
a·poc·a·lypse *n.* apocalipsis
a·pol·o·gize *v.* disculparse
a·pol·o·gy *n.* apología; disculpa
ap·o·plec·tic *adj.* apoplético
ap·o·plex·y *n.* apoplejía
a·port *adv.* a babor
a·pos·tate *n.* apóstata
a·pos·ta·tize *v.* apostatar
a·pos·tle *n.* apóstol
ap·os·tol·ic *adj.* apostólico
a·pos·tro·phe *n.* apóstrofo
a·poth·e·car·y *n.* boticario
ap·pall, ap·pal *v.* aterrar
ap·pa·rat·us *n.* aparato
ap·pa·rel *n.* ropa
ap·par·ent *adj.* claro; aparente
ap·pa·ri·tion *n.* fantasma
ap·peal *n.* apelación
ap·pear *v.* parecer
ap·pear·ance *n.* apariencia
ap·pease *v.* apaciguar
ap·pel·lant *n.* apelante
ap·pel·la·tion *n.* nombre
ap·pend *v.* anexar
ap·pen·dage *n.* apéndice
ap·pen·dec·to·my *n.* apendectomía
ap·pen·di·ci·tis *n.* apendicitis
ap·pen·dix *n.* apéndice
ap·per·tain *v.* pertenecer
ap·pe·tite *n.* gana
ap·pe·tiz·ing *adj.* apetitoso; apetitivo
ap·plaud *v.* aplaudir
ap·plause *n.* aplauso
ap·ple *n.* manzana

ap·pli·cant *n.* suplicante
ap·pli·ca·tion *n.* aplicación
ap·ply *v.* aplicar
ap·point *v.* señalar; nombrar
ap·point·ment *n.* cita;
nombramiento
ap·por·tion *v.* repartir
ap·po·si·tion *n.* aposición
ap·prais·al *n.* valoración
ap·praise *v.* valorar
ap·pre·ci·ate *v.* apreciar;
valorar; agradecer
ap·pre·ci·a·tion *n.* aprecio;
aumento en valor
ap·pre·hend *v.* entender
ap·pre·hen·sion *n.*
aprehensión
ap·pren·tice *n.* aprendiz; *v.*
poner de aprendiz
ap·prise, ap·prize *v.*
informar
ap·proach *v.* aproximarse
ap·pro·ba·tion *n.*
aprobación
ap·prov·al *n.* aprobación
ap·prove *v.* aprobar
ap·prox·i·mate *v.* aproximar
ap·ri·cot *n.* albaricoque
A·pril *n.* abril
a·pron *n.* delantal; *m.*
ap·ro·pos of *prep.*
a propósito de
apt *adj.* apto; listo
ap·ti·tude *n.* aptitud
a·quar·i·um *n.* acuario
a·quat·ic *adj.* acuático
aq·ue·duct *n.* acueducto
a·que·ous *adj.* ácueo
aq·ui·line *adj.* aguileño
Ar·ab *n., adj.* árabe; *m., f.*
Ar·a·bic nu·me·rals *n.*
números arábigos
ar·a·ble *adj.* arable;
cultivable
ar·bi·ter *n.* árbitro
ar·bi·trar·y *adj.* arbitrario
ar·bi·trate *v.* arbitrar
ar·bi·tra·tion *n.* arbitraje
ar·bo·re·tum *n.* jardín
botánico
arc *n.* **arco** *v.* formar un arco
voltaico
ar·cade *n.* arcada; galería
arch *n.* **arco** *v.* arquear
arch *prefix* principal
ar·chae·ol·o·gy,
ar·che·ol·o·gy *n.*

arqueología
ar·cha·ic *adj.* arcaico
arch·an·gel *n.* arcángel
arch·bish·op *n.* arzobispo
arch·duch·ess *n.*
archiduquesa
arch·duke *n.* archiduque
arch·er *n.* arquero
ar·cher·y *n.* ballestería
ar·che·type *n.* arquetipo
ar·chi·pel·a·go *n.*
archipiélago
ar·chi·tect *n.* arquitecto
ar·chi·tec·tur·al *adj.*
arquitectónico
ar·chi·tec·ture *n.*
arquitectura
ar·chive *n.* archivo
arch·priest *n.* arcipreste
arc·tic *adj.* ártico
ar·dent *adj.* ardiente;
fervoroso
ar·dor *n.* ardor
ar·du·ous *adj.* arduo; difícil
a·re·na *n.* arena
ar·gon *n.* argo
ar·got *n.* jerga
ar·gue *v.* razonar
ar·gu·ment *n.* disputa
ar·gu·men·ta·tive *adj.*
argumentador
ar·id *adj.* árido
a·rid·i·ty *n.* aridez
a·rise *v.* alzarse; surgir
ar·is·toc·ra·cy *n.*
aristocracia
a·ris·to·crat *n.* aristócrata
a·ris·to·crat·ic *adj.*
aristocrático
a·rith·me·tic *n.* aritmética
a·rith·me·ti·cian *n.*
aritmético
ark *n.* arca
arm *n.* brazo
ar·ma·da *n.* armada
ar·ma·dil·lo *n.* armadillo
ar·ma·ment *n.* armamento
arm·ful *n.* brazado
ar·mi·stice *n.* armisticio
ar·moire *n.* armario
ar·mor *n.* armadura
ar·mored *adj.* blindado
ar·mor·y *n.* armería
arm·pit *n.* sobaco
ar·my *n.* ejército
a·ro·ma *n.* aroma
ar·o·mat·ic *adj.* aromático

a·round *adv.* alrededor
a·rouse *v.* despertar; excitar
ar·range *v.* arreglar; prevenir
ar·range·ment *n.* orden
ar·ray *n.* orden; formación;
adorno; *v.* colocar; ataviar
ar·rest *v.* detener
ar·ri·val *v.* llegar
ar·ro·gance *n.* arrogancia
ar·ro·gant *adj.* arrogante
ar·row *n.* flecha
ar·row·head *n.* punta de
flecha
ar·sen·al *n.* arsenal
ar·sen·ic *n.* arsénico
ar·son *n.* incendio premeditado
art *n.* arte
ar·te·ri·al *adj.* arterial
ar·ter·y *n.* arteria
art·ful *adj.* ingenioso; astuto
ar·thrit·ic *adj.* artrítico
ar·thri·tis *n.* artritis
ar·ti·cle *n.* artículo; objeto
ar·tic·u·late *v.* articular
ar·tic·u·la·tion *n.*
articulación
ar·ti·fi·cial *adj.* artificial
ar·til·ler·y *n.* artillería
art·ist *n.* artista
ar·tis·tic *adj.* artístico
as *conj., adv.* como
as·bes·tos, as·bes·tus *n.*
asbesto
as·cend *v.* subir; ascender
as·cen·sion *n.* ascensión
as·cent *n.* subida; cuesta
as·cer·tain *v.* averiguar
as·ce·tic *adj.* ascético; *n.*
asceta
as·cet·i·cism *n.* ascetismo
as·cribe *v.* atribuir
a·sex·u·al *adj.* asexual
ash *n.* ceniza
a·shamed *adj.* avergonzado
a·side *adv.* a un lado; *n.*
aparte
as·i·nine *adj.* asnal
ask *v.* rogar; preguntar
a·skance *adv.* con recelo
a·slant *adv.* a través; *prep.*
a través de
a·sleep *adv., adj.* dormido
asp *n.* áspid
as·par·a·gus *n.* espárrago
as·pect *n.* aspecto; aire
as·per·i·ty *n.* aspereza

as·per·sion *n.* calumnia
as·phalt *n.* asfalto
as·phyx·i·ate *v.* asfixiar
as·pi·ra·tion *n.* aspiración;
anhelo
as·pire *v.* aspirar
as·pi·rin *n.* aspirina
ass *n.* burro; tonto
as·sail *v.* acometer
as·sail·ant *n.* asaltador
as·sas·sin *n.* asesino
as·sas·si·na·tion *n.*
asesinato
as·sault *v.* atacar
as·sem·ble *v.* juntar
as·sem·bly *n.* asamblea
as·sent *n.* asentimiento
as·sert *v.* afirmar
as·sess *v.* fijar; tasar
as·set *n.* haber
as·sev·er·ate *v.* aseverar
as·sid·u·ous *adj.* asiduo
as·sign *v.* asignar
as·sign·ment *n.* asignación
as·sim·i·late *v.* asimilar
as·sist *v.* ayudar
as·sist·ance *n.* ayuda
asth·ma *n.* asma
asth·mat·ic *adj.* asmático
as·ton·ish *v.* asombrar
as·ton·ish·ment *n.* asombro
as·trol·o·gy *n.* astrología
as·tron·o·my *n.* astronomía
at *prep.* a; en
ath·lete *n.* atleta
ath·let·ic *adj.* atlético
at·om *n.* átomo
a·tom·ic *adj.* atómico
a·top *prep.* sobre
at·tach *v.* pegar; sujetar
at·tack *v.* atacar
at·tempt *v.* intentar
at·tend *v.* asistir
at·ten·tion *n.* atención
a·typ·i·cal *adj.* atípico
au·di·ence *n.* público
au·di·tion *n.* audición
au·di·to·ry *adj.* auditivo
Au·gust *n.* agosto
aunt *n.* tía
au·then·tic·i·ty *n.*
autenticidad
au·thor *n.* autor
au·thor·i·ty *n.* autoridad
au·thor·ize *v.* autorizar
au·to·bi·og·ra·pher *n.*
autobiógrafo

au·to·bi·og·ra·phy *n.* autobiografía

au·to·ma·tic *adj.* automático

au·to·ma·tion *n.* automatización

au·to·mo·bile *n.* automóvil; coche

au·ton·o·mous *adj.* autónomo

a·venge *v.* vengar

av·e·nue *n.* avenida

a·ver *v.* afirmar

av·er·age *adj.* medio

a·vert *v.* apartar

a·wait *v.* esperar

a·wake *v.* despertar(se)

a·way *adv.* lejos

aw·ful *adj.* horrible

awk·ward *adj.* embarazoso

ax·i·om *n.* axioma

ax·i·o·mat·ic *adj.* axiomático

ax·is *n.* axis; eje

ax·le *n.* eje

aye, ay *interj., n.* sí

az·ure *adj., n.* azul celeste

B

bab·ble *v.* murmurar; barbotar; susurrar

ba·boon *n.* mandril

ba·bush·ka *n.* pañuelo

ba·by *n.* niño

ba·by·hood *n.* infancia

ba·by·ish *adj.* infantil

bac·cha·nal *n.* bacanal

bach·e·lor *n.* soltero

bach·e·lor·hood *n.* soltería

ba·cil·lus *n.* bacilo

back *n.* espalda

back·ache *n.* dolor de espalda

back·bit·ing *n.* murmuración

back·bone *n.* espinazo

back·break·ing *adj.* agobiador

back·date *v.* antedatar

back·er *n.* promotor

back·gam·mon *n.* juego de chaquete

back·ground *n.* fondo

back·hand·ed *adj.* revés

back·lash *n.* sacudida

back·pack *n.* mochila

back·side *n.* trasero

back·stairs *adj.* furtivo

back·track *v.* desandar

back·up *n.* suplente; reserva

back·ward *adv.* atrás

back·ward·ness *n.* retraso

ba·con *n.* tocino

bac·te·ri·al *adj.* bacteriano

bac·te·ri·cide *n.* bactericida

bac·ter·i·um *n.* bacteria

bad *adj.* malo

badge *n.* insignia

bad·ger *n.* tejón

bad·ly *adv.* mal

bad·min·ton *n.* juego de volante

baf·fle *v.* desconcertar; confundir

baf·fle·ment *n.* confusión

baf·fling *adj.* desconcertante

bag *n.* bolso; saco

bag·gage *n.* equipaje

bag·pipe *n.* gaita

bail *v.* afianzar

bail·iff *n.* alguacil

bail·or *n.* fiador

bait *n.* carnada

bake *v.* cocer en horno

bak·er *n.* panadero

bak·er·y *n.* panadería

bak·ing *n.* cocción

bal·ance *n.* equilibrio

bal·anced *adj.* balanceado

bal·co·ny *n.* balcón

bald *adj.* calvo

bald·ness *n.* calvicie

bale *n.* bala

bale·ful *adj.* funesto

balk *v.* oponerse

ball *n.* pelota

bal·lad *n.* balada

bal·le·ri·na *n.* bailarina

bal·let *n.* ballet

bal·lis·tic *adj.* balístico

bal·loon *n.* globo

bal·lot *n.* votación

balm *n.* bálsamo

bal·sa *n.* balsa

bam·boo *n.* bambú

ban *v.* prohibir

ba·nal *adj.* vulgar

ba·nan·a *n.* plátano

band *n.* banda

band·age *v.* vendar

ban·dit *n.* bandido

ban·do·leer *n.* bandolera

bane·ful *adj.* nocivo

bang *v.* golpear

bangs *n.* flequillo

ban·gle *n.* esclava

ban·ish *v.* desterrar

ban·ish·ment *n.* proscripción; exilio

ban·is·ter *n.* baranda

ban·jo *n.* banjo

bank *n.* banco

bank·er *n.* banquero

bank·ing *n.* banca

bank·rupt *adj.* arruinado

ban·ner *n.* bandera

ban·quet *n.* banquete

ban·ter *f.* broma

bap·tism *n.* bautismo

bap·tist *n.* bautista

bap·tis·ter·y *n.* baptisterio

bap·tize *v.* bautizar

bar *v.* excluir

bar·bar·i·an *adj.* bárbaro

bar·bar·ic *adj.* bárbaro

bar·bar·i·ty *n.* barbaridad

bar·ba·rous *adj.* bárbaro

bar·ber *n.* peluquero

bar·ber·shop *n.* peluquería

bar·bi·tu·ric *n.* barbitúrico

bare *adj.* desnudo; *v.* desnudar

bare·faced *adj.* descarado

bare·ly *adv.* simplemente; apenas

bar·gain *n.* ganga; convenio

bar·gain·ing *n.* negociación

barge *n.* gabarra

bar·i·tone *n.* barítono

bar·i·um *n.* bario

bark *v.* ladrar; *n.* ladrido

bar·ley *n.* cebada

bar·maid *n.* cantinera

barn *n.* granero

bar·na·cle *n.* percebe

ba·rom·et·er *n.* barómetro

bar·o·met·ric *adj.* barométrico

bar·on *n.* barón

bar·on·ess *n.* baronesa

ba·roque *adj.* barroco

bar·racks *n.* barraca

bar·rel *n.* barril

bar·ren *adj.* infecundo; infructuoso; yermo

bar·ri·cade *n.* barricada

bar·ri·er *n.* barrera

bar·tend·er *n.* camarero

bar·ter *v.* trocar

ba·sal *adj.* básico

ba·salt *n.* basalto

base *n.* base

base·ball *n.* béisbol

base·board *n.* zócalo

base·less *adj.* infundado

base·ment *n.* sótano

bash *v.* golpear

bash·ful *adj.* tímido

ba·sic *adj.* básico

ba·sic·i·ty *n.* basicidad

bas·il *n.* albahaca

ba·sil·i·ca *n.* basílica

ba·sin *n.* jofaina

ba·sis *n.* base

bask *v.* tomar el sol

bas·ket *n.* cesta

bas·ket·ball *n.* baloncesto

bas·ket·ry *n.* cestería

baste *v.* hilvanar

bat *v.* golpear; *n.* mazo

batch *n.* hornada

bate *v.* disminuir

bath *n.* baño

bathe *v.* bañar(se)

bath·ing·suit *n.* traje de baño

bath·tub *n.* bañera

ba·ton *n.* batuta

bat·tal·ion *n.* batallón

bat·ter *v.* estropear; golpear

bat·ter·y *n.* batería

bat·tle *v.* luchar; *n.* lucha

bat·tle·ground *n.* campo de batalla

bat·tle·ship *n.* acorazado

bau·ble *n.* baratija

baud *n.* baudio

bawl *v.* llorar

bay *n.* bahía

bay·o·net *n.* bayoneta

ba·zaar *n.* bazar

ba·zoo·ka *n.* bazuca

be *v.* estar; ser

beach *n.* playa

bea·con *n.* almenara; faro

bead *n.* abalorio

beak *n.* pico

beam *n.* rayo

bean *n.* fríjol; habichuela

bear *n.* oso; *v.* llevar

bear·a·ble *adj.* soportable

beard *n.* barba

beard·ed *adj.* barbudo

bear·er *n.* portador

bear·ing *n.* porte

beast *n.* bestia
beast·ly *adj.* bestial
beat *v.* vencer; golpear
beat·en *adj.* derrotado
beat·er *n.* batidor
be·a·tif·ic *adj.* beatífico
be·at·i·fy *v.* beatificar
beat·ing *n.* latido; paliza
be·at·i·tude *n.* beatitud
beau·ti·ful *adj.* hermoso
beau·ti·ful·ly *adj.*
  bellamente
beau·ti·fy *v.* embellecer
beau·ty *n.* belleza
bea·ver *n.* castor
be·cause *conj.* porque
beck·on *v.* llamar
be·come *v.* hacer(se)
be·com·ing *adj.* apropiado
bed *n.* cama
be·daz·zle *v.* deslumbrar
bed·cham·ber *n.* alcoba
bed·lam *n.* alboroto
bed·room. *n.* alcoba
bed·side *adj.* (de) cabecera
bee *n.* abeja
beech *n.* haya
beef·y *adj.* musculoso
bee·hive *n.* colmena
beer *n.* cerveza
bees·wax *n.* cera
beet *n.* remolacha
bee·tle *n.* escarabajo
be·fit *v.* convenir
be·fit·ting *adj.* conveniente
be·fore *prep.* antes de;
  adv. delante
be·fore·hand
  adv. de antemano
be·fud·dle *v.* confundir
beg *v.* pedir
beg·gar *n.* pobre
beg·gar·ly *adj.* miserable
be·gin *v.* comenzar
be·gin·ner *n.* novato
be·gin·ning *n.* comienzo
be·grudge *v.* envidiar
be·guile *v.* seducir
be·have *v.* funcionar;
  comportarse
be·hav·ior *n.*
  comportamiento
be·head *v.* descabezar
be·hind *adv.* atrás; detrás;
  prep. detrás de
be·hold *v.* contemplar
be·hold·en *adj.* obligado

be·hoove *v.* convenir
beige *adj.* beige
be·ing *n.* ser
be·la·bor *v.* machacar
be·lat·ed *adj.* tardío
be·lief *n.* fe
be·liev·a·ble *adj.* creíble
be·lieve *v.* creer
be·liev·er *n.* creyente
bell *n.* cascabel
bellflower *n.* campanilla
bel·lig·er·ence *n.*
  beligerancia
bel·lig·er·ent *adj.*
  beligerante
be·llow *v.* rugir
bel·ly *n.* estómago
be·long *v.* pertenecer
be·long·ings *n.* pertenencias
be·lov·ed *adj.* querido
be·low *adv.* abajo; *prep.*
  debajo de
belt *n.* cinturón
be·moan *v.* lamentar
bench *n.* banco
bend *v.* doblar; inclinar
bend·er *n.* juerga
be·neath *prep.* debajo de
ben·e·dic·tion *n.* bendición
ben·e·fac·tor *n.* bienhechor
ben·e·fice *n.* beneficio
ben·ef·i·cent *adj.* benéfico
ben·e·fi·cial *adj.* beneficioso
ben·e·fi·ci·ar·y *n.*
  beneficiario
ben·e·fit *n.* beneficio
be·nev·o·lence *n.*
  benevolencia
be·nev·o·lent *adj.* benévolo
be·nign *adj.* benigno
bent *adj.* empeñado; torcido
be·numb *v.* entorpecer
be·queath *v.* legar
be·quest *n.* legado
be·rate *v.* reprender
be·reave·ment *n.* duelo
be·reft *adj.* privado
ber·ry *n.* baya
berth *n.* camarote
be·ryl·li·um *n.* berilio
be·seech *v.* implorar
be·set *v.* acosar
be·side *prep.* cerca
be·sides *prep.* además de
be·siege *v.* asediar
be·smirch *v.* manchar
best *adj.* mejor

bes·tial *adj.* bestial
bes·ti·al·i·ty *n.* bestialidad
be·stow *v.* conceder
bet *n.* apuesta
be·to·ken *v.* presagiar
be·tray *v.* revelar
be·tray·al *n.* traición
be·trothed *n.* novio
bet·ter *adv., adj.* mejor
bet·ter·ment *n.*
  mejoramiento
bet·tor *n.* apostador
be·tween *adv.* en medio;
  prep. entre
bev·eled *adj.* biselado
bev·er·age *n.* bebida
bev·y *n.* grupo
be·wail *v.* lamentar
be·wil·der *v.* aturdir
be·wil·der·ment *n.*
  aturdimiento
be·witch *v.* hechizar
be·witch·ment *n.* hechizo
be·yond *prep.* después de
bi·an·nu·al *adj.* semestral
bi·as *n.* prejuicio
bib *n.* babero
Bi·ble *n.* Biblia
Bib·li·cal *adj.* bíblico
bib·li·og·ra·pher *n.*
  bibliógrafo
bib·li·og·ra·phy *n.*
  bibliografía
bib·li·o·phile *n.* bibliófilo
bi·car·bon·ate *n.*
  bicarbonato
bi·cen·ten·ni·al *adj.*
  bicentenario
bi·ceps *n.* bíceps
bi·cy·cle *n.* bicicleta
bi·cy·clist *n.* biciclista
bid *n.* oferta; *v.* mandar
bid·ding *n.* oferta
bi·en·ni·al *adj.* bienal
bi·fo·cal *adj.* bifocal
bi·fur·cate *v.* bifucarse
bi·fur·ca·tion *n.* bifurcación
big *adj.* grande
big·a·mist *n.* bígamo
big·a·my *n.* bigamia
big·ness *n.* grandeza
bike *n.* bicicleta
bik·er *n.* motociclista
bi·lat·er·al *adj.* bilateral
bile *n.* bilis
bi·lin·gual *adj.* bilingüe
bil·ious *adj.* bilioso

bilk *v.* defraudar
bill *n.* pico; cuenta
bill·board *n.* cartelera
bil·let *v.* alojar
bill·fold *n.* cartera
bil·liards *n.* billar
bil·lion *n.* billón
bil·lion·aire *n.* billonario
bil·low *n.* oleada
bil·low·y *adj.* ondulante
bi·month·ly *adj.* bimestral
bin *n.* cajón
bi·na·ry *adj.* binario
bind *v.* encuadernar; atar
bind·er *n.* atadura;
  encuadernador
bind·ing *n.* ecuadernación
bin·oc·u·lar *n.* gemelos
bi·no·mi·al *adj.* binomio
bi·o·chem·i·cal *adj.*
  bioquímico
bi·o·chem·ist *n.* bioquímico
bi·o·chem·is·try *n.*
  bioquímica
bi·og·ra·pher *n.* biógrafo
bi·o·graph·ic *adj.* biográfico
bi·og·ra·phy *n.* biografía
bi·o·log·ic *adj.* biológico
bi·ol·o·gist *n.* biólogo
bi·ol·o·gy *n.* biología
bi·on·ics *n.* biónica
bi·o·phys·ics *n.* biofísica
bi·op·sy *n.* biopsia
bi·par·tite *adj.* bipartito
bi·ped *adj.* bípedo
bi·plane *n.* biplano
birch *n.* abedul
bird *n.* pájaro
bird·cage *n.* jaula
bird·seed *n.* alpiste
birth *n.* nacimiento
birth·day *n.* cumpleaños
bis·cuit *n.* bizcocho
bi·sect *v.* bisecar
bi·sec·tion *n.* bisección
bish·op *n.* obispo
bis·muth *n.* bismuto
bi·son *n.* bisonte
bit *n.* pedazo
bite *v.* picar
bit·ing *adj.* mordaz; cortante
bit·ter *adj.* cortante;
  implacable; amargo
bit·ter·ness *n.* rencor;
  encarnizamiento
bit·ter·sweet *adj.* agridulce
bi·tu·mi·nous *adj.*

bituminoso

bi·va·lent *adj.* bivalent

bi·valve *adj.* bivalvo

bi·week·ly *adj.* quincenal

bi·zarre *adj.* raro

blab·ber *v.* cotorrear

black *adj.* negro

black-and-blue *adj.* amoratado

black·ber·ry *n.* zarzamora

black·bird *n.* mirlo

black·board *n.* pizarra

black·en *v.* difamar

black·head *n.* espinilla

black·mail *v.* chantajear

black·mail·er *n.* chantajista

black·smith *n.* herrero

black·top *n.* asfalto

blad·der *n.* vejiga

blade *n.* pala; hoja

blame *v.* culpar

bland *adj.* suave

blank *n., adj.* blanco

blan·ket *n.* manta

blare *v.* resonar

blas·pheme *v.* blasfemar

blas·phe·mous *adj.* blasfemo

blas·phe·my *n.* blasfemia

blast *v.* destruir; *n.* explosión

blast·ed *adj.* maldito

bla·tant *adj.* ruidoso

blaze *n.* hoguera; llamarada; *v.* arder

bleach *n.* lejía; *v.* blanquear

bleach·ers *n.* gradas

blear *adj.* nublado

bleat *v.* balar

bleed *v.* sangrar

blem·ish *v.* manchar

blend *n.* mezcla; *v.* mezclar

blend·er *n.* licuadora

bless *v.* bendecir

bless·ed *adj.* santo

bless·ing *n.* bendición

blind *v.* cegar; *adj.* ciego

blind·ers *n.* anteojeras

blind·ing *adj.* cegador

blind·ly *adv.* ciegamente

blind·ness *n.* ceguera

blink *v.* pestañear; ceder

blink·ing *adj.* parpadeante

bliss *n.* felicidad

bliss·ful *adj.* feliz

blis·ter *v.* ampollar(se)

blis·ter·ing *adj.* forzado; abrasador

bliz·zard *n.* ventisca

block *n.* manzana; bloque

block·ade *n.* obstrucción

blond *adj.* rubio

blonde *adj.* rubia

blood *n.* sangre

blood·less *adj.* exangüe

blood·thirst·y *adj.* sanguinario

blood·y *adj.* sangriento

bloom *v.* florecer

blos·som *n.* flor

blot *n.* mancha

blotch *n.* mancha

blouse *n.* blusa

blow *v.* inflar; soplar

blow·gun *n.* cerbatana

blow·torch *n.* soplete

blow·up *n.* explosión

bludg·eon *v.* aporrear

blue *adj.* azul

blue·bell *n.* campanilla

blue·print *n.* cianotipo

blunt *adj.* abrupto

blur·ry *adj.* confuso

blush *n.* sonrojo

blus·ter *v.* bramar

boar *n.* verraco

board *n.* consejo

board·er *n.* pensionista

board·ing·house *n.* pensión

boast *v.* alardear

boast·ful *adj.* jactancioso

boast·ing *n.* jactancia

boat *n.* barco

boat·man *n.* lanchero

bob·ber *n.* flotador

bob·bin *n.* bobina

bod·ice *n.* cuerpo

bod·i·ly *adj.* corporal

bod·y *n.* cuerpo

bod·y·guard *n.* guardaespaldas

bog *n.* ciénaga

bo·gus *adj.* falso

boil *v.* cocer; hervir

boil·er *n.* caldera

boil·ing *adj.* hirviente

bois·ter·ous *adj.* ruidoso; bullicioso

bold *adj.* descarado; intrépido

bol·ster *v.* apoyar

bolt *n.* pestillo; rayo

bomb *n.* bomba

bom·bard *v.* acosar; bombardear

bom·bard·ment *n.* bombardeo

bomb·er *n.* bombardero

bomb·ing *n.* bombardero

bomb·shell *n.* bomba

bo·nan·za *n.* bonanza

bond *n.* atadura; bono

bone *n.* hueso

bon·fire *n.* hoguera

bon·net *n.* gorra

bo·nus *n.* sobresueldo

bon·y *adj.* huesudo

book *n.* libro

book·bind·ing *n.* encuadernación

book·end *n.* sujetalibros

book·ing *n.* reservación

book·sell·er *n.* librero

book·store *n.* librería

boom *n.* prosperidad

boo·mer·ang *n.* bumerang

boor *n.* patán

boor·ish *adj.* tosco

boost *v.* levantar

boot *n.* bota

booth *n.* puesto; cabina

boot·leg *v.* contrabandear

boo·ty *n.* botín

bor·der *n.* borde; frontera

bor·der·line *n.* frontera

bore *v.* aburrir

bore·dom *n.* aburrimiento

bor·ing *adj.* aburrido

born *adj.* nacido

bor·ough *n.* municipio

bor·row *v.* apropiarse

bor·row·er *n.* prestatario

bos·om *n.* pecho

boss *n.* jefe

bo·tan·ic *adj.* botánico

bot·a·nist *n.* botánico

botch *v.* chapucear

both *adj.* los dos

both·er *v.* molestar(se)

both·er·some *adj.* molesto

bot·tle *n.* botella

bot·tom *n.* base; fondo

bot·tom·less *adj.* sin fondo

bot·u·lism *n.* botulismo

bough *n.* rama

bouil·lon *n.* caldo

boul·e·vard *n.* avenida

bounce *v.* rebotar

bounc·ing *adj.* fuerte

bound *v.* saltar

bound·a·ry *n.* límite

bound·less *adj.* ilimitado

boun·te·ous *adj.* abundante

boun·ti·ful *adj.* generoso

boun·ty *n.* generosidad

bou·quet *n.* ramo

bour·geois *n.* burgués

bout *n.* ataque

bo·vine *n.* bovino

bow *v.* inclinarse; doblegarse

bow·el *n.* intestino

bowl *n.* tazón; fuente

bowl·ing *n.* bolos

box *n.* caja

box·er *n.* boxeador

box·ing *n.* boxeo

boy *n.* chico; niño

boy·cott *v.* boicotear

boy·friend *n.* novio

bra *n.* sostén

brace *n.* puntal

brace·let *n.* brazalete

brac·ing *adj.* fortificante

brack·et *n.* corchete

brack·ish *adj.* salobre

brag *v.* jactarse

brain *n.* cerebro

brain·y *adj.* listo

brake *v.* frenar

bran *n.* salvado

branch *n.* rama

brand *n.* modo; marca

brand·ing *n.* hierra

bran·dish *v.* blandir

bran·dy *n.* coñac

brash *adj.* insolente; impetuoso

brass *n.* latón

bras·siere *n.* sostén

brass·y *adj.* descarado

brave *adj.* valiente

brav·er·y *n.* valor

brawn·y *adj.* musculoso

bra·zen *adj.* descarado

bra·zier *n.* brasero

breach *n.* ruptura; violación

bread *n.* pan

bread·bas·ket *n.* panera

breadth *n.* extensión

break *v.* quebrar; romper

break·a·ble *adj.* rompible

break·age *n.* rotura

break·down *n.* depresión; desglose

break·fast *n.* desayuno

break·through *n.* adelanto

break·up *n.* desintegración; separación

breast *n.* pecho

breast·bone n. esternón
breath n. respiración
breathe v. respirar
breath·ing n. respiración
breath·tak·ing adj. impresionante
breed v. criar; reproducirse
breed·er n. criador
breed·ing v. crianza
breeze n. brisa
breez·y adj. ventoso
brev·i·ty n. brevedad
brew·er n. cervecero
brew·er·y n. cervecería
bribe n. soborno
brick n. ladrillo
brick·lay·er n. albañil
bri·dal n. boda
bride n. novia
bridge n. puente
bri·dle n. brida
brief adj. breve
brief·case n. cartera
brief·ing n. reunión
bri·gade n. brigada
bright adj. brillante
bright·en v. iluminar(se)
bright·ness n. lustre
bril·liance n. brillo
bril·liant adj. brillante
brim n. borde
bring v. traer
bri·quet n. briqueta
brisk adj. vigoroso
bris·tle n. cerda
brit·tle adj. frágil
broach n. broche
broad adj. extenso; ancho
broad·cast v. transmitir; emitir
broad·cast·ing n. trasmisión
broad·en v. ensanchar(se)
broad·mind·ed adj. comprensivo
bro·cade n. brocado
broc·co·li n. brécol
bro·chure n. folleto
bro·ken adj. roto; quebrado
bro·ken·down adj. decrépito
bro·ker·age n. corretaje
bro·mide n. bromuro
bro·mine n. bromo
bron·chi·al adj. bronquial
bron·chi·tis n. bronquitis
bronze n. bronce

brook n. arroyo
broom n. escoba
broth n. caldo
broth·el n. burdel
broth·er n. hermano
broth·er·hood n. fraternidad
broth·er·in·law n. cuñado
broth·er·ly adj. fraterno
brow n. ceja
brown adj. moreno
brown·out n. parcial
browse v. pacer; curiosear
bruise n. contusión
brunt n. impacto
brush n. cepillo
bru·tal adj. brutal
bru·tal·i·ty n. brutalidad
bru·tal·ize v. brutalizar
brute n. bruto
buc·ca·neer n. bucanero
buck·et n. balde
buck·le n. hebilla
bud n. yema
bud·dy n. compadre
budge v. ceder
budg·et v. presupuestar
buf·fa·lo n. búfalo
buff·er n. interceser
buf·fet n. bofetada
buf·foon n. bufón
bug n. bicho
bu·gle n. clarín
build v. construir
build·er n. constructor
build·ing n. contrucción
bulb n. bulbo
bulge n. bulto
bulk·y adj. pesado
bull n. toro
bull·dog n. buldog
bull·doz·er n. excavadora
bul·let n. bala
bul·le·tin n. boletín
bull·fight·er n. torero
bul·rush n. espadaña
bul·wark n. baluarte
bum·ble·bee n. abejorro
bump n. choque
bump·y adj. agitado
bun n. bollo
bunch n. racimo
bun·dle n. fajo; bulto
bun·ny n. conejito
buoy n. boya
buoy·ant adj. boyante
bur n. erizo

bur·den n. carga
bu·reauc·ra·cy n. burocracia
bu·reau·crat n. burócrata
burg·er n. hamburguesa
bur·glar n. ladrón
bur·glar·ize v. robar
bur·i·al n. entierro
bur·lap n. arpillera
bur·ly adj. robusto
burn v. incendiar
burn·er n. quemador
burn·ing adj. ardiente
burn·out n. extinción
burnt adj. quemado
burp n. eructo
bur·ro n. burro
burst v. romper
bur·y v. enterrar
bus n. autobús
bus·boy n. ayudante
bush n. arbusto
bushed adj. agotado
busi·ness n. oficio
but conj. pero
but·ter n. mantequilla
but·ter·fly n. mariposa
buy v. comprar
buy·er n. comprador
by adv. cerca; prep. cerca de; por

C

cab n. taxi
ca·bal n. cábala
cab·a·la n. cábala
cab·a·ret n. cabaret
cab·bage n. col
cab·driv·er n. taxista
cab·in n. cabaña
cab·i·net n. gabinete
cab·i·net·mak·er n. ebanista
cab·i·net·work n. ebanistería
ca·ble n. cable
ca·ble·gram n. cablegrama
ca·ca·o n. cacao
cack·le n. cacareo
cac·tus n. cacto
ca·dav·er n. cadáver
ca·dav·er·ous adj. cadavérico
cad·die n. caddy
ca·dence n. cadencia

ca·det n. cadete
cad·mi·um n. cadmio
ca·du·ce·us n. caduceo
ca·fe n. café
caf·e·te·ri·a n. cafetería
caf·feine n. cafeína
caf·tan n. túnica
cage n. jaula
ca·jole v. engatusar
cake n. pastel
cal·a·bash n. calabaza
cal·a·mine n. calamina
ca·lam·i·ty n. calamidad
cal·ci·fi·ca·tion n. calcificación
cal·ci·fy v. calcificar
cal·ci·um n. calcio
cal·cu·late v. calcular
cal·cu·lat·ed adj. intencional
cal·cu·lat·ing adj. calculador
cal·cu·la·tion n. cálculo
cal·cu·la·tor n. calculadora
cal·dron n. caldera
cal·en·dar n. calendario
cal·i·ber n. calibre
cal·i·brate v. calibrar
cal·i·bra·tion n. calibración
cal·i·co n. calicó
ca·liph n. califa
cal·is·then·ics n. calistenia
ca·lix n. cavidad
call v. llamar
cal·lig·ra·pher n. calígrafo
cal·lig·ra·phy n. caligrafía
call·ing n. vocación
cal·lous v. encallecerse
cal·low adj. inmaduro
cal·lus n. callo
calm v. calmar(se); n. calma
calm·ness n. traquilidad
ca·lor·ic adj. calórico
cal·o·rie n. caloría
ca·lum·ni·ate v. calumniar
cal·va·ry n. calvario
ca·lyx n. cáliz
ca·ma·ra·der·ie n. camaradería
cam·bi·um n. cambium
cam·el n. camello
ca·mel·lia n. camelia
cam·e·o n. camefeo
cam·er·a n. cámara
cam·ou·flage n. camuflaje
camp v. acampar
cam·paign n. capaña

camp·er *n.* campista
cam·phor *n.* alcanfor
can *v.* poder
ca·nar·y *n.* canario
can·cel *v.* cancelar; matar; anular
can·cel·la·tion *n.* cancelación
can·cer *n.* cáncer
can·cer·ous *adj.* canceroso
can·did *adj.* franco
can·di·da·cy *n.* candidatura
can·di·date *n.* candidato
can·died *adj.* escarchado
can·dle *n.* cirio; vela
can·dle·hold·er *n.* candelero
can·dle·stick *n.* candelero
can·dor *n.* franqueza
can·dy *n.* azúcar
cane *n.* caña; bastón
ca·nine *adj.* canino
can·is·ter *n.* lata
canned *adj.* enlatado
can·ni·bal *n.* caníbal
can·ni·bal·ism *n.* canibalismo
can·ni·bal·is·tic *adj.* caníbal
can·non *n.* cañón
ca·noe *n.* canoa
ca·non·i·za·tion *n.* canonización
can·on·ize *v.* canonizar
can·ta·loupe *n.* cantalupo
can·teen *n.* cantina
can·vas *n.* lona
can·yon *n.* cañón
cap *n.* tapa
ca·pa·bil·i·ty *n.* capacidad
ca·pa·ble *adj.* capaz
ca·pa·cious *adj.* espacioso
ca·pac·i·ty *n.* capacidad
ca·per *n.* cabriola
cap·il·lar·y *n.* capilar
cap·i·tal *n., adj.* capital
cap·i·tal·ism *n.* capitalismo
cap·i·tal·ist *n.* capitalista
cap·i·tal·is·tic *adj.* capitalista
cap·i·tal·i·za·tion *n.* capitalización
cap·i·tal·ize *v.* capitalizar
cap·i·tal·ly *adv.* admirablemente
cap·i·tol *n.* capitolio
ca·pi·tu·late *v.* capitular
ca·price *n.* capricho
ca·pri·cious *adj.* caprichoso

cap·sule *n.* cápsula
cap·tain *n.* capitán
cap·tion *n.* subtítulo
cap·tious *adj.* capcioso
cap·ti·vate *v.* cautivar
cap·ti·va·tion *n.* encanto
cap·tive *adj.* cautivo
cap·tiv·i·ty *n.* cautividad
cap·tor *n.* captor
cap·ture *v.* capturar
car *n.* coche
car·a·mel *n.* caramelo
car·at *n.* quilate
car·a·van *n.* caravana
car·bide *n.* carburo
car·bine *n.* carabina
car·bo·hy·drate *n.* carbohidrato
car·bon *n.* carbono
car·bun·cle *n.* carbunclo
car·bu·re·tor *n.* carburador
car·cin·o·gen·ic *adj.* cancerígeno
card *n.* tarjeta
car·di·ac *adj.* cardíaco
car·di·nal *adj.* cardinal
car·di·o·gram *n.* cardiograma
car·di·ol·o·gy *n.* cardiología
care *v.* cuidar
ca·reer *n.* carrera
care·free *adj.* despreocupado
care·ful *adj.* cuidadoso
care·less *adj.* espontáneo; descuidado
ca·ress *n.* caricia
care·tak·er *n.* portero
car·go *n.* carga
car·i·ca·ture *n.* caricatura
car·nage *n.* carnicería
car·nal *adj.* carnal
car·ni·val *n.* carnaval
car·ni·vore *n.* carnívoro
car·niv·o·rous *adj.* carnívoro
ca·rous·al *n.* jarana
car·ou·sel *n.* carrusel
car·pen·try *n.* carpintería
car·pet *n.* alfombra
car·riage *n.* carruaje
car·ri·er *n.* carrero
car·rot *n.* zanahoria
car·ry *v.* logra; llevar
car·sick *adj.* mareado
cart *n.* carro
cart·age *n.* acarreo
car·tel *n.* cartel

car·ti·lage *n.* cartílago
cart·load *n.* carretado
car·toon *n.* tira
car·toon·ist *n.* caricaturista
car·tridge *n.* cartucho
carve *v.* esculpir
carv·ing *n.* escultura
case *n.* caja
cash *n.* efectivo
cash·ew *n.* anacardo
cash·ier *n.* cajero
cash·mere *n.* cachemira
ca·si·no *n.* casino
cask *n.* barril
cas·se·role *n.* cacerola
cas·sette *n.* casete
cast *v.* dar; fundir; echar
cas·ta·nets *n.* castañuelas
caste *n.* casta
cas·ti·gate *v.* castigar
cas·tle *n.* castillo
cas·trate *v.* castrar
cas·tra·tion *n.* castración
ca·su·al *adj.* casual
cas·u·al·ly *adv.* casualmente
ca·su·ist·ry *n.* casuística
cat *n.* gato
ca·tab·o·lism *n.* catabolismo
cat·a·log *n.* catálogo
cat·a·lyst *n.* catalizador
cat·a·lyt·ic *adj.* catálítico
cat·a·lyze *v.* catapulta
cat·a·ract *n.* catarata
ca·tas·tro·phe *n.* catástrofe
cat·a·stroph·ic *adj.* catastrófico
cat·a·ton·ic *adj.* catatónico
catch *v.* prender; coger
catch·er *n.* receptor
catch·ing *adj.* contagioso
catch·y *adj.* capcioso
cat·e·chism *n.* catecismo
cat·e·gor·ic *adj.* categórico
cat·e·gor·i·cal·ly *adv.* categóricamente
cat·e·go·rize *v.* clasificar
cat·e·go·ry *n.* categoría
cat·er·pil·lar *n.* oruga
cat·er·waul *v.* chillar
ca·thar·sis *n.* catarsis
ca·the·dral *n.* catedral
cath·ode *n.* cátodo
cath·o·lic *adj.* católico
ca·thol·i·cism *n.* catolicismo
cat·nip *n.* nébeda
cat·tail *n.* espadaña
cat·tle *n.* ganado

cat·tle·man *n.* ganadero
cau·li·flow·er *n.* coliflor
cau·sa·tion *n.* causalidad
caus·a·tive *adj.* causativo
cause *n.* razón; causa
cause·way *n.* elevada
caus·tic *adj.* cáustico
cau·ter·ize *v.* cauterizar
cau·tion *v.* amonestar
cau·tion·ar·y *adj.* preventivo
cau·tious *adj.* cauteloso
cav·al·ry *n.* cabellería
cave *n.* cueva
cav·ern *n.* caverna
cav·ern·ous *adj.* cavernoso
cav·i·ty *n.* cavidad
ca·vort *v.* cabriolar
cay *n.* cayo
cease *v.* suspender
cease·less *adj.* continuo
ce·dar *n.* cedro
cede *v.* ceder
ceil·ing *n.* techo
cel·e·brant *n.* celebrante
cel·e·brate *v.* celebrar
cel·e·brat·ed *adj.* célebre
cel·e·bra·tion *n.* celebración
ce·leb·ri·ty *n.* celebridad
cel·er·y *n.* apio
ce·les·tial *adj.* celestial
cel·i·ba·cy *n.* celibato
cel·i·bate *adj.* célibe
cell *n.* celda
cel·lar *n.* sótano
cel·lo·phane *n.* celofán
cel·lu·lar *adj.* celular
cel·lu·loid *n.* celuloide
cel·lu·lose *n.* celulosa
ce·ment *n.* cemento
cem·e·ter·y *n.* cementerio
cen·ser *n.* incensario
cen·sor *n.* censor
cen·so·ri·ous *adj.* censurado
cen·sor·ship *n.* censura
cen·sure *v.* censurar
cen·sus *n.* censo
cent *n.* centavo
cen·taur *n.* centauro
cen·ten·ni·al *adj.* centenario
cen·ter *n.* centro
cen·ti·grade *adj.* centígrado
cen·ti·gram *n.* centigramo
cen·ti·li·ter *n.* centilitro
cen·ti·me·ter *n.* centímetro
cen·tral *adj.* central
cen·tral·ize *v.* centralizar(se)

cen·tric *adj.* céntrico

cen·trif·u·gal *adj.* centrífugo

cen·tu·ry *n.* siglo

ce·phal·ic *adj.* cefálico

ce·ram·ic *adj.* cerámico

ce·re·al *n.* cereal

cer·e·bral *adj.* cerebral

cer·e·brum *n.* cerebro

cer·e·mo·ni·al *adj.* ceremonial

cer·e·mo·ni·ous *adj.* ceremonioso

cer·e·mo·ny *n.* ceremonia

cer·tain *adj.* seguro; cierto

cer·tain·ly *adv.* ciertamente

cer·tain·ty *n.* certeza

cer·ti·fi·a·ble *adj.* certificable

cer·tif·i·cate *n.* certificado

cer·ti·fi·ca·tion *n.* certificación

cer·ti·fied *adj.* certificado

cer·ti·fy *v.* certificar

cer·ti·tude *n.* certidumbre

cer·vix *n.* cerviz

ces·sa·tion *n.* cesación

ces·sion *n.* cesión

chafe *v.* frotar; rozar

cha·grin *v.* desilusionar

chain *n.* cadena

chair *n.* silla

chair·man *n.* presidente

chair·man·ship *n.* presidencia

chair·wo·man *n.* presidenta

cha·let *n.* chalet

chal·ice *n.* cáliz

chalk *n.* tiza

chalk·board *n.* pizarra

chal·lenge *v.* desafiar

chal·leng·er *n.* desafiador

cham·ber·lain *n.* chambelán

cha·me·leon *n.* camaleón

champ *n.* campeón

cham·pi·on·ship *n.* campeonato

chance *n.* oportunidad; casualidad

chan·cel·ler·y *n.* cancillería

chan·cel·lor *n.* canciller

change *v.* transformar; cambiar

change·a·ble *adj.* cambiable

change·o·ver *n.* cambio

chang·er *n.* cambiador

chan·nel *n.* canal

chant *n.* canto

cha·os *n.* caos

cha·ot·ic *adj.* caótico

chap·el *n.* capilla

chap·er·one *n.* carabina

chap·lain *n.* capellán

chap·ter *n.* capítulo

char·ac·ter *n.* carácter

char·ac·ter·is·tic *n.* característica

char·ac·ter·ize *v.* caracterizar

char·coal *n.* carboncillo

charge *v.* pedir; cargar

cha·ris·ma *n.* carisma

char·i·ta·ble *adj.* caritativo

char·i·ty *n.* caridad

charm *n.* encanto

charm·er *n.* encantador

chart *v.* trazar

char·ter *n.* carta

chase *v.* perseguir

chaste *adj.* casto

chas·ten *v.* castigar

chas·ti·ty *n.* castidad

chat *v.* charlar

chau·vin·ist *n.* chauvinista

chau·vin·is·tic *adj.* chauvinista

cheap *adj.* barato

cheap·ness *n.* tacañería

cheat *v.* engañar

cheat·er *n.* tramposo

check *n.* cheque; parada; cuenta

check·book *n.* chequera

check·ered *adj.* a cuadros

cheek *n.* mejilla

cheep *n.* gorjeo

cheer *v.* alegrar; alentar

cheer·ful *adj.* alegre

cheer·i·ly *adv.* alegremente

cheer·less *adj.* triste

cheese *n.* queso

cheese·cake *n.* quesadilla

chef *n.* cocinero

chem·i·cal *n.* químico

chem·ist *n.* químico

chem·is·try *n.* química

che·mo·ther·a·py *n.* quimioterapia

cher·ish *v.* abrigar; querer

cher·ry *n.* cerezo

cher·ub *n.* querubín

che·ru·bic *adj.* querúbico

chess *n.* ajedrez

chest *n.* pecho

chest·nut *n.* castaña

chew *v.* masticar

chew·ing *n.* masticación

chick·en *n.* pollo

chick·pea *n.* garbanzo

chief *n.* jefe

chif·fon *n.* gasa

child *n.* hijo; niño

child·birth *n.* parto

child·ish *adj.* aniñado

child·like *adj.* infantil

chil·i *n.* chile

chill *n.* frío

chill·ing *adj.* frío

chime *n.* campaneo

chim·ney *n.* chimenea

chim·pan·zee *n.* chimpancé

chin *n.* barba

chi·na *n.* china

chip *n.* astilla; *v.* astillar

chip·per *adj.* jovial

chi·ro·prac·tor *n.* quiropráctico

chirp *v.* gorjear

chis·el *n.* cincel

chis·el·er *n.* cincelador

chiv·al·rous *adj.* caballeresco

chiv·al·ry *n.* cabellerosidad

chive *n.* cebollino

chlo·ride *n.* cloruro

choc·o·late *n.* chocolate

choice *adj.* selecto; *n.* preferencia

choir *n.* coro

choke *v.* ahogar; atorar; estrangular

chol·er·a *n.* cólera

chol·er·ic *adj.* colérico

cho·les·ter·ol *n.* colesterol

chomp *v.* ronzar

choose *v.* escoger

choos·ing *n.* selección

chop *v.* cortar

cho·ral *n.* coral

cho·re·og·ra·pher *n.* coreógrafo

cho·re·og·ra·phy *n.* coreografía

cho·sen *adj.* escogido

chow *n.* comida

Christ *n.* Cristo

chris·ten *v.* bautizar

chris·ten·ing *n.* cristiano

Chris·tian *n.* cristiano

Chris·ti·an·i·ty *n.* cristianismo

Christ·mas *n.* Navidad

chro·mat·ic *adj.* cromático

chrome *n.* cromo

chro·mi·um *n.* cromo

chro·mo·some *n.* cromosoma

chron·ic *adj.* crónico

chron·i·cle *n.* crónica

chron·o·log·ic *adj.* cronológico

chro·nol·o·gy *n.* cronología

chrys·a·lis *n.* crisálida

chry·san·the·mum *n.* crisantemo

chum *n.* compañero

chunk *n.* trozo

church *n.* iglesia

church·man *n.* clérigo

churn *n.* mantequera

chute *n.* conducto; rampa

ci·ca·da *n.* cigarra

ci·der *n.* sidra

ci·gar *n.* puro

cig·a·rette *n.* cigarrillo

cinch *n.* cincha

cin·der *n.* carbonilla

cin·e·ma *n.* cine

cin·e·mat·ic *adj.* fílmico

cin·e·ma·tog·ra·phy *n.* cinematografía

cin·na·mon *n.* canela

ci·pher *v.* cifrar

cir·cle *n.* ciclo

cir·cuit *n.* circuito

cir·cu·lar *adj.* circular

cir·cu·lat·ing *adj.* circulante

cir·cu·la·tion *n.* circulación

cir·cum·cise *v.* circuncidar

cir·cum·cised *adj.* circunciso

cir·cum·ci·sion *n.* circuncisión

cir·cum·fer·ence *n.* circunferencia

cir·cum·nav·i·gate *v.* circunnavegar

cir·cum·scribe *v.* circunscribir

cir·cum·spect *adj.* circunspecto

cir·cum·stance *n.* circunstancia

cir·cum·stan·tial *adj.* circunstancial

cir·cus *n.* circo

cir·rho·sis *n.* cirrosis

cir·rus *n.* cirro

cis·tern *n.* cisterna
cit·a·del *n.* ciudadela
ci·ta·tion *n.* citación
cite *v.* citar
cit·i·zen *n.* ciudadano
cit·ric *adj.* cítrico
cit·y *n.* ciudad
civ·et *n.* civeta
civ·ic *adj.* cívico
civ·il *adj.* civil
ci·vil·i·ty *n.* civilidad
civ·i·li·za·tion *n.* civilización
civ·i·lize *v.* civilizar
claim *v.* merecer; reclamar
clair·voy·ance *n.* clarividencia
clair·voy·ant *adj.* clarividente
clam *n.* almeja
clam·or *n.* clamor
clam·or·ous *adj.* clamoroso
clamp *n.* abrazadera
clan *n.* clan
clan·gor *n.* estruendo
clap *v.* aplaudir
clap·per *n.* badajo
clap·ping *n.* aplausos
clar·et *n.* clarete
clar·i·fi·ca·tion *n.* clarificación
clar·i·fy *v.* clarificar
clar·i·net *n.* clarinete
clar·i·on *adj.* sonoro
clar·i·ty *n.* claridad
clash *v.* entrechocarse
class *n.* clase
clas·sic *adj.* clásico
clas·si·cal *adj.* clásico
clas·si·cism *n.* clasicismo
clas·si·cist *n.* clasicista
clas·si·fi·ca·tion *n.* clasificación
clas·si·fied *adj.* clasificado
clas·si·fy *v.* clasificar
class·y *adj.* elegante
clause *n.* cláusula
claus·tro·pho·bi·a *n.* claustrofobia
clav·i·chord *n.* clavicordio
clav·i·cle *n.* clavícula
claw *n.* garra
clay *n.* arcilla
clean *v.* limpiar
clean·cut *adj.* definido
clean·er *n.* limpiador
clean·ing *n.* limpieza
cleanse *v.* limpiar

cleans·er *n.* limpiador
clear *adj.* despejado; transparente
clear·cut *adj.* claro
clear·ing *n.* claro
clear·ly *adv.* claramente
cleav·age *n.* división
cleave *v.* adherir; partir
cleav·er *n.* cuchilla
clem·en·cy *n.* clemencia
cler·gy *n.* clero
cler·gy·man *n.* clérigo
cler·ic *adj.* clérigo
cler·i·cal *adj.* clerical
clerk *n.* oficinista
clev·er *adj.* listo
clev·er·ness *n.* inteligencia
cli·ent *n.* cliente
cli·mac·tic *adj.* culminante
cli·mate *n.* clima
cli·mat·ic *adj.* climático
cli·max *n.* clímax
climb *v.* trepar
climb·er *n.* alpinista
climb·ing *adj.* trepador
clin·ic *n.* clínica
clin·i·cal *adj.* clínico
cli·ni·cian *n.* clínico
clip *v.* cortar
cloak *n.* manto
clock *n.* reloj
clog *n.* atasco
clois·ter *n.* claustro
clone *n.* clón
close *v.* cerrar
closed *adj.* cerrado; vedado
close·down *n.* cierre
close·ly *adv.* atentamente; de cerca
close·ness *n.* proximidad
close·out *n.* liquidación
clos·et *n.* armario
clos·ing *n.* cierre
clot *n.* cóagulo
cloth *n.* tela
clothe *n.* tela
clothe *v.* arropar
clothes *n.* ropa
cloth·ing *n.* ropa
cloud *n.* nube
cloud·burst *n.* aguacero
cloud·y *adj.* nuboso
clout *n.* bofetada
clo·ver *n.* trébol
clown *n.* payaso
club *n.* palo
clue *n.* pista

clump *n.* grupo
clum·sy *adj.* pesado
coach *n.* vagón; coche
coach·man *n.* cochero
co·ag·u·late *v.* coagular(se)
co·ag·u·la·tion *n.* coagulación
coal *n.* carbón
co·a·lesce *v.* unirse
co·a·li·tion *n.* coalición
coarse *adj.* tosco
coars·en *v.* vulgarizar
coarse·ness *n.* vulgaridad
coat *n.* pelo
coat·ed *adj.* bañado
coat·ing *n.* capa; baño
coat·tail *n.* faldón
coax *v.* engatusar
coax·ing *n.* engatusamiento
cob *n.* elote
co·balt *n.* cobalto
cob·bler *n.* zapatero
co·bra *n.* cobra
cob·web *n.* telaraña
co·caine *n.* cocaína
coc·cyx *n.* cóccix
cock *n.* gallo
cock·ade *n.* escarapela
cock·a·too *n.* cacatúa
cock·i·ness *n.* presunción
cock·le *n.* berberecho
cock·pit *n.* cancha
cock·roach *n.* cucaracha
cock·tail *n.* coctel
co·coa *n.* cacao
co·co·nut *n.* coco
co·coon *n.* capullo
code *n.* código
co·de·fend·ant *n.* coacusado
co·deine *n.* codeína
cod·fish *n.* bacalao
cod·i·fy *v.* codificar
co·di·rec·tion *n.* codirección
co·ed *adj.* coeducacional
co·ed·u·ca·tion *n.* coeducación
co·ed·u·ca·tion·al *adj.* coeducacional
co·ef·fi·cient *n.* coeficiente
co·erce *v.* coercer
co·er·cion *n.* coerción
co·ex·ist *v.* coexistir
co·ex·is·tence *n.* coexistencia
co·ex·ten·sive *adj.* coextenso
cof·fee *n.* café

cof·fer *n.* cofre
cof·fin *n.* ataúd
cog *n.* diente
cog·i·tate *v.* meditar
cog·nac *n.* coñac
cog·ni·tion *n.* cognición
cog·ni·zance *n.* conocimiento
cog·ni·zent *adj.* enterado
co·hab·it *v.* cohabitar
co·here *v.* adherirse
co·her·ence *n.* coherencia
co·her·ent *adj.* coherente
co·he·sion *n.* cohesión
co·he·sive *adj.* cohesivo
co·hort *n.* cohorte
coil *n.* rollo
coin *v.* acuñar; *n.* moneda
co·in·cide *v.* coincidir
co·in·ci·dence *n.* coincidencia
co·in·ci·den·tal *adj.* coincidente
co·la *n.* cola
col·an·der *n.* colador
cold *n., adj.* frío
cold·blood·ed *adj.* de sangrefria
cold·heart·ed *adj.* insensible
cold·ness *n.* frialdad
col·ic *n.* cólico
col·i·se·um *n.* coliseo
co·li·tis *n.* colitis
col·lab·o·rate *v.* colaborar
col·lab·o·ra·tion *n.* colaboración
col·lab·o·ra·tion·ist *n.* colaboracionista
col·lab·o·ra·tive *adj.* cooperativo
col·lab·o·ra·tor *n.* colaborador
col·lage *n.* collage
col·lapse *v.* desplomarse; caerse
col·laps·i·ble *adj.* plegable
col·lar *n.* cuello
col·lar·bone *n.* clavícula
col·late *v.* colacionar
col·lat·er·al *adj.* colateral
col·league *n.* colega
col·lect *v.* recoger; reunir; coleccionar
col·lect·ed *adj.* sosegado
col·lec·tion *n.* colección
col·lec·tive *adj.* colectivo

col·lec·tiv·ist n. colectivista
col·lec·tiv·ize v. colectivizar
col·lec·tor n. colector
col·lege n. colegio
col·le·gian n. estudiante
col·le·giate adj.
  universitario
col·lide v. chocar
col·li·sion n. choque
col·loid n. coloide
col·lo·qui·al adj. familiar
col·lo·qui·um n. coloquio
col·lude v. confabularse
col·lu·sion n. cofabulación
co·logne n. colonia
colo·nel n. coronel
co·lo·ni·al adj. colonial
co·lo·ni·al·ist n. colonialista
col·o·nist n. colonizador
col·o·ni·za·tion n.
  colonización
col·o·nize v. colonizar
col·o·niz·er n. colonizador
col·on·nade n. columnata
col·o·ny n. colonia
col·or v. colerear; n. color
col·or·a·tion n. coloración
col·ored adj. coloreado
col·or·ful adj. pintoresco
col·or·ing n. coloración
col·or·less adj. incoloro
co·los·sal adj. coloso
co·los·to·my n. colostomía
col·umn n. columna
col·umn·ist n. columnista
co·ma n. coma
co·ma·tose adj. comatoso
comb v. peinar; n. peine
com·bat v. combatir
com·bat·ant n. combatiente
com·bi·na·tion n.
  combinación
com·bine v. combinar
com·bo n. conjunto
com·bus·ti·ble adj.
  combustible
com·bus·tion n. combustión
come v. llegar; venir
come·back n. reaparición
co·me·di·an n. comediante
co·me·di·enne n.
  comedianta
com·e·dy n. comedia
come-on n. incentivo
com·et n. cometa
com·fort v. confortar
com·fort·a·ble adj.

confortable
com·fort·er n. consolador
com·ic adj. cómico
com·i·cal adj. cómico
com·ing adj. venidero
com·ma n. coma
com·mand n. mando;
  v. mandar
com·man·dant n.
  comandante
com·mand·er n.
  comandante
com·mand·ing adj.
  imponente
com·man·do n. comando
com·mem·o·rate v.
  conmemorar
com·mem·o·ra·tion n.
  conmemoración
com·mence v. comenzar
com·mence·ment n.
  comienzo
com·mend v. encomendar
com·men·da·tion n.
  recomendación
com·men·su·rate adj.
  proporcionado
com·ment n. observación
com·men·tar·y n.
  comentario
com·men·tate v. comentar
com·merce n. comercio
com·mer·cial adj. comercial
com·mer·cial·ism n.
  comercialismo
com·mer·cial·ize v.
  comercializar
com·mis·er·ate v.
  compadecerse
com·mis·sar n. comisario
com·mis·sar·y n.
  economato
com·mis·sion v. encargar;
  n. comisión
com·mis·sion·er n.
  comisario
com·mit v. entregar
com·mit·ment n.
  compromiso
com·mit·tal n. obligación
com·mit·ee n. comité
com·mode n. cómoda
com·mo·dore n. comodoro
com·mon adj. común
com·mon·place adj.
  ordinario
com·mon·wealth n.

comunidad
com·mo·tion n. tumulto
com·mu·nal adj. comunal
com·mune v. comulgar
com·mu·ni·ca·ble adj.
  comunicable
com·mu·ni·cate v.
  comunicar(se)
com·mu·ni·ca·tion n.
  comunicación
com·mu·ni·ca·tive adj.
  comunicativo
com·mu·ni·ca·tor n.
  comunicante
com·mun·ion n. comunión
com·mu·nism n.
  comunismo
com·mun·ist n. comunista
com·mu·nis·tic adj.
  comunista
com·mu·ni·ty n. comunidad
com·mu·ta·tive adj.
  conmutativo
com·mute v. conmutar
com·pact adj. compacto
com·pan·ion n. compañero
com·pan·ion·ship n.
  compañerismo
com·pa·ny n. compañía
com·pa·ra·ble adj.
  comparable
com·par·a·tive adj.
  comparativo
com·pare v. comparar
com·par·i·son n.
  comparación
com·part·ment n.
  compartimiento
com·pass n. compás
com·pas·sion n. compasión
com·pas·sion·ate adj.
  compasivo
com·pat·i·ble adj.
  compatible
com·pa·tri·ot n.
  compatriota
com·pel v. obligar; imponer
com·pel·ling adj.
  incontestable
com·pen·sate v. compensar
com·pen·sa·tion n.
  compensación
com·pete v. competir
com·pe·tence n.
  competencia
com·pe·tent adj.
  competente

com·pe·ti·tion n.
  competencia
com·pe·ti·tive adj.
  competitivo
com·pe·ti·tor n. competidor
com·pi·la·tion n.
  compilación
com·pile v. compilar
com·plain v. quejarse
com·plain·ant n.
  demandante
com·plaint n. queja
com·plai·sant adj.
  complaciente
com·ple·ment n.
  complemento
com·ple·men·ta·ry adj.
  complementario
com·plete adj. completo
com·ple·tion n. terminación
com·plex adj. complejo
com·plex·ion n. carácter
com·plex·i·ty n.
  complejidad
com·pli·ance n.
  conformidad
com·pli·ant adj. obediente
com·pli·cate v. complicar
com·pli·cat·ed adj.
  complicado
com·pli·ca·tion n.
  complicación
com·plic·i·ty n. complicidad
com·pli·ment n. honor;
  elogio
com·pli·men·tar·y adj.
  elogioso
com·ply v. obedecer
com·po·nent n.
  componente
com·port·ment n.
  comportamiento
com·pose v. redactar
com·posed adj. tranquilo
com·pos·er n. compositor
com·pos·ite adj. compuesto
com·po·si·tion n.
  composición
com·po·sure n. serenidad
com·pound adj. compuesto
com·pre·hend v.
  comprender
com·pre·hen·si·ble adj.
  comprensible
com·pre·hen·sive adj.
  comprensivo; general
com·press n. compresa

com·pressed *adj.*
comprimido
com·pres·sion *n.*
compresión
com·prise *v.* constar de;
comprender
com·pro·mise *n.*
compromiso; *v.* componer
com·pro·mis·ing *adj.*
comprometedor
com·pul·sion *n.* compulsión
com·pul·so·ry *adj.*
compulsorio
com·pu·ta·tion *n.* cálculo
com·pute *v.* computar
com·pu·ter *n.* computador
com·put·er·ize *v.*
computarizar
com·rade *n.* camarada
con *adv.* contra
con·cave *adj.* cóncavo
con·ceal *v.* ocultar
con·ceal·ment *n.*
encubrimiento
con·cede *v.* conceder
con·ceit·ed *adj.* vanidoso
con·ceiv·a·ble *adj.*
concebible
con·ceive *v.* concebir
con·cen·trate *v.*
concentrar(se)
con·cen·tra·tion *n.*
concentración
con·cen·tric *adj.*
concéntrico
con·cept *n.* concepto
con·cep·tion *n.* concepción
con·cep·tu·al *adj.*
conceptual
con·cern *v.* concernir
con·cerned *adj.* preocupado
con·cern·ing *prep.*
acerca de
con·cert *n.* concierto
con·cert·ed *adj.* conjunto
con·ces·sion *n.* concesión
con·cil·i·ate *v.* conciliar
con·cil·i·a·tion *n.*
conciliación
con·cise *adj.* conciso
con·clude *v.* concluir
con·clu·sion *n.* conclusión
con·clu·sive *adj.*
concluyente
con·coc·tion *n.* confección
con·cord *n.* concordia
con·crete *adj.* concreto

con·cur *v.* concurrir
con·cur·rence *n.*
concurrencia
con·cur·rent *adj.*
concurrente
con·cus·sion *n.* concusión
con·dem·na·ble *adj.*
condenable
con·den·sa·tion *n.*
condensación
con·dense *v.* condensar(se)
con·dens·er *n.* condensador
con·de·scend·ing *adj.*
condescendiente
con·di·ment *n.* condimento
con·di·tion *v.* condicionar
con·done *v.* condonar
con·duc·tor *n.* cobrador
con·fed·er·a·cy *n.*
confederación
con·fer *v.* conferenciar
con·fess *v.* confesar
con·fide *v.* confiar
con·fi·dence *n.* confianza
con·fi·den·tial *adj.*
confidencial
con·firm *v.* confirmar
con·flict *v.* chocar
con·form·i·ty *n.*
conformidad
con·fron·ta·tion *n.*
confrontación
con·fuse *v.* confundir
con·fu·sion *n.* confusión
con·gest *v.* acumular
con·ges·tion *n.* congestión
con·glom·er·a·tion *n.*
conglomeración
con·grat·u·la·tion *n.*
felicitación
con·gre·gate *v.*
congregar(se)
con·junc·tion *n.* conjución
con·jure *v.* conjurar
con·nect *v.* conectar
con·no·ta·tion *n.*
connotación
con·note *v.* connotar
con·sec·u·tive *adj.*
consecutivo
con·serv·a·to·ry *n.*
conservatorio
con·serve *v.* conservar
con·sid·er *v.* considerar
con·sid·er·a·tion *n.*
consideración
con·sist *v.* consistir

con·sol·i·date *v.* consolidar
con·sol·i·da·tion *n.*
consolidación
con·sist *v.* consistir
con·stan·cy *n.* constancia
con·stant *adj.* continuo
con·sti·tu·tion *n.*
constitución
con·struc·tion *n.*
construcción
con·sult *v.* consultar
con·sume *v.* consumir
con·sump·tion *n.* consumo
con·tain *v.* contener
con·tam·i·na·tion *n.*
contaminación
con·tem·plate *v.* proyectar
con·tem·po·rar·y *n.*
contemporáneo
con·tend *v.* afirmar;
contender
con·ti·nen·tal *adj.*
continental
con·tin·gen·cy *n.*
contingencia
con·tin·ue *v.* seguir;
continuar
con·trac·tion *n.* contracción
con·tra·dict *v.* contradecir
con·trast *v.* contrastar
con·tri·bu·tion *n.*
contribución
con·trol *v.* dirigir; controlar
con·va·lesce *v.* convalecer
con·verge *v.* convergir
con·ver·sa·tion *n.*
conversación
con·verse *v.* conversar
con·ver·sion *n.* conversión
con·vey *v.* llevar
con·vic·tion *n.* convicción
con·vince *v.* convencer
con·vul·sion *n.* convulsión
cook *n.* cocinero; *v.* cocinar
cook·ie *n.* galleta
cool *adj.* fresco
co·or·di·nate *v.* coordinar
co·or·di·na·tion *n.*
coordinación
cop·per *n.* cobre
cop·y *v.* copiar
cor·dial·i·ty *n.* cordialidad
corn *n.* maíz
cor·po·ral *adj.* corporal
cor·po·ra·tion *n.*
corporación
cor·pu·lent *adj.* gordo

cor·pus·cu·lar *adj.*
corpuscular
cor·ral *v.* acorralar
cor·rect *v.* corregir
cor·rec·tion *n.* corrección
cor·re·spond *v.* escribir
cor·re·spond·ence *n.*
correspondencia
cor·rode *v.* corroer
cor·ro·sion *n.* corrosión
cor·rup·tion *n.* corrupción
cos·met·ic *n.* cosmético
cos·mic *adj.* cósmico
cost *v.* costar; *n.* precio
couch *n.* sofá
count *n.* cuenta; *v.* contar
coun·try *n.* campo; país
cou·ple *n.* pareja
cou·ra·geous *adj.* valiente
course *n.* plato; dirección
cous·in *n.* prima; primo
cov·er *n.* cubierta; *v.* cubrir
cow *n.* vaca
cow·boy *n.* vaquero
coy·o·te *n.* coyote
crab *n.* cangrejo
crack·er *n.* galleta
cra·dle *v.* mecer
crash *n.* choque; estallido
crate *n.* cajón
cra·ter *n.* cráter
crave *v.* ansiar
crav·ing *n.* anhelo
crawl *v.* gatear; arrastrarse
cray·on *n.* lápiz de color
craze *v.* enloquecer
crazed *adj.* loco
cra·zy *adj.* loco
cream *n.* crema
cream·y *adj.* cremoso
crease *v.* doblar
cre·ate *v.* producir; crear
cre·a·tion *n.* creación
cre·a·tive *adj.* creador
cre·a·tiv·i·ty *n.* originalidad
cre·a·tor *n.* creador
crea·ture *n.* criatura
cre·dence *n.* crédito
cre·den·tial *n.* credencial
cred·i·ble *adj.* creíble
cred·it *n.* crédito;
reconocimiento
cred·it·a·ble *adj.* loable
cred·u·lous *adj.* crédulo
creed *n.* credo
creep·y *adj.* espeluznante
cre·mate *v.* incinerar

cre·ma·tion *n.* incineración
crepe *n.* crespón
cres·cent *n.* medialuna
crest *n.* cresta
cre·tin *n.* cretino
crew *n.* equipo
crib *n.* pesebre
crick·et *n.* grillo
crime *n.* crimen
crim·i·nal *n., adj.* criminal
crin·kle *v.* arrugar(se)
crip·ple *v.* mutilar
cri·sis *n.* crisis
crisp *adj.* crespo
crisp·y *adj.* crujiente
crit·ic *n.* crítico
crit·i·cism *n.* crítica
crit·i·cize *v.* criticar
cri·tique *n.* crítica
croc·o·dile *n.* cocodrilo
cro·cus *n.* azafrán
crook *n.* curba, ladrón
crook·ed *adj.* corvo
cross *v.* cruzar; *n.* cruz
cross·beam *n.* traviesa
cross·bow *n.* ballesta
cross·cur·rent *n.*
  contracorriente
cross·ex·am·ine *v.*
  interrogar
cross·ing *n.* cruce
cross·word puz·zle *n.*
  crucigrama
crouch *v.* acuclillarse
crow *v.* cacarear
crowd *n.* gentío; multitud
crowd·ed *adj.* concurrido
crown *n.* corona
crown·ing *n.* coronación
cru·ci·ble *n.* crisol
cru·ci·fix *n.* crucifijo
cru·ci·fix·ion *n.* crucifixión
cru·ci·fy *v.* crucificar
crude *adj.* tosco; ordinario;
  crudo
crude·ness *n.* tosquedad
cru·el *adj.* cruel
cru·el·ty *n.* crueldad
cruise *v.* navegar
crumb *n.* migaja
crum·ble *v.* desmigajar(se)
crum·ple *v.* estrujar(se)
crunch·y *adj.* crujiente
cru·sade *n.* cruzada
cru·sad·er *n.* cruzado
crush *v.* aplastar
crust *n.* costra; corteza

crus·ta·cean *n.* crustáceo
crust·y *adj.* costroso
cry *v.* llorar
crypt *n.* cripta
crys·tal *n.* cristal
crys·tal·line *adj.* cristalino
crys·tal·lize *v.* cristalizar(se)
crys·tal·log·ra·phy *n.*
  cristalografía
cube *n.* cubo
cu·bic *adj.* cúbico
cu·bi·cle *adj.* cubículo
cu·bi·cle *n.* compartimiento
cub·ist *n.* cubista
cu·cum·ber *n.* pepino
cud·dle *v.* abrazar(se)
cue *n.* taco
cu·li·nar·y *adj.* culinario
cul·mi·nate *v.* culminar
cul·pa·ble *adj.* culpable
cul·prit *n.* culpable
cult *n.* culto
cul·ti·vate *v.* cultivar
cul·ti·va·tion *n.* cultivo
cul·ti·va·tor *n.* cultivador
cul·tur·al *adj.* cultural
cul·ture *n.* cultura
cul·tured *adj.* culto
cum·ber *v.* embarazar
cum·ber·some *adj.*
  embarazoso
cu·mu·late *v.* acumular
cu·mu·la·tive *adj.*
  acumulativo
cun·ning *adj.* hábil; astuto
cup *n.* taza
cup·ful *n.* taza
cur·a·ble *adj.* curable
curb *n.* bordillo
curd *n.* cuajada
cure *n.* cura
cu·ri·os·i·ty *n.* curiosidad
cu·ri·ous *adj.* curioso
curl *v.* enrollar(se); rizar(se)
cur·ren·cy *n.* moneda
cur·rent *n., adj.* corriente
cur·rent·ly *adj.* actualmente
curse *n.* desgracia; maldición
curs·ed *adj.* maldito
cur·sor *n.* cursor
cur·tain *n.* telón
cur·va·ture *n.* curvatura
curve *n.* curva
curved *n.* curva
curved *adj.* curvo
cus·to·di·an *n.* custodio
cus·to·dy *n.* custodia

cus·tom *n.* costumbre
cus·tom·ar·i·ly *adv.*
  acostumbrada mente
cut *adj.* cortado; *n.,*
  cortadura; *v.* cortar
cu·ta·ne·ous *adj.* cutáneo
cute *adj.* mono
cu·ti·cle *n.* cutícula
cut·ler·y *n.* cubiertos
cy·a·nide *n.* cianuro
cy·cle *n.* ciclo
cy·clic *adj.* cíclico
cy·clist *n.* ciclista
cy·clone *n.* ciclón
cyl·in·der *n.* cilindro
cy·lin·dri·cal *adj.* cilíndrico
cym·bal *n.* címbalo
cyn·i·cal *adj.* cínico
cyn·i·cism *n.* cinismo
cy·press *n.* ciprés
cyst *n.* quiste
cys·tic *adj.* cístico
cys·ti·tis *n.* cistitis
cy·to·plasm *n.* citoplasma
czar *n.* zar
cza·ri·na *n.* zarina

D

dab *v.* tocar ligeramente
dab·ble *v.* salpicar
dad *n.* papá
daft *adj.* loco
dag·ger *n.* puñal
dai·ly *adj.* diario
dain·ti·ness *n.* delicadeza
dain·ty *adj.* delicado
dair·y *n.* lechería; quesería
dair·y·man *n.* lechero
da·is *n.* estrado
dale *n.* valle
dal·li·ance *n.* diversión
dal·ly *v.* perder tiempo;
  entretenerse
dam *v.* represar; *n.* presa
dam·age *v.* dañar; perjudicar
damn *v.* condenar
dam·na·ble *adj.* detestable
damned *adj.* condenado
damp *adj.* húmedo
damp·en *v.* mojar
dance *n.* baile; *v.* bailar
dan·cer *n.* bailador
dan·druff *n.* caspa
dan·ger *n.* peligro
dan·ger·ous *adj.* peligroso

dan·gle *v.* colgar
dank *adj.* húmedo
dap·pled *adj.* rodado
dare *v.* arriesgarse
dar·ing *n.* atrevimiento
dark *n.* oscuridad; *adj.*
  oscuro
dark·en *v.* oscurecer
dark·ness *n.* oscuridad
darl·ing *n.* querido
darn *v.* zurcir
dash *v.* precipitarse; romper
dash·board *n.* tablero de
  instrumentos
date *n.* cita; fecha
daub *v.* pintarrajear
daugh·ter *n.* hija
daugh·ter-in-law *n.* nuera
daunt·less *adj.* impávido
daw·dle *v.* perder el tiempo
dawn *v.* amanecer
day *n.* día
day·break *n.* amanecer
day·dream *n.* ensueño
day·light *n.* luz del día
day·time *n.* día
daze *v.* aturdir
daz·zle *v.* deslumbrar
dea·con *n.* diácono
dea·con·ry *n.* diaconía
dead *adj.* muerto
dead·en *v.* amortiguar
dead-end *n.* calle sin salida
dead·ly *adj.* mortal
deaf *adj.* sordo
deaf·en *v.* ensordecer
deal *n.* cantidad; trato;
  reparto
deal·er *n.* tratante
dean *n.* decano; deán
dear *adj.* querido; caro
dear·ness *n.* carestía
death *n.* muerte
death·less *adj.* inmortal
death·ly *adj.* mortal
de·ba·cle *n.* fracaso
de·bar *v.* prohibir
de·bate *v.* debatir
de·bauch *v.* corromper
de·bauch·er·y *n.* libertinaje
de·bil·i·tate *v.* debilitar
de·bil·i·ta·tion *n.*
  debilitación
de·bil·it·y *n.* debilidad
deb·it *n.* debe
deb·o·nair *adj.* cortés;
  elegante

de·bris *n.* escombros
debt *n.* deuda
debt·or *n.* deudor
de·but, de·but *n.* presentación; estreno
deb·u·tant, deb·u·tante *n.* debutante
de·cade *n.* decenio
dec·a·dence *n.* decadencia
dec·a·dent *adj.* decadente
de·can·ter *n.* garrafa
de·cay *v.* decaer; cariarse; deteriorar
de·cease *v.* morir
de·ceased *adj.* muerto
de·ceit·ful *adj.* engañoso
de·ceive *v.* engañar
De·cem·ber *n.* diciembre
de·cen·cy *n.* decencia
de·cent *adj.* decente
de·cep·tion *n.* fraude
de·cide *v.* decidir
de·cid·ed·ly *adv.* decididamente
dec·i·mal *n.* decimal
de·ci·pher *v.* descifrar
de·ci·sion *n.* decisión; firmeza
de·ci·sive *adj.* decisivo
de·ci·sive·ly *adv.* con resolución
deck *v.* adornar
dec·la·ra·tion *n.* declaración
de·clare *v.* declarar
de·cline *v.* rehusar
de·com·pose *v.* descomponer(se)
de·com·po·si·tion *n.* descomposición
dec·o·rate *v.* adornar; condecorar
dec·o·ra·tion *n.* decoración; ornato
dec·o·ra·tor *n.* decorador
de·coy *n.* señuelo
de·crease *v.* disminuir(se)
de·creas·ing·ly *adv.* en disminución
de·cree *n.* decreto
de·crep·it *adj.* decrépito
de·cry *v.* rebajar
de·duce *v.* deducir
de·duct *v.* restar
de·duc·tion *n.* descuento
deed *n.* hecho
deem *v.* juzgar
deep *adj.* profundo

deep·en *v.* intensificar
de·face *v.* desfigurar
def·a·ma·tion *n.* difamación
de·fame *v.* difamar
de·fault *n.* a falta de
de·feat *n.* derrota; *v.* vencer; frustrar
de·fect *n.* defecto
de·fec·tion *n.* defección
de·fec·tive *adj.* defectuoso
de·fend *v.* defender
de·fend·ant *n.* demandado
de·fense, de·fence *n.* defensa
de·fen·sive *adj.* defensivo
de·fer *v.* diferir; aplazar
def·er·ence *n.* deferencia
de·fer·ment *n.* aplazamiento
de·fi·ance *n.* desafío
de·fi·ant *adj.* provocativo
de·fi·cien·cy *n.* deficiencia
de·fi·cient *adj.* insuficiente
def·i·cit *n.* déficit
de·file *v.* manchar
de·fine *v.* definir
def·i·nite *adj.* concreto; definido
def·i·ni·tion *n.* definición
de·fin·i·tive *adj.* definitivo
de·flate *v.* desinflar
de·fla·tion *n.* desinflación
de·flect *v.* desviar
de·form·i·ty *n.* deformidad
de·fraud *v.* defraudar; estafar
de·fray *v.* pagar
deft *adj.* diestro
deft·ness *n.* habilidad
de·funct *adj.* difunto
de·fy *v.* desafiar; contravenir
de·gen·er·ate *v.* degenerar
deg·ra·da·tion *n.* degradación
de·grade *v.* degradar
de·gree *n.* rango
de·hy·drate *v.* deshidratar
de·hy·dra·tion *n.* deshidratación
de·i·fy *v.* deificar
deign *v.* dignarse
de·i·ty *n.* deidad
de·ject·ed *adj.* abatido
de·jec·tion *n.* melancolía; abatimiento
de·lay *v.* aplazar; demorar
de·lec·ta·ble *adj.* deleitable
del·e·gate *v.* delegar
del·e·ga·tion *n.* diputación

de·lete *v.* tachar
de·le·tion *n.* supresión; borradura
de·lib·er·ate *v.* deliberar
del·i·ca·cy *n.* delicadeza
del·i·cate *adj.* delicado; fino
de·li·cious *adj.* delicioso
de·light *v.* deleitar
de·light·ful *adj.* encantador
de·lin·e·ate *v.* delinear
de·lin·e·a·tion *n.* bosquejo
de·lin·quen·cy *n.* delincuencia
de·lin·quent *adj.* delincuente
de·lir·i·ous *adj.* delirante
de·lir·i·um *n.* delirio
de·liv·er *v.* entregar
de·liv·er·y *n.* entrega
del·ta *n.* delta
de·lude *v.* engañar
del·uge *n.* diluvio
de·lu·sion *n.* engaño; ilusión
de·luxe *adj.* de lujo
delve *v.* cavar
de·mand *v.* demandar; exigir
de·moc·ra·cy *n.* democracia
dem·o·crat *n.* demócrata
dem·o·crat·ic *adj.* democrático
dem·on·strate *v.* demostrar
dem·on·stra·tion *n.* demostración
de·mor·al·ize *v.* desmoralizar
den *n.* estudio
de·nom·i·na·tion *n.* denominación
de·nom·i·na·tor *n.* denominador
de·note *v.* denotar
de·nounce *n.* denunciar
dense *adj.* denso
den·si·ty *n.* densidad
den·tist *n.* dentista
de·nun·ci·ate *v.* denunciar
de·nun·ci·a·tion *n.* denuncia
de·par·ture *n.* salida
de·pend·en·cy *n.* dependencia
de·port *v.* deportar
de·por·ta·tion *n.* deportación
de·prave *v.* depravar
de·praved *adj.* depravado
de·pres·sion *n.* desaliento

depth *n.* fondo
de·ride *v.* mofar
de·ri·sion *n.* irrisión
der·i·va·tion *n.* derivación
de·rive *v.* derivar(se)
der·rick *n.* grúa
de·scend *v.* bajar; descender
de·scend·ant *n.* descendiente
de·scribe *v.* describir
de·scrip·tion *n.* descripción
de·scrip·tive *adj.* descriptivo
des·ert *n.* desierto
de·sert·er *n.* desertor
de·serve *v.* merecer
de·sign *v.* idear; diseñar
des·ig·nate *v.* señalar; nombrar
des·ig·na·tion *n.* nombramiento
de·sign·er *n.* diseñador; dibujante
de·sire *v.* desear
de·sist *v.* desistir
desk *n.* pupitre
des·o·la·tion *n.* desolación
de·spair *v.* desesperar
des·per·ate *adj.* desesperado; arriesgado
des·per·a·tion *n.* desesperación
des·pi·ca·ble *adj.* despreciable
de·spise *v.* despreciar
de·spite *prep.* a pesar de
des·sert *n.* postre
de·stroy *v.* destruir
de·struct·i·ble *adj.* destructible
de·struc·tion *n.* destrucción
de·tain *v.* retener
de·ter *v.* disuadir
de·ter·mi·na·tion *n.* determinación
de·test·a·ble *adj.* detestable
de·val·u·a·tion *n.* devaluación
dev·as·tate *v.* devastar
dev·as·ta·tion *n.* devastación
de·vel·op *v.* desenvolver
de·vice *n.* ingenio; estratagema
dev·il *n.* diablo
de·vi·ous *adj.* tortuoso
de·vise *v.* inventar

de·void *adj.* desprovisto
de·vote *v.* dedicar
dev·o·tee *n.* devoto
dev·o·tion *n.* devoción; lealtad
de·vour *v.* devorar
di·a·be·tes *n.* diabetes
di·a·bet·ic *adj.* diabético
di·ag·nose *v.* diagnosticar
di·a·bol·ic *adj.* diabólico
di·a·dem *n.* diadema
di·ag·nose *v.* diagnosticar
di·ag·no·sis *n.* diagnóstico
di·ag·o·nal *adj., n.* diagonal
di·a·gram *n.* diagrama
di·a·lect *n.* dialecto
di·am·e·ter *n.* diámetro
di·a·met·ric *adj.* diametral
dia·mond *n.* diamante
dia·per *n.* pañal
di·a·phragm *n.* diafragma
di·ar·rhe·a *n.* diarrea
di·a·ry *n.* diario
dice *n.* dados
dick·er *v.* regatear
dic·tate *v.* mandar; dictar
dic·ta·tion *n.* dictado
dic·ta·tor *n.* dictador
dic·tion·ar·y *n.* diccionario
die *v.* morir
dif·fer·ence *n.* diferencia
dif·fer·ent *adj.* diferente
dif·fi·cult *adj.* difícil
dif·fi·cul·ty *n.* dificultad
dig *n.* excavación; *v.* extraer
di·ges·tion *n.* digestión
dig·it *n.* dedo
dig·ni·fy *v.* dignificar
di·lem·ma *n.* dilema
dil·i·gence *n.* diligencia
dil·i·gent *adj.* diligente
di·lute *v.* diluir
di·lu·tion *n.* dilución
dim *adj.* oscuro
di·min·ish *v.* disminuir(se)
dine *v.* cenar
din·ner *n.* cena
di·plo·ma·cy *n.* diplomacia
dip·lo·mat *n.* diplomático
dip·lo·mat·ic *adj.* diplomático
di·rect *v.* dirigir; *adj.* directo
di·rec·tion *n.* dirección
di·rec·tor *n.* director
dis·a·ble *v.* inutilizar
dis·ap·pear *v.* desaparecer
dis·ap·pear·ance *n.*

desaparición
dis·as·trous *adj.* desastroso
dis·a·vow *v.* desconocer
dis·charge *v.* despedir
dis·ci·pli·nar·y *adj.* disciplinario
dis·ci·pline *v.* disciplinar; *n.* castigo
dis·con·nect *v.* desconectar
dis·con·tin·u·ous *adj.* discontinuo
dis·cov·er *v.* descubrir
dis·crep·an·cy *n.* discrepancia
dis·cus·sion *n.* discusión
dis·ease *n.* enfermedad
dis·guise *n.* disfraz; *v.* disfrazar
dish *n.* plato
dis·hon·or *v.* deshonrar
dis·hon·or·a·ble *adj.* deshonroso
dis·in·fect·ant *n.* desinfectante
dis·in·ter·est *n.* desinterés
disk *n.* disco
dis·lo·cate *v.* dislocar
dis·lo·ca·tion *n.* dislocación
dis·o·bey *v.* desobedecer
dis·or·der *n.* desorden
dis·pense *v.* dispensar
dis·play *n.* demostrar
dis·pute *n.* disputa; *v.* disputar
dis·qual·i·fy *v.* descalificar
dis·solve *v.* disolver(se)
dis·suade *v.* disuadir
dis·sua·sion *n.* disuasión
dis·tance *n.* distancia
dis·tant *adj.* distante
distill *v.* destilar
dis·till·er·y *n.* destilería
dis·tinc·tion *n.* distinción
dis·tin·guish *v.* distinguir
dis·tract *v.* distraer
dis·trac·tion *n.* distracción
dis·tri·bu·tion *n.* distribución
dis·turb *v.* perturbar
dis·turb·ance *n.* disturbio
di·verge *v.* divergir
di·ver·gence *n.* divergencia
di·ver·sion *n.* diversión
di·vert *v.* divertir
di·ver·si·ty *n.* diversidad
di·vide *v.* dividir(se)
di·vin·i·ty *n.* divinidad

di·vide *v.* dividir(se)
diz·zy *adj.* mareado
do *v.* cumplir; hacer
doc·tor *n.* médico
doc·u·ment *n.* document; *v.* documentar
dog *n.* perro
dog·mat·ic *adj.* dogmático
doll *n.* muñeca
dol·lar *n.* dólar
do·mes·tic *adj.* doméstico
do·mes·ti·cate *v.* domesticar
dom·i·nant *v.* dominar
dom·i·na·tion *n.* dominación
dom·i·neer *v.* tiranizar
dom·i·neer·ing *adj.* dominante
do·min·ion *n.* dominio
don *v.* ponerse
do·nate *v.* donar
done *adj.* hecho
do·nor *n.* donante
doom *n.* juicio; suerte
door *n.* puerta
dope *n.* narcótico
dor·mi·to·ry *n.* dormitorio
dor·sal *adj.* dorsal
dos·age *n.* dosificación
dose *n.* dosis
dot *n.* punto
dot·age *n.* chochez
dou·ble *v.* doblar(se)
doubt *n.* duda; *v.* dudar
dough *n.* maza
dough·nut *n.* buñuelo
dour *adj.* austero
douse *v.* mojar; zambullir
dow·a·ger *n.* viuda de un titulado
dow·dy *adj.* desaliñado; poco elegante
down *prep., adv.* abajo
down·cast *adj.* abatido
down·fall *n.* caída
down·heart·ed *adj.* desanimado
down·ward *adv.* hacia abajo
doze *v.* dormitar
doz·en *n.* docena
drab *adj.* monótono
draft *n.* giro
drag *v.* arrastrar
drag·on *n.* dragón
drain *v.* agotar; desaguar

drain·age *n.* desagüe; drenaje
dra·ma *n.* drama
dra·mat·ic *adj.* dramático
dram·a·tist *n.* dramaturgo
dram·a·tize *v.* dramatizar
drape *v.* poner colgaduras
dra·per·y *n.* colgadura
dras·tic *adj.* drástico; enérgico
draw *v.* sacar; dibujar; arrastrar
draw·back *n.* desventaja
draw·bridge *n.* puente levadizo
draw·er *n.* cajón
dread *v.* temer
dread·ful *adj.* terrible
dream *v.* soñar; *n.* sueño
dream·er *n.* soñador
dredge *v.* dragar
dreg *n.* heces
drench *v.* empapar
dress *n.* vestido; *v.* vestir(se)
dress·er *n.* aparador
drib·ble *v.* caer gota a gota
drift *n.* impulso de la corriente; montón
drift·wood *n.* madera llevada por el agua
drill *v.* taladrar
drink *n.* bebida; *v.* beber
drip *v.* gotear
drive *v.* manejar; empujar; conducir
driz·zle *v.* lloviznar
droll *adj.* gracioso
drone *n.* zángano
drool *v.* babear
droop *v.* inclinar
drop *n.* gota; declive
drop·sy *n.* hidropesía
dross *n.* escoria
drought *n.* sequía
drown *v.* ahogar; anegar
drowse *v.* adormecer(se)
drow·sy *adj.* soñoliento
drudg·er·y *n.* faena penosa
drug *n.* droga
drug·gist *n.* farmacéutico; boticario
drum *n.* tambor
drum·stick *n.* baqueta
drunk *adj.* borracho
drunk·ard *n.* borracho
drunk·en *adj.* borracho
du·al·i·ty *n.* dualidad

dub *v.* armar; apodar
du·bi·ous *adj.* dudoso
duch·ess *n.* duquesa
duck *n.* pato
duct *n.* conducto
dude *n.* petimetre
due *adj.* debido; oportuno
duel *n.* duelo
du·et *n.* dúo
duke *n.* duque
dull *adj.* embotado; torpe
dumb *adj.* mudo
dum·found *v.* pasmar
dum·my *n.* maniquí
dump *v.* descargar
dump·ling *n.* bola de masa
dunce *n.* zopenco
dune *n.* duna
dung *n.* estiércol
dun·geon *n.* mazmorra
du·pli·cate *adj.* duplicado;
    v. duplicar
du·pli·ca·tion *n.* duplicación
du·ra·tion *n.* duración
dur·ing *prep.* durante
dusk *n.* crepúsculo
dusk·y *adj.* oscuro
dust *n.* polvo
du·ti·ful *adj.* obediente
du·ty *n.* derechos
dwell *v.* habitar
dwell·ing *n.* morada
dwin·dle *v.* disminuir
dye *n.* tinte
dy·nam·ic *adj.* dinámico
dy·na·mite *n.* dinamita
dy·na·mo *n.* dinamo
dy·nas·ty *n.* dinastía
dys·en·ter·y *n.* disentería

E

each *adv.* para cada uno
ea·ger *adj.* impaciente
ea·ger·ness *n.* ansia
ea·gle *n.* águila
ear *n.* oído; oreja
ear·drum *n.* tímpano del
    oído
earl *n.* conde
ear·li·ness *n.* precocidad
ear·ly *adj.* primitivo; *adv.*,
    adj. temprano
earn *v.* merecer
ear·nest *adj.* fervoroso; serio
ear·nest·ly *adv.* con

seriedad
earn·ings *n.* sueldo
ear·ring *n.* pendiente
ear·shot *n.* alcance del oído
earth *n.* mundo; tierra
earth·en·ware *n.* loza de
    barro
earth·ly *adj.* mundano
earth·quake *n.* terremoto
earth·y *adj.* terroso
ease *v.* facilitar; *n.* facilidad
ea·sel *n.* caballete
eas·i·ly *adv.* fácilmente
eas·i·ness *n.* facilidad
east *n.* este
east·ern *adj.* del este
east·ward *adv.* hacia el este
eas·y *adj.* fácil
eas·y·go·ing *adj.*
    acomodadizo; demanga
    ancha
eat *v.* gustar; comer
eat·a·ble *adj.* comestible
eaves *n.* alero
eaves·drop *v.* escuchar a
    escondidas; espiar
ebb *v.* menguar; decaer
eb·on·y *n.* ébano
ec·cen·tric *adj.* excéntrico
ec·cen·tric·i·ty *n.*
    excentricidad
ec·cle·si·as·tic *adj.,* *n.*
    eclesiástico
ech·o *n.* eco
e·clipse *v.* eclipsar
e·clip·tic *adj.* eclíptico
ec·o·lo·gic *adj.* ecológico
e·col·o·gist *n.* ecólogo
e·col·o·gy *n.* ecología
e·co·nom·ic *adj.* económico
e·co·nom·ic·al *adj.*
    económico
e·co·nom·ics *n.* economía
e·con·o·mist *n.* economista
e·con·o·mize *v.* economizar
e·con·o·my *n.* economía
ec·sta·sy *n.* éxtasis
ec·stat·ic *adj.* extático
ec·u·men·i·cal *n.* ecuménico
ec·ze·ma *n.* eczema; eccema
ed·dy *n.* remolino
e·den·tate *adj.* desdentado
edge *n.* filo; agudeza; borde
ed·i·ble *adj.* comestible
e·dict *n.* edicto
ed·i·fi·ca·tion *n.* edificación
ed·i·fice *n.* edificio

ed·i·fy *v.* edificar
ed·it *v.* editar
e·di·tion *n.* edición
ed·i·tor *n.* editor
ed·i·to·ri·al *n.* editorial
ed·i·to·ri·al·ist *n.*
    editorialista
ed·u·cate *v.* educar
ed·u·ca·tion *n.* educación
eel *n.* anguila
ee·rie *adj.* espantoso;
    fantástico
ef·face *v.* borrar
ef·fect *v.* efectuar; *n.*
    resultado
ef·fec·tive *adj.* efectivo;
    eficaz
ef·fec·tu·al *adj.* eficaz
ef·fem·i·nate *adj.*
    afeminado
ef·fer·vesce *v.* estar en
    efervescencia
ef·fer·ves·cence *n.*
    efervescencia
ef·fer·ves·cent *adj.*
    efervescente
ef·fi·ca·cious *adj.* eficaz
ef·fi·cien·cy *n.* eficiencia
ef·fi·cient *adj.* eficiente
ef·fi·gy *n.* efigie
ef·fort *n.* esfuerzo
ef·fort·less *adj.* sin esfuerzo
ef·fuse *v.* derramar
ef·fu·sion *n.* efusión
ef·fu·sive *adj.* expansivo;
    efusivo
egg *n.* huevo
e·go *n.* el yo
e·go·tist *n.* egotista
e·gress *n.* salida
eight *adj.* ocho
eight·een *adj.* dieciocho
eighth *adj.* octavo
eight·y *adj.* ochenta
ei·ther *adv.* tampoco;
    también; *adj.* cualquier
e·ject *v.* echar; expulsar
e·jec·tion *n.* expulsión
eke *v.* aumentar
e·lab·o·rate *v.* elaborar
e·lab·or·a·tion *n.*
    elaboración
e·lapse *v.* pasar
e·last·ic *adj.* elástico
e·las·tic·i·ty *n.* elasticidad
e·late *v.* alegrar
e·la·tion *n.* regocijo

el·bow *n.* codo
eld·er *adj.* mayor
eld·er·ly *adj.* de edad
eld·est *adj.* el mayor
e·lect *v.* elegir
e·lec·tion *n.* elección
e·lec·tive *adj.* electivo
e·lec·tor *n.* elector
e·lec·tor·ate *n.* electorado
e·lec·tric *adj.* eléctrico; vivo
e·lec·tri·cian *n.* electricista
e·lec·tro·cute *v.* electrocutar
e·lec·trode *n.* electrodo
e·lec·tron *n.* electrón
e·lec·tron·ic *adj.* electrónico
el·e·gance *n.* elegancia
el·e·gant *adj.* elegante
el·e·gy *n.* elegía
el·e·ment *n.* elemento
el·e·men·ta·ry *adj.*
    elemental
el·e·phant *n.* elefante
el·e·vate *v.* elevar
el·e·va·tion *n.* elevación
el·e·va·tor *n.* ascensor
e·lev·en *adj.* once
e·lev·enth *adj.,* *n.*
    undécimo
elf·in *a.* elfo
e·lic·it *v.* sacar
el·i·gi·bil·i·ty *n.* elegibilidad
el·i·gi·ble *adj.* elegible;
    deseable
e·lim·i·nate *v.* eliminar
e·lim·i·na·tion *n.*
    eliminación
e·lite *n.* lo mejor
e·lix·ir *n.* elixir
elk *n.* alce
el·lipse *n.* elipse
el·lip·ti·cal *adj.* elíptico
elm *n.* olmo
el·o·cu·tion *n.* elocución
e·lon·gate *v.* alargar
e·lope *v.* fugarse
e·lope·ment *n.* fuga
el·o·quence *n.* elocuencia
el·o·quent *adj.* elocuente
else *adv.* otro; más
e·lu·ci·date *v.* elucidar
e·lude *v.* eludir; escapar de
e·lu·sive *adj.* esquivo
e·ma·ci·ate *v.*
    enflaquecer(se)
e·man·ci·pate *v.* emancipar
e·man·ci·pa·tion *n.*
    emancipación

em·balm v. embalsamar
em·bar·go n. embargo
em·bark v. embarcar(se)
em·bar·rass v. desconcertar
em·bas·sy n. embajada
em·ber n. ascua
em·bez·zle v. desfalcar
em·blem n. emblema
em·boss v. realzar
em·brace v. abrazar; aceptar; abarcar
em·broi·der v. recamar
em·bry·o n. embrión
em·er·ald n. esmeralda
e·merge v. salir
e·mer·gence n. salida
e·mer·gen·cy n. crisis
em·er·y n. esmeril
em·i·grant n. emigrante
em·i·gra·tion n. emigración
em·i·nence n. eminencia
em·i·nent adj. eminente
em·is·sar·y n. emisario
e·mis·sion n. emisión
e·mit v. emitir
e·mo·tion n. emoción
em·per·or n. emperador
em·pha·sis n. énfasis
em·pha·size v. acentuar; recalcar
em·phat·ic adj. enfático
em·pire n. imperio
em·ploy v. emplear
em·ploy·ee n. empleado
em·ploy·er n. amo; patrón
em·ploy·ment n. empleo; colocación
em·pow·er v. autorizar
em·press n. emperatriz
emp·ti·ness n. vacuidad; vacío
emp·ty v. vaciar; adj. desocupado
em·u·late v. emular
e·mul·sion n. emulsión
e·mul·sive adj. emulsivo
en·a·ble v. hacer que; permitir
en·act v. decretar; hacer el papel de
e·nam·el n. esmalte
en·am·or v. enamorar
en·case v. encerrar; encajar
en·chant v. encantar
en·chant·ing adj. encantador
en·chant·ment n. encanto

en·cir·cle v. ceñir
en·close v. encerrar; incluir
en·clo·sure n. cercamiento; carta adjunta
en·com·pass v. cercar; abarcar
en·core n. repetición
en·coun·ter n. encuentro
en·cour·age v. animar; fomentar
en·croach v. usurpar; pasar los límites
en·cum·ber v. estorbar; gravar
en·cy·clo·pe·dia n. enciclopedia
end n. final; fin
en·dan·ger v. poner en peligro
en·dear v. hacer querer
en·deav·or n. esfuerzo
end·ing f. fin
en·dorse v. endosar
en·dorse·ment n. endoso
en·dow v. dotar
en·dur·ance n. resistencia
en·dure v. durar
en·e·my n. enemigo
en·er·get·ic adj. enérgico
en·er·gy n. energía
en·force v. hacer cumplir; exigir
en·gage v. engranar; apalabrar
en·gage·ment n. obligación
en·gine n. motor; locomotora
en·gi·neer n. ingeniero
en·gi·neer·ing n. ingeniería
Eng·lish n. inglés
en·grave v. grabar
en·gross v. absorber; monopolizar
en·hance v. aumentar
e·nig·ma n. enigma
en·join v. imponer
en·joy v. disfrutar
en·joy·ment n. disfrute
en·large v. extender(se)
en·large·ment n. aumento; ampliación
en·light·en v. iluminar; instruir
en·list v. alistar(se)
en·liv·en v. avivar
en·mi·ty n. enemistad
e·nor·mous adj. enorme

e·nough adv. bastante
en·slave v. esclavizar
en·ter·tain·ment n. espectáculo
en·thu·si·asm n. entusiasmo
en·thu·si·ast n. entusiasta
en·tire adj. entero
en·tire·ly adv. totalmente
en·trance n. entrada
en·trust v. entregar
en·try n. partida; entrada
en·vel·op v. envolver
en·zyme n. enzima
ep·i·dem·ic n. epidemia
ep·i·sode n. episodio
ep·och n. época
eq·ua·bil·i·ty n. uniformidad
eq·ua·ble adj. uniforme
e·qual v. igualar; n. igual
e·qual·i·ty adj. igualdad
e·qual·ly adv. igualmente
e·qual·ize v. igualar
e·qua·nim·i·ty n. ecuanimidad
e·quate v. comparar
e·qua·tion n. ecuación
e·qua·tor n. ecuador
e·ques·tri·enne n. jineta
e·qui·lib·ri·um n. equilibrio
e·quip v. proveer; equipar
e·quip·ment n. equipo
eq·ui·ta·ble adj. equitativo
eq·ui·ty n. equidad
e·quiv·a·lent adj. equivalente
e·ra n. era
e·rad·i·cate v. desarraigar
e·rase v. borrar
e·ras·er n. borrador
ere conj. antes de que
e·rect v. erigir
e·rec·tion n. erección
er·mine n. armiño
e·rode v. corroer
e·ro·sion n. erosión
e·rot·ic adj. erótica
e·rot·ic adj. erótico
err v. vagar; errar
er·rand n. recado
er·rant adj. errante
er·ror n. error
er·u·dite adj. erudito
er·u·di·tion n. erudición
e·rup·tion n. erupción
es·ca·la·tor n. escalera móvil

es·ca·pade n. aventura
es·cape v. escapar; huir
es·chew v. evitar
es·cort v. acompañar; n. acompañante
e·soph·a·gus,
oe·soph·a·gus n. esófago
es·o·ter·ic adj. esotérico
es·pe·cial adj. especial
es·pe·cial·ly adv. especialmente
es·pi·o·nage n. espionaje
es·pouse v. adherirse a; casarse
es·py v. divisar; percibir
es·say n. ensayo
es·sence n. esencia; perfume
es·sen·tial adj. esencial
es·tab·lish v. establecer; probar; fundar
es·tab·lish·ment n. establecimiento
es·tate n. finca; propiedad
es·teem v. estimar
es·thet·ic adj. estético
es·ti·mate v. calcular; estimar
es·ti·ma·tion n. juicio; aprecio
es·trange v. apartar
es·tu·ar·y n. estuario
et·cet·er·a n. etcétera
etch v. grabar al agua fuerte
etch·ing n. aguafuerte
e·ter·nal adj. eterno
e·ter·nal·ly adv. eternamente
e·ter·ni·ty n. eternidad
e·ther n. éter
e·the·re·al adj. etéreo
eth·i·cal adj. ético
eth·ics n. ética
eth·nol·o·gy n. etnología
et·i·quette n. etiqueta
e·tude n. estudio
eu·lo·gize v. elogiar
eu·lo·gy n. elogio
eu·pho·ri·a n. euforia
eu·phor·ic adj. eufórico
e·vac·u·ate v. evacuar
e·vac·u·a·tion n. evacuación
e·vade v. evadir
e·val·u·a·tion evaluación
e·van·gel·i·cal adj. evangélico

e·van·ge·list n. evangelista
e·vap·o·rate v. evaporar(se)
e·vap·o·ra·tion n. evaporación
e·va·sion n. evasión
e·va·sive adj. evasivo
eve n. víspera
e·ven adj. igualar
eve·ning n. tarde
e·vent n. suceso
e·vent·ful adj. memorable
e·ven·tu·al·i·ty n. eventualidad
ev·er adv. siempre; nunca; jamás
eve·ry adj. todo
e·vict v. expulsar
e·vic·tion n. desahucio
ev·i·dence n. evidencia
e·vil n. mal
e·vil·do·er n. malhechor
e·voke v. evocar
ev·o·lu·tion n. desarrollo; evolución
e·volve v. desarrollar
ewe n. oveja
ew·er n. aguamanil
ex·act adj. exacto
ex·act·ing adj. exigente
ex·ag·ger·ate v. exagerar
ex·ag·ger·a·tion n. exageración
ex·alt v. exaltar; honrar
ex·al·ta·tion n. exaltación
ex·am·i·na·tion n. examen
ex·am·ine v. examinar
ex·am·in·er n. examinador
ex·am·ple n. ejemplo
ex·as·per·ate v. exasperar
ex·as·per·a·tion n. exasperación
ex·ca·vate v. excavar
ex·ca·va·tion n. excavación
ex·ceed v. superar; exceder
ex·ceed·ing·ly adv. sumamente
ex·cel v. sobresalir; aventajar
ex·cel·lence n. excelencia
ex·cel·lent adj. excelente
ex·cept v. exceptuar
ex·cep·tion n. excepción
ex·cep·tion·al adj. excepcional
ex·cerpt v. citar un texto
ex·cess n. exceso
ex·change v. cambiar
ex·cise n. impuestos sobre ciertos artículos

ex·cit·a·ble adj. excitable
ex·cite v. excitar
ex·cite·ment n. agitación; emoción
ex·cit·ing adj. emocionante
ex·claim v. exclamar
ex·cla·ma·tion n. exclamación
ex·clude v. excluir
ex·clu·sion n. exclusión
ex·clu·sive adj. exclusivo
ex·com·mu·ni·cate v. excomulgar
ex·com·mu·ni·ca·tion n. excomunión
ex·cre·ment n. excremento
ex·cur·sion n. viaje; excursión
ex·cuse v. excusar; perdonar
ex·e·cute v. ejecutar; llevar a cabo
ex·e·cu·tion n. ejecución
ex·ec·u·tive adj. ejecutivo
ex·ec·u·tor n. albacea
ex·em·pla·ry adj. ejemplar
ex·er·cise n. ejercicio
ex·hale v. exhalar; expirar
ex·haust v. agotar
ex·hib·it v. mostrar; presentar
ex·hi·bi·tion n. exposición
ex·hil·a·rate v. vigorizar; alegrar
ex·hort v. exhortar
ex·i·gent adj. exigente
ex·ile n. exilado; destierro
ex·ist v. existir
ex·ist·ence n. existencia
ex·it n. salida
ex·o·dus n. éxodo
ex·or·bi·tant adj. excesivo
ex·ot·ic adj. exótico
ex·pand v. extender; ensanchar
ex·panse n. extensión
ex·pan·sion n. expansión
ex·pan·sive adj. expansivo
ex·pect v. esperar; contar con
ex·pect·an·cy n. expectación
ex·pect·ant adj. expectante
ex·pec·ta·tion n. expectación
ex·pe·di·en·cy n. conveniencia
ex·pe·di·ent adj. conveniente

ex·pe·dite v. facilitar; acelerar
ex·pe·di·tion n. expedición
ex·pel v. expulsar
ex·pend v. expender
ex·pend·i·ture n. gasto
ex·pe·ri·ence v. experimentar
ex·per·i·ment n. experimento
ex·pire v. terminar
ex·pla·na·tion n. explicación
ex·pli·cit adj. explícito
ex·plode v. estallar; volar
ex·ploit n. hazaña
ex·plo·ra·tion n. exploración
ex·plore v. explorar; examinar
ex·plor·er n. explorador
ex·plo·sion n. explosión
ex·po·nent n. exponente
ex·port v. exportar
ex·por·ta·tion n. exportación
ex·pose v. exponer; desenmascarar
ex·press v. expresar
ex·pres·sion n. expresión
ex·pres·sive adj. expresivo
ex·tend v. extender
ex·ten·sion n. extensión
ex·te·ri·or adj. exterior
ex·tinct adj. extinto
ex·tinc·tion n. extinción
ex·tra n. extra
ex·tra·or·di·nar·y adj. extraordinario
ex·treme adj. extremo
ex·ul·ta·tion n. exultación
eye n. ojo
eye·let n. ojete
eye·sight n. vista
eye·tooth n. colmillo
eye·wit·ness n. testigo ocular

F

fa·ble n. fábula
fab·ric n. tela
fab·ri·cate v. inventar

fab·u·lous adj. fabuloso
fa·cade n. fachada
face n. cara
fa·cial adj. facial
fa·cile adj. fácil
fa·cil·i·tate v. facilitar
fa·cil·i·ty n. facilidad
fac·sim·i·le n. facsímile
fact n. hecho
fac·tion n. facción
fac·tor n. factor
fac·to·ry n. fábrica
fac·tu·al adj. basado en datos
fac·ul·ty n. facultad
fad n. novedad
fade v. descolorar(se)
fag v. fatigar
fag·ot n. haz de leña
Fahr·en·heit adj. de Fahrenheit
fail v. acabar; faltar
fail·ure n. fracaso
faint v. desmayarse
faint·ness n. debilidad
fair adj. justo; rubio
fair·ly adv. justamente
fair·y n. hada
faith n. fe
faith·ful adj. fiel
faith·less adj. desleal
fake n. impostura
fal·con n. halcón
fall v. caer(se)
fal·la·cious adj. engañoso
fal·la·cy n. error; falacia
fal·li·ble adj. falible
fal·low adj. en barbecho
false adj. falso
false·hood n. mentira
false·ly adv. falsamente
fal·si·fy v. falsificar
fal·si·ty n. falsedad
fal·ter v. vacilar; titubear
fame n. fama
fa·mil·iar adj. familiar
fa·mil·i·ar·i·ty n. familiaridad
fam·i·ly n. familia
fam·ine n. hambre
fam·ish v. morirse de hambre
fa·mous adj. famoso
fan n. aficionado
fa·nat·ic n., adj. fanático
fa·nat·i·cism n. fanatismo
fan·ci·er n. aficionado
fan·ci·ful adj. fantástico

fan·cy *n.* fantasía
fan·fare *n.* toque de trompetas
fang *n.* colmillo
fan·tas·tic *adj.* fantástico
fan·ta·sy *n.* fantasía
far *adv.* lejos
far·a·way *adj.* remoto
farce *n.* farsa
far·ci·cal *adj.* rídiculo
fare *v.* pasarlo
fare·well *v.* adiós
far·fetched *adj.* improbable
farm *n.* granja
farm·house *n.* alquería
far·off *adj.* lejano
fas·ci·nate *v.* fascinar
fas·cism *n.* fascismo
fas·cist *n.* fascista
fash·ion *n.* estilo; moda; uso
fash·ion·a·ble *adj.* de moda
fast *adj.* rápidamente; rápido
fas·ten *v.* abrochar; asegurar
fas·tid·i·ous *adj.* fino; quisquilloso
fat *adj.* gordo
fa·tal *adj.* fatal
fa·tal·ism *n.* fatalismo
fa·tal·ist *n.* fatalista
fa·tal·i·ty *n.* fatalidad
fate *n.* suerte
fate·ful *adj.* fatal
fa·ther *n.* padre
fa·ther·hood *n.* paternidad
fa·ther·in·law *n.* suegro
fath·om *n.* braza; *v.* penetrar
fa·tigue *n.* fatiga
fat·ten *v.* engordar
fau·cet *n.* grifo
fault *n.* culpa; falta
fault·y *adj.* defectuoso
fa·vor *n.* favor
fa·vor·a·ble *adj.* favorable
fa·vored *adj.* favorecido
fa·vor·ite *adj.* favorito
fa·vor·it·ism *n.* favoritismo
fawn *n.* cervato
faze *v.* perturbar
fear *n.* miedo
fear·ful *adj.* temeroso
fear·less *adj.* intrépido
fear·some *adj.* temible
fea·si·bil·i·ty *n.* viabilidad
fea·si·ble *adj.* factible
feast *n.* banquete; fiesta
feat *n.* proeza
feath·er *n.* pluma

feath·er·y *adj.* plumoso
fea·ture *n.* facción; rasgo
Feb·ru·ar·y *n.* febrero
fe·ces *n.* excrementos
fe·cund *adj.* fecundo
fed·er·al *adj.* federal
fed·er·a·tion *n.* federación
fee *n.* honorario
fee·ble *adj.* débil
fee·bly *adv.* flojamente
feed *v.* alimentar
feel *v.* sentir(se)
feel·er *n.* antena
feel·ing *n.* emoción
feign *v.* fingir
feint *n.* treta
fe·lic·i·tate *v.* felicitar
fe·lic·i·tous *adj.* oportuno; feliz
fe·lic·i·ty *n.* felicidad
fe·line *adj.* felino
fell *v.* talar
fel·low *n.* compañero
fel·low·ship *n.* compañerismo
fel·on *n.* criminal
fel·o·ny *n.* crimen
felt *n.* fieltro
fe·male *n.* hembra
fem·i·nine *adj.* femenino
fe·mur *n.* fémur
fence *v.* esgrimir
fenc·ing *n.* esgrima
fend *v.* rechazar
fen·der *n.* guardafango
fer·ment *v.* fermentar
fer·men·ta·tion *n.* fermentación
fern *n.* helecho
fe·ro·cious *adj.* feroz
fe·ro·ci·ty *n.* ferocidad
fer·ret *n.* hurón
fer·ry *n.* transbordador
fer·tile *adj.* fecundo; fértil
fer·til·i·ty *n.* fecundidad
fer·ti·lize *v.* fertilizar
fer·ti·liz·er *n.* abono
fer·vid *adj.* férvido
fer·vor *n.* fervor
fes·ter *v.* enconarse
fes·ti·val *n.* fiesta
fes·tive *adj.* festivo
fes·tiv·i·ty *n.* regocijo; fiesta
fes·toon *n.* festón
fetch *v.* ir por
fetch·ing *adj.* atractivo
fete *n.* fiesta

fet·id *adj.* fétido
fet·ish *n.* fetiche
fet·ter *n.* grillos
fet·tle *n.* condición
fe·tus *n.* feto
feud *n.* enemistad
feu·dal *adj.* feudal
feu·dal·ism *n.* feudalismo
fe·ver *n.* fiebre
fe·ver·ish *adj.* febril
few *adj.* pocos
fi·an·ce *n.* novio
fi·an·cee *n.* novia
fi·as·co *n.* fiasco
fi·at *n.* fíat
fib *v.* mentir
fi·ber, fi·bre *n.* fibra
fi·brous *adj.* fibroso
fick·le *adj.* inconstante
fic·tion *n.* ficción
fic·tion·al *adj.* novelesco
fic·ti·tious *adj.* ficticio
fid·dle *n.* violín
fi·del·i·ty *n.* fidelidad
fidg·et *v.* inquietar
fidg·et·y *adj.* inquieto; azogado
field *n.* prado; campo
fiend *n.* demonio
fiend·ish *adj.* diabólico
fierce *adj.* feroz
fier·y *adj.* ardiente; apasionado
fif·teen *adj.* quince
fif·teenth *adj.* decimoquinto
fifth *adj.* quinto
fif·ti·eth *adj.* quincuagésimo
fif·ty *adj.* cincuenta
fig *n.* higo
fight *v.* pelear; luchar; *n.* pelea; lucha
fight·er *n.* guerrero
fig·ment *n.* invención
fig·ur·a·tive *adj.* figurativo
fig·ure *n.* tipo; figura
fig·ure·head *n.* mascarón de proa
fig·ur·ine *n.* figurín
fil·a·ment *n.* filamento
filch *v.* ratear
file *n.* lima; archivo; fila
fi·let *n.* filete also **fil·let**
fil·i·bus·ter *n.* obstruccionista
fil·i·gree *n.* filigrana
fil·ings *n.* limaduras
fill *v.* llenar

fill·ing *n.* empaste; relleno
fil·ly *n.* potra
film *n.* película
fil·ter *n.* filtro
filth *n.* inmundicia
filth·y *adj.* sucio
fin *n.* aleta
fi·nal *adj.* final
fi·na·le *n.* final
fi·nal·ist *n.* finalista
fi·nal·i·ty *n.* finalidad
fi·nal·ly *adv.* finalmente; por fin
fi·nance *n.* finanzas
fi·nan·cial *adj.* financiero
fin·an·cier *n.* financiero
finch *n.* pinzón
find *v.* hallar; encontrar
fine *adj.* fino; admirable; *n.* multa; *v.* multar
fin·er·y *n.* adornos
fi·nesse *n.* sutileza; diplomacia
fin·ger *n.* dedo
fin·ger·nail *n.* uña
fin·ger·print *n.* huella dactilar
fin·ish *v.* terminar; acabar
fi·nite *adj.* finito
fir *n.* abeto
fire *n.* fuego
fire·arm *n.* arma de fuego
fire·crack·er *n.* petardo
fire·en·gine *n.* bomba de incendios
fire·fly *n.* luciérnaga
fire·man *n.* bombero
fire·place *n.* hogar
firm *adj.* firme
fir·ma·ment *n.* firmamento
firm·ly *adj.* firmemente
firm·ness *n.* firmeza
first *adj.* primero
first·class *adj.* de primera clase
first·hand *adj.* de primera mano
first·rate *adj.* de primera clase
fis·cal *adj.* fiscal
fish *n.* pez
fish·er·man *n.* pescador
fish·ery *n.* pesquera
fish·y *adj.* sospechoso
fis·sion *n.* fisión
fis·sure *n.* grieta
fist *n.* puño

fist·i·cuffs *n.* puñetazo
fit *v.* probar; acomodar; *adj.* adecuado
fit·ful *adj.* espasmódico
fit·ting *n.* ajuste; *adj.* propio; conveniente
five *adj.* cinco
fix *v.* arreglar
fix·a·tion *n.* fijación
fix·ed *adj.* fijo
fix·ture *n.* cosa o instalación fija
fla·bby *adj.* flojo; débil
flag *n.* bandera
flag·on *n.* jarro; frasco
fla·grant *adj.* notorio
flag·stone *n.* losa
flail *n.* mayal
flair *n.* instinto
flake *n.* escama; *v.* formar hojuelas
flak·y *adj.* escamoso
flam·boy·ant *adj.* llamativo
flame *n.* llama; *v.* flamear
flam·ma·ble *adj.* inflamable
flank *n.* ijada; lado; *v.* lindar; flanquear
flap *v.* ondear
flare *v.* brillar; fulgurar; *n.* bengala
flash *n.* relámpago; ráfaga; *v.* lanzar
flash·light *n.* linterna eléctrica
flash·y *adj.* charro
flask *n.* frasco
flat *adj.* plano; llano
flat·ter·y *n.* adulación
flaunt *v.* lucir
fla·vor *n.* sabor
fla·vor·ing *n.* condimento
flaw *n.* imperfección
flax *n.* lino
flay *v.* desollar
flea *n.* pulga
fleck *n.* mancha
flee *v.* fugarse; huir
fleece *n.* vellón
fleec·y *adj.* lanudo
fleet *adj.* veloz
fleet·ing *adj.* fugaz
flesh *n.* carne
flex *v.* doblar
flex·i·ble *adj.* flexible
flick *n.* golpecito
fli·er *n.* aviador
flight *n.* vuelo

flim·sy *adj.* endeble
flinch *v.* acobardarse
fling *v.* arrojar
flint *n.* pedernal
flip *n.* capirote
flip *v.* mover de un tirón
flip·pant *adj.* ligero
flirt *v.* flirtear; coquetear
flit *v.* revolotear
float *v.* flotar; hacer flotar
flock *n.* rebaño
floe *n.* témpano
flog *v.* azotar
flood *n.* diluvio
floor *n.* suelo; piso
flop *v.* caer pesadamente; fracasar
flo·ra *n.* flora
flo·ral *adj.* floral
flor·id *adj.* florido
flo·rist *n.* florista
floss *n.* seda floja
flo·til·la *n.* flotilla
flounce *v.* moverse airadamente
floun·der *v.* tropezar
flour *n.* harina
flour·ish *v.* florecer; blandir
flout *v.* mofarse
flow *v.* fluir
flow·er *n.* flor
flu *n.* gripe
fluc·tu·ate *v.* fluctuar
flue *n.* cañón de chimenea
flu·en·cy *n.* fluidez
flu·ent *adj.* facundo
fluff·y *adj.* plumosa
flu·id *adj.* fluido
fluke *n.* chiripa
flunk *v.* no aprobar
flu·o·res·cent *adj.* fluorescente
flur·ry *n.* ráfaga; agitación
flush *adj.* nivelado
flus·ter *v.* aturdir
flute *n.* flauta
flut·ter *n.* aleteo; *v.* revolotear
flux *n.* mudanza; flujo
fly *v.* volar, *n.* mosca
fly·er *n.* aviador
fly·wheel *n.* rueda volante
foal *n.* potro
foam *n.* espuma
fo·cus *v.* enfocar
fod·der *n.* forraje
foe *n.* enemigo

fog *n.* niebla
fo·gey *n.* persona de ideas anticuadas
foi·ble *n.* flaco
foil *n.* hoja; florete
foist *v.* encajar
fold *v.* plegar; doblar
fold·er *n.* carpeta
fo·li·age *n.* follaje
folk *n.* gente
folk·lore *n.* folklore
fol·li·cle *n.* folículo
fol·low *v.* perseguir; seguir
fol·low·er *n.* seguidor
fol·ly *n.* locura; tontería
fo·ment *v.* fomentar
fond *adj.* cariñoso
fon·dle *v.* acariciar
fond·ly *adv.* afectuosamente
food *n.* alimento
fool *n.* tonto
fool·har·dy *adj.* temerario
fool·ish *adj.* necio
fool·proof *adj.* infalible
foot *n.* pata; pie
foot·ball *n.* fútbol
foot·note *n.* nota
foot·print *n.* huella
foot·step *n.* paso
fop *n.* petimetre
for *conj.* pues, *prep.* para; por
for·age *n.* forraje
for·ay *n.* correría
for·bear *v.* contenerse
for·bid *v.* prohibir
for·bid·den *adj.* prohibido
for·ceps *n.* fórceps
for·ci·ble *adj.* enérgico; eficaz
ford *n.* vado
fore *adj.* anterior
fore·arm *n.* antebrazo
fore·bode *v.* presagiar
fore·cast *v.* pronosticar
fore·fa·ther *n.* antepasado
fore·fin·ger *n.* dedo índice
fore·go *v.* renunciar
fore·gone *adj.* predeterminado
fore·ground *n.* primer plano
fore·head *n.* frente
for·eign *adj.* extranjero
for·eign·er *n.* extranjero
fore·man *n.* capataz
fore·most *adj.* primero
fore·run·ner *n.* precursor
fore·see *v.* prever

fore·sight *n.* previsión; perspicacia
fore·skin *n.* prepucio
for·est *n.* bosque
fore·tell *v.* predecir
for·ev·er *adv.* siempre
fore·word *n.* prefacio
for·feit *v.* perder
forge *n.* fragua
for·ger·y *n.* falsificación
for·get *v.* olvidar(se)
for·get·ful *adj.* olvidadizo
for·give *v.* perdonar
fork *n.* tenedor
for·lorn *adj.* abandonado
form *n.* forma
for·mal *adj.* ceremonioso
for·mal·i·ty *n.* formalidad
for·mat *n.* formato
for·ma·tion *n.* formación
for·mer *adj.* anterior
for·mer·ly *adv.* antiguamente
for·mi·da·ble *adj.* formidable
for·mu·la *n.* fórmula
for·ni·cate *v.* fornicar
for·ni·ca·tion *n.* fornicación
for·sake *v.* abandonar
fort *n.* fuerte
forth *adv.* en adelante
forth·com·ing *adj.* próximo
forth·right *adj.* directo
for·ti·fi·ca·tion *n.* fortificación
for·tune *n.* fortuna
for·ty *adj.* cuarenta
for·ward *adv.* adelante
fos·sil *n.* fósil
foul *adj.* sucio
foun·da·tion *n.* fundación
foun·tain *n.* fuente
four *adj.* cuatro
four·teen *adj.* catorce
fourth *adj.* cuarto
fox *n.* zorra
fra·cas *n.* riña
frac·tion *n.* fracción
frac·ture *v.* quebrar; *n.* fractura
frag·ile *adj.* frágil
frag·ment *n.* fragmento
fra·grance *n.* fragancia
fra·grant *adj.* oloroso
frail *adj.* débil; frágil
frail·ty *n.* fragilidad
frame *n.* estructura; marco

frame·work *n.* esqueleto
franc *n.* franco
fran·chise *n.* derecho de sufragio
frank *adj.* franco
frank·in·cense *n.* incienso
frank·ly *adv.* francamente
frank·ness *n.* franqueza
fran·tic *adj.* frenético
fra·ter·ni·ty *n.* fraternidad
fraud *n.* fraude
fraught *adj.* lleno de
fray *v.* deshilacharse
freak *n.* monstruosidad; fenómeno
freck·le *n.* peca
free *v.* libertar; *adj.* libre
free·dom *n.* libertad
free·way *n.* autopista
freeze *v.* helar(se); congelar
freight *n.* flete
freight·er *n.* buque de carga
French *n., adj.* francés
fre·net·ic *adj.* frenético
fren·zy *n.* frenesí
fre·quen·cy *n.* frecuencia
fre·quent *adj.* frecuente
fresh *n.* fresco
fresh·en *v.* refrescar
fret *v.* apurarse
fri·ar *n.* fraile
fric·tion *n.* fricción
Friday *n.* viernes
friend *n.* amigo; amiga
friend·ly *adj.* amistoso
frieze *n.* friso
fright *n.* susto
fright·en *v.* asustar
frig·id *adj.* frío
frill *n.* lechuga
fringe *n.* orla; margen
frisk *v.* retozar
fro *adv.* atrás
frock *n.* vestido
frog *n.* rana
from *prep.* desde; de
front *n.* frente
fron·tal *adj.* frontal
frown *n.* ceño
fru·gal *adj.* frugal
fruit *n.* fruta
frus·trate *v.* frustrar
frus·tra·tion *n.* frustración
fry *v.* freír
fu·gi·tive *n., adj.* fugitivo
full *adj.* completo; lleno
ful·ly *adv.* completamente

func·tion *v.* funcionar
func·tion·al *adj.* funcional
fun·da·men·tal *adj.* fundamental
fun·ny *adj.* cómico
fur *n.* piel
fu·ri·ous *adj.* furioso
fur·ni·ture *n.* mueblaje
fur·ther *adj., adv.* mas lejos
fuse *n.* fusible; espoleta
fu·tile *adj.* inútil
fuzz *n.* pelusa

G

gab·ar·dine *n.* garbardina
gad *v.* andorrear
gad·get *n.* aparato
gaff *n.* arpón
gag *v.* amordazar
gai·e·ty *n.* alegría
gai·ly *adv.* alegremente
gain *v.* amordazar
gain·say *v.* contradecir
gait *n.* modo de andar
ga·la *n.* fiesta
gal·ax·y *n.* galaxia
gale *n.* ventarrón
gall *n.* bilis
gal·lant *adj.* valeroso
gal·lant·ry *n.* galantería
gal·ler·y *n.* galería
gal·ley *n.* galera; fogón
gal·lon *n.* galón
gal·lop *n.* galope
gal·lows *n.* horca
gal·va·nize *v.* galvanizar
gam·bit *n.* gambito
gam·ble *v.* jugar
gam·bol *v.* brincar
game *n.* partido; juego
gam·ut *n.* gama
gan·der *n.* ganso
gang *n.* pandilla
gan·grene *n.* gangrena
gang·ster *n.* gángster; pistolero
gang·way *n.* pasillo
gap *n.* hueco
ga·rage *n.* garaje
garb *n.* vestido
gar·bage *n.* basura
gar·ble *v.* mutilar
gar·den *n.* jardín
gar·gan·tu·an *adj.* colosal
gar·gle *v.* gargarizar

gar·ish *v.* llamativo
gar·land *n.* guirnalda
gar·ment *n.* prenda de vestir
gar·ner *n.* granero
gar·net *n.* granate
gar·nish *v.* adornar
gar·ret *n.* guardilla
gar·ri·son *n.* guarnición
gar·ru·lous *adj.* gárrulo
gar·ter *n.* liga
gas *n.* gasolina
gas·e·ous *adj.* gaseoso
gash *n.* cuchillada
gas·o·line *n.* gasolina
gasp *v.* boquear
gas·tric *adj.* gástrico
gas·tron·o·my *n.* gastronomía
gate *n.* puerta
gate·way *n.* paso
gath·er *v.* fruncir; reunir
gauche *adj.* torpe
gaud·y *adj.* chillón
gauge *n.* norma de medida; indicador
gaunt *adj.* flaco
gaunt·let *n.* guantelete
gauze *n.* gasa
gawk·y *adj.* desgarbado
gay *adj.* alegre; vistoso
gaze *v.* mirar
ga·zelle *n.* gacela
ga·zette *n.* gaceta
gaz·et·teer *n.* diccionario geográfico
gear *v.* engranar
gel·a·tin *n.* gelatina
ge·lat·i·nous *adj.* gelatinoso
geld *v.* castrar
gem *n.* joya; gema
gen·der *n.* género
gene *n.* gen
ge·ne·al·o·gy *n.* genealogía
gen·er·al *adj.* general
gen·er·al·i·ty *n.* generalidad
gen·er·al·ize *v.* generalizar
gen·er·ate *v.* generar
gen·er·a·tion *n.* generador
ge·ner·ic *adj.* genérico
gen·er·os·i·ty *n.* generosidad
gen·er·ous *adj.* generoso
gen·e·sis *n.* génesis
ge·net·ic *adj.* genético
gen·ial *adj.* afable
gen·i·tal *adj.* genital
gen·ius *n.* genio

gen·o·cide *n.* genocidio
gen·teel *adj.* elegante; bien criado
gen·til·i·ty *n.* gentileza
gen·tle *adj.* suave; apacible
gen·tle·man *n.* caballero
gen·tly *adv.* suavemente
gen·u·ine *adj.* genuino; sincero
ge·nus *n.* género
ge·o·gra·pher *n.* geógrafo
ge·o·pra·phic,
ge·o·graph·i·cal *adj.* geográfico
ge·o·gra·phy *n.* geografía
ge·o·log·ic *adj.* geológico
ge·ol·o·gist *n.* geólogo
ge·ol·o·gy *n.* geología
ge·o·met·ric *adj.* geométrico
ge·om·e·try *n.* geometría
ge·o·phys·i·cal *adj.* geofísico
ge·o·phys·ics *n.* geofísica
ger·i·at·rics *n.* geriatría
germ *n.* germen
ger·mane *adj.* relativo
ger·mi·na·tion *n.* germinación
ger·und *n.* gerundio
ges·tic·u·late *v.* gesticular
ges·ture *n.* gesto
get *v.* lograr; obtener
gey·ser *n.* géiser
ghast·ly *adj.* horrible
gher·kin *n.* pepinillo
ghost *n.* fantasma
ghost·ly *adj.* espectral
ghoul *n.* demonio
GI *n.* soldado
giant *adj.* gigantesco
gib·ber·ish *n.* galimatías; jerga
gib·bon *n.* gibón
gib·let *n.* menudillos
gid·di·ness *n.* vértigo
gid·dy *adj.* mareado; ligero
gift *n.* regalo; don
gi·gan·tic *adj.* gigantesco
gig·gle *n.* risa sofocada
gild *v.* dorar
gill *n.* agalla
gilt *adj.* dorado
gim·mick *n.* truco
gin *n.* desmotadera de algodón; ginebra
gin·ger·ale *n.* cerveza de

jengibre
gin·ger·bread *n.* pan de
  jengibre
gin·ger·ly *adj.* cauteloso
gip·sy *n.* gitano
gi·raffe *n.* jirafa
gird *v.* ceñir
gird·er *n.* viga
gir·dle *n.* cinto; faja
girl *n.* chica; niña
girl·ish *adj.* de niña
girth *n.* cincha
gist *n.* esencial; clave
give *v.* entregar; dar
giv·en *adj.* citado
giz·zard *n.* molleja
gla·cial *n.* glacial
glad *adj.* alegre
glade *n.* claro
glad·ly *adv.* con mucho
  gusto
glad·ness *n.* alegría
glad·i·o·lus *n.* gladiolo
glam·our, glam·or *n.*
  encanto
glam·our·ous *adj.*
  encantador
glance *v.* rebotar; mirar
gland *n.* glándula
glan·du·lar *adj.* glandular
glare *v.* relumbrar
glar·ing *adj.* evidente
glass *n.* vidrio; vaso
glass·y *adj.* vítreo
glau·co·ma *n.* glaucoma
glaze *v.* vidriar
glean *n.* espigar
glee *n.* júbilo
glen *n.* cañada
glide *v.* deslizarse
glim·mer *v.* brillar
  débilmente
glimpse *n.* vislumbre
glint *v.* destellar
glis·ten *v.* relucir
glit·ter *v.* relucir
gloat *v.* manifestar
  satisfacción maligna
globe *n.* globo; esfera
glob·ule *n.* glóbulo
gloom *n.* tristeza
gloom·y *adj.* lóbrego;
  melancólico
glo·ri·fy *v.* glorificar
glo·ri·ous *adj.* glorioso
glo·ry *n.* gloria
gloss *n.* lustre

glos·sa·ry *n.* glosario
gloss·y *adj.* lustroso
glot·tis *n.* glotis
glove *n.* guante
glow *v.* brillar
glow·er *v.* mirar con ceño
glow·worm *n.* luciérnaga
glue *v.* encolar
glum *adj.* abatido
glut *v.* hartar
glut·ton *n.* glotón
glut·ton·y *n.* gula
gnarl *v.* torcer
gnash *v.* rechinar
gnat *n.* jején
gnaw *v.* roer
gnome *n.* gnomo
go *v.* ir
goad *n.* aguijada; incitar
goal *n.* meta; gol
goat *n.* cabra
gob·ble *v.* engullir
gob·let *n.* copa
gob·lin *n.* duende
God *n.* Dios
god·child *n.* ahijado
god·daugh·ter *n.* ahijada
god·dess *n.* diosa
god·fa·ther *n.* padrino
god·ly *adj.* piadoso
god·moth·er *n.* madrina
god·par·ent *n.* padrino;
  madrina
god·send *n.* buena suerte
god·son *n.* ahijado
gog·gles *n.* anteojos
go·ing *n.* ida; estado del
  camino
gold *n.* oro
golf *n.* golf
gon·do·la *n.* góndola
gon·do·lier *n.* góndolero
gong *n.* gong
gon·or·rhe·a *n.* gonorrea
good *n.* bien
good·by *int.* adiós
good·heart·ed *adj.* amable
good·look·ing *adj.* guapo
good·ly *adj.* agradable;
  considerable
good·ness *n.* bondad
good·y *n.* golosina
goose *n.* ganso
goose·ber·ry *n.* uva espina
gore *n.* sangre
gorge *n.* barranco
gor·geous *adj.* magnífico;

vistoso
gos·pel *n.* evangelio
gos·sa·mer *n.* gasa
gos·sip *n.* chisme; comadre
gouge *n.* gubia
gourd *n.* calabaza
gour·met *n.* gastrónomo
gout *n.* gota
gov·ern *v.* gobernar
gov·ern·ess *n.* institutriz
gov·ern·ment *n.* gobierno
gov·er·nor *n.* gobernador
gown *n.* vestido
grab *v.* asir; arrebatar
grace *n.* gracia
grace·ful *adj.* gracioso
gra·cious *adj.* agradable
gra·da·tion *n.* gradación
grade *n.* grado; clase
grad·u·al *adj.* gradual
grad·u·al·ly *adv.* poco a
  poco
grad·u·ate *v.* graduar(se)
grad·u·a·tion *n.* graduación
graft *n.* injerto; soborno
grain *n.* grano; fibra
gram *n.* gramo
gram·mar *n.* gramática
gram·mat·i·cal *adj.*
  gramatical
gra·na·ry *n.* granero
grand *adj.* magnífico;
  grandioso
grand·child *n.* nieto
grand·daugh·ter *n.* nieta
grand·fa·ther *n.* abuelo
grand·par·ent *n.* abuelo
grand·son *n.* nieto
grange *n.* cortijo
grant *v.* conferir; otorgar
gran·u·late *v.* granular
gran·ule *n.* gránulo
grape *n.* uva
grape·fruit *n.* toronja;
  pomelo
graph *n.* gráfica
graph·ic *adj.* gráfico
graph·ite *n.* grafito
grap·nel *n.* arpeo
grap·ple *n.* lucha; garfio
grasp *v.* agarrar; comprender
grasp·ing *adj.* codicioso
grass *n.* hierba
grass·hop·per *n.*
  saltamontes
grass·y *adj.* herboso
grate *n.* parrilla de hogar

grate·ful *adj.* agradecido
grat·i·fi·ca·tion *n.*
  gratificación; placer
grat·i·fy *v.* complacer;
  satisfacer
grat·ing *n.* reja
gra·tis *adj.* gratis
grat·i·tude *n.*
  reconocimiento
gra·tu·i·tous *adj.* gratuito;
  injustificado
gra·tu·i·ty *n.* propina
grave *n.* sepultura
grav·el *n.* cascajo
grav·en *adj.* grabado
grave·yard *n.* cementerio
grav·i·tate *v.* gravitar
grav·i·ta·tion *n.* gravitación
grav·i·ty *n.* seriedad;
  gravedad
gra·vy *n.* salsa
gray, grey *adj.* gris
graze *v.* pacer; rozar
grease *n.* grasa
greas·y *adj.* grasiento
great *adj.* grande; gran
greed *n.* avaricia; codicia
greed·y *adj.* avaro; codicioso;
  goloso
green *adj., n.* verde
green·er·y *n.* verdura
greet *v.* saludar
greet·ing *n.* saludo
gre·gar·i·ous *adj.* gregario
gre·nade *n.* granada de
  mano
grid *n.* reja; parrilla
grid·dle *n.* tortera
grid·i·ron *n.* campo de
  fútbol; parrilla
grief *n.* pesar
griev·ance *n.* agravio
grieve *v.* afligirse
griev·ous *adj.* grave; penoso
grif·fin, grif·fon *n.* grifo
grill *v.* asar a la parrilla
grille, grill *n.* verja
grim *adj.* inflexible; severo
grim·ace *n.* visaje
grime *n.* mugre
grim·y *adj.* mugriento
grin *v.* sonreír
grind *v.* moler; pulverizar
grind·stone *n.* muela
grip *n.* agarro; apretón; saco
  de mano
grippe *n.* gripe

gris·ly *adj.* horroroso
gris·tle *n.* cartílago
grit *n.* arena; firmeza
grit·ty *adj.* arenoso
griz·zled, griz·zly *adj.* gris
groan *v.* gemir
gro·cer *n.* abacero
gro·cer·y *n.* abacería
groin *n.* ingle
groom *n.* novio; mozo de caballos
groove *n.* estría
grope *v.* buscar a tientas
gross *adj.* bruto; grosero; grueso
gro·tesque *adj.* grotesco
grot·to *n.* gruta
grouch *v.* refunfuñar
ground *n.* tierra; terreno; razón; poso
ground·work *n.* fundamento
group *n.* grupo
grouse *v.* quejarse
grove *n.* arboleda
grov·el *v.* arrastrarse
gus·to *n.* entusiasmo
gym *n.* gimnasio
gym·nast *n.* gimnasta
gym·nas·tic *adj.* gimnástico
gy·ne·col·o·gy *n.* ginecología
gyp *v.* estafar
gyp·sum *n.* yeso

H

hab·it *n.* costumbre
hab·it·a·ble *adj.* habitable
hab·i·tat *n.* habitación
hab·i·ta·tion *n.* habitación
ha·bit·u·al *adj.* habitual
ha·bit·u·ate *v.* acostumbrarse
hack *v.* acuchillar
hack·neyed *adj.* trillado
had *v. pt.* and *pp.* of have
hag *n.* bruja
hag·gard *adj.* ojeroso
hag·gle *v.* regatear
hail *n.* granizo; *v.* granizar
hail·stone *n.* piedra de granizo
hair *n.* pelo; cabello

hair·breadth *n.* ancho de un pelo
hair·dress·er *n.* peluquero
hair·pin *n.* horquilla
hale *adj.* robusto
half *n.* mitad
half·way *n.* a medio camino
hall *n.* sala
hal·le·lu·jah *interj.* aleluya
hal·low *v.* consagrar
hal·lu·cin·a·tion *n.* alucinación
hall·way *n.* passillo
hal·o *n.* halo; aureola
halt *v.* parar
hal·ter *n.* cabestro
halve *v.* partir por mitad
ham *n.* jamón
ham·burg·er *n.* hamburguesa
ham·let *n.* aldehuela
ham·mer *v.* martillar; *n.* martillo
ham·mock *n.* hamaca
ham·per *v.* impedir
hand *n.* mano
hand·bag *n.* bolso
hand·book *n.* manual
hand·cuff *n.* esposas
hand·ful *n.* puñado
hand·i·cap *n.* desventaja
hand·ker·chief *n.* pañuelo
han·dle *n.* mango; manubrio
hand·some *adj.* hermoso
hand·y *adj.* conveniente; próximo; hábil
hang *v.* pegar; colgar
hang·er·on *n.* pegote
hank·er *v.* anhelar
hap·haz·zard *adj.* fortuito
hap·pen *v.* pasar
hap·pen·ing *n.* acontecimiento
hap·pi·ly *adv.* alegremente
hap·pi·ness *n.* alegría
hap·py *adj.* feliz
har·bor *n.* puerto
hard *adj.* firme
har·dy *adj.* robusto
harm *v.* dañar
harm·ful *adj.* dañino
har·mo·ni·ous *adj.* armonioso
har·mo·ny *n.* armonía
harsh *adj.* severo
harsh·ness *n.* severidad
har·vest *v.* cosechar

hat *n.* sombrero
hatch *v.* empollar; *n.* portezuela
hatch·et *n.* hacha
hate *n.* odio; *v.* odiar
hate·ful *adj.* odioso
have *v.* tener
hawk *n.* halcón
haz·ard *v.* arriesgar; *n.* azar
he *pron.* él
head *n.* cabeza
head·ache *n.* dolor de cabeza
head·ing *n.* título
head·land *n.* promontorio
head·light *n.* faro
head·quar·ters *n.* cuartel general
head·way *n.* progreso
heal *v.* sanar; curar
health *n.* salud
health·ful *adj.* sano
heap *n.* montón
hear *v.* oír
hear·ing *n.* oído
hearse *n.* coche fúnebre
heart *n.* corazón
heart·ache *n.* angustia
heart·break *n.* angustia
heart·en *v.* alentar
heart·felt *adj.* sincero
hearth *n.* hogar
heat *v.* calentar; *n.* calor
heat·er *n.* calentador
heath *n.* brezal
heave *v.* levantar
heav·en *n.* cielo
heav·y *adj.* fuerte
heck·le *v.* interrumpir
hec·tic *adj.* febril
hedge *n.* seto
heed *v.* escuchar
heel *n.* talón
heft *n.* bulto
heif·er *n.* vaquilla
height *n.* altura
height·en *v.* elevar
hei·nous *adj.* atroz
heir *n.* heredero
heir·ess *n.* heredera
heir·loom *n.* herencia; reliquia de familia
hel·i·cop·ter *n.* helicóptero
he·li·um *n.* helio
he·lix *n.* hélice
hell *n.* infierno
hell·ish *adj.* infernal

hel·lo *interj.* hola
helm *n.* timón
hel·met *n.* casco
help *n.* ayuda; *v.* ayudar
help·ful *adj.* útil
help·ing *n.* ración
help·less *adj.* incapaz
hem *n.* dobladillo
hem·i·sphere *n.* hemisferio
hem·i·spher·ic *adj.* hemisférico
hem·or·rhage *n.* hemorragia
hem·or·rhoid *n.* hemorroides
hemp *n.* cáñamo
hen *n.* gallina
hence *adv.* de aquí; por lo tanto
her *pron. obj.* and *poss.* she
her·ald *n.* heraldo; precursor
he·ral·dic *adj.* heráldico
herb *n.* hierba
her·ba·ceous *adj.* herbáceo
her·cu·le·an *adj.* hercúleo
herds·man *n.* pastor
here *adv.* aquí
here·af·ter *adv.* en el futuro
he·red·i·tar·y *adj.* hereditiario
he·red·i·ty *n.* herencia
here·in *adv.* incluso
her·e·sy *n.* herejía
here·to·fore *adv.* hasta ahora
her·it·age *n.* herencia
her·mit *n.* ermitaño
her·mit·age *n.* ermita
her·ni·a *n.* hernia
he·ro *n.* héroe
he·ro·ic *adj.* heroico
her·o·ine *n.* heroína
her·o·ism *n.* heroísmo
her·on *n.* garza
hers *pron. poss.* she
her·self *pron.* ella misma; sí misma
hes·i·tant *adj.* vacilante
hes·i·tate *v.* vacilar
het·er·o·ge·ne·ous *adj.* heterogéneo
hew *v.* tajar
hex·a·gon *n.* hexágono
hex·ag·o·nal *adj.* hexagonal
hi·ber·nate *v.* invernar
hic·cup *n.* hipo
hide *v.* ocultar(se)

hid·e·ous *adj.* horrible; feo
hi·er·ar·chy *n.* jerarquía
hi·er·o·glyph·ic *adj.* jeroglífico
high *adj.* alto
hike *n.* caminata
hi·lar·i·ous *adj.* alegre
hi·lar·i·ty *n.* alegría
hill *n.* colina
hilt *n.* puño
him *pron. obj.* of he
him·self *pron.* el mismo
hind *adj.* trasero
hin·der *v.* impedir
hind·most *adj.* postrero
hinge *n.* gozne
hint *n.* indirecta
hip *n.* cadera
hip·po·pot·a·mus *n.* hipopótamo
hire *v.* alquilar
hire·ling *n.* mercenario
his *pron.* suyo
hiss *v.* silbar
his·to·ri·an *n.* historiador
his·tor·ic *adj.* histórico
his·to·ry *n.* historia
hit *n.* golpe; *v.* golpear
hitch *v.* atar
hitch·hike *v.* hacer autostop
hith·er *adv.* acá
hive *n.* colmena
hoard *n.* provisión
hoarse *adj.* ronco
hoax *n.* engaño
hob·ble *v.* cojear
hob·by *n.* pasatiempo
ho·bo *n.* vagabundo
hoe *n.* azadón
hog *n.* puerco
hoist *v.* alzar
hold *v.* contener; tener
hold·ing *n.* tenencia
hole *n.* hoyo
hol·i·day *n.* día de fiesta
hol·low *adj.* vacío
hol·ly *n.* acebo
hol·o·caust *n.* holocausto
hol·ster *n.* pistolera
hom·age *n.* homenaje
home *n.* casa
home·ly *adj.* feo
home·sick *adj.* nostálgico
home·ward *adv.* hacia casa
home·y *adj.* cómodo
hom·i·cide *adj.* homicidio
hom·i·ly *n.* homilía

ho·mo·gen·e·ous *adj.* homogéneo
hone *n.* piedra de afilar
hon·est *adj.* honrado
hon·es·ty *n.* honradez
hon·ey *n.* miel
hon·ey·comb *n.* panal
hon·ey·moon *n.* luna de miel
hon·ey·suck·le *n.* madreselva
hon·or *v.* honrar; *n.* honor
hon·or·a·ble *adj.* honorable
hon·or·ar·y *adj.* honorario
hood *n.* capucha
hood·lum *n.* matón
hood·wink *v.* engañar
hoof *n.* casco
hook *n.* gancho; *v.* enganchar; encorvar
hoop *n.* aro
hoot *v.* ulular; *n.* grito
hop *n.* salto; *v.* saltar
hope *v.* desear; *n.* esperanza
hope·less *adj.* desesperado
horde *n.* horda
ho·ri·zon *n.* horizonte
hor·i·zon·tal *adj.* horizontal
hor·mone *n.* hormona
horn *n.* cuerno
hor·o·scope *n.* horóscopo
hor·ri·ble *adj.* horrible
hor·ri·fy *v.* horrorizar
hor·ror *n.* horror
horse *n.* caballo
horse·man *n.* jinete
horse·pow·er *n.* caballo de fuerza
horse·rad·ish *n.* rábano picante
horse·shoe *n.* herradura
hor·ti·cul·ture *n.* horticultura
hose *n.* medias
hose *n.* manga
ho·sier·y *n.* calcetería
hos·pi·ta·ble *adj.* hospitalario
hos·pi·tal *n.* hospital
hos·pi·tal·i·ty *n.* hospitalidad
host *n.* anfitrión; patrón; multitud
hos·tage *n.* rehén
host·ess *n.* anfitriona
hos·tile *adj.* hostil
hos·til·i·ty *n.* hostilidad

hot *adj.* caliente
ho·tel *n.* hotel
hot·house *n.* invernáculo
hound *n.* podenco; *v.* perseguir
hour *n.* hora
house *n.* casa
house·keep·er *n.* ama de llaves
hous·ing *n.* alojamiento
how *adv.* cómo
how·ev·er *adv.* en todo caso; *conj.* sin embargo
howl *v.* aullar
hub *n.* cubo
hud·dle *v.* amontonar(se)
hue *n.* color; matiz
hug *v.* abrazar
huge *adj.* enorme
hull *n.* cáscara; casco
hum *v.* zumbar; canturrear
hu·man *n.* humano
hu·man·i·ty *n.* humanidad
hum·ble *adj.* humilde
hu·mid·i·ty *n.* humedad
hu·mil·i·ate *v.* humillar
hu·mil·i·a·tion *n.* humillación
hum·ming·bird *n.* colibrí
hu·mor *n.* complacer
hump *n.* giba; joroba
hunch *v.* corazonada
hunch·back *n.* jorobado
hun·dred *adj.* ciento
hun·dredth *adj.* centésimo
hun·ger *n.* hambre
hun·gry *adj.* hambriento
hunt *v.* cazar
hunt·er *n.* cazador
hur·dle *n.* valla; zarzo
hurl *v.* lanzar
hur·ri·cane *n.* huracán
hur·ry *v.* apresurar; darse prisa
hurt *v.* hacer daño; doler; dañar
hus·band *n.* esposo
husk *n.* cáscara
husk·y *adj.* ronco
hus·sy *n.* pícara
hus·tle *v.* empujar
hy·brid *n.* híbrido
hy·drant *n.* boca de riego
hy·dro·gen *n.* hidrógeno
hy·e·na *n.* hiena
hy·giene *n.* higiene
hymn *n.* himno

hyp·no·sis *n.* hipnosis
hyp·no·tize *v.* hipnotizar
hyp·o·crite *n.* hipócrita
hy·po·der·mic *adj.* hipodérmico
hy·pot·e·nuse *n.* hipotenusa
hy·poth·e·sis *n.* hipótesis
hy·po·thet·i·cal *adj.* hipotético
hys·te·ri·a *n.* histerismo
hys·ter·ic *adj.* histérico

I

I *pron.* yo
i·bis *n.* ibis
ice *n.* hielo
ice·berg *n.* iceberg
ice cream *n.* helado
i·ci·cle *n.* carámbano
ic·ing *n.* garapiña
i·con *n.* icono
i·con·o·clast *n.* iconoclasta
i·cy *adj.* helado
i·de·a *n.* idea
i·de·al *adj.* ideal
i·de·al·ize *v.* idealizar
i·den·ti·cal *adj.* idéntico
i·den·ti·fi·ca·tion *n.* identificación
i·den·ti·fy *v.* identificar
i·den·ti·ty *n.* identidad
i·de·ol·o·gy *n.* ideología
id·i·om *n.* idiotismo
id·i·o·mat·ic *adj.* idiomático
id·i·o·syn·cra·sy *n.* idiosincrasia
id·i·ot *n.* idiota
i·dle *adj.* ocioso
i·dol *n.* ídolo
i·dol·a·try *n.* idolatría
i·dol·ize *v.* idolatrar
if *conj.* si
ig·nite *v.* encender(se)
ig·no·ble *adj.* innoble
ig·no·min·y *n.* ignominia
ig·no·rance *n.* ignorancia
ig·no·rant *adj.* ignorante
ig·nore *v.* no hacer caso de
ill *adj.* enfermo
il·le·gal *adj.* ilegal
il·leg·i·ble *adj.* ilegible

il·le·git·i·ma·cy *n.*
ilegitimidad

il·le·git·i·mate *adj.*
ilegítimo

il·lic·it *adj.* ilícito

il·lit·er·ate *adj., n.*
analfabeto

ill·ness *n.* enfermedad

il·lu·mi·nate *v.* iluminar

il·lu·sion *n.* ilusión

il·lus·trate *v.* ilustrar

il·lus·tra·tion *n.* ilustración;
ejemplo

im·age *n.* imagen

im·ag·i·nar·y *adj.*
imaginario

im·ag·i·na·tion *n.*
imaginación

im·ag·ine *v.* imaginar

im·be·cile *n., adj.* imbécil

im·i·tate *v.* imitar

im·i·ta·tion *n.* imitación;
copia

im·ma·ture *adj.* inmaduro

im·meas·ur·a·ble *adj.*
inmensurable

im·me·di·ate *adj.* inmediato

im·mense *adj.* inmenso

im·mer·sion *n.* inmersión

im·mi·grant *n.* inmigrante

im·mi·grate *v.* inmigrar

im·mi·gra·tion *n.*
inmigración

im·mi·nent *adj.* inminente

im·mo·bile *adj.* inmóvil

im·mo·dest *adj.* impúdico

im·mor·al *adj.* inmoral

im·mor·tal *adj.* inmortal

im·mune *adj.* inmune

im·mu·ni·ty *n.* inmunidad

imp *n.* diablillo

im·pact *n.* impacto

im·pair *v.* deteriorar

im·part *v.* comunicar; relatar;
dar

im·par·tial *n.* imparcial

im·pa·tient *adj.* impaciente

im·peach *v.* acusar

im·pec·a·ble *adj.* impecable

im·pede *v.* impedir; estorbar

im·ped·i·ment *n.*
impedimento; estorbo

im·pel *v.* impulsar

im·pe·ri·al *adj.* imperial

im·pe·ri·ous *adj.* imperioso

im·per·son·al *adj.*
impersonal

im·per·ti·nent *adj.*
impertinente

im·pe·tus *n.* ímpetu

im·pi·e·ty *n.* impiedad

im·ple·ment *n.* herramienta

im·pli·cate *v.* implicar

im·plore *v.* implorar

im·ply *v.* dar a entender;
significar

im·po·lite *adj.* descortés

im·port *v.* importar

im·por·tance *n.* importancia

im·por·tant *adj.* importante

im·pose *v.* imponer

im·pos·si·ble *adj.* imposible

im·pos·tor *n.* impostor

im·po·tence *n.* impotencia

im·pov·er·ish *v.* empobrecer

im·prac·ti·cal *adj.*
impracticable

im·press *v.* estampar;
imprimir; impresionar

im·pres·sion *n.* impresión

im·print *v.* imprimir

im·prove *v.* mejorar

im·prove·ment *n.* mejora

im·pro·vise *n.* improvisar

im·pulse *n.* impulso

in *adv.* dentro; *prep.* durante,
en

in·a·bil·i·ty *n.* inhabilidad

in·ca·pac·i·tate *v.*
incapacitar

inch *n.* pulgada

in·ci·den·tal *adj.* incidental

in·cin·er·ate *v.* incinerar

in·ci·sion *n.* incisión

in·cite *v.* incitar

in·cli·na·tion *n.* inclinación

in·clu·sion *n.* inclusión

in·com·pa·ra·ble *adj.*
incomparable

in·com·plete *adj.*
incompleto

in·cor·rect *adj.* incorrecto

in·crease *v.* crecer;
acrecentar

in·crim·i·nate *v.* incriminar

in·de·cen·cy *n.* indecencia

in·de·cent *adj.* indecente

in·deed *adv.* de veras

in·def·i·nite *adj.* indefinido

in·dem·ni·ty *n.*
indemnización

in·dent *v.* mellar

in·den·ta·tion *n.* mella

in·de·pend·ence *n.*
independencia

in·de·pend·ent *adj.*
independiente

in·de·struct·i·ble *adj.*
indestructible

in·dex *n.* índice

in·di·cate *v.* indicar

in·di·ca·tion *n.* indicación

in·dict *v.* acusar

in·dif·fer·ent *adj.*
indiferente

in·dig·e·nous *adj.* indígena

in·di·gent *adj.* indigente

in·di·ges·tion *n.* indigestión

in·dig·ni·ty *n.* indignidad

in·di·go *n.* añil

in·di·rect *adj.* indirecto

in·dis·creet *adj.* indiscreto

in·dis·cre·tion *n.*
indiscreción

in·dis·pen·sa·ble *adj.*
imprescindible

in·di·vid·u·al *n.* individuo

in·di·vid·u·al·i·ty *n.*
individualidad

in·doc·tri·nate *v.* adoctrinar

in·do·lent *adj.* indolente

in·door *adj.* interior; de
puertas adentro

in·doors *adv.* dentro

in·duce *v.* inducir

in·duct *v.* iniciar

in·dulge *v.* satisfacer;
consentir

in·dus·tri·al *adj.* industrial

in·er·tia *n.* inercia

in·ev·i·ta·ble *adj.* inevitable

in·fa·my *n.* infamia

in·fan·cy *n.* infancia

in·fect *v.* infectar

in·fec·tion *n.* infección

in·fe·ri·or *adj.* inferior

in·fi·del·i·ty *n.* infidelidad

in·fil·trate *v.* infiltrarse

in·fi·nite *adj.* infinito

in·fin·i·tive *n.* infinitivo

in·fin·i·ty *n.* infinidad

in·fir·ma·ry *n.* enfermería

in·flame *v.* inflamar;
provocar

in·flam·ma·ble *adj.*
inflamable

in·flate *v.* inflar

in·fla·tion *n.* inflación

in·flec·tion *n.* inflexión

in·flict *v.* infligir; imponer

in·flu·ence *n.* influencia

in·flu·en·za *n.* gripe

in·form *v.* informar

in·for·mal *adj.*
sin ceremonia

in·for·ma·tion *n.*
información

in·for·ma·tive *adj.*
informativo

in·fre·quent *adj.* infrecuente

in·fu·ri·ate *v.* enfurecer

in·fuse *v.* infundir

in·fu·sion *n.* infusión

in·gen·ious *adj.* ingenioso

in·ge·nu·i·ty *n.* ingeniosidad

in·got *n.* lingote

in·gre·di·ent *n.* ingrediente

in·hab·it *v.* habitar

in·hab·i·tant *n.* habitante

in·hale *v.* inhalar; aspirar

in·her·ent *adj.* inmanente;
inherente

in·her·it *v.* heredar

in·her·it·ance *n.* herencia

in·hib·it *v.* inhibir

in·hi·bi·tion *n.* inhibición

in·hu·man *adj.* inhumano;
cruel

in·iq·ui·ty *n.* iniquidad

in·i·tial *adj.* inicial

in·i·ti·ate *v.* iniciar

in·i·ti·a·tion *n.* iniciación

in·i·ti·a·tive *n.* iniciativa

in·ject *v.* inyectar

in·jec·tion *n.* inyección

in·jure *v.* hacer daño a;
ofender

in·ju·ry *n.* daño; injuria

in·jus·tice *n.* injusticia

ink *n.* tinta

ink·ling *n.* sospecha

in·let *n.* entrada; ensenada

in·mate *n.* inquilino

inn *n.* posada

in·nate *adj.* innato

in·ner *adj.* interior

in·no·cence *n.* inocencia

in·no·cent *adj.* inocente

in·no·va·tion *n.* innovación

in·nu·en·do *n.* indirecta

in·nu·mer·a·ble *adj.*
innumerable

in·oc·u·late *v.* inocular

in·oc·u·la·tion *n.*
inoculación

in·quest *n.* pesquisa judicial

in·quire *v.* preguntar

in·quir·y *n.* indagación;

pregunta
in·qui·si·tion *n.* inquisición
in·sane *adj.* insensato; loco
in·san·i·ty *n.* locura
in·scribe *v.* inscribir
in·scrip·tion *n.* inscripción
in·sect *n.* insecto
in·se·cure *adj.* inseguro;
   precario
in·sert *v.* insertar; meter
in·ser·tion *n.* inserción
in·side *n.* interior
in·sight *n.* perspicacia
in·sig·ni·a *n.* insignias
in·sig·nif·i·cance *n.*
   insignificancia
in·sin·u·ate *v.* insinuar
in·sin·u·a·tion *n.*
   insinuación; indirecta
in·sip·id *adj.* insípido
in·sist *v.* insistir
in·sist·ent *adj.* insistente;
   porfiado
in·so·lence *n.* insolencia
in·so·lent *adj.* insolente
in·som·ni·a *n.* insomnio
in·spect *v.* examinar;
   inspeccionar
in·spec·tion *n.* inspección
in·spi·ra·tion *n.* inspiración
in·spire *v.* inspirar; estimular
in·stall *v.* instalar
in·stall·ment *n.* plazo;
   entrega
in·stance *n.* ejemplo
in·stant *n.* instante
in·stan·ta·ne·ous *adj.*
   instantáneo
in·stead *adv.* en lugar; en
   vez de
in·step *n.* empeine
in·sti·gate *v.* instigar
in·stinct *n.* instinto
in·stinc·tive *adj.* instinctivo
in·sti·tute *v.* instituir;
   empezar
in·sti·tu·tion *n.* institución
in·struct *v.* instruir; enseñar
in·struc·tion *n.* instrucción
in·stru·ment *n.* instrumento
in·suf·fi·cient *adj.*
   insuficiente
in·su·late *v.* aislar
in·su·la·tion *n.* aislamiento
in·su·lin *n.* insulina
in·sult *n.* insulto; ultraje
in·sur·ance *n.* seguro

in·sure *v.* asegurar
in·sur·rec·tion *n.*
   insurrección
in·tact *adj.* intacto
in·te·ger *n.* número entero
in·te·grate *v.* integrar
in·te·gra·tion *n.* integración
in·teg·ri·ty *n.* integridad
in·tel·lect *n.* intelecto
in·tel·li·gence *n.*
   inteligencia
in·tel·li·gent *adj.* inteligente
in·tend *v.* proponerse; querer
   decir
in·tense *adj.* intenso
in·ten·si·ty *n.* intensidad
in·tent *adj.* atento; absorto
in·ter *v.* enterrar
in·ter·cede *v.* interceder
in·ter·cept *v.* interceptar
in·ter·ces·sion *n.*
   intercesión
in·ter·change *v.*
   intercambiar
in·ter·course *n.* comercio;
   trato; coito
in·ter·est *n.* interés
in·ter·fere *v.* intervenir;
   meterse
in·ter·im *n.* ínterin
in·ter·jec·tion *n.*
   interjección
in·ter·lude *n.* intermedio
in·ter·me·di·ate *adj.*
   intermedio
in·ter·mis·sion *n.*
   intermisión
in·tern *n.* interno
in·ter·nal *adj.* interior
in·ter·na·tion·al *adj.*
   internacional
in·ter·play *n.* interacción
in·ter·pose *v.* interponer
in·ter·pret *v.* explicar;
   interpretar; entender
in·ter·pre·ta·tion *n.* inter
   pretación
in·ter·ro·gate *v.* interrogar
in·ter·ro·ga·tion *n.*
   interrogación
in·ter·rupt *v.* interrumpir
in·ter·rup·tion *n.*
   interrupción
in·ter·twine *n.* entretejer(se)
in·ter·val *n.* intervalo
in·ter·vene *v.* intervenir
in·ter·view *n.* entrevista

in·tes·tine *n.* intestino
in·ti·mate *v.* intimar
in·tim·i·date *v.* intimidar
in·to *prep.* en
in·tol·er·ant *adj.* intolerante
in·to·na·tion *n.* entonación
in·tox·i·cate *v.* embriagar;
   intoxicar
in·tran·si·tive *adj.*
   intransitivo
in·tra·ve·nous *adj.*
   intravenoso
in·trep·id *adj.* intrépido
in·tri·ca·cy *n.* complejidad;
   enredo
in·tri·cate *adj.* intrincado
in·trigue *v.* intrigar; fascinar
in·trin·sic *adj.* intrínseco
in·tro·duce *v.* introducir
in·tro·duc·tion *n.*
   introducción
in·trude *v.* entremeterse
in·tu·i·tion *n.* intuición
in·ure *v.* habituar
in·vade *v.* invadir
in·va·lid *adj.* inválido
in·var·i·a·ble *adj.* invariable
in·va·sion *n.* invasión
in·vent *v.* inventar
in·ven·tion *n.* invención
in·ven·to·ry *n.* inventario
in·ver·sion *n.* inversión
in·vert *v.* invertir
in·ver·te·brate *adj., n.*
   invertebrado
in·vest *v.* investir
in·ves·ti·ga·tion *n.*
   investigación
in·vig·or·ate *v.* vigorizar
in·vin·ci·ble *adj.* invencible
in·vis·i·ble *adj.* invisible
in·vi·ta·tion *n.* invitación
in·vite *v.* invitar
in·vo·ca·tion *n.* invocación
in·voice *n.* factura
in·voke *v.* invocar; implorar
in·vol·un·tar·y *adj.*
   involuntario
in·volve *v.* complicar;
   comprometer; enredar
in·ward *adv.* hacia dentro
i·o·dine *n.* yodo
i·on *n.* ion
i·ron *v.* planchar; *n.* plancha
i·ron·ic *adj.* irónico
i·ro·ny *n.* ironía
ir·ra·di·ate *v.* irradiar

ir·ra·tion·al *adj.* irracional
ir·rec·on·cil·a·ble *adj.*
   irreconciliable
ir·ref·u·ta·ble *adj.*
   irrefutable
ir·reg·u·lar *adj.* irregular
ir·rel·e·vant *adj.* inaplicable
ir·re·sist·i·ble *adj.*
   irresistible
ir·re·spon·si·ble *adj.*
   irresponsable
ir·ri·gate *v.* regar
ir·ri·tate *v.* irritar; provocar;
   molestar
is·land *n.* isla
isle *n.* isla
i·so·late *v.* aislar
i·so·ce·les *adj.* isósceles
is·sue *v.* publicar; salir;
   n. resultado; emisión
isth·mus *n., pl.* istmo
it *pron.* le; la; lo; ello; ella; el
i·tal·ic *n.* usu. pl. letra
   bastardilla
i·tal·i·cize *v.* imprimir en
   bastardilla
itch *v.* picar
itch·y *adj.* que da picazón;
   impaciente
i·tem *n.* artículo; partida
i·tem·ize *v.* detallar
it·er·ate *v.* iterar; repetir
i·tin·er·ar·y *n.* itinerario
it *pron.* el, ella, ello
i·vo·ry *n., pl.* marfil
i·vy *n.* hiedra

J

jab *v.* golpear
jab·ber *v.* farfullar
jack *n.* mozo; marinero; gato;
   sota
jack·al *n.* chacal
jack·ass *n.* burro
jack·et *n.* chaqueta
jack·knife *n.* navaja
jack·pot *n.* bote
jade *n.* jade
jag·uar *n.* jaguar
jail *v.* encarcelar; *n.* cárcel
jam *v.* apiñar; atascar
jamb *n.* jamba
jam·bo·ree *n.* francachela
jangle *n.* sonido discordante
jan·i·tor *n.* portero

Jan·u·ar·y *n.* enero
jar *n.* jarra
jar·gon *n.* jerga
jas·mine *n.* jazmín
jaun·dice *n.* ictericia
jaunt *n.* excursión
jave·lin *n.* jabalina
jaw *n.* quijada
jay *n.* arrendajo
jazz *n.* jazz
jeal·ous *adj.* celoso
Jeep *n.* trademark; jeep
jeer *v.* mofarse; befar
jell *v.* cuajar(se)
jel·ly *n.* jalea
jel·ly·fish *n.* medusa
jeop·ar·dize *v.* arriesgar
jeop·ar·dy *n.* peligro
jer·kin *n.* justillo
jer·sey *n.* jersey
jest *n.* chanza
jet *n.* chorro; surtidor; avión a
    reacción; azabache
jet·sam *n.* echazón
jet·ti·son *n.* echazón
jet·ty *n.* malecón; muelle
jew·el *n.* joya
jew·el·er *n.* joyero
jew·el·ry *n.* joyas
jif·fy *n.* instante
jib *n.* jiga
jig·saw *n.* sierra de vaivén
jig·saw puzzle *n.*
    rompecabezas
jilt *v.* dar calabazas
jim·my *n.* palanqueta
jin·gle *v.* tintinear
jinx *n.* gafe
jit·ters *n.* inquietud
job *n.* trabajo
jock·ey *n.* jockey
jo·cose *adj.* jocoso
joc·u·lar *adj.* jocoso
joc·und *adj.* alegre
jog *v.* empujar; correr;
    despacio
join *v.* unir(se)
joint *n.* juntura; unión
joist *n.* viga
joke *n.* chiste; broma
jok·er *n.* bromista
jol·ly *adj.* alegre
jolt *v.* sacudir
jon·quil *n.* junquillo
jour·nal *n.* periódico
jour·nal·ism *n.* periodismo
jour·nal·ist *n.* periodista

jour·ney *v.* viajar; *n.* viaje
joy·ous *adj.* alegre
judge *n.* juez; *v.* juzgar
ju·di·cial *adj.* judicial
jug·gle *v.* hacer juegos
    malabares
jug·u·lar *adj.* yuqular
juice *n.* jugo
July *n.* julio
jum·ble *v.* mezclar
jump *n.* salto; *v.* saltar
jump·er *n.* saltador
junc·tion *n.* juntura;
    empalme
junc·ture *n.* juntura;
    coyuntura
June *n.* junio
jun·gle *n.* selva
jun·ior *adj.* más joven; menor
ju·ni·per *n.* enebro
junk *n.* trastos viejos; junco
ju·ris·dic·tion *n.* jurisdicción
ju·ris·pru·dence *n.*
    jurisprudencia
ju·rist *n.* jurista
ju·ror *n.* jurado
ju·ry *n.* jurado
just *adj.* justo; imparcial
jus·ti·fy *v.* justificar
ju·ve·nile *adj.* joven

K

ka·lei·do·scope *n.*
    caleidoscopio
kan·ga·roo *n.* canguro
kar·at *n.* quilate
keel *n.* quilla
keen *adj.* agudo; perspicaz;
    entusiasta; afilado
keep *v.* detener; tener;
    cumplir
keep·ing *n.* custodia
keg *n.* cuñete
ken *n.* alcance
ken·nel *n.* perrera
ker·chief *n.* pañuelo
ker·nel *n.* almendra; núcleo
ker·o·sene *n.* queroseno
ketch *n.* queche
ketch·up *n.* salsa picante de
    tomate
ket·tle *n.* tetera
key *n.* llave
key·board *n.* teclado
key·stone *n.* piedra clave

kha·ki *n.* caqui
kick *v.* dar patadas; dar un
    puntapié
kid *n.* cabrito
kid·nap *v.* secuestrar
kid·ney *n.* riñón
kill *v.* matar
kiln. *n.* honor
kil·o·cy·cle *n.* kilociclo
kil·o·gram *n.* kilogramo
kil·o·me·ter *n.* kilómetro
kil·o·watt *n.* kilovatio
kin *n.* parientes
kind *adj.* bueno; *n.* género
kin·der·gar·ten *n.* jardín de
    la infancia
kind·heart·ed *adj.*
    bondadoso
kin·dle *v.* encender
kind·ly *adj.* bondadoso
kind·ness *n.* benevolencia
kin·dred *n.* parientes
king *n.* rey
king·dom *n.* reino
kink *n.* coca; peculiaridad
kin·ship *n.* parentesco
kins·man *n.* pariente
kiss *n.* beso; *v.* besar
kit *n.* equipo; avíos
kitch·en *n.* cocina
kite *n.* cometa
kith *n.* amigos
kit·ten *n.* gatito
knack *n.* maña
knap·sack *n.* mochila
knave *n.* bribón
knav·er·y *n.* bellaquería
knav·ish *adj.* bellaco
knead *v.* amasar
knee *n.* rodilla
knee·cap *n.* rótula
kneel *n.* arrodillar
knee·pad *n.* rodillera
knell *n.* doble
knick·ers *n.* bombachos
knick·knack *n.* chuchería
knife *v.* acuchillar; *n.* cuchillo
knight *n.* caballero
knight·hood *n.*
    caballerosidad
knit *v.* hacer punto; tejer
knit·ting *n.* tejido
knob *n.* tirador; pomo; puño
knock *v.* golpear
knock·down *adj.*
    que derriba
knock·er *adj.* golpeador

knock·ing *n.* llamada
knoll *n.* otero
knot *v.* anudar
knot·hole *n.* agujero
knot·ted *adj.* anudado;
    nudoso
knot·ty *adj.* enredado;
    nudoso
know *v.* saber; conocer
know·a·ble *adj.* conocible
know·how *n.* pericia
know·ing *adj.* astuto; hábil
know·ing·ly *adv.* a
    sabiendas
knowl·edge *n.* saber
knowl·edge·a·ble *adj.*
    erudito
known *adj.* conocido
know·noth·ing *n.* ignorante
knuck·le *n.* nudillo
ko·a·la *n.* koala
kook *n.* excéntrico
Ko·ran *n.* Alcorán; Corán
ko·sher *adj.* legítimo;
    conforme a las reglas
kow·tow *v.* postarse

L

lab *n.* laboratorio
la·bel *v.* marcar; *n.* etiqueta;
    rótulo
la·bi·al *adj.* labial
la·bor *v.* trabajar; *n.* trabajo
lab·o·ra·to·ry *n.* laboratorio
la·borer *n.* peón; trabajador;
    jornalero
la·bo·ri·ous *adj.* laborioso
lab·y·rinth *n.* laberinto
lac *n.* laca
lace *v.* encordonar; *n.* encaje
lac·er·ate *v.* lacerar
lac·er·ation *n.* laceración
lach·ry·mal *adj.* lagrimal
lack *v.* faltar; hacer falta;
    n. falta
lack·ey *n.* lacayo
lack·ing *adj.* deficiente;
    prep. sin
lack·lus·ter *adj.* deslustrado
la·con·ic *adj.* lacónico
lac·quer *n.* laca
lac·tase *n.* lactasa
lac·tate *v.* lactar
lac·ta·tion *n.* lactancia
lac·tic *adj.* láctico

lac·tose *n.* lactosa
la·cu·na *n.* laguna
lac·y *adj.* de encaje
lad *n.* chico
lad·der *n.* escalera
lad·die *n.* chico
lade *v.* agobiar
lad·en *adj.* agobiado; cargado
la·dle *n.* cucharón
la·dy *n.* dama
la·dy·bug *n.* mariquita
lag *v.* atrasarse; rezagarse
lag·gard *adj.* rezagado
la·goon *n.* laguna
la·ic *adj.* laico
lair *n.* madriguera
la·i·ty *n.* laicos
lake *n.* lago
lamb *n.* cordero
lame *v.* encojar; *adj.* renco; cojo
la·me *n.* lame
la·ment *v.* deplorar; lamentar
la·men·ta·ble *adj.* lamentable
lam·en·ta·tion *n.* lamentación
la·ment·ed *adj.* lamentado
lam·i·na *n.* lámina
lam·i·nate *v.* laminar
lam·i·nat·ed *adj.* laminado
lam·i·na·tion *n.* laminación
lamp *n.* lámpara
lam·poon *v.* satirizar; *n.* sátira
lam·prey *n.* lamprea
lance *n.* lanza
lan·cet *n.* lanceta
land *v.* país; tierra
land·ed *adj.* hacendado
land·fall *n.* recalada
land·hold·er *n.* terrateniente
land·ing *n.* aterrizaje; desembarco
land·lord *n.* arrendador
land·mark *n.* mojón
land·own·er *n.* terrateniente
land·scape *n.* panorama
lane *n.* ruta; vereda; camino
lan·guage *n.* lenguaje
lan·guid *adj.* lánguido
lan·guish *v.* decaer; languidecer
lan·guish·ing *adj.* lánguido
lan·guor *n.* languidez
lan·guor·ous *adj.* lánguido
lan·o·lin *n.* lanolina

lan·tern *n.* linterna
lap *n.* falda; *v.* plegar; doblar
la·pel *n.* solapa
lap·i·dar·y *n.* lapidario
lapse *v.* faltar; caer; decaer; deslizarse
lapsed *adj.* caduco
lar·ce·ny *adj.* robo
lard *n.* lardo
large *adj.* grande
lar·gess *n.* donativo; generosidad
lar·va *n.* larva
lar·val *adj.* larval
lar·yn·gi·tis *n.* laringitis
lar·ynx *n.* laringe
la·ser *n.* laser
lash *n.* látigo; azote; latigazo
lash·ing *n.* fustigación; azotaína
lass *n.* muchacha
las·si·tude *n.* lasitud
las·so *n.* lazo
last *adv.* finalmente; *adj.* final
last·ing *adj.* duradero
last·ly *adv.* finalmente
latch *n.* aldabilla
late *adj.* tarde
late·ly *adv.* últimamente
la·ten·cy *n.* latencia
late·ness *n.* tardanza
la·tent *adj.* latente
la·ter *adj.* posterior
lat·er·al *adj.* lateral
lat·est *adj.* último
la·tex *n.* látex
lath·er *n.* espuma
lat·i·tude *n.* latitud
la·trine *n.* letrina
lat·ter *adj.* último
lat·ter·day *adj.* reciente
lat·tice *n.* celosía; *v.* enrejar
lat·tice·work *n.* enrejado
laud *v.* alabar; elogiar
laud·a·able *adj.* laudable
laud·a·tor·y *adj.* laudatorio
laugh *n.* risa; *v.* reír(se)
laugh·a·ble *adj.* absurdo; cómico
laugh·ing *adj.* risueño
laugh·ter *n.* risa
launch *v.* lanzar; iniciar; botar
launch·er *n.* lanzador
launch·ing *n.* lanzamiento
laun·der *v.* lavar(se)

laun·dered *adj.* lavado
laun·der·er *n.* lavandero
laun·dry *n.* lavandería
lau·rel *n.* laurel
la·va *n.* lava
lav·en·der *n.* lavanda
lav·ish *adj.* espléndido; generoso
law *n.* derecho; ley
law·ful *adj.* legítimo
law·less *adj.* sin leyes
law·mak·er *n.* legislador
lawn *n.* césped
law·yer *n.* abogado
lax *adj.* laxo
lax·a·tive *n.* laxante
lax·i·ty *n.* laxitud
lay *v.* acostar; poner
lay·er *n.* estrato
lay·out *n.* disposición
la·zi·ness *n.* pereza
la·zy *adj.* perezoso
lead *v.* mandar; conducir
lead·en *adj.* plomizo
lead·er *n.* líder
lead·er·ship *n.* mando
lead·ing *n.* emplomado
leaf *n.* hoja
leaf·let *n.* panfleto
leaf·y *adj.* hojoso
league *n.* liga
leak *v.* gotear; salir(se); *n.* gotera; agujero
lean *adj.* magro
lean·ing *n.* inclinación
leap *v.* saltar
learn *v.* aprender
learn·ed *adj.* erudito
learn·er *n.* principiante
learn·ing *n.* aprendizaje
lease·hold *n.* arrendamiento
lease·hold·er *n.* arrendador
leash *n.* traílla
leas·ing *n.* arrendamiento
least *adv.* menos; *adj.* menor
leath·er *n.* cuero
leath·er·y *adj.* curtido
leave *v.* salir; dejar; irse
leav·en *n.* levadura
leav·ing *n.* salida
lech·er·ous *adj.* lujurioso
lech·er·y *n.* lujuria
lec·tor *n.* lector
lec·ture *v.* sermonear; reprender, *n.* reprimenda; conferencia

lec·tur·er *n.* conferenciante
leech *n.* sanguijuela
leek *n.* puerro
left *adj.* izquierdo
left·over *adj.* sobrante
left·y *n.* zurdo
leg *n.* pierna
leg·a·cy *n.* herencia
le·gal *adj.* legal
le·gal·ist *n.* legalista
le·gal·is·tic *adj.* legalista
le·gal·i·ty *n.* legalidad
le·gal·ize *v.* legalizar
leg·ate *n.* legado
le·ga·tion *n.* legación
leg·end *n.* leyenda
leg·end·ar·y *adj.* legendario
leg·gings *n.* polainas
leg·i·bil·i·ty *n.* legibilidad
leg·i·ble *adj.* legible
le·gion *n.* legión
le·gion·ar·y *n.* legionario
le·gion·aire *n.* legionario
leg·is·late *v.* legislar
leg·is·la·tion *n.* legislación
leg·is·la·tor *n.* legislador
le·git·i·ma·cy *n.* legitimidad
le·git·i·mate *adj.* legitimar
lei·sure *n.* ocio
lem·on *n.* limón
lem·on·ade *n.* limonada
lend *v.* impartir; prestar
lend·er *n.* prestador
length *n.* extensión; longitud; tramo; largo
length·en *v.* prolongar(se); alargar(se)
length·y *adj.* prolongado
le·nient *adj.* indulgente
lens *n.* lente
len·til *n.* lenteja
le·o·nine *adj.* leonino
leop·ard *n.* leopardo
lep·er *n.* leproso
lep·ro·sy *n.* lepra
lep·rous *adj.* leproso
le·sion *n.* lesión
less *adv., adj.* menos
less·en *v.* disminuir
less·er *adj.* menor
les·son *n.* lección
let *v.* dejar; permitir
let·down *n.* desilusión
le·thal *adj.* letal
le·thar·gic *adj.* letárgico
leth·ar·gy *n.* letargo
let·ter *n.* carta

let·tered *adj.* letrado
let·ter·ing *n.* rótulo
let·tuce *n.* lechuga
leu·ke·mi·a *n.* leucemia
lev·el *n.* llano; nivel
lev·i·ta·tion *n.* levitación
lev·y *v.* recaudar; exigir
lewd *adj.* lujurioso
lewd·ness *n.* lujuria
lex·i·cog·ra·phy
　n. lexicografía
lex·i·con *n.* léxico
li·a·bil·i·ty *n.* obligación
li·a·ble *adj.* sujeto;
　responsable
li·ar *n.* mentiroso
li·ba·tion *n.* libación
lib·er·al *adj.* liberal
lib·er·ate *v.* libertar
lib·er·ty *n.* libertad
li·brar·y *n.* biblioteca
lie *v.* mentir; acostarse
life *n.* vida
lift *v.* levantar(se) elevar
light *n.* lámpara; luz
light·ly *adv.* ligeramente
like *n.* gusto; *v.* gustar
like·ness *n.* semejanza
li·lac *n.* lila
lil·y *n.* lirio
lim·bo *n.* limbo
lime *n.* lima
lim·it *v.* limitar
lim·ou·sine *n.* limousina
line *v.* alinear; rayar;
　n. raya; línea
li·on *n.* león
lip *n.* labio
liq·uid *n.* líquido
liq·ui·date *v.* liquidar
liq·uor *n.* licor
list *n.* lista
lit·er·al *adj.* literal
lit·er·ar·y *adj.* literario
lit·er·a·ture *n.* literatura
lit·tle *n., adj., adv.* poco;
　adj. pequeño
live *v.* vivir
liz·ard *n.* lagarto
lob·ster *n.* langosta
lo·cal *adj.* local
lo·cal·i·ty *n.* localidad
lo·cate *v.* encontrar
lone *adj.* solitario
lone·ly *adj.* solo
long *adj.* largo
look *n.* mirada; *v.* buscar;
　mirar
loose *v.* soltar; *adj.* disoluto;
　suelto
lost *adj.* perdido
lo·tion *n.* loción
loud *adj.* alto
love *v.* amar; querer; *n.* amor
love·ly *adj.* hermoso
low *adv., adj.* bajo;
　adv. abajo
low·er *v.* bajar
loy·al *adj.* fiel
loy·al·ty *n.* fidelidad
lu·bri·cant *n.* lubricante
lu·bri·cious *adj.* lúbrico
lu·cent *adj.* luciente
lu·cid *adj.* cuerdo; lúcido
lu·cid·i·ty *n.* lucidez
luck *n.* suerte
luck·less *adj.* desafortunado
luck·y *adj.* afortunado
lu·cra·tive *adj.* lucrativo
lu·di·crous *adj.* ridículo
lug *v.* halar
lug·gage *n.* equipaje
luke·warm *adj.* tibio
lull *v.* sosegar; embaucar
lum·bar *adj.* lumbar
lum·ber·ing *adj.* torpe;
　pesado
lu·mi·nance *n.* luminancia
lu·mi·na·ry *n.* luminar
lum·i·nes·cence
　n. luminescente
lu·mi·nous *adj.* luminoso
lump *n.* masa; terrón
lu·na·cy *n.* locura
lu·nar *adj.* lunar
lunch *v.* almorzar;
　n. almuerzo
lus·ter *n.* lustre
lus·ty *adj.* robusto
lute *n.* laúd
lux·u·ri·ant *adj.* lozano
lux·u·ry *n.* lujo
lye *n.* lejía
lymph *n.* linfa
lynch *n.* linchar
lynx *n.* lince
lyre *n.* lira
lyr·ic *adj.* lírico

M

ma·ca·bre *adj.* macabro

mac·a·ro·ni *n.* macarrones
mac·a·roon *n.* mostachón
ma·caw *n.* guacamayo
mac·er·ate *v.* macerar(se)
ma·chet·e *n.* machete
mach·i·nate *v.* maquinar
mach·i·na·tion
　n. maquinación
ma·chine *n.* máquina
ma·chine·gun
　n. ametralladora
ma·chin·er·y *n.* maquinaria
ma·chin·ist *n.* maquinista
mack·er·el *n.* caballa
mac·ra·me *n.* macramé
mac·ro·bi·ot·ics
　n. macrobiótica
mac·ro·cosm
　n. macrocosmo
mac·ro·scop·ic
　adj. macroscópico
mad *adj.* furioso
mad·cap *adj.* alocado
mad·den *v.* enloquecer
mad·den·ing
　adj. enloquecedor
made·up *adj.* inventado
mad·ness *n.* locura
mag·a·zine *n.* revista
mag·got *n.* gusano
mag·ic *n.* magia
mag·i·cal *adj.* mágico
ma·gi·cian *n* mago
mag·is·te·ri·al
　adj. magistral
mag·is·trate *n.* magistrado
mag·nate *n.* magnate
mag·ne·si·um *n.* magnesio
mag·net·ic *adj.* magnético
mag·net·ism *n.* magnetismo
mag·net·ize *v.* magnetizar
mag·ni·fi·ca·tion
　n. ampliación
mag·nif·i·cence
　n. magnificencia
mag·nif·i·cent
　adj. magnífico
mag·ni·fi·er *n.* amplificador
mag·ni·fy *v.* aumentar
mag·ni·tude *n.* magnitud
ma·hog·a·ny *n.* caoba
maid *n.* soltera
mail *n.* correo
mail·box *n.* buzón
mail·man *n.* cartero
main·tain *v.* mantener
main·te·nance *n.*
　mantenimiento
ma·jes·tic *adj.* majestuoso
maj·es·ty *n.* majestad
ma·jor *adj.* mayor
ma·jor·i·ty *n.* mayoría
make *v.* ganar; crear; hacer
mak·er *n.* fabricante
mak·ing *v.* fabricación
mal·a·dy *n.* dolencia
ma·lar·i·a *n.* malaria
mal·con·tent
　adj. malcontento
male *adj.* masculino; macho
mal·e·dic·tion *n.* maldición
ma·lev·o·lent *adj.* malévolo
mal·fun·tion
　v. funcionar mal
mal·ice *n.* malicia
ma·li·cious *adj.* malicioso
ma·lig·nan·cy *n.* malignidad
ma·lig·nant *adj.* maligno
mall *n.* alameda
mal·le·a·ble *adj.* maleable
mal·nour·ished
　adj. desnutrido
mal·nu·tri·tion
　n. desnutrición
malt *n.* malta
mal·treat *v.* maltratar
mal·treat·ment
　n. maltratamiento
mam·mal *n.* mamífero
mam·ma·li·an
　adj. mamífero
mam·ma·ry *adj.* mamario
man *n.* hombre
man·age *v.* manejar
man·age·a·ble
　adj. manejable
man·age·ment *n.* gerencia
man·da·rin *n.* mandarín
man·date *n.* mandato
man·da·to·ry *adj.* mandate
man·do·lin *n.* mandolina
ma·neu·ver *v.* maniobrar
ma·neu·ver·a·ble
　adj. maniobrable
man·ga·nese *n.* manganeso
man·gle *v.* mutilar
man·go *n.* mango
man·hood *n.* madurez
ma·ni·a *n.* manía
ma·ni·ac *adj.* maníaco
ma·ni·a·cal *adj.* maníaco
man·ic *adj.* maníaco
man·i·cure *n.* manicura
man·i·cur·ist *n.* manicuro

man·i·fest *adj.* manifiesto
man·i·fes·ta·tion *n.* manifestación
man·i·fes·to *n.* manifiesto
ma·ni·kin *n.* maniquí
ma·nip·u·late *v.* manipular
ma·nip·u·la·tion *n.* manipulación
ma·nip·u·la·tive *adj.* manipulativo
ma·nip·u·la·tor *n.* manipulador
man·li·ness *n.* hombría
man·ly *adj.* masculino
man·ne·quin *n.* maniquí
man·ner *n.* manera
man·nered *adj.* amanerado
man·ner·ism *n.* amaneramiento
man·nish *adj.* hombruno
man·tel *n.* manto
man·tle *n.* manto
man·u·al *n.* manual
man·u·fac·ture *n.* manufactura
man·u·fac·tured *adj.* manufacturado
man·u·fac·tur·ing *adj.* manufacturero
man·u·script *n.* manuscrito
man·y *adj.* muchos
map *n.* mapa
ma·ple *n.* arce
map·mak·er *n.* cartógrafe
mar *v.* desfigurar
mar·a·thon *n.* maratón
ma·raud·er *n.* merodeador
mar·ble *n.* mármol
mar·bled *adj.* jaspeado
mar·bling *n.* marmoración
march *v.* marchar
March *n.* marzo
mar·ga·rine *n.* margarina
mar·gin *n.* márgen
mar·gin·al *adj.* marginal
mar·i·gold *n.* maravilla
ma·ri·na *n.* marina
mar·i·nate *v.* marinar
ma·rine *n.* marino
mar·i·ner *n.* marinero
mar·i·tal *adj.* marital
mar·i·time *adj.* marítimo
mark *n.* marca
marked *adj.* marcado
mark·er *n.* marcador
mar·ket *v.* vender; *n.* mercado

mar·ket·a·ble *adj.* vendible
mar·ket·er *n.* vendedor
mar·king *n.* marca
mar·ma·lade *n.* mermelada
ma·roon *v.* abandonar
mar·quis *n.* marqués
mar·riage *n.* matrimonio
mar·ried *adj.* casado
mar·row *n.* médula
mar·ry *v.* casar(se)
marsh *n.* pantano
mar·shal *n.* mariscal
marsh·y *adj.* pantanoso
mar·su·pi·al *adj.* marsupial
mart *n.* mercado
mar·tial *adj.* marcial
mar·tyr *n.* mártir
mar·tyr·dom *n.* martirio
mar·vel *n.* maravilla
mar·vel·lous *adj.* maravilloso
mas·cot *n.* mascota
mas·cu·line *adj.* masculino
mas·cu·lin·i·ty *n.* masculinidad
mash *v.* majar
mash·er *n.* majador
mask *n.* máscara
mas·och·ism *n.* masoquismo
mas·och·ist *n.* masoquista
mas·och·is·tic *adj.* masoquista
ma·son·ry *n.* albañilería
mas·quer·ade *n.* mascarada
mass *n.* masa
mas·sa·cre *n.* matanza
mas·sage *v.* masajear
mas·sive *adj.* masivo
mast *n.* mástil
mas·tec·to·my *n.* mastectomía
mas·ter *n.* maestro
mas·ter·ful *adj.* hábil
mas·ter·ly *adj.* magistral
mas·ter·y *n.* maestría
mas·tic *adj.* pegante
mas·ti·cate *v.* masticar
mas·toid *n.* mastoides
mat *n.* estera
mate *n.* hembra; compañero
ma·te·ri·al *adj., n.* material
ma·te·ri·al·ist *n.* materialista
ma·te·ri·al·ist·ic *adj.* materialista
ma·te·ri·al·i·ty

n. materialidad
math *n.* matemáticas
math·e·mat·i·cal *adj.* matemático
math·e·ma·ti·cian *n.* matemático
math·e·mat·ics *n.* matemáticas
mat·i·nee *n.* funcion de tarde
mat·ri·arch *n.* matriarca
ma·tri·ar·chal *adj.* matriarcal
ma·tri·ar·chy *n.* matriarcado
ma·tric·u·late *v.* matricular(se)
ma·tric·u·la·tion *n.* matrícula
mat·ri·mon·ial *adj.* matrimonial
mat·ri·mo·ny *n.* matrimonio
ma·trix *n.* matriz
ma·tron *n.* matrona
ma·tron·ly *adj.* matronal
mat·ted *adj.* estera
mat·ter *n.* materia
mat·ting *n.* estera
mat·tress *n.* colchón
mat·u·ra·tion *n.* maduración
ma·ture *v.* madurar; *adj.* maduro
ma·tur·i·ty *n.* madurez
maul *v.* maltratar
mauve *n.* malva
max·im *n.* máxima
max·i·mal *adj.* máximo
max·i·mum *adj.* máximo
May *n.* mayo
may *v.* poder
may·be *adv.* tal vez
may·on·naise *n.* mayonesa
may·or *n.* alcade
may·or·al·ty *n.* alcaldía
me *pron.* mí; me
mead·ow *n.* pradera
mea·ger *adj.* pobre; magro
meal *n.* comida
mean *v.* intentar
me·an·der *v.* vagar
mean·ing *n.* significado
mean·ing·ful *adj.* significativo
mean·ing·less *adj.* insignificante
mea·sles *n.* rubéola

meas·ure *v.* medir
meas·ured *adj.* mesurado
meas·ure·ment *n.* medida
meat *n.* carne
meat·y *adj.* carnoso
me·chan·ic *n.* mecánico
me·chan·i·cal *adj.* mecánico
mech·a·nism *n.* mecanismo
mech·a·nize *v.* mecanizar
med·al *n.* medalla
me·dal·lion *n.* medallón
med·dle *v.* entremeterse
med·dler *n.* entremetido
me·di·an *adj.* mediano
me·di·ate *v.* mediar
me·di·a·tion *n.* mediación
me·di·a·tor *n.* mediador
med·ic *n.* médico
med·i·cal *adj.* médico
med·i·cate *v.* medicinar
med·i·ca·tion *n.* medicación
med·i·cine *n.* medicina
me·di·e·val *adj.* medieval
me·di·o·cre *adj.* mediocre
me·di·oc·ri·ty *n.* mediocridad
med·i·tate *v.* meditar
med·i·ta·tion *n.* meditación
meet *v.* reunirse; encontrar(se)
mel·o·dy *n.* melodía
mel·on *n.* melón
mem·ber *n.* miembro
mem·o·ra·ble *adj.* memorable
men·tal *adj.* mental
men·tion *v.* mencionar; *n.* mención
mer·cu·ry *n.* mercurio
mer·it *v.* merecer
mer·ry *adj.* festivo
mes·sage *n.* mensaje; comunicación
mes·sen·ger *n.* mensajero
met·al *n.* metal
me·te·or·ol·o·gy *n.* meteorología
meth·od *n.* método
mi·crobe *n.* microbio
mi·cro·phone *n.* micrófono
mid·dle *n., adj.* medio
mid·night *n.* medianoche
mi·grate *v.* emigrar
mil·i·tar·y *adj.* militar
mi·li·tia *n.* milicia
milk *n.* leche
mil·lion *n.* millón

mil·lion·aire *n.* millonario
mind *v.* obedecer; *n.* mente
min·er·al *n.* mineral
min·is·ter *n.* ministro
mi·nor *adj.* menor
mi·nor·i·ty *n.* minoría
mi·nus *prep.* menos
mir·a·cle *n.* milagro
mir·ror *n.* espejo
mis·chie·vous
  adj. malicioso
miss *v.* perder
mis·sion *n.* misión
mis·sion·ar·y *n.* misionero
mis·take *v.* equivocar(se)
mis·ter *n.* señor
mis·treat *v.* maltratar
mit·i·gate *v.* mitigar
mit·ten *n.* mitón
mix *n.* mezcla; *v.* mezclar(se)
mix·ture *n.* mezcla
mod·el *v.* modelar;
  n. modelo
mod·er·ate *v.* moderar;
  adj. moderno
mod·ern *n.* moderno
mod·est *adj.* modesto
mod·i·fi·ca·tion
  n. modificación
mod·i·fy *v.* modificar
mod·u·late *v.* modular
moist *adj.* húmedo
mois·ten *v.* humedecer(se)
moist·ness *n.* humedad
mois·ture *n.* humedad
mois·tur·iz·er *v.* humedecer
mo·lar *n.* molar
mo·las·ses *n.* melaza
mold *v.* moldear; *n.* molde
mold·er *v.* desmoronar(se)
mold·ing *n.* mohoso
mo·lec·u·lar *adj.* molecular
mol·e·cule *n.* molécula
mole·hill *n.* topera
mol·li·fy *v.* molificar
mol·lusk *n.* molusco
mol·ten *adj.* fundido
mom *n.* mamá
mo·ment *n.* momento
mo·men·tar·i·ly
  adv. momentáneamente
mo·men·tar·y
  adj. momentáneo
mo·men·tum *n.* momento
mon·arch *n.* monarca
mo·nar·chic
  adj. monárquico

mon·ar·chist *n.* monárquico
mon·ar·chy *n.* monarquía
mon·as·ter·y *n.* monasterio
mo·nas·tic *adj.* monástico
Mon·day *n.* lunes
mon·e·tar·y *adj.* monetario
mon·ey *n.* dinero
mon·eyed *adj.* adinerado
mon·goose *n.* mangosta
mo·ni·tion *n.* admonición
mon·i·tor *n.* monitor
mon·i·to·ry *adj.* monitorio
monk *n.* monje
mon·key *n.* mono
monk·hood *n.* monacato
monk·ish *adj.* monacal
mon·o·chro·mat·ic
  adj. monocromático
mo·noc·u·lar *adj.* monóulo
mo·nog·a·my
  n. monogamia
mo·no·gram *n.* monograma
mo·no·graph *n.* monografía
mon·o·lith *n.* monolito
mon·o·lith·ic
  adj. monolítico
mon·o·plane *n.* monoplano
mo·nop·o·lize
  v. monopolizar
mo·nop·o·ly *n.* monopolio
mon·o·rail *n.* monocarril
mo·no·tone *n.* monotonía
mo·not·o·nous
  adj. monótono
mo·not·o·ny *n.* monotonía
mon·ox·ide *n.* monóxido
mon·soon *n.* monzón
mon·ster *n.* monstruo
mon·stros·i·ty
  n. monstruosidad
mon·strous *adj.* monstruoso
mon·tage *n.* montaje
month *n.* mes
month·ly *adj.* mensual
mon·u·ment *n.* monumento
mon·u·men·tal
  adj. monumental
moo *v.* mugir
mood *n.* humor
moon *n.* luna
moor *v.* amarrar
moor·age *n.* amarraje
moor·ing *n.* amarradero
moose *n.* anta
mop *n.* estropajo
mo·ped *n.* ciclomotor
mor·al *adj.* moral

mo·rale *n.* moral
mor·al·ist *n.* moralista
mor·al·is·tic
  adj. moralizador
mo·ral·it·y *n.* moralidad
mor·al·ize *v.* moralizar
mor·bid *adj.* morboso
mor·bid·i·ty *n.* morbosidad
more *n., adv.* más
more·o·ver *adv.* además
morn·ing *n.* mañana
mor·phine *n.* morfina
mor·phol·o·gy
  n. morfología
mor·tal *n., adj.* mortal
mor·tal·i·ty *n.* mortalidad
mor·tu·ar·y *n.* mortuorio
mos·qui·to *n.* mosquito
most *adj.* muy; más
moth *n.* polilla
moth·er *n.* madre
moth·er·hood
  n. maternidad
moth·er-in-law *n.* suegra
mo·tor·cy·cle *n.* motocicleta
moun·tain *n.* montaña
mouse *n.* ratón
mouth *n.* boca
move *v.* mudar; mover
mov·ie *n.* película
Mr. *n.* señor
Mrs. *n.* señora
Ms. *n.* señora
much *adj.* muy; *n.,*
  adv., adj. mucho
mul·ti·ple *adj.* múltiple
mul·ti·pli·ca·tion
  n. multiplicación
mul·ti·ply *v.* multiplicar
mul·ti·pur·pose
  adj. multiuso
mul·ti·tude *n.* multitud
mum·ble *v.* mascullar
mum·my *n.* momia
munch *v.* ronzar
mun·dane *adj.* mundano
mu·nic·i·pal *adj.* municipal
mu·nic·i·pal·i·ty
  n. municipalidad
mu·ni·fi·cence
  n. munificencia
mu·nif·i·cent
  adj. munificente
mur·der *v.* asesinato
mur·der·er *n.* asesino
mur·der·ous *adj.* asesino
mur·mur *v.* murmurar

mus·cle *n.* músculo
mus·cu·lar *adj.* musculoso
muse *v.* meditar
mu·se·um *n.* museo
mu·sic *n.* música
mu·si·cal *adj.* musical
mu·si·cal·i·ty *n.* musicalidad
mu·si·cian *n.* músico
mus·ing *n.* contemplación
mus·ket *n.* mosquete
mus·ket·eer *n.* mosquetero
mus·lin *n.* muselina
mus·sel *n.* mejillón
must *v.* deber
mus·tache *n.* bigote
mu·ti·late *v.* mutilar
muz·zle *n.* hocico; boca
my *adj.* mi
myr·i·ad *n.* miríada
my·self *pron.* yo mismo
mys·te·ri·ous
  adj. misterioso
mys·ter·y *n.* misterio
mys·tic *adj.* místico
mys·ti·cism
  n. misticismo; mística
myth *n.* mito
myth·ic *adj.* mítico
my·thol·o·gy *n.* mitología

N

nab *v.* prender
na·dir *n.* nadir
nag *n.* jaca
nail *v.* clavar; *n.* clavo
na·ive *adj.* ingenuo
name *v.* apellido; nombre
name·less *adj.* anónimo
name·ly *adv.* a saber
name·sake *n.* tocayo
nap *n.* siesta
nape *n.* nuca
nap·kin *n.* servilleta
nar·cis·sism *n.* narcisismo
nar·cis·sus *n.* narciso
nar·cot·ic *n.* narcótico
nar·rate *v.* narrar
nar·ra·tive *adj.* narrativo
nar·ra·tor *n.* narrador
nar·row *adj.* estrecho;
  limitado; angosto
nar·row·ing *n.* limitación
na·sal *adj.* nasal

na·sal·i·ty *n.* nasalidad
nas·ty *adj.* antipático; sucio; obsceno
na·tal *adj.* natal
na·tal·i·ty *n.* natalidad
na·tion *n.* nación
na·tion·al *n., adj.* nacional
na·tion·al an·them *n.* himno nacional
na·tion·al·ist *n.* nacionalista
na·tion·al·is·tic *adj.* nacionalista
na·tion·al·i·ty *n.* nacionalidad
na·tion·al·ize *v.* nacionalizar
na·tive *adj.* natal; innato; nativo
na·tiv·i·ty *n.* natividad
nat·u·ral *adj.* natural
nat·ur·al·ist *n.* naturalista
nat·u·ral·is·tic *adj.* naturalista
nat·u·ral·ize *v.* naturalizar(se)
nat·u·ral·ly *adv.* naturalmente
na·ture *n.* género; naturaleza
naught *n.* nada
naugh·ty *adj.* verde; travieso
nau·se·a *n.* náusea
nau·se·ate *v.* dar náuseas a
nau·se·at·ing *adj.* nauseabundo
nau·seous *adj.* nauseabundo
nau·ti·cal *adj.* náutico
na·val *adj.* naval
nav·i·ga·ble *adj.* navegable
nav·i·gate *v.* navegar
nav·i·ga·tion *n.* navegación
nav·i·ga·tor *n.* navegante
nay *adv.* no
near *prep.* cerca de; *adv.* cerca; *adj.* próximo
near·by *adj.* próximo
near·ly *adj.* casi
neat *adj.* claro; limpio; fantástico
neb·u·la *n.* nebulosa
nec·es·sar·y *adj.* necesario
ne·ces·si·tate *v.* necesitar
ne·ces·si·ty *n.* necesidad
neck *n.* cuello
neck·lace *n.* collar
neck·line *n.* escote
ne·crol·o·gy *n.* necrología
ne·cro·sis *n.* necrosis
nec·tar *n.* néctar

nec·tar·ine *n.* nectarino
need *v.* necesitar
need·ful *adj.* necessario
nee·dle *n.* aguja
need·less *adj.* superfluo
need·y *adj.* necesitado
ne·far·i·ous *adj.* nefario
ne·gate *v.* negar
ne·ga·tion *n.* negación
neg·a·tive *n.* negativa
ne·glect *v.* descuidar
ne·glect·ful *adj.* negligente
neg·li·gence *n.* negligencia
neg·li·gent *adj.* negligente
neg·li·gi·ble *adj.* insignificante
ne·go·ti·able *adj.* negociable
ne·go·ti·ate *v.* negociar
ne·go·ti·a·tion *n.* negociación
ne·go·ti·a·tor *n.* negociador
neigh·bor *n.* prójimo; vecino
neigh·bor·hood *n.* barrio
neigh·bor·ing *adj.* vecino
neigh·bor·ly *adj.* amable
nei·ther *pron.* ninguno; *conj.* tampoco; ni
ne·ol·o·gism *n.* neologismo
ne·ol·o·gist *n.* neólogo
ne·on *n.* neón
ne·o·phyte *n.* neófito
neph·ew *n.* sobrino
nep·o·tism *n.* nepotismo
nerve *n.* nervio
nerve·less *adj.* sin nervios
nerv·ous *adj.* nervioso
nerv·ous·ness *n.* nerviosidad
nest *n.* nido
net *n.* red
net·ting *n.* red
net·tle *n.* ortiga
net·work *n.* red
neu·ral·gia *n.* neuralgia
neu·ral·gic *adj.* neurálgico
neu·ri·tis *n.* neuritis
neu·ro·sis *n.* neurosis
neu·rol·o·gist *n.* neurólogo
neu·rol·o·gy *n.* neurología
neu·rot·ic *adj.* neurótico
neu·tral *adj.* neutral
neu·tral·i·ty *n.* neutralidad
neu·tral·ize *v.* neutralizar
neu·tral·iz·er *n.* neutralizador
neu·tron *n.* neutrón

nev·er *adv.* jamás; nunca
nev·er·more *adv.* nunca más
nev·er·the·less *adv.* sin embargo
new *adj.* nuevo
new·found *adj.* nuevo
new·ly *adv.* nuevamente
news *n.* nuevas
news·cast *n.* noticiario
news·cast·er *n.* locutor
news·pa·per *n.* diario
news·y *adj.* informativo
newt *n.* tritón
new·ton *n.* neutonio
next *adj.* próximo
nib·ble *v.* mordiscar
nice *adj.* agradable; amable
ni·cety *n.* delicadeza; precisión
niche *n.* nicho
nick *n.* muesca; mella
nick·el *n.* níquel
nick·name *n.* apodo
nic·o·tine *n.* nicotina
niece *n.* sobrina
nigh *adv.* cerca
night *n.* noche
night·fall *n.* anochecer
night·gown *n.* camisón
night·in·gale *n.* ruiseñor
night·light *n.* lamparilla
night·ly *adj.* nocturno
night·mare *n.* pesadilla
night·time *n.* noche
nine *adj.* nueve
nine·teen *adj.* diecinueve
nine·ty *adj.* noventa
ninth *adj.* noveno
no *n., adv.* no
no·bod·y *n., pron.* nadie
noise *n.* ruido
nois·y *adj.* ruidoso
none *pron.* nadie; nada
noon *n.* mediodía
nor *conj.* ni
nor·mal *adj.* normal
nor·mal·ly *adv.* normalmente
north *n.* norte
north·east *n.* nordeste
north·west *n.* noroeste
nose *n.* nariz
not *adv.* no
no·ta·ble *adj.* notable
no·ta·tion *n.* notación
note *v.* notar; *n.* nota

no·ti·fy *v.* notificar
no·tion *n.* noción
no·to·ri·ous *adj.* notorio
No·vem·ber *n.* noviembre
now *adv.* ahora
nu·cle·ar *adj.* nuclear
nude *n., adj.* desnudo
num·ber *v.* numerar; *n.* número
nu·mer·i·cal *adj.* numérico
num·er·ous *adj.* numeroso
nut *n.* nuez
nu·tri·tion *n.* nutrición
nu·tri·tious *adj.* nutritivo
nu·tri·tive *adj.* nutritivo
nuz·zle *v.* hocicar
ny·lon *n.* nilón

O

oak *n.* roble
oak·en *adj.* de roble
oar *n.* remo
o·a·sis *n.* oasis
oat *n.* avena
oath *n.* juramento
oat·meal *n.* gachas de avena
ob·du·ra·cy *n.* obstinación
ob·du·rate *adj.* obstinado; insensible
o·be·di·ence *n.* obediencia
o·be·di·ent *adj.* obediente
ob·e·lisk *n.* obelisco
o·bese *adj.* obeso
o·be·si·ty *n.* obesidad
o·bey *v.* obedecer
ob·fus·cate *v.* ofuscar
ob·fus·ca·tion *n.* ofuscación
o·bit·u·ar·y *n.* obituario
ob·ject *v.* desaprobar; *n.* objeto
ob·jec·tion *n.* objeción
objec·tion·a·ble *adj.* ofensivo
ob·jec·tive *n., adj.* objetivo
ob·li·gate *v.* obligar
ob·li·ga·tion *n.* obligación
o·blig·a·to·ry *adj.* obligatorio
o·blige *v.* obligar
o·blig·ing *adj.* complaciente
o·blique *adj.* oblicuo
o·blit·er·ate *v.* aniquilar; arrasar
o·bliv·i·on *n.* olvido
o·bliv·i·ous *adj.* olvidadizo

ob·long *adj.* oblongo

ob·nox·ious *adj.* insoportable; desagradable

o·boe *n.* oboe

ob·scene *adj.* obsceno

ob·scen·i·ty *n.* obscenidad

ob·scure *adj.* imperceptible; oscuro

ob·scu·ri·ty *n.* oscuridad

ob·se·qui·ous *adj.* servil

ob·ser·vance *n.* observación; cumplimiento

ob·ser·vant *adj.* observador

ob·ser·va·tion *n.* observación

ob·ser·va·to·ry *n.* observatorio

ob·serve *v.* cumplir; observar

ob·serv·er *n.* observador

ob·sess *v.* obsesionar

ob·session *n.* obsesión

ob·ses·sive *adj.* obsesivo

ob·so·lete *adj.* obsoleto

ob·sta·cle *n.* obstáculo

ob·stet·ric *adj.* obstétrico

ob·sti·na·cy *n.* obstinación

ob·sti·nate *adj.* obstinado

ob·struct *v.* obstruir

ob·struc·tion *n.* obstrucción

ob·struc·tion·ist *n.* obstruccionista

ob·tain *v.* obtener

ob·trude *v.* introducir

ob·tru·sion *n.* intrusión

ob·tuse *adj.* obtuso

ob·vi·ate *v.* obviar

ob·vi·ous *adj.* obvio

ob·vi·ous·ly *adj.* claro

oc·ca·sion *n.* ocasión

oc·ca·sion·al *adj.* ocasional

oc·clude *v.* ocluir

oc·cu·pan·cy *n.* ocupación

oc·cu·pant *n.* pasajero; inquilino

oc·cu·pa·tion *n.* ocupación

oc·cu·pa·tion·al *adj.* ocupacional

oc·cu·pied *adj.* ocupado

oc·cu·py *v.* ocupar

oc·cur *v.* ocurrir

oc·cur·rence *n.* presencia; suceso

o·cean *n.* océano

o·ce·an·ic *adj.* oceánico

oc·ta·gon *n.* octágono

oc·tag·o·nal *adj.* octagonal

oc·tane *n.* octano

oc·tave *n.* octavo

Oc·to·ber *n.* octubre

oc·to·ge·nar·i·an *adj.* octogenario

oc·to·pus *n.* pulpo

oc·u·lar *adj.* ocular

oc·u·list *n.* oculista

odd *adj.* raro

odd·i·ty *n.* rareza

odds *n.* probabilidades

o·di·ous *adj.* odioso

o·di·um *n.* odio

o·dom·e·ter *n.* odómetro

o·dor *n.* olor

o·dor·less *adj.* inodoro

od·ys·sey *n.* odisea

of *prep.* de

off *adv.* fuera

of·fend *v.* ofender

of·fend·er *n.* infractor

of·fense *n.* ofense

of·fen·sive *adj.* ofensivo

of·fer *n.* ofrecimiento; *v.* ofrecer

of·fer·ing *n.* ofrecimiento

of·fice *n.* oficina

of·fi·cer *n.* oficial

of·fi·cial *n., adj.* oficial

of·fi·ci·ate *v.* oficiar

of·fi·cious *adj.* oficioso

off·set *v.* compensar

of·ten *adv.* a menudo

oil *n.* aceite

oil·can *n.* aceitera

oiled *adj.* aceitado

oil·y *adj.* aceitoso

oint·ment *n.* pomada

o·kra *n.* okra

old *adj.* anciano; viejo

old·en *adj.* pasado

old·fash·ioned *adj.* anticuado

ol·fac·to·ry *adj.* olfativo

ol·ive *n.* oliva

om·in·ous *adj.* ominoso

o·mis·sion *n.* omisión

o·mit *v.* omitir

om·ni·bus *n.* ómnibus

om·nip·o·tence *n.* omnipotencia

om·nip·o·tent *adj.* omnipotente

on *prep.* sobre

once *n., adv.* una vez

on·col·o·gy *n.* oncología

on·com·ing *adj.* que viene

one *adj.* uno; un

one·di·men·sion·al *adj.* unidimensional

on·er·ous *adj.* oneroso

one·self *pron.* uno

one·sid·ed *adj.* desigual

on·ion *n.* cebolla

on·look·er *n.* espectador

on·ly *adj., adv.* solo

on·rush *n.* embestida

on·to *prep.* sobre; en

on·ward *adj.* hacia adelante

on·yx *n.* onix

o·pac·i·ty *n.* opacidad

o·pal *n.* ópalo

o·pal·es·cence *n.* opalescencia

o·paque *adj.* opaco

o·pen *v.* abrir; *adj.* abierto

o·pen·er *n.* abridor

o·pen·ing *n.* abertura

o·pen·mind·ed *adj.* receptivo

o·per·a *n.* ópera

op·er·a·ble *adj.* operable

op·er·ate *v.* operar; actuar; manejar

op·er·at·ing *adj.* de mantenimiento

op·er·a·tion *n.* operación

op·er·a·tion·al *adj.* de operación

op·er·a·tive *adj.* operante

oph·thal·mol·ogy *n.* oftalmología

o·pi·ate *n.* opiato

o·pine *v.* opinar

o·pin·ion *n.* opinión

o·pi·um *n.* opio

op·po·nent *n.* adversario

op·por·tune *adj.* oportuno

op·por·tun·ist *n.* oportunista

op·por·tu·ni·ty *n.* oportunidad

op·pose *v.* oponerse

op·po·site *adj.* opuesto

op·po·si·tion *n.* oposición

op·press *v.* oprimir

op·pres·sive *adj.* opresivo

op·pres·sor *n.* opresor

opt *v.* optar

op·tic *adj.* óptico

op·ti·cal *adj.* óptico

op·ti·cian *n.* óptico

op·ti·mal *adj.* óptimo

op·ti·mism *n.* optimismo

op·ti·mist *n.* optimista

op·ti·mis·tic *adj.* optimista

op·tion *n.* opción

op·tion·al *adj.* opcional

op·tom·e·try *n.* optometría

op·u·lent *adj.* opulento

or *conj.* u; o

o·ral *adj.* oral

or·ange *adj.* anaranjado; *n.* naranja

o·ra·tion *n.* oración

or·ches·tra *n.* orquesta

or·der *n.* orden

or·din·ar·y *adj.* ordinario

or·gan·ism *n.* organismo

or·gan·i·za·tion *n.* organización

or·gan·ize *v.* organizar

o·rig·i·nal *adj.* original

o·rig·i·nate *v.* originar

os·ten·ta·tion *n.* ostentación

oth·er *prep.* el otro; *adj.* otro

ounce *n.* onza

our *adj.* nuestro

out *prep.* fuera de; *adv.* fuera

out·er *adj.* externo

out·fit *n.* traje

out·line *v.* bosquejar; *n.* bosquejo

out·side *adv.* fuera; *n.* exterior

out·ward *adj.* exterior

o·va·ry *n.* ovario

o·va·tion *n.* ovación

ov·en *n.* horno

o·ver *adj.* otra vez; *prep.* sobre; encima de

o·ver·lap *v.* solapar

o·ver·night *adj.* de noche

o·ver·sight *n.* olvido

o·vert *adj.* público

o·ver·turn *v.* volcar

o·ver·weight *adj.* gordo

o·vum *n.* óvulo

owe *v.* tener deudas

owl *n.* búho

own *v.* reconocer

ox·ide *n.* óxido

ox·i·dize *v.* oxidar(se)

ox·y·gen *n.* oxígeno

ox·y·gen·ate *v.* oxigenar

oys·ter *n.* ostra

o·zone *n.* ozono

P

pa *n.* papá
pace *n.* paso
pa·cif·ic *adj.* pacífico
pac·i·fism *n.* pacifismo
pac·i·fy *v.* pacificar
pack *n.* fardo
pack·age *n.* paquete
pact *n.* pacto
pad *n.* almohadilla
pad·dle *n.* canalete
pad·lock *n.* candado
pa·gan *n.* pagano
page *n.* página
pag·eant *n.* espectáculo
pa·go·da *n.* pagoda
pail *n.* cubo
pain *v.* doler; *n.* dolor
pain·ful *adj.* doloroso
pains·tak·ing *adj.* laborioso;
  esmerado
paint *n.* pintura; *v.* pintar
paint·ing *n.* pintura
pair *n.* pareja; par
pa·jam·as *n.* pijama
pal·ace *n.* palacio
pal·ate *n.* paladar
pale *adj.* pálido; claro
pa·le·on·tol·o·gy
  n. paleontología
pal·ette *n.* paleta
pal·i·sade *n.* palizada
pall *v.* perder su sabor
pal·lid *adj.* pálido
pal·lor *n.* palidez
palm *n.* palma
palm·is·try *n.* quiromancia
pal·pa·ble *adj.* palpable
pal·pi·ta·tion *n.* palpitación
pal·try *adj.* miserable
pam·per *v.* mimar
pam·phlet *n.* folleto
pan *n.* cazuela
pan·a·ce·a *n.* panacea
pan·cake *n.* hojuela
pan·cre·as *n.* páncreas
pan·de·mo·ni·um
  n. pandemónium
pane *n.* hoja de vidrio
pan·el *n.* panel
pang *n.* punzada; dolor
pan·han·dle *v.* mendigar
pan·ic *n.* terror; pánico
pan·o·ram·a *n.* panorama
pan·sy *n.* pensamiento

pant *n., pl.* pantalones
pan·the·ism *n.* panteísmo
pan·ther *n.* pantera
pan·to·mime *n.* pantomima
pan·try *n.* despensa
pa·pa *n.* papá
pa·pa·cy *n.* papado;
  pontificado
pa·per *n.* papel
pa·pier·ma·che *n.* cartón
  piedra
pa·poose *n.* crío
pa·py·rus *n.* papiro
par *n.* par
par·a·ble *n.* parábola
par·a·chute *n.* paracaídas
pa·rade *n.* parada
par·a·dise *n.* paraíso
par·a·dox *n.* paradoja
par·af·fin *n.* parafina
par·a·graph *n.* párrafo
par·al·lel *adj.* paralelo
par·a·lyze *v.* paralizar
pa·ram·e·ter *n.* parámetro;
  límite
par·a·noi·a *n.* paranoia
par·a·pher·nal·ia *n.* arreos
par·a·phrase *n.* paráfrasis
par·a·site *n.* parásito
par·a·troop·er
  n. paracaidista
par·cel *n.* paquete; bulto
parch *v.* secar
parch·ment *n.* pergamino
par·don *n.* perdón;
  v. perdonar
pare *v.* cortar
par·ent *n.* madre; padre
par·en·the·sis *n.* paréntesis
pa·ri·ah *n.* paria
par·ish *n.* parroquia
park *v.* aparcar; *n.* parque
par·ley *v.* parlamentar
par·lia·ment *n.* parlamento
par·lor *n.* sala de recibo
pa·ro·chi·al *adj.* parroquial;
  estrecho
par·o·dy *n.* parodia
pa·role *n.* libertad bajo
  palabra
par·ox·ysm *n.* paroxismo
par·rot *n.* loro
par·ry *v.* parar
pars·ley *n.* perejil
par·son *n.* clérigo
part *v.* separar(se); partir(se);
  n. parte

par·take *v.* tomar parte
par·tial *adj.* parcial
par·tial·i·ty *n.* parcialidad
par·tic·i·pant *adj.* partícipe
par·tic·i·pate *v.* participar
par·tic·i·pa·tion
  n. participación
par·ti·ci·ple *n.* participio
par·ti·cle *n.* partícula
par·tic·u·lar *adj.* particular
par·tic·u·lar·i·ty
  n. particularidad
part·ing *adj.* despedida
par·ti·san *n.* partidario
par·ti·tion *n.* partición;
  tabique
part·ner *n.* socio
par·tridge *n.* perdiz
par·ty *n.* fiesta
pass *v.* aprobar; pasar
pas·sage *n.* pasaje; travesía;
  pasadizo
pas·sen·ger *n.* pasajero;
  viajero
pas·sion *n.* pasión
pas·sion·ate
  adj. apasionado
pas·sive *adj.* pasivo
pass·port *n.* pasaporte
pass·word *n.* santo y seña
past *n.* pasado
paste *n.* engrudo; pasta
paste·board *n.* cartón
pas·teur·i·za·tion
  n. pasteurización
pas·teur·ize *v.* pasteurizar
pas·time *n.* pasatiempo
pas·tor *n.* pastor
pas·try *n.* pasteles
pas·ture *n.* pasto
pat *n.* golpecito; pastelillo
patch *n.* pedazo
pat·ent *n.* patente
pa·ter·nal *adj.* paterno
pa·ter·ni·ty *n.* paternidad
path *n.* senda
pa·thet·ic *adj.* patético
pa·thol·o·gy *n.* patología
pa·tience *n.* paciencia
pa·tient *adj.* paciente
pa·ti·o *n.* patio
pa·tri·ar·chy *n.* patriarcado
pat·ri·mo·ny *n.* patrimonio
pa·tri·ot *n.* patriota
pa·trol *v.* patrullar
pa·tron *n.* cliente
pat·tern *n.* patrón

pau·per *n.* pobre
pause *n.* pausa
pave *v.* empedrar; pavimentar
pave·ment *n.* pavimento
pa·vil·ion *n.* pabellón
paw *v.* manosear; *n.* pata
pawn *v.* empeñar
pay *v.* pagar; ser provechoso
pay·roll *n.* nómina
pea *n.* guisante
peace *n.* paz
peace·ful *adj.* tranquilo
peach *n.* melocotón
pea·cock *n.* pavo real; pavón
peak *n.* pico; cumbre
peal *v.* repicar
pea·nut *n.* cacahuete
pear *n.* pera
pearl *n.* perla
peas·ant *n.* campesino
peb·ble *n.* guijarro
pec·ca·dil·lo *n.* pecadillo
pe·cu·liar *adj.* peculiar
pe·cu·li·ar·i·ty
  n. peculiaridad
ped·al *n.* pedal
ped·dle *v.* vender por las
  calles
ped·dler *n.* buhonero
ped·es·tal *n.* pedestal
pe·des·tri·an *n.* peatón
ped·i·gree *n.* geneología
peel *v.* pelar
peer *n.* par
peg *n.* clavija; estaca
pel·let *n.* bolita; pella
pelt *n.* piel
pel·vis *n.* pelvis
pen *n.* pluma
pe·nal *adj.* penal
pen·al·ty *n.* pena; castigo
pen·cil *n.* lápiz
pend·ant *n.* pendiente
pend·ing *adj.* pendiente
pen·du·lum *n.* péndulo
pen·e·trate *v.* penetrar
pen·i·cil·lin *n.* penicilina
pen·in·su·la *n.* península
pen·i·tent *n.* penitente
pen·i·ten·tia·ry *n.* presidio
pen·ny *n.* centavo
pen·sion *n.* pensión
pen·sive *adj.* pensativo
pen·ta·gon *n.* pentágono
pe·on *n.* peón
pe·o·ny *n.* peonía
peo·ple *n.* gente; pueblo

pep·per *n.* pimienta; pimiento

pep·per·mint *n.* menta

per *prep.* por

per·ceive *v.* percibir

per·cent *n.* por ciento

per·cent·age *n.* porcentaje

per·cep·tion *n.* percepción

perch *n.* percha; perca

per·di·tion *n.* perdición

per·en·ni·al *adj.* perenne

per·fect *adj.* perfecto

per·fec·tion *n.* perfección

per·fo·rate *v.* perforar

per·form *v.* efectuar; hacer; representar

per·for·mance *n.* representación; función

per·fume *n.* perfume

per·il *n.* peligro

pe·rim·e·ter *n.* perímetro

pe·ri·od *n.* período

pe·ri·od·i·cal *n.* publicación periódica

pe·riph·er·y *n.* periferia

per·i·scope *n.* periscopio

per·ish *n.* perecer

per·jure *v.* perjurar(se)

per·ju·ry *n.* perjurio

per·ma·nent *adj.* permanente

per·mis·sion *n.* permiso

per·mit *v.* permitir; tolerar

per·pen·dic·u·lar *adj.* perpendicular

per·pet·u·al *adj.* perpetuo; continuo

per·plex *v.* confundir

per·se·cute *v.* perseguir

per·se·cu·tion *n.* persecución

per·sist *v.* persistir

per·son *n.* persona

per·son·al·i·ty *n.* personalidad

per·son·nel *n.* personal

per·spec·tive *n.* perspectiva

per·spi·ra·tion *n.* sudor

per·suade *v.* persuadir

per·spire *v.* sudar

per·ver·sion *n.* perversión

pe·ti·tion *n.* petición

phar·ma·cy *n.* farmacia

phi·los·o·phy *n.* filosofía

pho·bi·a *n.* fobia

pho·to·cop·y *n.* fotocopia

pho·to·graph *n.* foto

pho·tog·ra·phy *n.* fotografía

phrase *n.* frase

phys·i·cal *adj.* físico

phy·si·cian *n.* médico

pi·an·o *n.* piano

pick *v.* picar; elegir

pic·ture *n.* foto; cuadro; película

pie *n.* pastel

piece *n.* pedazo

pig *n.* cerdo

pi·geon *n.* paloma

pil·lar *n.* pilar

pine *n.* pino

pink *adj.* rosado

pipe *n.* pipa

pis·tol *n.* pistola

pit·y *n.* lástima

place *v.* poner; *n.* posición; sitio

plac·id *adj.* plácido

plague *n.* plaga

plain *adj.*, *n.* llano

plan *v.* planear; *n.* plano

plane *n.* avión; plano

plan·et *n.* planeta

plas·ma *n.* plasma

plas·tic *n.*, *adj.* plástico

plate *n.* plato

play *v.* tocar; jugar; *n.* juego

plea *n.* defensa

plead *v.* suplicar; defender

pleas·ure *n.* placer

plen·ti·ful *adj.* abundante

plen·ty *n.* abundancia

plum *n.* ciruela

plum·age *n.* plumaje

plu·ral *n.*, *adj.* plural

pock·et *n.* bolsillo

po·em *n.* poema

po·et *n.* poeta

po·et·ic *adj.* poético

point *n.* punto

po·lice *n.* policía

po·lit·i·cal *adj.* político

pol·i·ti·cian *n.* político

pol·i·tics *n.* política

pol·lu·tion *n.* polución

pomp·ous *adj.* pomposo

pond *n.* estanque

po·ny *n.* jaca

pool *n.* piscina

poor *n.* pobre

pop·u·lar *adj.* popular

pop·u·late *v.* poblar

pop·u·la·tion *n.* población

port *n.* puerto

por·tion *n.* parte

pose *v.* plantear

po·si·tion *n.* posición

pos·i·tive *adj.* positivo

pos·sess *v.* poseer

pos·ses·sion *n.* posesión

pos·si·bil·i·ty *n.* posibilidad

pos·si·ble *adj.* posible

post *n.* poste; puesto; correo

post·age *n.* porte; franqueo

post·card *n.* tarjeta

post·er *n.* cartel

pos·te·ri·or *adj.* posterior

post·man *n.* cartero

post·mark *n.* matasellos

post·me·rid·i·an *adj.* postmeridiano

post·mor·tem *n.* autopsia

post·pone *v.* aplazar

post·script *v.* postdata

pos·ture *n.* postura

pot *n.* olla; tiesto

po·tas·si·um *n.* potasio

po·ta·to *n.* patata

po·tent *adj.* potente; fuerte

po·ten·tial *adj.* potencial

po·tion *n.* poción

pot·ter·y *n.* alfarería

pouch *n.* bolsa

poul·try *n.* aves de corral

pound *n.* libra

pour *v.* diluviar

pout *v.* hacer pucheros

pov·er·ty *n.* pobreza

pow·der *n.* polvo

pow·er *n.* fuerza; poder

pow·er·ful *adj.* potente; poderoso

prac·ti·cal *adj.* práctico

prac·tice *v.* practicar; ejercer

prag·mat·ic *adj.* pragmático

prai·rie *n.* pradera

praise *v.* alabar

prank *n.* travesura

pray *v.* rezar

prayer *n.* oración

preach *v.* predicar

pre·am·ble *n.* preámbulo

pre·cau·tion *n.* precaución

pre·cede *v.* preceder

prec·e·dent *n.* precedente

pre·cinct *n.* recinto; distrito electoral

pre·cious *adj.* precioso

prec·i·pice *n.* precipicio

pre·cip·i·ta·tion *n.* precipitación

pre·cise *adj.* preciso; exacto

pre·co·cious *adj.* precoz

pre·cur·sor *n.* precursor

pred·e·ces·sor *n.* predecesor

pre·des·ti·na·tion *n.* predestinación

pre·dic·a·ment *n.* apuro

pre·dict *v.* pronosticar

pre·dic·tion *n.* pronóstico

pre·dom·i·nant *adj.* predominante

pref·ace *n.* prólogo; prefacio

pre·fer *v.* preferir

pref·er·ence *n.* preferencia

pre·fix *n.* prefijo

preg·nan·cy *n.* embarazo

preg·nant *adj.* embarazada

pre·his·tor·ic *adj.* prehistórico

prej·u·dice *n.* prejuicio

pre·lim·i·nar·y *n.* preliminar

pre·lude *n.* preludio

pre·med·i·tate *v.* premeditar

pre·miere *n.* estreno

pre·mi·um *n.* prima

pre·mo·ni·tion *n.* presentimiento

pre·oc·cu·pied *adj.* preocupada

prep·a·ra·tion *n.* preparación

pre·pare *v.* preparar(se)

prep·o·si·tion *n.* preposición

pre·pos·ter·ous *adj.* absurdo

pre·req·ui·site *n.* requisto previo

pre·rog·a·tive *n.* prerrogativa

pre·scribe *v.* prescribir

pre·scrip·tion *n.* receta

pres·ence *n.* presencia

pre·sent *adj.* presente; *v.* presentar, *n.* regalo

pres·en·ta·tion *n.* presentación

pre·serv·a·tive *n.* preservativo

pre·serve *v.* preservar; conservar

pre·side *v.* presidir

pres·i·dent *n.* presidente

press *n.* prensa; imprenta

pres·sure *n.* presión; urgencia

pres·ti·dig·i·ta·tion *n.* prestidigitación

pres·tige *n.* prestigio

pre·sume *v.* presumir; suponer

pre·tend *v.* pretender

pre·tense *n.* pretexto

pret·ty *adj.* guapo; bonito; mono

pre·vail *v.* prevalecer; predominar

pre·vent *v.* impedir

pre·vi·ous *adj.* previo

prey *n.* presa

price *n.* precio

price·less *adj.* inapreciable

prick *v.* punzar

pride *n.* orgullo

priest *n.* sacerdote

prim *adj.* estirado

pri·ma·ry *adj.* primario

prime *adj.* primero

prim·i·tive *adj.* primitivo

pri·mo·gen·i·ture *n.* primogenitura

prince *n.* príncipe

prin·cess *n.* princesa

prin·ci·pal *n., adj.* principal

prin·ci·pal·i·ty *n.* principado

prin·ci·ple *n.* principio

print *v.* imprimir

print·ing *n.* imprenta

pri·or *adj.* anterior

pri·or·i·ty *n.* prioridad

pri·or·y *n.* priorato

prism *n.* prisma

pris·on *n.* cárcel

pri·va·cy *n.* soledad

pri·vate *adj.* privado

priv·i·lege *n.* privilegio

prize *n.* premio

prob·a·bil·i·ty *n.* probabilidad

prob·a·ble *adj.* probable

probe *n.* sonda

prob·lem *n.* problema

pro·ce·dure *n.* procedimiento

pro·ceed *v.* proceder

proc·ess *n.* proceso

pro·claim *v.* proclamar

pro·cliv·i·ty *n.* proclividad; inclinación

pro·cras·ti·nate *v.* dilatar; aplazar

pro·cure *v.* obtener; alcahuetear

prod *v.* punzar

prod·i·gal *adj.* pródigo

pro·di·gy *n.* prodigio

pro·duce *v.* producir

prod·uct *n.* producto

pro·fane *adj.* profano

pro·fan·i·ty *n.* profanidad

pro·fes·sion *n.* profesión

pro·fes·sor *n.* profesora; profesor

pro·fi·cien·cy *n.* pericia

pro·file *n.* perfil

prof·it *n.* ganancia; beneficio

pro·found *adj.* profundo

pro·fuse *adj.* profuso

pro·fu·sion *n.* profusión

prog·e·ny *n.* progenie

prog·no·sis *n.* pronóstico

pro·gram *n.* programa

prog·ress *n.* progreso; desarrollo

pro·gres·sive *adj.* progresivo

pro·hib·it *v.* prohibir

pro·hi·bi·tion *n.* prohibición

pro·ject *n.* proyecto; *v.* proyectar

pro·jec·tile *n.* proyectile

pro·lif·ic *adj.* prolífico

pro·logue *n.* prolongar

prom·i·nent *adj.* prominente

pro·mis·cu·ous *adj.* promiscuo; libertino

prom·ise *v.* prometer; *n.* promesa

prom·on·to·ry *n.* promontorio

pro·mote *v.* promover; fomentar; ascender

pro·mo·tion *n.* promoción

prompt *adj.* puntual; pronto

pro·noun *n.* pronombre

pro·nounce *v.* pronunciar(se)

pro·nounced *adj.* marcado

pro·nun·ci·a·tion *n.* pronunciación

proof *n.* prueba

proof·read·er *n.* corrector de pruebas

prop *n.* apoyo

prop·a·gan·da *n.* propaganda

pro·pel *v.* propulsar

pro·pel·ler *n.* hélice

pro·pen·si·ty *n.* propensión; inclinación

prop·er *adj.* propio; apropiado; decente

prop·er·ty *n.* propiedad

proph·e·cy *n.* profecía

proph·e·sy *v.* profetizar

proph·et *n.* profeta

pro·phy·lac·tic *adj.* profiláctico

pro·pi·tious *adj.* propicio

pro·por·tion *n.* proporción

pro·pose *v.* proponer(se); declararse

prop·o·si·tion *n.* proposición; propuesta

pro·pri·e·tor *n.* propietario

pro·pri·e·ty *n.* corrección; decoro

pro·scribe *v.* proscribir

prose *n.* prosa

pros·e·cute *v.* proseguir

pros·pect *n.* perspectiva

pros·per *v.* prosperar

pros·per·i·ty *n.* prosperidad

pros·ti·tute *n.* prostituta; ramera

pros·trate *v.* postrar(se); derribar

pro·tag·o·nist *n.* protagonista

pro·tect *v.* proteger

pro·tein *n.* proteína

pro·test *n.* protesta; *v.* protestar

pro·to·col *n.* protocolo

pro·ton *n.* protón

pro·to·plasm *n.* protoplasma

pro·trude *v.* salir fuera

proud *adj.* orgulloso; arrogante

prove *v.* probar

pro·verb *n.* proverbio

pro·vide *v.* proveer

prov·ince *n.* provincia

pro·vi·sion *n.* provisión

pro·voc·a·tive *adj.* provocativa; provocador

pro·voke *v.* provocar

prow *n.* proa

prox·y *n.* poder; apoderado

prude *n.* gazmoña

prune *n.* ciruela

pry *v.* meterse; fisgonear

psalm *n.* salmo

pseu·do·nym *n.* seudónimo

psych·e·del·ic *adj.* psiquedélico

psy·chi·a·trist *n.* psiquiatra

psy·chi·a·try *n.* psiquiatría

psy·cho·a·nal·y·sis *n.* psicoanálisis

psy·cho·an·a·lyze *v.* psicoanalizar

psy·cho·log·i·cal *adj.* psicológico

psy·chol·o·gy *n.* psicología

psy·cho·sis *n.* psicosis

pto·maine *n.* ptomaína

pub *n.* taberna

pu·ber·ty *n.* pubertad

pub·lic *n., adj.* público

pub·li·ca·tion *n.* publicación

pub·lish *v.* publicar

pub·lish·er *n.* editor

puck·er *v.* arrugar

pud·ding *n.* pudín

pud·dle *n.* charco

puff *v.* soplar; inflar

pug·na·cious *adj.* pugnaz

puke *v.* vomitar

pull *v.* tirar; arrastrar

pul·ley *n.* polea

pul·mo·nar·y *adj.* pulmonar

pulp *n.* pulpa

pul·pit *n.* púlpito

pulse *n.* pulso

pul·ver·ize *v.* pulverizar

pum·ice *n.* piedra pómez

pump *n.* bomba

pump·kin *n.* calabaza

pun *n.* juego de palabras o vocablos

punch *v.* punzar

punc·tu·al *adj.* puntual

punc·tu·a·tion *n.* puntuación

punc·ture *v.* pinchazo

pun·ish *v.* castigar

pu·ny *adj.* encanijado

pu·pa *n.* crisálida

pu·pil *n.* estudiante; pupila

pup·pet *n.* títere

pur·chase *v.* comprar

pure *adj.* puro

pur·ga·to·ry *n.* purgatorio

pu·ri·fy *v.* purificar

pu·ri·tan *n.* puritano

pur·ple *adj.* purpúreo

pur·pose *n.* fin; propósito; resolución

purr *n.* ronroneo

purse *n.* bolsa
pur•sue *v.* perseguir
pur•suit *n.* perseguimiento; busca; ocupación
pus *n.* pus
push *v.* empujar; apretar
puss•y *n.* gatito
put *v.* meter; poner(se)
pu•tre•fy *v.* pudrir
pu•trid *adj.* podrido
put•ty *n.* masilla
pyr•a•mid *n.* pirámide
pyre *n.* pira
py•thon *n.* pitón

Q

quack *v.* graznar; *n.* graznido
quad•ran•gle *n.* cuadrángulo
quad•rant *n.* cuadrante
quad•rate *adj.* cuadrante
quad•rat•ic *adj.* cuadrático
quad•ri•ceps *n.* cuadriceps
quad•ri•lat•er•al *n., adj.* cuadrilátero
quad•ri•ple•gi•a *n.* cuadriplejia
quad•ri•ple•gic *adj.* cuadripléjico
quad•ru•ple *v.* cuadruplicar(se)
quag•mire *n.* pantano
quail *n.* codorniz
quake *v.* temblar
qual•i•fi•ca•tion *n.* calificación
qual•i•fied *adj.* acreditado; capacitado
qual•i•fi•er *n.* calificativo
qual•i•fy *v.* habilitar
qual•i•fy•ing *adj.* eliminatoria
qual•i•ta•tive *adj.* cualitativo
qual•i•ty *n.* calidad
qualm *n.* duda
quan•ti•ta•tive *adj.* cuantitativo
quan•ti•ty *n.* cantidad
quar•an•tine *n.* cuarentena
quar•rel *n.* riña
quar•rel•er *n.* pendenciero
quar•rel•some *adj.* pendeciero
quar•ry *n.* cantera
quart *n.* cuarto
quar•ter *n.* cuarto

quar•ter•deck *n.* alcázar
quar•ter•ly *adj.* trimestral
quar•tet *n.* cuarteto
quartz *n.* cuarzo
qua•ver *v.* temblar
queen *n.* reina
quench *v.* matar; apagar
quench•a•ble *adj.* apagar
ques•tion *n.* pregunta
quick *adj.* listo; rápido
qui•et *adj.* silencio
quit *v.* dejar; irse
quo•ta•tion *n.* cita
quote *v.* citar

R

rab•bi *n.* rabino
rab•bit *n.* conejo
rab•ble *n.* chusma
rab•id *adj.* rabioso
ra•bies *n.* rabia
rac•coon *n.* mapache
race *v.* correr de prisa; *n.* raza
rac•er *n.* corredor
race•track *n.* pista
ra•cial *adj.* racial
rac•ism *n.* racismo
ra•cist *n.* racista
rack *n.* potro
rack•et *n.* raqueta
rac•y *adj.* picante
ra•dar *n.* radar
ra•di•al *adj.* radial
ra•di•ance *n.* resplandor
ra•di•ant *adj.* radiante
ra•di•ate *v.* radiar; emitir; brillar
ra•di•a•tion *n.* radiación
ra•di•a•tor *n.* radiador
rad•i•cal *n., adj.* radical
rad•i•cle *n.* radícula
ra•di•o *n.* radio
ra•di•o•ac•tive *adj.* radioactivo
ra•di•o•ac•tiv•i•ty *n.* radioactividad
ra•di•o•broad•cast *v.* radiar
ra•di•o•gram *n.* radiograma
ra•di•o•graph *n.* radiografía
ra•di•ol•o•gist *n.* radiólogo
ra•di•ol•o•gy *n.* radiología
rad•ish *n.* rábano
ra•di•um *n.* radio
ra•di•us *n.* radio
ra•don *n.* radón

raff•ish *adj.* ostentoso
raf•fle *n.* rifa
raft *n.* balsa
raft•er *n.* cabrio
rag *n.* trapo
rage *v.* enfurecerse
rag•ged *adj.* desigual
raid *v.* atacar
rail *n.* carril
rail•ing *n.* baranda
rail•road *n.* ferrocarril
rail•way *n.* ferrocarril
rain *v.* llover; *n.* lluvia
rain•bow *n.* arco iris
rain•coat *n.* impermeable
rain•drop *n.* gota de lluvia
rain•fall *n.* precipitación
rain•wear *n.* ropa impermeable
rain•y *adj.* lluvioso
raise *v.* criar; levantar
raised *adj.* repujado
rai•sin *n.* pasa
rake *v.* rastrillar; *n.* rastro
ral•ly *n.* reunión; *v.* reunir(se)
ram *n.* carnero
ram•ble *v.* divagar
ram•bler *n.* vagabundo
ram•bunc•tious *adj.* alborotador
ram•i•fi•ca•tion *n.* ramificación
ramp *n.* rampa
ram•page *n.* alboroto
ramp•ant *adj.* destartalado
ranch *n.* hacienda
ranch•er *n.* hacendado
ran•cid *adj.* rancio
ran•cor *n.* rencor
ran•cor•ous *adj.* rencoroso
ran•dom *adj.* fortuito
range *v.* colocar; alinear
rang•er *n.* guardabosques
rank *n.* rango; fila
rank•ing *adj.* superior
ran•kle *v.* enconarse
ran•sack *v.* saquear
ran•som *v.* rescatar; *n.* rescate
rant *v.* vociferar
rap *v.* golpear
ra•pa•cious *adj.* rapaz
ra•pac•i•ty *n.* rapacidad
rape *v.* violar; *n.* violación
rap•id *adj.* rápido
ra•pid•i•ty *n.* rapidez
rap•ine *n.* rapiña

rap•ist *n.* violador
rap•port *n.* relación
rapt *adj.* absorto
rap•ture *n.* rapto
rap•tur•ous *adj.* extasiado
rare *adj.* poco; raro
rar•e•fied *adj.* refinado
rar•e•fy *v.* enrarecer(se)
rar•ing *adj.* impaciente
rar•i•ty *n.* rareza
ras•cal *n.* bribón
rash *n.* erupción
rash•er *n.* tocino
rasp•ber•ry *n.* frambuesa
rasp•ing *adj.* áspero
rat *n.* rata
rate *v.* tasar; *n.* razón
rath•er *adv.* más bien
rat•i•fy *v.* ratificar
rat•ing *n.* popularidad; clasificación
ra•tio *n.* proporción
ra•ti•o•ci•nate *v.* raciocinar
ra•tion *n.* ración
ra•tion•al *adj.* racional
ra•tion•ale *n.* explicación; razón
ra•tion•al•i•ty *n.* racionalidad
ra•tion•al•i•za•tion *n.* racionalización
ra•tion•al•ize *v.* racionalizar
ra•tion•ing *n.* racionamiento
rat•tle *n.* ruido
rat•trap *n.* ratonera
raun•chy *adj.* sucio
rav•age *v.* destruir; *n.* estrago
rave *v.* delirar
rav•el *v.* deshilar(se)
ra•ven *n.* cuervo
ra•ven•ous *adj.* voraz
ra•vine *n.* barranco
rav•ing *adj.* extraordinario
rav•ish *v.* raptar
rav•ish•ing *adj.* encantador
raw *adj.* novato; crudo
ray *n.* rayo
ray•on *n.* rayón
reach *n.* alcance; *v.* extenderse; alargar
re•act *v.* reaccionar
re•ac•tion *n.* reacción
re•ac•tion•ar•y *n.* reaccionario
re•ac•tor *n.* reactor
read *v.* decir; leer

read·ing *n.* lección
re·ad·just *v.* reajustar
read·y *adj.* pronto; listo
re·al *adj.* real
re·al·i·ty *n.* realidad
re·al·ize *v.* realizar
re·al·ly *adv.* realmente
realm *n.* reino
ream *n.* resma
rea·son *v.* razonar; *n.* razón
rea·son·a·ble *adj.* razonable
reb·el *adj., n.* rebelde
re·bel·lion *n.* rebelión
re·buke *n.* reprimenda
re·call *v.* retirar; hacer
re·cant *v.* retractar(se)
re·cede *v.* retroceder
re·ceipt *n.* ingresos
re·ceive *v.* acoger; recibir
re·cent *adj.* reciente
re·cep·ta·cle *n.* receptáculo
re·cess *n.* nicho
re·ces·sion *n.* retroceso
rec·i·pe *n.* receta
re·cip·ro·cal *adj.* recíproco
re·cit·al *n.* recital
rec·i·ta·tion *n.* recitación
re·cite *v.* recitar
reck·on *v.* considerar
re·claim *v.* reclamar
re·cline *v.* recostar(se)
rec·luse *n.* recluso
rec·og·ni·tion
  n. reconocimiento
rec·om·pense
  n. recompensa
re·con·cile *v.* reconciliar
re·con·struct *v.* reconstruir
re·cord *n.* disco; *v.* registrar
re·course *n.* recurso
re·cov·er *v.* recobrar
re·cruit *n.* recluta
rec·tan·gle *n.* rectángulo
rec·ti·fy *v.* rectificar
re·cu·per·ate *v.* recuperar
re·cu·per·a·tion
  n. recuperación
red *adj.* rojo
red·dish *adj.* rojizo
re·deem *v.* redimir
re·demp·tion *n.* redención
re·do *v.* rehacer
re·duce *v.* disminuir; reducir
re·duc·tion *n.* reducción
reef *n.* escollo
reek *n.* olor
re·fer *v.* referir(se)

ref·er·ee *n.* árbitro
ref·er·ence *n.* referencia
re·fill *v.* rellenar
re·fine *v.* refinar
re·fin·er·y *n.* refinería
re·flect *v.* reflejar
re·flec·tion *n.* reflejo
re·flex *adj.* reflejo
re·flex·ive *adj.* reflexivo
re·form *n.* reforma;
  v. reformarse
re·form·a·to·ry
  n. reformatorio
re·fract *v.* refractar
re·frain *v.* refrenar
re·fresh *v.* refrescar
re·fresh·ment *n.* refresco
re·frig·er·ate *v.* refrigerar
ref·uge *n.* refugio
ref·u·gee *n.* refugiado
re·fund *n.* reembolso
re·fuse *v.* refusar
re·gain *v.* recobrar
re·gard *v.* considerar
re·gen·er·ate *v.* regenerar
re·gent *n.* regente
re·gime *n.* régimen
reg·i·men *n.* régimen
reg·i·ment *n.* regimiento
re·gion *n.* región
reg·is·ter *v.* registrar;
  n. registro
re·gret *n.* sentimiento
reg·u·lar *adj.* regular
reg·u·la·tion *n.* regulación
re·ha·bil·i·tate *v.* rehabilitar
re·ha·bil·i·ta·tion
  n. rehabilitación
re·hearse *v.* ensayar
reign *v.* reinar; *n.* reinado
re·im·burse *v.* reembolsar
rein *n.* rienda
re·in·car·na·tion
  n. reencarnación
re·in·force *v.* reforzar
re·it·er·ate *v.* reiterar
re·ject *v.* rechazar
re·lapse *n.* recaída;
  v. reincidir
re·late *v.* relatar
re·lat·ed *adj.* afín
re·la·tion *n.* relación
re·lax *v.* relajar
re·lease *n.* descargo
re·lent *v.* ceder
re·li·a·ble *adj.* confiable
rel·ic *n.* reliquia

re·lief *n.* alivio
re·lieve *v.* aliviar
re·li·gion *n.* religión
re·lig·ious *adj.* religioso
rel·ish *n.* apetencia; *v.* gustar
re·ly *v.* contar; confiar
re·main *v.* quedar(se)
rem·e·dy *n.* remedio
re·mem·ber *v.* acordarse de
re·mem·brance *n.* recuerdo
re·mind *v.* recordar
rem·i·nis·cence
  n. reminiscencia
re·miss *adj.* descuidado
re·mit *v.* remitir
re·mit·tance *n.* remesa
re·morse *n.* remordimiento
re·mote *adj.* remoto
re·move *v.* apartar(se);
  quitar(se)
ren·ais·sance
  n. renacimiento
rend *v.* rasgar
ren·der *v.* volver
ren·dez·vous *v.* reunirse
ren·e·gade *n.* renegado
re·new *v.* renovar(se)
re·nounce *v.* renunciar
re·nown *n.* renombre
rent *v.* alquilar; *n.* alquiler
re·pair *v.* remendar; reparar
re·pay *v.* pagar; recompensar
re·peat *v.* repetir(se)
re·pel *v.* repeler
re·per·cus·sion
  n. repercusión
rep·er·toire *n.* repertorio
re·place *v.* reponer
re·ply *v.* respuesta
re·port *v.* informar
rep·re·hen·si·ble
  adj. reprensible
rep·re·sen·ta·tion
  n. representación
re·press *v.* reprimir
rep·ri·mand *v.* reprender
re·proach *n.* reproche
re·pro·duce *v.* reproducir
rep·tile *n.* reptil
re·pub·lic *n.* república
re·pulse *n.* repulsa
rep·u·ta·tion *n.* reputación
re·quest *v.* rogar
re·quire *v.* necesitar; exigir
res·cue *n.* rescate
re·search *v.* investigar
re·sent *v.* resentirse de

res·er·va·tion *n.* reservación
re·serve *v.* reservar
re·side *v.* vivir; residir
res·i·dent *n., adj.* residente
re·sign *v.* resignarse
res·ig·na·tion *n.* resignación
res·in *n.* resina
re·sist *v.* resistir
re·sist·ance *n.* resistencia
res·o·lu·tion *n.* resolución
re·solve *v.* resolver(se)
re·sort *n.* recurso
re·source *n.* recurso
re·spect *n.* respeto
re·spect·a·ble *adj.* respetable
re·spect·ful *adj.* respetuoso
re·spect·ing *prep.* respecto
re·spec·tive *adj.* respectivo
res·pi·ra·tion *n.* respiración
res·pi·ra·tor *n.* respirador
res·pi·ra·to·ry
  adj. respiratorio
re·spire *v.* respirar
res·pite *n.* respiro
re·splen·dent
  adj. resplandesciente
re·spond *v.* responder
re·spon·dent
  adj. resplandesciente
re·sponse *n.* respuesta
re·spon·si·bil·i·ty
  n. responsabilidad
re·spon·si·ble
  adj. responsable
rest *n.* descansar
res·tau·rant *n.* restaurante
rest·ful *adj.* sosegado
res·ti·tute *v.* restituir
res·ti·tu·tion *n.* restitución
rest·less *adj.* inquieto
res·to·ra·tion *n.*
  restauración
re·store *v.* restaurar
re·strain *v.* refrenar
re·strict *v.* restringir
re·stric·tion *n.* restricción
re·sult *n.* resultado;
  v. resultar
re·sus·ci·tate *v.* resucitar
re·tain *v.* retener
re·tard *v.* retardar
ret·i·na *n.* retina
re·tire *v.* retirarse
re·tract *v.* retractar(se)
re·trieve *v.* recobrar
ret·ro·ac·tive *adj.*
  retroactivo

re·turn *v.* volver
re·un·ion *n.* reunión
re·veal *v.* revelar
rev·e·la·tion *n.* revelación
re·venge *v.* vengar(se)
re·verse *adj.* inverso
re·view *n.* reseña
re·vise *v.* repasar; revisar
re·vi·sion *n.* revisión
re·vive *v.* revivir
re·voke *v.* revocar
rev·o·lu·tion *n.* revolución
rev·o·lu·tion·ary *n., adj.*
   revolucionario
re·volve *v.* revolverse
re·volv·er *n.* revólver
re·ward *n.* recompensa
rhap·so·dy *n.* rapsodia
rhe·tor·i·cal *adj.* retórico
rheu·mat·ic *adj.* reumático
rheu·ma·tism
   n. reumatismo
rhyme *v.* rimar; *n.* rima
rhythm *n.* ritmo
rib *n.* costilla
rib·bon *n.* cinta
rice *n.* arroz
rich *adj.* fértil; rico
rid *v.* librar(se)
rid·dle *n.* acertijo
ride *v.* montar
rid·i·cule *v.* ridiculizar
ri·dic·u·lous *adj.* ridículo
ri·fle *n.* rifle
right *adj.* exacto; derecho
rig·id *adj.* rígido
rig·or·ous *adj.* riguroso
rind *n.* piel
ring *v.* sonar; *n.* anillo
rink *n.* pista
rip *v.* arrancar; rasgar
ripe *adj.* maduro
rise *v.* subir; levantarse
risk *n.* riesgo
rite *n.* rito
rit·u·al *n., adj.* ritual
ri·val·ry *n.* rivalidad
riv·er *n.* río
roach *n.* cucaracha
road *n.* camino
roar *v.* rugir

S

Sab·bath *n.* domingo
sa·ber *n.* sable

sa·ble *n.* cebellina
sab·o·tage *v.* sabotear;
   n. sabotaje
sac·cha·rin *n.* sacarina
sack *n.* saco
sac·ra·ment *n.* sacramento
sacred *adj.* sagrado
sac·ri·fice *v.* sacrificar;
   n. sacrificio
sac·ri·lege *n.* sacrilegio
sad *adj.* triste
sad·den *v.* entristecer
sad·dle *n.* ensillar
sad·ism *n.* sadismo
sa·fa·ri *n.* safari
safe *adj.* seguro
safe·ty *n.* seguridad
sag *v.* combar(se)
sa·ga *n.* saga
sage *n., adj.* sabio
sail *v.* navegar; *n.* vela
sail·or *n.* marinero
saint *n.* santo
sake *n.* consideración; motivo
sal·ad *n.* ensalada
sal·a·man·der
   n. salamandra
sal·a·ry *n.* salario
sale *n.* venta
sa·line *n.* salino
sa·li·va *n.* saliva
sal·low *n.* cetrino
sal·ly *n.* salida
salm·on *n.* salmón
sa·lon *n.* salón
sa·loon *n.* salón
salt *n.* sal
sal·u·tar·y *adj.* saludable
sal·u·ta·tion *n.* saludo
sa·lute *v.* saludar
sal·vage *n.* salvamento
sal·va·tion *n.* salvación
salve *n.* ungüento
sal·vo *n.* salva
same *adj.* mismo
sam·ple *v.* probar
san·a·to·ri·um *n.* sanatorio
sanc·ti·fy *v.* santificar
sanc·tion *n.* sanción
sanc·ti·ty *n.* santidad
sanc·tu·ar·y *n.* santuario
sand *n.* arena
san·dal *n.* sandalia
sand·stone *n.* arenisca
sand·wich *n.* bocadillo
sand·y *adj.* arenoso

san·gui·nar·y
   adj. sanguinario
san·i·tar·i·um *n.* sanatorie
san·i·tar·y *adj.* sanitario
san·i·ta·tion *n.* sanidad;
   saneamiento
san·i·ty *n.* juicio sano
sap *n.* savia
sa·pi·ent *adj.* sabio
sap·phire *n.* zafiro
sar·casm *n.* sarcasmo
sar·cas·tic *adj.* sarcástico
sar·coph·a·gus *n.* sarcófago
sar·dine *n.* sardina
sa·ri, sa·ree *n.* sari
sash *n.* faja
sas·sy *adj.* descarado
sa·tan *n.* Satanás
sa·tan·ic *adj.* satánico
sate *v.* saciar; hartar
sat·el·lite *n.* satélite
sa·ti·ate *v.* saciar
sat·in *n.* raso
sa·tire *n.* sátira
sat·is·fac·tion
   n. satisfacción
sat·is·fy *v.* satisfacer
sat·u·rate *v.* saturar
Sat·ur·day *n.* sábado
sa·tyr *n.* sátiro
sauce *n.* salsa
sau·cer *n.* platillo
sau·sage *n.* salchicha
sav·age *n., adj.* salvaje
save *v.* ahorrar; salvar
sav·ing *n.* economía
sav·ior *n.* salvador
sa·vor *n.* sabor
saw *n.* sierra
sax·o·phone *n.* saxofón
say *v.* decir
say·ing *n.* dicho
scab *n.* costra
scaf·fold *n.* andamio
scald *v.* escaldar
scale *n.* escala
scal·lop *n.* venera; festón
scalp *n.* pericráneo; cuero
   cabelludo
scal·pel *n.* escalpelo
scan *v.* escudriñar
scan·dal *n.* escándalo
scan·dal·ize *v.* escandalizar
scant *adj.* escaso
scant·y *adj.* escaso
scape·goat *n.* cabeza de
   turco

scar *n.* cicatriz
scarce *adj.* escaso
scare *v.* asustar
scare·crow *n.* espantajo;
   espantapájaros
scarf *n.* bufanda
scar·let *n.* escarlata
scat·ter *v.* esparcir
scav·en·ger *n.* basurero
scene *n.* vista; escena
scen·er·y *n.* paisaje
scent *n.* pista; olor
sched·ule *n.* horario
scheme *v.* intrigar
schism *n.* cisma
schiz·o·phre·ni·a
   n. esquizofrenia
schol·ar *n.* erudito; alumno
schol·ar·ship *n.* erudición;
   beca
schol·as·tic *adj.* escolar
school *n.* escuela
sci·ence *n.* ciencia
sci·en·tist *n.* científico
scim·i·tar *n.* cimitarra
scis·sors *n.* tijeras
scoff *v.* mofarse
scold *v.* regañar
scoop *n.* paleta
scoot·er *n.* patinete
scope *n.* alcance
scorch *v.* chamuscar
score *n.* cuenta
scorn *n.* desdén
scor·pi·on *n.* escorpión
scotch *n.* frustrar
scoun·drel *n.* canalla
scour *v.* fregar; recorrer
scout *n.* explorador
scowl *v.* poner mal gesto
scraggy *adj.* escarnido
scram·ble *v.* revolver
scrap *n.* fragmento; sobras
scrape *v.* raer
scratch *v.* rayar; rasguñar;
   rascar
scrawl *n.* garabatos
scream *n.* grito
screen *n.* biombo; pantalla
screw *v.* atornillar;
   n. tornillo
scrib·ble *v.* garabatear
scrim·mage *n.* arrebatiña
script *n.* letra cursiva; guión
scrip·ture *n.* Sagrada
   Escritura

scroll *n.* rollo de pergamino
scrub *v.* fregar
scru·ple *n.* escrúpulo
scru·ti·nize *v.* escudriñar
scru·ti·ny *n.* escrutinio
scuf·fle *v.* pelear
sculp·tor *n.* escultor
sculp·ture *v.* esculpir;
 n. escultura
scum *n.* espuma
scur·ry *v.* darse prisa
scur·vy *n.* escorbuto
scut·tle *v.* echar a pique
scythe *n.* guadaña
sea *n.* mar
seal *n.* foca
seal *n.* sello; *v.* cerrar
seam *n.* costura
sea·man *n.* marinero
seam·stress *n.* costurera
seam·y *adj.* asqueroso
se·ance *n.* sesión de
 espirtistas
sea·port *n.* puerto de mar
sear *v.* marchitar; chamuscar
search *v.* buscar
sea·shore *n.* orilla del mar
sea·sick·ness *n.* mareo
sea·son *n.* estación
sea·son·ing *n.* condimento
seat *v.* sentar; *n.* asiento
sea·weed *n.* alga marina
se·clude *v.* aislar
se·clu·sion *n.* retiro
sec·ond *n., adj.* segundo
sec·ond·ar·y *adj.* secundario
sec·ond·hand *adj.* de
 segunda mano
sec·ond·rate *adj.* inferior
se·cre·cy *n.* secreto
se·cret *n., adj.* secreto
sec·re·tar·y *n.* secretario
se·crete *v.* secretar; ocultar
se·cre·tion *n.* secreción
sect *n.* secta
sec·tion *n.* sección
sec·tor *n.* sector
sec·u·lar *adj.* secular
se·cure *adj.* seguro
se·cu·ri·ty *n.* seguridad
se·date *adj., v.* sosegado
sed·a·tive *n., adj.* sedativo
sed·en·tar·y *adj.* sedentario
sed·i·ment *n.* sedimento
se·di·tion *n.* sedición
se·duce *v.* seducir
se·duc·tion *n.* seducción

see *v.* percibir; ver
seed *n.* semilla; simiente
seed·y *adj.* desharrapado
seek *v.* buscar; solicitar
seem *v.* parecer
seem·ly *adj.* decoroso;
 correcto
seep *v.* rezumar
se·er *n.* profeta
seg·ment *n.* segmento
seg·re·gate *v.* segregar
seg·re·ga·tion
 n. segregación
seis·mo·graph
 n. sismógrafo
seize *v.* apoderarse de; asir
sei·zure *n.* asimiento
sel·dom *adv.* raramente
se·lect *adj.* selecto; *v.* elegir
se·lec·tion *n.* selección
self *n.* sí mismo
self-cen·tered
 adj. egocéntrico
self-com·mand *n.* dominio
 de sí mismo
self-con·fi·dence
 n. confianza en sí mismo
self-ev·i·dent *adj.* patente
self-ex·plan·a·to·ry
 adj. evidente; obvio
self-gov·ern·ment
 n. autonomía
self-im·por·tance
 n. presunción
self·ish *adj.* egoísta;
 interesado
self·less *adj.* desinteresado
self-re·li·ance *n.* confianza
 en sí mismo
self·same *adj.* mismo
self-suf·fi·cient
 adj. independiente
self-will *n.* terquedad
sell *v.* vender
se·man·tics *n.* semántica
sem·blance *n.* parecido;
 apariencia
se·men *n.* semen
sem·es·ter *n.* semestre
sem·i·cir·cle *n.* semicírculo
sem·i·co·lon *n.* punto y
 coma
sem·i·fi·nal *adj.* semifinal
sem·i·nar *n.* seminario
sem·i·nar·y *n.* seminario
sem·i·of·fi·cial
 adj. semioficial

sem·i·pre·cious
 adj. semiprecioso
sem·i·week·ly
 adj. bisemanal
sen·ate *n.* senado
sen·a·tor *n.* senador
send *v.* mandar; enviar
se·nile *adj.* senil
sen·ior *adj.* superior
sen·ior·i·ty *n.* antigüedad
sen·sa·tion *n.* sensación
sense *v.* percibir; *n.* sentido
sense·less *adj.* sin sentido;
 insensato
sen·si·bil·i·ty *n.* sensibilidad
sen·si·ble *adj.* razonable
sen·si·tive *adj.* delicado
sen·si·tiv·i·ty *n.* delicadeza
sen·so·ry *adj.* sensorio
sen·su·al *adj.* sensual
sen·su·ous *adj.* sensorio
sen·tence *n.* frase
sen·ti·ment *n.* sentimiento
sen·ti·nel *n.* centinela
sen·try *n.* centinela
se·pal *n.* sépalo
sep·a·rate *v.* separar(se)
sep·a·ra·tion *n.* separación
Sep·tem·ber *n.* septiembre
sep·tic *adj.* séptico
sep·ul·cher *n.* sepulcro
se·quel *n.* resultado
se·quence *n.* sucesión
se·ques·ter *v.* separar; aislar
se·ques·tered *adj.* aislado
se·quin *n.* lentejuela
ser·aph *n.* serafín
ser·e·nade *n.* serenata
se·rene *n.* sereno
se·ren·i·ty *n.* serenidad
serf *n.* siervo
se·ri·al *adj.* en serie
se·ries *n.* serie
se·ri·ous *adj.* serio
ser·mon *n.* sermón
ser·pent *n.* serpiente
se·rum *n.* suero
serv·ant *n.* sirviente; servidor
serve *v.* servir
serv·ice *n.* servicio
serv·ice·man *n.* militar
ser·vile *adj.* servil
ses·sion *n.* sesión
set *v.* fijar; poner(se)
set·back *n.* revés
set·ting *n.* engaste
set·tle *v.* arreglar; resolver

set·tle·ment *n.* colonización
set·ler *n.* colono
sev·en *adj.* siete
sev·en·teen *adj.* diecisiete
sev·enth *adj.* séptimo
sev·en·ty *adj.* setenta
sev·er *v.* cortar
sev·er·al *adj.* varios; diversos
se·vere *adj.* severo
sev·er·i·ty *n.* severidad
sew *v.* coser
sew·er *n.* albañal; cloaca
sex *n.* sexo
sex·tet *n.* sexteto
sex·u·al *adj.* sexual
sex·y *adj.* provocativo
shab·by *adj.* raído; en mal
 estado
shack *n.* choza
shack·le *n.* grillete
shade *v.* sombrear;
 n. sombra
shad·ing *n.* degradación
shad·ow *n.* sombra
shad·ow·y *adj.* umbroso;
 vago
shad·y *adj.* sombreado
shaft *n.* eje; pozo
shag·gy *adj.* velludo
shake *v.* estrechar; temblar
shak·y *adj.* poco profundo;
 tembloroso
sham *v.* fingir(se);
 adj. fingido
sham·bles *n.* desorden
shame *n.* vergüenza
shame·less
 adj. desvergonzado
sham·poo *n.* champú
shan·ty *n.* choza
shape *v.* formar; *n.* forma
shape·ly *adj.* bien formado
share *n.* parte
shark *n.* tiburón
sharp *adj.* vivo; cortante
sharp·en *v.* afilar; sacar
 punta
shat·ter *v.* hacer(se) pedazos
shave *v.* afeitar(se)
shav·er *n.* máquina de afeitar
shawl *n.* chal
she *pron.* ella
shears *n.* tijeras grandes
shed *v.* quitarse; verter
sheen *n.* lustre
sheep *n.* oveja
sheep·ish *adj.* tímido

sheer *adj.* escarpado
sheet *n.* sábana; hoja; lámina
shiek, sheikh *n.* jeque
shelf *n.* estante
shell *n.* cáscara
shel·lac, shel·lack *n.* goma laca
shell·fish *n.* marisco
shel·ter *n.* refugio
shep·herd *n.* pastor
sher·bet *n.* sorbete
sher·iff *n.* aguacil
sher·ry *n.* jerez
shield *n.* escudo
shift *v.* mover(se); cambiar
shil·ly·shal·ly *v.* vacilar
shim·mer *v.* rielar
shin *n.* espinilla
shine *v.* pulir; brillar
shin·gle *n.* tablilla; placa; teja
shin·y *adj.* brillante
ship *n.* barco
ship·ment *n.* embarque; envío
ship·shape *adj.* en buen orden
ship·wreck *n.* naufragio
shirk *v.* evitar; esquivar
shirt *n.* camisa
shiv·er *v.* temblar
shock *n.* susto; choque; postración
shod·dy *adj.* de pacotilla; falso
shoe *n.* zapato
shoe·horn *n.* calzador
shoe·lace *n.* cordón
shoot *v.* espigar; disparar
shoot·ing *n.* tiro; caza con escopeta
shoot·ing star *n.* estrella fugaz
shop *n.* taller; tienda
shop·keep·er *n.* tendero
shore *n.* playa
short *adj.* breve; corto
short·age *n.* deficiencia; escasez
short·com·ing *n.* defecto
short·cut *n.* atajo
short·en *v.* acortar(se)
short·hand *n.* taquigrafía
short·lived *adj.* de breve duración
short·tem·pered *adj.* de mal genio
shot *n.* tiro; tirador

shot·gun *n.* escopeta
shoul·der *n.* hombro
shout *v.* gritar; *n.* grito
shov·el *n.* pala
show *v.* mostrar(se)
show·er *v.* duchar(se); *n.* ducha
show·man *n.* director de espectáculos
shred *v.* hacer tiras
shrew *n.* arpía
shrewd *adj.* sagaz; prudente
shriek *n.* chillar
shrill *adj.* estridente
shrimp *n.* camarón
shrine *n.* relicario
shrink *v.* encoger(se)
shriv·el *v.* encoger(se); secar(se)
shroud *n.* mortaja
shrub *n.* arbusto
shrub·bery *n.* arbustos
shrug *v.* encogerse de hombros
shud·der *v.* extremecerse
shuf·fle *v.* arrastrar los pies; (cards) barajar
shun *v.* evitar; apartarse de
shut *v.* cerrar(se)
shut·ter *n.* contraventana
shut·tle *n.* lanzadera
shy *adj.* tímido
sic *v.* atacar
sick *adj.* enfermo
sick·en *v.* enfermar(se)
sick·le *n.* hoz
sick·ness *n.* enfermedad
side *n.* partido; lado
side·burns *n.* patillas
side·long *adj.* lateral
side·track *v.* desviar
side·walk *n.* acera
side·ways *adv.* oblicuamente
siege *n.* sitio; cerco
sieve *n.* coladera; tamiz
sift *v.* tamizar
sigh *n.* suspiro; *v.* suspirar
sight *n.* visión; vista
sight·less *adj.* ciego
sight·see·ing *n.* visita de puntos de interés
sign *n.* signo; señal
sig·nal *n.* señal
sig·na·ture *n.* firma
sig·nif·i·cance *n.* significación

sig·ni·fy *v.* significar
si·lence *n.* silencio
si·lent *adj.* silencioso
sil·hou·ette *n.* silueta
sil·i·ca *n.* sílice
sil·i·con *n.* silicio
silk *n.* seda
silk·y *adj.* sedoso
sil·ly *adj.* bobo
si·lo *n.* silo
silt *n.* sedimento
sil·ver *n.* plata
sil·ver·smith *n.* platero
sil·ver·ware *n.* vajilla de plata
sim·i·an *adj.* símico
sim·i·lar *adj.* similar
sim·i·lar·i·ty *n.* semejanza
sim·mer *v.* hervir a fuego lento
sim·per *v.* sonreírse afectadamente
sim·ple *adj.* simple; fácil
sim·pli·fy *v.* simplificar
sim·ply *adv.* sencillamente
sim·u·late *v.* simular
si·mul·ta·ne·ous *adj.* simultáneo
sin *n.* pecado; transgresión
since *conj.* puesto que; *prep.* después; desde
sin·cere *adj.* sincero
sin·cer·i·ty *n.* sinceridad
si·ne·cure *n.* sinecura
sin·ew *n.* tendón
sing *v.* cantar
sing·er *n.* cantante
sin·gle *adj.* único; soltero
sin·gle·hand·ed *adj.* sin ayuda
sin·gu·lar *adj.* singular
sin·is·ter *adj.* siniestro
sink *v.* hundir(se)
sin·ner *n.* pecador
si·nus *n.* seno
sip *n.* sorbo; *v.* sorber
sir *n.* señor
sire *n.* padre
si·ren *n.* sirena
sir·loin *n.* solomillo
sis·ter *n.* hermana
sis·ter-in-law *n.* cuñada
sit *v.* sentar(se)
site *n.* sitio
sit·u·a·tion *n.* situación
six *adj., n.* seis
six·teen *adj., n.* dieciséis

sixth *adj,. n.* sexto
six·ty *adj., n.* sesenta
size *n.* talla
siz·zle *v.* chisporrotear
skate *v.* patinar
skel·e·ton *n.* esqueleto
skep·tic *n.* escéptico
skep·ti·cal *adj.* escéptico
sketch *n.* esbozo; bosquejo
skew·er *n.* broqueta
ski *v.* esquiar
skid *n.* patinazo
skill *n.* destreza; habilidad
skil·let *n.* sartén
skim *v.* espumar; desnatar; hojear
skin *n.* piel
skin·ny *adj.* flaco
skip *v.* saltar; pasar por alto
skir·mish *n.* escaramuza
skirt *n.* falda
skit *n.* parodia
skull *n.* cráneo
skunk *n.* mofeta
sky *n.* cielo
sky·rock·et *n.* cohete
sky·scrap·er *n.* rascacielos
slab *n.* tabla; plancha
slack *adj.* flojo; negligente
slack·en *v.* aflojar
slacks *n.* pantalones
slag *n.* escoria
slam *v.* cerrarse de golpe
slan·der *v.* calumniar; *n.* calumnia
slang *n.* argot
slant *v.* inclinar(se); sesgar(se)
slap *v.* pegar
slash *v.* acuchillar
slat *n.* tablilla
slate *n.* pizarra; lista de candidatos
slaugh·ter *v.* matar
slave *n.* esclavo
slav·er·y *n.* esclavitud
slay *v.* matar
sled *n.* trineo
sleek *adj.* liso; pulcro
sleep *v.* dormir
sleep·y *adj.* soñoliento
sleet *n.* aguanieve
sleeve *n.* manga
sleigh *n.* trineo
slen·der *adj.* delgado
sleuth *n. inf.* detective
slice *v.* tajar; *n.* tajada
slide *v.* deslizarse

slight *adj.* pequeño; de poca importancia

slim *adj.* delgado

slime *n.* lodo; cieno

sling *v.* tirar; suspender

slip *v.* introducir; deslizar(se); resbalar; escaparse

slip·knot *n.* nudo corredizo

slip·per *n.* zapatilla

slip·per·y *adj.* resbaladizo

slip·up *n. inf.* equivocación

slit *v.* cortar

sliv·er *n.* astilla

slob·ber *v.* babear; babosear

slo·gan *n.* mote

slop *v.* verter

slope *v.* inclinar(se); *n.* inclinación

slot *n.* ranura

slov·en·ly *adj.* descuidado; desaseado

slow *adj.* torpe; lento

slow·ly *adv.* despacio

slug *n.* posta

slug·gish *adj.* perezoso; lento

slum *n.* barrio bajo

slump *v.* hundirse; caer

slur *v.* comerse palabras; calumniar

slut *n.* pazpuerca; perra

sly *n.* astuto; disimulado

smack *v.* pegar

small *adj.* pequeño

small·pox *n.* viruelas

smart *adj.* listo; fresco

smash *v.* romper(se)

smear *v.* manchar; untar

smell *v.* oler

smile *n.* sonrisa; *v.* sonreír(se)

smirk *n.* sonrisa afectada

smith *n.* herrero

smock *n.* blusa de labrador

smog *n.* niebla y humo mezclados

smoke *v.* fumar; *n.* humo

smol·der *v.* arder sin llamas

smooch *v. inf.* besar

smooth *adj.* suave

smooth·er *v.* ahogar(se); sofocar(se)

smudge *n.* mancha

smug *adj.* pagado de sí mismo

smug·gle *v.* pasar de (o hacer) contrabando

snack *n.* merienda

snag *n.* obstáculo; rasgón

snail *n.* caracol

snake *n.* culebra

snap·shot *n.* foto

snare *n.* trampa

snatch *n.* fragmento; trocito

sneak *v.* moverse a hurtadillas

sneer *v.* mofarse

sneeze *n.* estornudo; *v.* estornudar

sniff *v.* husmear; oler

snip *v.* tijeretear

snob *n.* esnob

snooze *v. infin.* dormitar

snore *n.* ronquido; *v.* roncar

snow *v.* nevar; *n.* nieve

snow·ball *n.* bola de nieve

snow·flake *n.* copo de nieve

snow·man *n.* figura de nieve

snub *v.* desairar

snug·gle *v.* arrimarse

so *conj.* por tanto; *adv.* así; tan

soak *v.* remojar

soap *n.* jabón

soar *v.* remontarse

sob *v.* sollozar

so·ber *adj.* sobrio

so·bri·quet, sou·bri·quet *n.* apodo

so·called *adj.* llamado; supuesto

soc·cer *n.* fútbol

so·cia·ble *adj.* sociable

so·cial *adj.* social

so·cial·ism *n.* socialismo

so·cial·ize *v.* socializar

so·ci·e·ty *n.* sociedad

so·di·um *n.* sodio

so·fa *n.* sofá

soil *v.* manchar; *n.* tierra

so·lar *adj.* solar

sol·dier *n.* soldado

sole·ly *adv.* solamente

sol·emn *adj.* solemne

so·lic·it *v.* solicitar

sol·id *n., adj.* sólido

sol·i·dar·i·ty *n.* solidaridad

sol·i·tar·y *adj.* solitario

sol·u·ble *adj.* soluble

so·lu·tion *n.* solución

solve *v.* resolver

sol·vent *n. adj.* solvente

som·ber *adj.* sombrío

some *pron.* algunos; *adj.* alguno

some·bo·dy *n. pron.* alguien

some·day *adv.* algún día

some·one *pron.* alguien

some·thing *n.* algo

some·times *adv.* a veces

son *n.* hijo

song *n.* canción

son-in-law *n.* yerno

soon *adv.* pronto

soothe *v.* calmar

so·pran·o *n.* soprano

sor·did *adj.* vil

sor·ry *adj.* triste

so·so *adv.* así así

soul *n.* alma

sound *n.* ruido

soup *n.* sopa

sour *adj.* agrio

south *n.* sur

south·east *n.* sudeste

south·ern *adj.* del sur

south·west *n.* sudoeste

sov·er·eign *n., adj.* soberano

space *v.* espaciar; *n.* espacio

spa·cious *adj.* espacioso

spa·ghet·ti *n.* espagueti

spasm *n.* espasmo

spas·mod·ic *adj.* espasmódico

spas·tic *adj.* espástico

spat·u·la *n.* espátula

speak *v.* decir; hablar

spear *n.* lanza

spe·cial *adj.* especial

spe·cial·ist *n.* especialista

spe·cial·ize *v.* especializar(se)

spe·cial·ty *n.* especialidad

spe·cies *n.* especie

spe·cif·ic *adj.* específico

spec·i·fy *v.* especificar

spec·ta·cle *n.* espectáculo

spec·tac·u·lar *adj.* espectacular

speech·less *adj.* mudo

speed *v.* apresurarse; acelerar

spell *n.* deletrear

spell·bind *v.* encantar

spell·ing *n.* ortografía

spend *v.* gastar

sperm *n.* esperma

sperm whale *n.* cachalote

sphere *n.* esfera

spher·i·cal *adj.* esférico

spice *n.* especia

spic·y *adj.* picante

spi·der *n.* araña

spill *v.* verter(se)

spin·ach *n.* espinaca

spi·nal *adj.* espinal

spine *n.* espinazo

spi·ral *adj., n.* espiral

spir·it *n.* espíritu

spir·it·u·al *adj.* espiritual

spir·it·u·al·ism *n.* espiritismo

spit *v.* escupir

spite *n.* rencor

splin·ter *n.* astilla

split *v.* dividir; separarse

spoil *v.* echar(se); estropear(se)

spo·ken *adj.* hablado

sponge *n.* esponja

spon·gy *adj.* esponjoso

spon·ta·ne·i·ty *n.* espontaneidad

spon·ta·ne·ous *adj.* espontáneo

spoon *n.* cuchara

spoon·ful *n.* cucharada

spo·rad·ic *adj.* esporádico

spore *n.* espora

sport *n.* deporte

sports·man *n.* deportista

spot *n.* mancha

spot·ty *adj.* manchado

spouse *n.* esposa; esposo

spread *v.* diseminar

spring *n.* primavera; *v.* saltar

spring·time *n.* primavera

spruce *n.* picea

spu·ri·ous *adj.* espurio

spy *v.* espiar

squad·ron *n.* escuadrón

squal·id *adj.* desaliñado

square *adj.* cuadrado

squeak *n.* chirrido; *v.* chillar

sta·bil·i·ty *n.* estabilidad

sta·ble *adj.* estable

sta·di·um *n.* estadio

stage *n.* etapa

stain *n.* mancha

stair *n.* escalón

stair·way *n.* escalera

stamp *n.* sello

stam·pede *n.* estampida

stand *v.* colocar

stand·ing *adj.* derecho

sta·ple *n.* grapa

sta·pler *n.* grapadora

star *n.* estrella
star·less *adj.* sin estrellas
star·ry *adj.* estrellado
start *v.* comenzar; empezar
state *n.* estado
stat·ic *adj.* estático
sta·tion *v.* estación
sta·tis·tic *n.* estadístico
stat·ue *n.* estatua
stay *v.* quedar(se)
steal *v.* robar
steam *v.* empañar; *n.* vapor
steam·y *adj.* vaporoso
stem *n.* tallo
step *n.* escalera
step·broth·er
    n. hermanastro
step·daugh·ter *n.* hijastra
step·fa·ther *n.* padrastro
step·moth·er *n.* madrastra
step·sis·ter *n.* hermanastra
step·son *n.* hijastro
ste·ril·i·ty *n.* esterilidad
stick *n.* palo
stick·y *adj.* viscoso
stiff *adj.* rígido
still *adj.* tranquilo
stim·u·lant *n.* estimulante
stim·u·late *v.* estimular
stink *v.* hedor
stip·u·late *v.* estipular
stip·u·la·tion *n.* estipulación
stock·ing *n.* media
sto·i·cal *adj.* estoico
stom·ach *n.* estómago
stone *n.* piedra
stop *v.* terminar
stop·light *n.* semáforo
store *n.* almacén; tienda
stork *n.* cigüeña
storm *n.* tempestad
sto·ry *n.* piso; historia
stove *n.* estufa
straight *adj.* directo
strange *adj.* extraño; raro
stra·te·gic *adj.* estratégico
strat·e·gy *n.* estrategia
straw *n.* pajilla
straw·ber·ry *n.* fresa
stream *n.* arroyo
street *n.* calle
strength *n.* vigor; fuerza
strict *adj.* estricto
strike *v.* atacar; golpear
string *n.* cordel
stripe *n.* raya
striped *adj.* rayado

strong *adj.* robusto; fuerte
struc·tur·al *adj.* estructural
stu·dent *n.* estudiante
stu·di·o *n.* estudio
stud·y *v.* estudiar
stu·pen·dous
    adj. estupendo
stu·pid *adj.* estúpido
style *n.* modo; estilo
sub·di·vide *v.* subdividir
sub·ject *adj., n.* sujeto
sub·jec·tive *adj.* subjetivo
sub·lease *v.* subarrendar
sub·let *v.* subarrendar
sub·li·mate *v.* sublimar
sub·li·ma·tion
    n. sublimación
sub·lime *adj.* sublime
sub·lim·it·y *n.* sublimidad
sub·ma·rine *n.* submarino
sub·merge *v.* sumergir(se)
sub·mer·sion *n.* sumersión
sub·mis·sion *n.* sumisión
sub·mis·sive *adj.* sumiso
sub·mit *v.* someter(se);
    presentar
sub·nor·mal *adj.* anormal
sub·or·di·nate *adj.*
    subordinado; secundario;
    dependiente
sub·or·di·na·tion
    n. subordinación
sub·poe·na *n.* citación;
    comparendo
sub·scribe *v.* subscribir(se)
sub·scrip·tion
    n. subscripción
sub·se·quent
    adj. subsiguiente
sub·ser·vi·ent *adj.* servil
sub·side *v.* bajar; calmarse
sub·sid·i·ar·y
    adj. subsidiario
sub·si·dize *v.* subvencionar
sub·si·dy *n.* subvención;
    subsidio
sub·sist *v.* subsistir; existir
sub·sis·tence *n.* subsistencia
sub·stance *n.* esencia;
    substancia
sub·stan·tial
    adj. substancial
sub·stan·ti·a·tion *n.*
    comprobación; justificación
sub·stan·tive *n.* substantivo
sub·sti·tute *n.* substituto,
    v. substituir

sub·sti·tu·tion
    n. substitución; reemplazo
sub·ter·fuge *n.* subterfugio
sub·ter·ra·ne·an
    adj. subterráneo
sub·ti·tle *n.* subtítulo
sub·tle *adj.* sutil; ingenioso;
    delicado; astuto
sub·tle·ty *n.* sutileza
sub·tract *v.* substraer
sub·trac·tion
    n. substracción; resta
sub·urb *n.* suburbio
sub·ur·ban *adj.* suburbano
sub·ver·sion *n.* subversivo
sub·ver·sive *adj.* sobversivo
sub·vert *v.* subvertir
sub·way *n.* metro
succeed *v.* suceder
suc·cess *n.* éxito
suc·cess·ful *adj.* próspero;
    afortunado
suc·ces·sion *n.* sucesión
suc·ces·sor *n.* sucesor
suc·cinct *adj.* sucinto
suc·cor *n.* socorro; auxilio
suc·cu·lent *adj.* suculento
suc·cumb *v.* sucumbir
such *adv.* tan; *pron.,*
    adj. tal
suck *v.* chupar; mamar
suck·er *n.* pirulí
suck·le *v.* lactar; amamantar
suc·tion *n.* succión
suf·fer *v.* sufrir
suf·fer·ance *n.* tolerancia
suf·fice *v.* bastar
suf·fi·cien·cy *n.* suficiencia
suf·fix *n.* sufijo
suf·fo·cate *v.* sofocar;
    asfixiar
suf·frage *n.* sufragio
suf·fuse *v.* extender; bañar
suf·fu·sion *n.* difusión
sug·ar *n.* azúcar
sug·ar·y *adj.* azucarado
sug·gest *v.* sugerir
sug·ges·tion *n.* sugestión
sug·ges·tive *n.* sugestivo
su·i·cide *n.* suicida
suit *n.* traje
suit·a·ble *adj.* apropiado
suit·case *n.* maleta
suite *n.* juego; serie
sul·fur, sul·phur *n.* azufre
sul·fu·ric ac·id *n.* ácido
    sulfúrico

sulk *v.* estar de mal humor
sul·len *adj.* hosco
sul·ly *v.* manchar
sul·tan *n.* sultán
sul·tan·ate *n.* sultanato
sul·try *adj.* bochornoso;
    sensual
sum *v.* sumar; *n.* suma
sum·ma·ry *adj.* sumario
sum·mer *n.* verano
sun *n.* sol
Sun·day *n.* domingo
sun·down *n.* puesta del sol
sun·flow·er *n.* girasol
sun·glass·es *n.* gafas de sol
sun·light *n.* luz del sol
sun·rise *n.* salida del sol
su·per·fi·cial *adj.* superficial
su·per·in·tend
    v. superentender
su·pe·ri·or *n., adj.* superior
su·pe·ri·or·i·ty
    n. superioridad
su·per·mar·ket
    n. supermercado
su·per·sti·tion
    n. superstición
su·per·sti·tious
    adj. supersticioso
su·pine *adj.* supino
sup·per *n.* cena
sup·ple·ment *n.* suplemento
sup·li·cate *v.* suplicar
sup·pose *v.* suponer
sup·pres·sion *n.* supresión
su·prem·a·cy *n.* supremacía
su·preme *adj.* supremo
sure *adj.* seguro
sure·ly *adv.* seguramente
sur·face *n.* superficie
sur·geon *n.* cirujano
sur·ger·y *n.* cirugía
sur·name *n.* apellido
sur·prise *v.* sorprender;
    n. sorpresa
sur·vive *v.* sobrevivir
sus·cep·ti·ble
    adj. susceptible
sus·pend *v.* suspender
sus·pense *n.* incertidumbre
sus·pen·sion
    adj. suspensión
sus·pi·cion *n.* sospecha;
    sombra
sus·pi·cious *adj.* sospechoso
sus·tain *v.* sustentar
sus·te·nance *n.* sustento

svelte *adj.* esbelto
swab *n.* algodón; tapón
swan *n.* cisne
swap *v.* cambiar
swarm *n.* enjambre
swash·buck·ler *n.* espadachín
swat *v.* matar
sway *v.* bambolearse; inclinar
swear *v.* jurar
swear·word *n.* palabrota
sweat *n.* sudor; *v.* sudar
sweat·y *adj.* sudoroso
sweet *adj.* dulce
sweet·en *v.* azucarar; endulzar
sweet·heart *n.* querida; novia
sweet·meat *n.* dulce
swell *v.* hinchar(se)
swerve *v.* torcer(se); desviar(se)
swift *adj.* veloz
swig *v.* beber a grandes tragos
swill *n.* bazofia
swim *n.* natación; *v.* nadar
swim·mer *n.* nadador
switch *v.* cambiar
swiv·el *n.* alacrán; torniquete; girar
swoon *n.* desmayo
sword *n.* espada
sword·belt *n.* talabarte
sword·fish *n.* pez espada
sword·play *n.* esgrima
swords·man *n.* espadachín
syc·a·more *n.* sicomoro
syc·o·phant *n.* adulador
syl·lab·i·cate *v.* silabear
syl·lab·i·ca·tion *n.* silabeo
syl·lab·i·fy *v.* silabear
syl·a·ble *n.* sílaba
syl·a·bus *n.* resumen; programa
syl·van *adj.* silvestre
sym·bol *n.* símbolo
sym·bol·ic *adj.* simbólico
sym·bol·ism *n.* simbolismo
sym·bol·ize *v.* simbolizar
sym·me·try *n.* simetría
sym·pa·thet·ic *adj.* compasivo; simpático
sym·pa·thy *n.* simpatía
sym·pho·ny *n.* sinfonía
symp·tom *n.* síntoma
syn·a·gogue *n.* sinagoga

syn·chro·nize *v.* sincronizar(se)
syn·di·cate *v.* sindicar
syn·od *n.* sínodo
syn·o·nym *n.* sinónimo
syn·on·y·mous *adj.* sinónimo
syn·op·sis *n.* sinopsis
syn·the·sis *n.* síntesis
syn·thet·ic *adj.* sintético
syph·i·lis *n.* sífilis
sy·ringe *n.* jeringa
sy·rup *n.* jarabe; almíbar
sys·tem *n.* sistema
sys·tem·at·ic *adj.* sistemático
sys·tem·a·tize *v.* sistematizar

T

tab *n.* cuenta
tab·er·nac·le *n.* tabernáculo
ta·ble *n.* mesa
ta·ble·spoon·ful *n.* cucharada
tab·let *n.* tableta
ta·boo, ta·bu *adj.* tabú
tab·u·lar *adj.* tabular
tab·u·late *v.* tabular
tac·it *adj.* tácito
tac·i·turn *adj.* taciturno
tack *n.* tachuela; virada
tack·le *n.* equipo; carga
tact *n.* tacto
tac·tics *n.* táctica
tad·pole *n.* renacuajo
taf·fe·ta *n.* tafetán
taf·fy *n.* caramelo
tag *n.* etiqueta; marbete
tail *n.* cola; rabo
tai·lor *n.* sastre
taint *v.* contaminar(se); corromper(se)
take *v.* coger; tomar; sacar
take·off *n.* despegue
tal·cum pow·der *n.* polvo de talco
tale *n.* cuenta
tal·ent *n.* talento
tal·ent·ed *adj.* talentoso
talk *v.* decir; hablar
talk·a·tive *adj.* hablador
tall *adj.* alto
tal·low *n.* sebo

tal·ly *n.* cuenta
tal·on *n.* garra
tam·bou·rine *n.* pandereta
tame *adj.* domesticado; manso; soso
tam·per *v.* estropear; falsificar
tan *v.* curtir; tostar
tan·dem *adv.* en tándem
tang *n.* sabor fuerte
tan·gent *n., adj.* tangente
tan·ge·rine *n.* naranja mandarina o tangerina
tan·gi·ble *adj.* tangible
tan·gle *v.* enredar(se)
tan·go *n.* tango
tank *n.* tanque
tan·ta·lize *v.* atormentar
tan·ta·mount *adj.* equivalente
tan·trum *n.* rabieta; berrinche
tap *n.* grifo; golpecito
tape *n.* cinta
ta·per *v.* afilar
tap·es·try *n.* tapiz
tape·worm *n.* tenia; solitaria
tap·i·o·ca *n.* tapioca
ta·pir *n.* tapir
tar *v.* alquitranar; embrear
ta·ran·tu·la *n.* tarántula
tar·dy *adj.* tardo; tardío
tar·get *n.* blanco
tar·iff *n.* tarifa
tar·nish *v.* deslustrar(se); empañar
tar·ry *v.* tardar; detenerse
tart *n.* tarta
tar·tar *n.* tártaro
task *n.* tarea; labor
task·mas·ter *n.* capataz
tas·sel *n.* borla
taste *n.* sabor
tast·y *adj.* sabroso
tat·ter *n.* andrajo
tat·tered *adj.* harapiento; andrajoso
tat·too *n.* tatuaje
taunt *n.* mofa; sarcasmo; escarnio
taut *adj.* tieso; tirante
tav·ern *n.* taberna
taw·dry *adj.* charro
taw·ny *adj.* leonado
tax *n.* impuesto; contribución; carga
tax·i *n.* taxi

tax·i·cab *n.* taxi
tea *n.* té
tea·bag *n.* sobre de té; muñeca de té
teach *v.* instruir
teach·er *n.* maestro; profesora; profesor
tea·cup *n.* taza para té
tea·ket·tle *n.* tetera
team *n.* equipo
team·mate *n.* compañero de equipo
team·ster *n.* camionero; camionista
team·work *n.* cooperación
tea·pot *n.* tetera
tear *n.* lágrima
tear *v.* rasgar(se); romper(se)
tease *v.* tomar el pelo; atormentar
tea·spoon *n.* cucharilla
tea·spoon·ful *n.* cucharadita
tech·ni·cal *adj.* técnico
tech·ni·cian *n.* técnico
tech·nol·o·gy *n.* tecnología
te·di·ous *adj.* aburrido; tedioso
tel·e·gram *n.* telegrama
tel·e·graph *n.* telégrafo
tel·eg·ra·phy *n.* telegrafía
tel·e·phone *n.* teléfono
tel·e·scope *n.* telescopio
tel·e·vi·sion *n.* televisión
tell *v.* mandar; decir
tem·per·a·men·tal *adj.* temperamental
tem·per·a·ture *n.* fiebre
tem·pes·tu·ous *adj.* tempestuoso
tem·ple *n.* templo
tem·po *n.* tiempo
tem·po·ral *adj.* temporal
temp·ta·tion *n.* tentación
ten *adj., n.* diez
tend *v.* tender
ten·den·cy *n.* tendencia
ten·der·ly *adv.* tiernamente
ten·don *n.* tendón
ten·nis *n.* tenis
tense *v.* tensar; *adj.* tenso
ten·sion *n.* tensión
ter·min·al *adj., n.* terminal
ter·min·ate *v.* terminar
ter·mi·nol·o·gy *n.* terminología
ter·rain *n.* terreno
ter·res·tri·al *adj.* terrestre

ter·ri·ble *adj.* terrible
ter·rif·ic *adj.* terrífico
ter·ror *n.* terror
ter·ror·ism *n.* terrorismo
ter·ror·ist *n.* terrorista
test *v.* examinar; *n.* examen
tes·ti·fy *v.* atestiguar
text *n.* texto
tex·ture *n.* textura
than *conj.* de; que
thanks *n.* gracias
that *adj.* aquella; aquel; esa; ese
the *def. art.* la; le; las; los; lo
the·a·ter *n.* teatro
them *pron.* las; les; los; ellas; ellos
then *adv.* luego; entonces
the·ol·o·gy *n.* teología
the·o·rize *v.* teorizar
the·o·ry *n.* teoría
there *adv.* ahí; allí; allá
ther·mal *adj.* termal
ther·mom·e·ter *n.* termómetro
the·sau·rus *n.* tesauro
these *pron.* éstas; éstos
they *pron.* ellas; ellos
thick *adj.* denso
thief *n.* ladrón
thigh *n.* muslo
thin *adj.* escaso; delgado
thing *n.* cosa
think *v.* creer; pensar
third *adj.* tercero
thirst *n.* sed
thir·teen *n., adj.* trece
thir·ty *n., adj.* treinta
this *adj.* esta; este; *pron.* esto; ésta; éste
thorn *n.* espina
thorn·y *adj.* espinoso
thor·ough *adj.* completo
though *adv.* sin embargo; *conj.* aunque
thought·ful *adj.* pensativo
thou·sand *n., adj.* mil
threat·en *v.* amenazar
three *n., adj.* tres
throat *n.* garganta
throne *n.* trono
through *prep.* por
throw *v.* lanzar; echar
thumb *n.* pulgar
Thurs·day *n.* jueves
tib·i·a *n.* tibia
tick·le *v.* cosquillear

tide *n.* marea
ti·ger *n.* tigre
till *prep.* hasta
tim·ber *n.* madero
time *n.* hora; tiempo; vez
tim·id *adj.* tímido
tim·id·i·ty *n.* timidez
tip *n.* propina
tire *v.* cansar(se)
tired *adj.* cansado
tire·some *adj.* molesto
tis·sue *n.* tisú
ti·tan·ic *adj.* titánico
tithe *n.* diezmo
ti·tle *v.* titular; *n.* título
tit·ter *v.* reír a medias
tit·u·lar *adj.* titular
TNT, T.N.T. *n.* explosivo
to *adv., prep.* hacia; *prep.* hasta; a
toad *n.* sapo
toad·stool *n.* hongo; hongo venenoso
toast *n.* tostar; brindar
to·bac·co *n.* tabacco
to·bog·gan *n.* tobogán
to·day *n., adv.* hoy
toe *n.* dedo del pie
tof·fee, tof·fy *n.* caramelo
toga *n.* toga
to·geth·er *adv.* juntos
toil *v.* trabajar asiduamente; afanarse
toi·let *n.* retrete; tocado
toi·let·ry *n.* artículo de tocador
to·ken *n.* indicio; prenda; señal
tol·er·a·ble *adj.* tolerable; regular
tol·er·ance *n.* tolerancia
tol·er·ant *adj.* tolerante
tol·er·ate *v.* permitir; tolerar
toll *n.* peaje
to·ma·to *n.* tomate
tomb *n.* tumba
tomb·stone *n.* lápida sepulcral
to·mor·row *adv., n.* mañana
ton *n.* tonelada
tone *n.* tono; tendencia
tongs *n.* tenazas
tongue *n.* lengua
ton·ic *n.* tónico
to·night *adv.* esta noche
ton·nage *n.* tonelaje

ton·sil *n.* amígdala; tonsila
ton·sil·li·tis *n.* amigdalitis
too *adv.* además; también
tool *n.* herramienta
tooth *n.* diente
tooth·ache *n.* dolor de muelas
tooth·brush *n.* cepillo de dientes
top *n.* tapa
to·paz *n.* topacio
top·coat *n.* sobretodo
top·hat *n.* chistera
top·ic *n.* tema
top·i·cal *adj.* tópico
to·pog·ra·phy *n.* topografía
top·ple *v.* venirse abajo
top·sy·tur·vy *adv.* patas arriba
torch *n.* antorcha; hacha
tor·ment *v.* atormentar
tor·na·do *n.* tornado
tor·pe·do *n.* torpedo
tor·rent *n.* torrente
tor·rid *adj.* tórrido
tor·so *n.* torso
tor·toise *n.* tortuga
tor·tu·ous *adj.* tortuoso
tor·ture *v.* torturar
toss *v.* echar
tot *n.* nene; nena
to·tal *n., adj.* total
to·tal·i·tar·i·an *adj.* totalitario
to·tal·ly *adv.* totalmente
tote *v. inf.* llevar
to·tem *n.* tótem
tot·ter *v.* bambolearse
touch *v.* tocar(se)
touch·y *adj.* irritable
tough *adj.* difícil
tough·en *v.* endurecer(se); hacer(se)
tour *n.* viaje; excursión
tour·ism *n.* turismo
tour·ist *n.* turista
tour·na·ment *n.* torneo
tour·ni·quet *n.* torniquete
tou·sle *v.* despeinar
tow *v.* llevar a remolque
to·ward *prep.* cerca de
tow·el *n.* toalla
tow·er *n.* torre
town *n.* pueblo; ciudad
tox·ic *adj.* tóxico
tox·in *n.* toxina
toy *n.* juguete

trace *n.* indicio; huella; rastro
tra·che·a *n.* tráquea
track *n.* vía; pista; senda
tract *n.* extensión; tratado
trac·tor *n.* tractor
trade *v.* comerciar
trade·mark *n.* marca de fábrica; marca registrada
trade un·ion *n.* sindicato
tra·di·tion *n.* tradición
tra·di·tion·al *adj.* tradicional
tra·duce *v.* calumniar
traf·fic *n.* tráfico
trag·e·dy *n.* tragedia
trag·ic *adj.* trágico
trail *v.* arrastrar(se); rastrear
trail·er *n.* remolque
train *n.* tren
trait *n.* característica; rasgo
trai·tor *n.* traidor
tra·jec·to·ry *n.* trayectoria
tramp *n.* andar con pasos pezados
tram·ple *v.* pisotear
trance *n.* arrobamiento; estado hipnótico
tran·quil *adj.* tranquilo
tran·quil·i·ty *n.* tranquilidad
tran·quil·ize *v.* tranquilizar
trans·act *v.* despachar
trans·ac·tion *n.* transacción
tran·scend *v.* sobresalir
tran·scribe *v.* transcribir
tran·script *n.* trasunto
tran·scrip·tion *n.* transcripción
trans·fer *v.* transferir; trasladar
trans·fer·ence *n.* transferencia
trans·form *v.* transformar
trans·for·ma·tion *n.* transformación
trans·form·er *n.* transformador
trans·fu·sion *n.* transfusión
trans·gress *v.* traspasar; pecar
trans·gres·sion *n.* transgresión
tran·sient *adj.* transitorio; pasajero
tran·sis·tor *adj., n.* transistor
trans·it *n.* tránsito
tran·si·tive *adj.* transitivo

tran·si·to·ry *adj.* transitorio
trans·late *v.* traducir
trans·la·tion *n.* traducción
trans·lu·cent *adj.* translúcido
trans·mis·sion *n.* transmisión
trans·mit *v.* transmitir
trans·mit·ter *n.* transmisor
tran·som *n.* travesaño
trans·par·ent *adj.* transparente; claro; obvio
tran·spire *v.* transpirar; suceder
trans·plant *v.* trasplantar
trans·port *n.* transporte; *v.* transportar
trans·por·ta·tion *n.* transportación
trans·pose *v.* transponer
trans·verse *adj.* transversal
trap *v.* entrampar
tra·peze *n.* trapecio
trap·e·zoid *n.* trapezoide
trash *n.* basura
tra·uma *n.* trauma
trau·mat·ic *adj.* traumático
trav·el *v.* viajar
trea·son *n.* traición
treas·ure *n.* tesoro
treas·ur·er *n.* tesorero
treas·ur·y *n.* tesoro
treat *v.* tratar
trea·tise *n.* tratado
treat·ment *n.* tratamiento
trea·ty *n.* tratado; pacto
tre·ble *adj.* triple
tree *n.* árbol
trek *v.* caminar
trel·lis *n.* enrejado; espaldera
trem·ble *v.* temblar
tre·men·dous *adj.* tremendo
trem·or *n.* temblor
trench *n.* foso; trinchera
tri·al *n.* prueba
tri·an·gle *n.* triángulo
tri·an·gu·lar *adj.* triangular
tri·bu·nal *n.* tribunal
trib·ute *n.* tributo
trick *n.* truco; trampa; engaño
trick·le *v.* gotear
tri·cy·cle *n.* triciclo
tried *adj.* probado
tri·fle *n.* bagatela
tri·fling *adj.* sin importancia
trig·ger *n.* gatillo

trig·o·nom·e·try *n.* trigonometría
tril·lion *n.* billón
trim *v.* guarnecer
trin·ket *n.* dije
tri·o *n.* trío
trip *n.* viaje
tri·ple *v.* triplicar(se)
trip·let *n.* trillizo
trip·li·cate *v.* triplicar
tri·pod *n.* trípode
trite *adj.* gastado
tri·umph *n.* triunfo
tri·um·phant *adj.* triunfante
triv·i·al *adj.* trivial; frívolo
triv·i·al·i·ty *n.* trivialidad
trol·ley *n.* tranvía
trom·bone *n.* trombón
troop *n.* tropa; escuadrón
troop·er *n.* soldado de caballería
tro·phy *n.* trofeo
trop·ic *n.* trópico
trop·i·cal *adj.* tropical
trot *v.* ir al trote; hacer trotar
trou·ba·dour *n.* trovador
trou·ble *v.* molestar(se)
trou·ble·some *adj.* molesto
trough *n.* abrevadero
troupe *n.* compañía
trou·sers *n.* pantalones
trous·seau *n.* ajuar
trout *n.* trucha
trow·el *n.* paleta; desplantador
tru·ant *n.* novillero
truce *n.* tregua
truck *n.* camión
true *adj.* verdadero
tru·ly *adv.* verdaderamente; realmente
trump *n.* triunfo
trum·pet *n.* trompeta
trun·cate *v.* truncar
trunk *n.* tronco; baúl
truss *v.* empaquetear
trust *v.* esperar; *n.* fideicomiso
trus·tee *n.* fideicomisario
trust·wor·thy *adj.* fidedigno; confiable
trust·y *adj.* seguro
truth *n.* verdad
truth·ful *adj.* veraz
try *v.* probar
try·ing *adj.* difícil; penoso
tryst *n.* cita

T-shirt *n.* camiseta
tub *n.* baño; tina
tu·ba *n.* tuba
tube *n.* tubo
tu·ber·cu·lo·sis *n.* tuberculosis
tuck *v.* alforzar
Tues·day *n.* martes
tuft *n.* copete
tug *v.* tirar con fuerza; remolcar
tug·boat *n.* remolcador
tu·i·tion *n.* enseñanza
tu·lip *n.* tulipán
tum·ble *v.* caer(se)
tum·bler *n.* volteador; vaso
tu·mor *n.* tumor
tu·mult *n.* tumulto
tu·mul·tu·ous *adj.* tumultuoso
tu·na *n.* atún
tun·dra *n.* tundra
tune *n.* aire; afinación
tu·nic *n.* túnica
tun·nel *n.* túnel
tur·ban *n.* turbante
tur·bid *adj.* túrbido
tur·bine *n.* turbina
tur·bu·lence *n.* turbulencia; confusión
tu·reen *n.* sopera
turf *n.* césped
tur·key *n.* pavo
tur·moil *n.* tumulto
turn *v.* volver(se); girar
turn·coat *n.* traidor
tur·nip *n.* nabo
turn·out *n.* concurrencia; producción
turn·pike *n.* autopista de peaje
turn·stile *n.* torniquete
tur·pen·tine *n.* trementina
tur·quoise *n.* turquesa
tur·ret *n.* torrecilla
tur·tle *n.* tortuga
tusk *n.* colmillo
tus·sle *n.* agarrada
tu·te·lage *n.* tutela
tu·tor *n.* tutor
tux·e·do *n.* smoking
TV *n.* televisión
twang *n.* tañido; timbre nasal
tweed *n.* mezcla de lana
twee·zers *n.* bruselas
twelfth *adj.* duodécimo
twelve *adj., n.* doce

twen·ty *adj., n.* veinte
twice *adv.* dos veces
twig *n.* ramita
twi·light *n.* crepúsculo
twill *n.* tela cruzada
twin *adj., n.* gemelo
twinge *n.* dolor agudo
twin·kle *v.* centellear
twirl *v.* girar; piruetear
twist *v.* torcer(se)
twitch *v.* crisparse
twit·ter *v.* gorjear
two *adj., n.* dos
two·faced *adj.* falso; hipócrita
ty·coon *n.* magnate
type *n.* tipo
type·write *v.* escribir a máquina
type·writ·er *n.* máquina de escribir
ty·phoid *n.* fiebre tifoidea
ty·phoon *n.* tifón
ty·phus *n.* tifus
typ·i·cal *adj.* típico
typ·i·fy *v.* simbolizar
typ·ist *n.* mecanógrafo
ty·pog·ra·phy *n.* tipografía
ty·ran·ni·cal *adj.* tiránico; despótico
tyr·an·nize *v.* tiranizar
tyr·an·ny *n.* tiranía

U

u·biq·ui·tous *adj.* ubicuo
u·biq·ui·ty *n.* ubicuidad
ud·der *n.* ubre
ug·li·ness *n.* fealdad
ug·ly *adj.* feo
u·ku·le·le *n.* ukelele
ul·cer *n.* úlcera
ul·cer·ate *v.* ulcerar(se)
ul·cer·ous *adj.* ulceroso
ul·na *n.* cúbito
ul·te·ri·or *adj.* ulterior
ul·ti·mate *adj.* último
ul·ti·ma·tum *n.* ultimátum
ul·tra *adj.* excesivo
ul·tra·mod·ern *adj.* ultramoderno
ul·tra·son·ic *adj.* ultrasónico
ul·tra·sound *n.* ultrasónico
ul·tra·vi·o·let *adj.* ultravioleta
ul·u·late *v.* ulular

um·bil·i·cal *adj.* umbilical
um·bil·i·cus *n.* ombligo
um·brel·la *n.* paraguas
um·pire *n.* árbitro
ump·teen *adj.* muchos
un·a·bashed *adj.* desvergonzado; descarado
un·a·ble *adj.* incapaz
un·a·bridged *adj.* no abreviado
un·ac·cent·ed *adj.* sin acento
un·ac·cept·a·ble *adj.* inaceptable
un·ac·count·a·ble *adj.* inexplicable
un·ac·cus·tomed *adj.* no acostumbrado
un·ac·knowl·edged *adj.* no reconocido
un·a·dorned *adj.* sin adorno
un·a·dul·ter·at·ed *adj.* no adulterado
un·af·fect·ed *adj.* sin afectación
un·a·fraid *adj.* sin terror
un·aid·ed *adj.* sin ayuda
un·am·big·u·ous *adj.* sin ambigüedad
u·nan·i·mous *adj.* unánime
un·an·swer·a·ble *adj.* incontestable
un·ap·proach·a·ble *adj.* inaccesible
un·armed *adj.* desarmado
un·as·sail·a·ble *adj.* inexpugnable
un·as·sist·ed *adj.* sin ayuda
un·as·sum·ing *adj.* modesto; sencillo
un·at·tached *adj.* suelto
un·at·tend·ed *adj.* desatendido
un·at·trac·tive *adj.* inatractivo
un·au·thor·ized *adj.* sin autorización
un·a·void·a·ble *adj.* inevitable
un·a·ware *adj.* ignorante
un·a·wares *adv.* de improviso
un·bal·anced *adj.* desequilibrado
un·beat·a·ble *adj.* invencible
un·beat·en *adj.* invicto

un·be·com·ing *adj.* que sienta mal
un·be·lief *n.* incredulidad
un·be·liev·a·ble *adj.* increíble
un·be·liev·er *n.* descreído
un·be·liev·ing *adj.* incrédulo
un·bend *v.* desencorvar; aflojar
un·bend·ing *adj.* inflexible
un·bi·ased *adj.* imparcial
un·bind *v.* desatar
un·blem·ished *adj.* puro
un·born *adj.* no nacido
un·bos·om *v.* revelar
un·bound·ed *adj.* ilimitado
un·bowed *adj.* recto
un·break·a·ble *adj.* irrompible
un·breath·a·ble *adj.* irrespirable
un·bri·dled *adj.* desenfrenado
un·bro·ken *adj.* inviolado; sin romper
un·buck·le *v.* deshebillar
un·bur·den *v.* descargar
un·but·ton *v.* desabotonar(se)
un·caged *adj.* suelto
un·called·for *adj.* inmerecido
un·can·ny *adj.* extraño; misterioso
un·cap *v.* destapar
un·ceas·ing *adj.* incesante
un·cer·e·mo·ni·ous *adj.* informal
un·cer·tain *adj.* indeciso
un·cer·tain·ty *n.* incertidumbre
un·change·a·ble *adj.* inalterable
un·changed *adj.* inalterado
un·chang·ing *adj.* inalterable
un·chart·ed *adj.* desconocido
un·civ·il *adj.* incivil; descortés
un·civ·i·lized *adj.* incivilizado; inculto
un·clad *adj.* desnudo
un·clasp *v.* separar
un·cle *n.* tío
un·clean *adj.* sucio

un·clear *adj.* confuso
un·clog *v.* sedatascar
un·com·fort·a·ble *adj.* incómodo
un·com·mon *adj.* raro
un·com·un·i·ca·tive *adj.* poco comunicativo
un·com·pro·mis·ing *adj.* inflexible
un·con·cern *n.* indiferencia
un·con·nect·ed *adj.* inconexo
un·con·scious *adj.* inconsciente
un·con·sid·ered *adj.* inconsiderado
un·con·trolled *adj.* desenfrenado
un·cooked *adj.* crudo
un·count·ed *adj.* innumerable
un·cross *v.* descruzar
un·de·cid·ed *adj.* indeciso
un·der·es·ti·mate *v.* subestimar
un·der·ground *adj.* subterráneo
un·der·line *v.* subrayar
un·der·neath *adv.* debajo; *prep.* bajo
un·der·wear *n.* ropa interior
un·do *v.* desatar
un·fin·ished *adj.* incompleto
un·fold *v.* extender; abrir
u·ni·form *n.* uniforme
un·ion *n.* unión
u·ni·ted *adj.* unido
u·ni·ver·sal *adj.* universal
un·luck·y *adj.* desdichado
un·rest *n.* inquietud
un·sa·vor·y *adj.* desagradable
un·seem·ly *adj.* indecoroso
un·skilled *adj.* inexperto
un·so·phis·ti·cat·ed *adj.* cándido
un·sta·ble *adj.* inestable
un·stead·y *adj.* inseguro
un·til *prep.* hasta
un·truth·ful *adj.* mentiroso
un·u·su·al *adj.* raro
un·wrap *v.* desenvolver
up *adj.* ascendente; *adv.* acabado; arriba
up·hill *adj.* ascendente
up·hol·ster·y *n.* tapicería
up·on *prep.* sobre; encima de

up·per *adj.* alto
up·per·cut *n.* gancho
up·roar *n.* alboroto
up·set *n.* trastorno; *v.* volcar
up·stairs *adj.* arriba
u·ra·ni·um *n.* uranio
U·ra·nus *n.* Urano
ur·ban *adj.* urbano
urge *n.* impulso; *v.* incitar
ur·gent *adj.* urgente
u·rine *n.* orina
urn *n.* urna
us *pron.* nosotras; nosotros; nos
use *n.* uso; *v.* utilizar; usar
use·less *adj.* inútil
u·su·al *adj.* usual
u·ten·sil *n.* utensilio
u·ter·us *n.* útero
u·til·i·ta·ri·an *n.* utilitario
u·til·i·ty *n.* utilidad
u·til·ize *v.* utilizar
ut·ter·ance *n.* expresión
ux·o·ri·ous *adj.* gurrumino

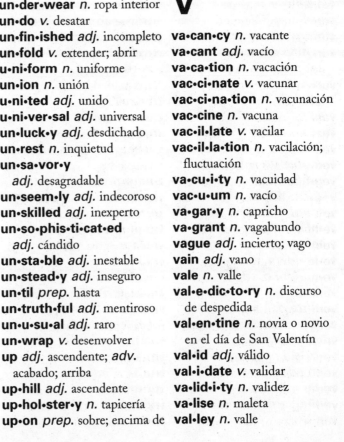

V

va·can·cy *n.* vacante
va·cant *adj.* vacío
va·ca·tion *n.* vacación
vac·ci·nate *v.* vacunar
vac·ci·na·tion *n.* vacunación
vac·cine *n.* vacuna
vac·il·late *v.* vacilar
vac·il·la·tion *n.* vacilación; fluctuación
va·cu·i·ty *n.* vacuidad
vac·u·um *n.* vacío
va·gar·y *n.* capricho
va·grant *n.* vagabundo
vague *adj.* incierto; vago
vale *n.* valle
val·e·dic·to·ry *n.* discurso de despedida
val·en·tine *n.* novia o novio en el día de San Valentín
val·id *adj.* válido
val·i·date *v.* validar
va·lid·i·ty *n.* validez
va·lise *n.* maleta
val·ley *n.* valle

val·or *n.* valor; valentía
val·u·a·ble *adj.* valioso; costoso; precioso
val·u·a·tion *n.* valuación; valorización
val·ue *v.* valuar; *n.* valor
valve *n.* válvula
vam·pire *n.* vampiro
van *n.* camión de mudanzas
van·dal *n.* vándalo
van·dal·ism *n.* vandalismo
vane *n.* veleta
van·guard *n.* vanguardia
va·nil·la *n.* vainilla
van·ish *v.* desaparecer
van·i·ty *n.* vanidad
van·quish *v.* vencer; conquistar
van·tage *n.* ventaja; provecho
vap·id *adj.* insípido
va·por *n.* vapor
va·por·ize *v.* vaporizar(se)
va·por·ous *adj.* vaporoso
var·i·a·bil·i·ty *n.* variabilidad
var·i·a·ble *n., adj.* variable
var·i·a·tion *n.* variación
var·i·cose *adj.* varicoso
var·ied *adj.* variado
va·ri·e·ty *n.* variedad
var·i·ous *adj.* variado
var·nish *n.* barniz
var·si·ty *n.* equipo principal de una universidad
var·y *v.* variar; desviarse; cambiar
vase *n.* jarrón
vast *adj.* vasto
veal *n.* ternera
veg·e·ta·ble *n.* legumbre
veg·e·tar·i·an *n.* vegetariano
veg·e·tate *v.* vegetar
veg·e·ta·tion *n.* vegetación
ve·hi·cle *n.* vehículo
vein *n.* vena
ve·lo·ci·ty *n.* velocidad
ve·nal·i·ty *n.* venalidad
vend *v.* vender
ven·er·a·ble *adj.* venerable
ven·er·a·tion *n.* veneración
ve·ni·al *adj.* venial
ven·om *n.* veneno
ven·om·ous *adj.* venenoso
ven·ti·late *v.* ventilar
ven·tral *adj.* ventral
ven·tri·cle *n.* ventrículo

ven·ture·some *adj.* aventurero
Ve·nus *n.* Venus
ve·ra·cious *adj.* veraz
verb *n.* verbo
ver·bal *adj.* verbal
ver·bose *adj.* verboso
ver·bos·i·ty *n.* verbosidad
ver·dict *n.* veredicto
ver·i·fy *v.* verificar
ver·mouth *n.* vermut
ver·nal *adj.* vernal
ver·sa·til·i·ty *n.* adaptabilidad
verse *n.* versículo
ver·sion *n.* versión
ver·te·bra *n.* vértebra
ver·te·brate *adj.* vertebrado
ver·ti·cal *adj.* vertical
ver·y *adj.* mismo; *adv.* muy
ves·sel *n.* vaso
vest *n.* chaleco
vet *n.* veterinario
vet·er·an *adj., n.* veterano
vet·er·i·nar·i·an *n.* veterinario
vet·er·i·nar·y *adj., n.* veterinario
vi·brant *adj.* vibrante
vi·brate *v.* oscilar
vi·bra·tion *n.* vibración
vic·ar *n.* vicario
vi·car·i·ous *adj.* substituto
vice *n.* vicio
vice pres·i·dent *n.* vicepresidente
vice·roy *n.* virrey
vice ver·sa *adv.* viceversa
vi·ci·ni·ty *n.* vecindad
vi·cious *adj.* depravado; vicioso; cruel
vic·tim *n.* víctima
vic·tim·ize *v.* hacer víctima
vic·to·ri·ous *adj.* victorioso
vic·to·ry *n.* victoria
view *v.* ver; *n.* escena
vig·i·lance *n.* vigilancia
vig·or *n.* vigor
vig·or·ous *adj.* vigoroso
vil·lage *n.* aldea
vin·di·cate *v.* vindicar
vine *n.* vid
vin·e·gar *n.* vinagre
vi·o·la *n.* viola
vi·o·la·tion *n.* violación
vi·o·lent *adj.* violento
vi·o·let *adj.* violado

vi·o·lin *n.* violín
vir·ile *adj.* viril
vi·ril·i·ty *n.* virilidad
vir·tu·al *adj.* virtual
vir·tu·al·ly *adv.* virtualmente
vir·u·lent *adj.* virulento
vi·rus *n.* virus
vis·cos·i·ty *n.* viscosidad
vis·count *n.* vizconde
vis·count·ess *n.* vizcondesa
vise *n.* tornillo
vis·i·bil·i·ty *n.* visibilidad
vis·i·ble *adj.* visible; conspicuo
vi·sion *n.* visión
vi·sion·ar·y *n.* visionario
vis·it *n.* visita; *v.* visitar
vis·it·a·tion *n.* visitación
vi·sor *n.* visera
vis·u·al *adj.* visual
vis·u·al·ize *v.* representarse en la mente
vi·tal *adj.* vital
vi·tal·i·ty *n.* vitalidad
vi·ta·min *n.* vitamina
vit·re·ous *adj.* vítreo
vit·ri·ol *n.* vitriolo
vi·tu·per·ate *v.* vituperar
vi·va·cious *adj.* vivaz; animado; vivaracho
vi·vac·i·ty *n.* vivacidad; animación
viv·id *adj.* intenso; vivo
vix·en *n.* arpía; zorra
vo·cab·u·lar·y *n.* vocabulario
vo·cal *adj.* vocal
vo·cal·ist *n.* cantante
vo·ca·tion *n.* vocación
vod·ka *n.* vodka
vogue *n.* moda; boga
voice *n.* voz
void *adj.* nulo; vacío
vol·can·ic *adj.* volcánico
vol·can·o *n.* volcán
vo·li·tion *n.* voluntad; volición
vol·ley *n.* descarga; voleo
volt *n.* voltio
volt·age *n.* voltaje
vol·u·ble *adj.* hablador
vol·ume *n.* cantidad; volumen
vol·un·tar·y *adj.* voluntario
vol·un·teer *n.* voluntario
vo·lup·tu·ar·y *n.* voluptuoso
vo·lup·tu·ous

adj. voluptuoso
vom·it *n.* vómito; *v.* vomitar
vom·it·ing *n.* vómito
voo·doo *n.* vudú
vo·ra·cious *adj.* voraz
vo·ra·ci·ty *n.* voracidad
vor·tex *n.* vórtice
vo·ta·ry *n.* devoto; partidario
vote *v.* votar; *n.* voto
vot·er *n.* votante
vot·ing *n.* votación
vo·tive *adj.* votivo; exvoto
vouch *v.* afirmar
vouch·er *n.* comprobante
vow·el *n.* vocal
voy·age *v.* viajar; *n.* viaje
vul·gar *adj.* vulgar
vul·gar·ize *v.* vulgarizar
vul·ner·a·ble *adj.* vulnerable
vul·ture *n.* buitre

W

wack·y *adj.* loco; chiflado
wad *n.* fajo; taco; rollo; bolita
wad·dle *v.* anadear
wade *v.* vadear; pasar con dificultad
wag *v.* menear(se)
wage *n.* salario
wag·er *v.* apostar
wag·on *n.* carro
waif *n.* niño abandonado
wail *v.* lamentarse; sollozar
wain·scot *n.* friso de madera
waist *n.* cintura
waist·coat *n.* chaleco
waist·line *n.* talle
wait *n.* espera; *v.* esperar
wait·er *n.* camarero
waive *v.* renunciar a; abandonar
waiv·er *n.* renuncia
wake *v.* despertar(se)
wake·ful *adj.* vigilante
wak·en *v.* despertar(se)
walk *n.* caminata; *v.* caminar; andar
walk·out *n.* huelga
walk·over *n.* triunfo fácil
wall *n.* pared
wall·board *n.* cartón de yeso
wal·let *n.* cartera
wal·lop *v.* zurrar
wal·low *v.* revolcarse
wall·pa·per *n.* papel pintado

wal·nut *n.* nogal

wal·rus *n.* morsa

waltz *n.* vals

wan *adj.* pálido

wan·der·lust *n.* deseo de viajar

wane *v.* disminuir; menguar

want *v.* querer; requerir; desear

want·ing *adj.* deficiente

wan·ton *adj.* lascivo; desenfrenado

war *v.* guerrear; *n.* guerra

war·ble *v.* trinar

war cry *n.* grito de guerra

ward *v.* desviar

war·den *n.* guardián; alcaide

ward·robe *n.* guardarropa; vestuario

ware *n.* mercancías

ware·house *n.* almacén

war·fare *n.* guerra

war·lock *n.* hechicero

warm *v.* calentar(se); *adj.* caluroso; caliente

warm·heart·ed *adj.* afectuoso

war·mon·ger *n.* belicista

warmth *n.* calor

warn *v.* advertir

warn·ing *n.* advertencia; aviso

warp *v.* alabearse; pervertir

war·rant *n.* autorización; garantía

war·ran·ty *n.* garantía

war·ren *n.* conejera

war·ri·or *n.* guerrero

wart *n.* verruga

war·y *adj.* cauteloso

wash *v.* lavar(se)

wash·cloth *n.* paño para lavarse

wash·er *n.* lavadora

wash·ing *n.* lavado

wash·room *n.* lavabo

wash·stand *n.* lavamanos

wash·tub *n.* tina

wasp *n.* avispa

wast·age *n.* desgaste; merma

waste *n.* pérdida; *v.* desperdiciar

wast·rel *n.* derrochador

watch *n.* reloj; *v.* mirar; observar

watch·ful *adj.* vigilante; desvelado

watch·man *n.* vigilante

watch·word *n.* santo y seña

wa·ter *n.* agua

wa·ter·co·lor *n.* acuarela

wa·ter·course *n.* corriente

wa·ter·fall *n.* cascada

wa·ter·fowl *n.* ave acuática

wa·ter·front *n.* terreno ribereño

wa·ter li·ly *n.* nenúfar

wa·ter·logged *adj.* anegado

wa·ter·mark *n.* nivel de agua; filigrana

wa·ter·mel·on *n.* sandía

wa·ter·proof *adj.* impermeable

wa·ter·side *n.* orilla del agua

wa·ter sof·ten·er *n.* ablandador químico de agua

wa·ter·spout *n.* tromba marina; boquilla

wa·ter·tight *adj.* estanco; seguro

wa·ter·way *n.* canal

wa·ter·y *adj.* insípido

watt *n.* vatio

wave *v.* ondular; *n.* onda

wa·ver *v.* oscilar; vacilar

wav·y *adj.* ondulado

wax *n.* cera

wax·en *adj.* de cera j pálido

wax·work *n.* figura de cera

way *n.* camino; modo; dirección

way·far·er *n.* viajero

way·lay *v.* asaltar

way·side *n.* borde del camino

way·ward *adj.* voluntarioso; travieso

we *pron.* nosotras; nosotros

weak *adj.* débil

weak·en *v.* debilitar(se)

weak·ling *n.* alfeñique

weak·ly *adj.* achacoso

weak·mind·ed *adj.* sin voluntad

weak·ness *n.* debilidad

wealth *n.* riqueza

wealth·y *adj.* rico

wean *v.* destetar

weap·on *n.* arma

weap·on·ry *n.* armas

wear *v.* desgastar(se); llevar

wear·ing *adj.* penoso

wea·ri·some *adj.* fastidioso

wea·ry *adj.* fatigado; aburrido

wea·sel *n.* comadreja

weath·er *n.* tiempo

weath·er·beat·en *adj.* curtido por la intemperie

weath·er·glass *n.* barómetro

weath·er·man *n.* pronosticador de tiempo

weave *v.* tejido

web *n.* tela

web·bing *n.* cincha

wed *v.* casar(se)

wed·ding *n.* boda

wedge *n.* cuña

wed·lock *n.* matrimonio

Wednes·day *n.* miércoles

wee *adj.* pequeñito

weed *v.* escardar

week *n.* semana

week·day *n.* día laborable o de trabajo

week·end *n.* fin de semana

week·ly *adj.* semanal

weep *v.* llorar

wee·vil *n.* gorgojo

weigh *v.* pesar

weight *n.* pesa

weight·y *adj.* pesado; importante

wel·come *adj.* agradable

weld *v.* soldar

wel·fare *n.* bienestar

well *adv.* pues; *n.* pozo

well-be·ing *n.* bienestar

well-bred *adj.* bien criado

well-dis·posed *adj.* bien dispuesto

well-known *adj.* famoso

well-off *adj.* adinerado

well-read *adj.* leído

well-thought-of *adj.* bien mirado

well-timed *adj.* oportuno

well-to-do *adj.* acaudalado

welt *n.* verduqón

wel·ter *v.* revolcar(se)

wench *n.* moza

were·wolf *n.* hombre que puede transformarse en lobo

west *n.* oeste

west·ern *adj.* occidental

wet *v.* mojar(se)

whack *v.* golpear

whale *n.* ballena

whale·bone *n.* ballena

what *pron.* qué; lo que; cuál

what·ev·er *pron.* todo lo que

what·not *n.* estante; juguetero

wheat *n.* trigo

whee·dle *v.* engatusar; halagar

wheel *n.* rueda

wheel·bar·row *n.* carretilla

wheel·chair *n.* silla de ruedas

wheeze *v.* respirar asmáticamente

when *conj.* cuando

whence *adv.* de dónde; de qué

when·ev·er *adv.* siempre que

where *conj.* donde; *adv.* adónde

where·a·bouts *n.* paradero

where·as *conj.* visto que

where·up·on *adv.* con lo cual

wher·ev·er *adv.* dondequiera

wheth·er *conj.* si

whey *n.* suero de la leche

which *pron.* lo que; cuál; la; le

which·ev·er *pron.* cualquiera

whiff *n.* olorcillo

while *conj.* mientras

whim *n.* capricho; lantojo

whim·per *v.* lloriquear

whim·si·cal *adj.* caprichoso

whine *v.* gimotear; gemir

whin·ny *n.* relincho

whip *v.* batir

whir *v.* zumbar; batir

whirl *v.* girar rápidamente

whirl·pool *n.* remolino

whirl·wind *n.* torbellino

whisk·ers *n.* barbas; bigotes

whis·key *n.* whisky

whis·per *n.* cuchicheo; *v.* cuchichear

whis·tle *v.* silbar

white *n., adj.* blanco

white-col·lar *adj.* oficinesco

whit·en *v.* blanquear

white·wash *n.* jalbegue

whith·er *conj.* adonde

whit·tle *v.* cortar poco a

poco

whiz *v.* silbar; rehilar

who *pron.* la; el; lo; quién; que

who·ev·er *pron.* quienquiera que

whole *n., adj.* todo

whole·heart·ed *adj.* sincero; incondicional

whole·sale *n.* venta al por menor

whole·some *adj.* saludable

whol·ly *adv.* completamente

whom *pron.* a quién

whom·ev·er *pron.* a quienquiera

whoop *n.* alarido

whore *n.* puta; prostituta

whose *pron.* cuyo

why *adv.* por qué

wick *n.* mecha

wick·ed *adj.* malicioso

wick·er *adj.* de mimbre

wide *adj.* ancho

wide·a·wake *adj.* despabilado

wid·en *v.* ensanchar(se)

wide·spread *adj.* extendido; difuso

wid·ow *n.* viuda

wid·ow·er *n.* viudo

width *n.* anchura

wield *v.* ejercer; mandar; manejar

wife *n.* esposa

wig *n.* peluca

wig·gle *v.* menear(se); cimbrearse

wild *adj.* descabellado

wild boar *n.* jabalí

wil·der·ness *n.* yermo; desierto

wile *n.* ardid

will *v.* querer

will·ful *adj.* voluntarioso; terco; premeditado

will·ing *adj.* dispuesto; complaciente

wil·low *n.* sauce

wil·low·y *adj.* esbelto

wilt *v.* marchitar(se)

win *n.* victoria; *v.* lograr; ganar

wince *v.* estremecerse; respingar

winch *n.* torno

wind *n.* viento

wind *v.* arrollar(se)

wind·fall *n.* ganancia inesperada

wind·mill *n.* molino de viento

win·dow *n.* ventana

win·dow·pane *n.* cristal

wind·shield *n.* parabrisas

wind·y *adj.* ventoso

wine *n.* vino

win·er·y *n.* lagar

wing *n.* ala

wink *v.* guiñar; pestañear

win·ner *n.* ganador

win·ning *n.* ganancias

win·now *v.* aventar

win·some *adj.* atractivo; alegre

win·ter *n.* invierno

win·try *adj.* invernal

wipe *v.* enjugar; secar; borrar

wire *n.* alambre

wire·tap *n.* intervenir

wir·ing *n.* instalación de alambres

wir·y *adj.* nervudo

wis·dom *n.* sabiduría

wise *adj.* acertado; sabio

wise·crack *n.* cuchufleta; pulla

wish *n.* deseo; *v.* desear

wish·ful *adj.* deseoso

wit *n.* ingenio; gracia

witch *n.* bruja

witch·craft *n.* brujería

with *prep.* con

with·draw·al *n.* retirada

with·drawn *adj.* ensimismado

with·er *v.* marchitar(se); secarse

with·hold *v.* retener

with·in *adv.* dentro

with·out *adv.* por fuera

with·stand *v.* resistir

wit·less *adj.* tonto

wit·ness *n.* testigo

wit·ti·cism *n.* dicho gracioso

wit·ty *adj.* salado; ingenioso

wiz·ard *n.* hechicero

wob·ble *v.* bambolear; bailar

woe *n.* aflicción; infortunio

wolf *n.* lobo

wo·man *n.* mujer

wom·an·kind *n.* sexo femenino

womb *n.* matriz

wom·en's rights *n.* derechos de la mujer

won·der *v.* asombrarse

won·der·ful *adj.* maravilloso

woo *v.* cortejar

wood *n.* madera

wood·en *adj.* de madera; sin expresión

wood·land *n.* monte

wood·peck·er *n.* pájaro carpintero

wood·y *adj.* leñoso

wool *n.* lana

wool·ly *adj.* lanudo

word *n.* palabra

work *v.* trabajar; *n.* obra; trabajo

work·book *n.* cuaderno

work·er *n.* trabajador

work·shop *n.* taller

world *n.* mundo

world·ly *adj.* mundano

world·wide *adj.* mundial

worm *n.* gusano

worm·eaten *adj.* carcomido

wormwood *n.* ajenjo

worn *adj.* usado

worrier *n.* aprensivo; pesimista

wor·ry *v.* inquietar(se)

wors·en *v.* empeorar

wor·ship *v.* venerar

worth *n.* valor

worth·less *adj.* despreciable

wound *v.* herir

wrap *v.* envolver

wreck *v.* naufragar; *n.* ruina

wrin·kle *v.* arrugar(se); *n.* arruga

wrist *n.* muñeca

write *v.* escribir

writ·er *n.* escritora; escritor

writ·ing *n.* escritura

wrong *adj.* equivocado

wrong·ful *adj.* injusto; falso

wrong·head·ed *adj.* terco

wrought *adj.* forjado; trabajado

wry *adj.* torcido; irónico; mueca

X

x·ray *v.* radiografiar; *n.* radiografía

Y

yank *v.* sacar de un tirón

Yan·kee *n.* yanqui

yard *n.* yarda

yard·goods *n.* tejidos

yard·stick *n.* vara de medir

yarn *n.* hilaza

yar·row *n.* milenrama

yawn *n.* bostezo; *v.* bostezar

ye *pron.* vosotros

yea *adv.* sí

year *n.* año

year·ling *n.* primal

year·ly *adj.* anualmente

yearn *v.* suspirar; anhelar

yearn·ing *n.* anhelo

yeast *n.* levadura

yell *n.* grito; *v.* gritar

yel·low *n., adj.* amarillo

yes *adv.* sí

yes·ter·day *n.* ayer

yet *adv.* todavía

yew *n.* tejo

yield *v.* rendir(se)

yolk *n.* yema

yon·der *adv.* allí; allá

you *n.* pron. vosotras; vosotros; tú

young *adj.* joven

young·ster *n.* jovencito

your *adj.* su(s); tu(s); vuestro(s); vuestra(s)

yours *pron.* deusted(es); el tuyo; elsuyo

your·self *pron.* usted mismo; tú mismo

youth *n.* jóvenes

youth·ful *adj.* juvenil

Z

zeal *n.* ardor

zeal·ous *adj.* celoso

ze·bra *n.* cebra

ze·nith *n.* cenit

ze·ro *n.* cero

ze·ro hour *n.* hora de ataque

zest *n.* gusto

zone *n.* zona

zoo *n.* jardín zoológico

zo·o·log·i·cal *adj.* zoológico

zuc·chi·ni *n.* cidracayote de verano

NOTES

APUNTES

NOTES

APUNTES

NOTES

APUNTES

NOTES

APUNTES

NOTES

APUNTES

NOTES

APUNTES

NOTES

APUNTES

NOTES

APUNTES

NOTES

APUNTES

NOTES